A KNITTER'S SKETCHBOOK

A KNITTER'S SKETCHBOOK

Design Inspiration for Twists and Cables

EMMA VINING

THE CROWOOD PRESS

First published in 2019 by
The Crowood Press Ltd
Ramsbury, Marlborough
Wiltshire SN8 2HR

www.crowood.com

British Library Cataloguing-in-Publication Data
A catalogue record for this book is available from the British Library.

ISBN 978 1 78500 537 4

Frontispiece: Tulip-bud scarf (*see* Chapter 13).

Typeset by Peggy & Co. Design Inc.
Printed and bound in Printed and bound in India by Parksons Graphics

CONTENTS

INTRODUCTION:
WHAT IS A KNITTER'S SKETCHBOOK?

The title of this book reflects a design-led approach to creating knitting stitch patterns. This method of design combines my love of knitting with an awareness of pattern inspiration at different scales and from diverse locations. Inspiration for twist and cable designs can be seen everywhere in the natural world and in the urban environment, from cracks in pavement to patterns in the walls of buildings and from posts and pillars. Sometimes just looking down at the ground can provide the best source material, from an elegant mosaic pattern in a town plaza to shadows cast by the sun shining on railings on a bridge.

Photographing and drawing this inspiration provides me with a reminder of what caught my eye. This can be a basic sketch, a detailed drawing or a simple written note. A sketch or note makes you really think about what you are observing. Along with knitted swatches, these images and sketches form the basis on my knitter's sketchbook. Using this kind of inspiration, combined with a wide range of knitting techniques, allows the development of new and original knitting stitch patterns. Figures 1, 2 and 3 summarize this approach, showing the design development from inspiration source to sketch to stitch pattern. In this example from Part 2: Line and Shape, the glass facade of a staircase is my inspiration source. My sketch captures the diamond and triangle shapes that attracted my attention. The resulting stitch pattern translates my ideas into

a design that is part of the Agora-wrap project in the chapter about diamond shapes (Chapter 6).

To get the most out of this book, all that is required is an open mind and a willingness to try out ideas. My aim is to encourage you to explore and experiment and to make new and beautiful knitting designs that reflect a personal interaction with the world around you.

How to use this book

This book can be used in many different ways: as a stitch library, as a collection of knitting patterns or as a starting point to inspire your own designs for your own personalized knitter's sketchbook. I have used many examples to show you my design process. These examples can be used to inspire your own new stitch patterns, or you can go straight to the knitting-pattern projects at the end of each chapter in Parts 2 and 3. Each of the ten accessory projects illustrates some of the twist and cable techniques that I use to interpret my source material. There is a progression in complexity within the book, from stitch patterns inspired by straight lines to designs full of complex curves. However, you can dip in and out of the chapters in whichever order you prefer.

The first part of this book, Part 1: Context, sets the scene for designing with twists and cables. A look back in time at historical knitting examples shows that the twist and cable patterns

Fig. 1   Glass facade of a staircase, Brussels, Belgium.

Fig. 2 Sketch of lines and shapes inspired by the glass facade of a staircase.

Fig. 3 Detail of Agora wrap.

now considered to be traditional are in fact part of a constantly evolving set of designs. Naming these different combinations of twist and cable designs has always played an important part in communicating knitting patterns, and the definitions and abbreviations used in this book are explored in detail in the chapter about terminology (Chapter 2). Chapter 3, about yarn and tools, highlights the importance of yarn choice, both in terms of fibre and weight, and reviews the knitting equipment needed to interpret inspiration sources for twists and cables.

The second and third parts of this book are all about designing stitch patterns by using inspiration-source images and sketches. In Part 2: Line and Shape, a range of twist and cable techniques is gradually built up, beginning with the knitting of straight and curved lines, then moving on to exploring the knitting of diamonds, hexagons and circles. All of the techniques are then put together in more complex combinations in the third part of this book, Part 3: Enhanced Twists and Cables. These chapters explore a selection of additional knitting techniques, such as those involving texture and openwork, using them to add detail to the twist and cable designs.

Throughout this book, I will show you how I look at inspirational source material as a way of developing designs. Looking

for pattern all around you leads to fascinating stitch combinations that can enhance and enrich any knitted project. I hope that this book will inspire your own creativity and be the launch pad for a multitude of amazing new knitting designs!

Creating a knitter's sketchbook

This section explains some of the steps involved in creating a knitter's sketchbook. The sketchbook will be both an individual record of inspiration and designs and a reference source for bringing ideas together and moving them on to even more creative designs. As well as knitted samples, rough sketches, photos and clippings from magazines, your knitter's sketchbook can also include an online element, by using sites such as Pinterest, Instagram and other online sources to help record and collect thoughts and ideas together.

As a collection of ideas builds up, a variety of ways to store them will be needed. Sketches and swatches can be stored in a folder, a ring binder or a larger sketchbook. Photographs and links to websites may all be kept in a digital folder. This will be very much a personal preference, and the most important aspect of the sketchbook is that it works for the individual designer. All of the parts of the sketchbook therefore do not need to be in the same place. For example, photographs may be stored digitally, but all of the sketches can be made in an A5-size paper notebook. I encourage you to experiment with different methods, to find the way of working that suits you best.

My own knitter's sketchbook includes my inspiration sources, my pen and pencil sketches and, most importantly, my knitted swatches. Knitted swatches are a response to all of the ideas that have been collected, and they form the basis for new stitch-pattern designs. Throughout this book, examples will illustrate ways to look at source material and demonstrate how to select knitting techniques that represent the lines and patterns present within the sources.

I have found it very helpful to use some specific approaches for recording ideas, building up a personalized stitch library and creating new projects. My favourite designs have been inspired by sources such as architecture and plants that have distinctive lines and shapes within them. I use my initial sketches and drawings to highlight the parts of the image that I want to translate into my knitted swatch. An example of this process is the Agora-wrap project in the diamonds chapter (Chapter 6) of Part 2: Line and Shape. Using this project as an example, let us take a closer look at the design process of a knitter's sketchbook.

Inspirational source material

The starting point for any new design is the inspirational source material. This source may be one image or a collection of ideas and sketches. The more information that is collected, the more ideas that can be generated. A photograph, image or sketch of the source is the key to the new design. The sketch does not need to be detailed; it just needs to contain enough information to remind you of what attracted your attention. To begin collecting ideas, the first tools needed are a camera, a pen or pencil and paper. Any pen or pencil and any piece of paper will do, as long as they are always available when needed. The most basic of drawings can be referred to and, if needed, redrawn later, but the first response to or idea about a source will capture the aspect that is key to your inspiration.

Figure 1 is one of several unplanned photographs that were taken on a phone during a walk through the European Parliament in Brussels. The simple sketch shown in Figure 2 was my way of identifying the design lines that I wished to focus on when planning the knitted swatch, shown in Figure 3.

Knitted swatches

The knitted swatches can be considered as the integral part of the sketchbook, as this is where the knitted lines are drawn, the knitted marks are made and the knitted response to the inspiration is created.

The knitted lines in the swatches can be viewed in the same way as the lines made with pencils and pens in a hand-drawn sketch. The twisted stitches are the fine lines, and the cables are the thicker lines made with marker pens. There is a cable or twist available to represent any line that is needed.

Thinking in terms of drawing allows the selection of appropriate lines, rather than allowing the technique to determine the design. The lines can be even more finely tuned by careful yarn selection. A twisted stitch worked in a fine, lace-weight yarn will allow a line made with a delicate touch on paper to be represented. A supersized cable in chunky yarn will create the dramatic effect across the knitting that is equivalent to a marker-pen stroke across paper. Conversely, a twisted stitch worked in chunky yarn allows the scaling up of a delicate detail, and using big cables in lace-weight yarn creates folds and depth in an otherwise flat and sheer knitted fabric. The wide range of yarn weights available means that a variety of lines can be knitted. Throughout this book, design sources are represented by using both yarn and stitch, to create new stitch patterns.

Fig. 4 Test swatch of staircase-inspired stitch pattern.

It can be helpful to label swatches with either a tie-on tag or a note next to them in the sketchbook. Include the knitting-needle size and the specific yarn, as well as its fibre content, that were used to knit the swatch; also record the date that it was knitted. Any comments about the swatch, even as simple as that it is too big or too small or that the fabric is too tight or too loose, can really help when looking back and reviewing.

Designs that at first appear not to work can also be very useful. Always try not to undo swatches, even if they do not appear to have any immediate use. It can be the so-called mistakes that result in the most interesting designs. Once the design has been ripped out, the precise details are lost. It can be very difficult to recreate any aspect of it, without a visual record. At the very least, if the emerging pattern is really not working, keeping the swatch along with detailed notes will help to avoid making the same mistake again. For example, in the swatch shown in Figure 4, a cabled border was experimented with. In the project for the diamonds chapter (Chapter 6), the Agora wrap, this has been changed to a reverse stocking stitch, ridged edge, to reflect the ridges throughout the wrap.

Throughout this book, the emphasis is on original ideas. However, everyone is influenced by the images and objects that surround them, from books and magazines to exhibitions and the general media. Work that has already been created can have a positive impact, as an inspiration, on new designs. However, if someone has already used a great idea in a design, that is to be admired and not copied. This book considers ways of creating new work. By looking for and using inspiration around you, a chance pattern, perhaps created by a shadow on paving stones, can result in truly original work that has never been made before. Please always respect other artists' and designers' copyright in the search for inspiration, and always credit the design sources that inspired your own work.

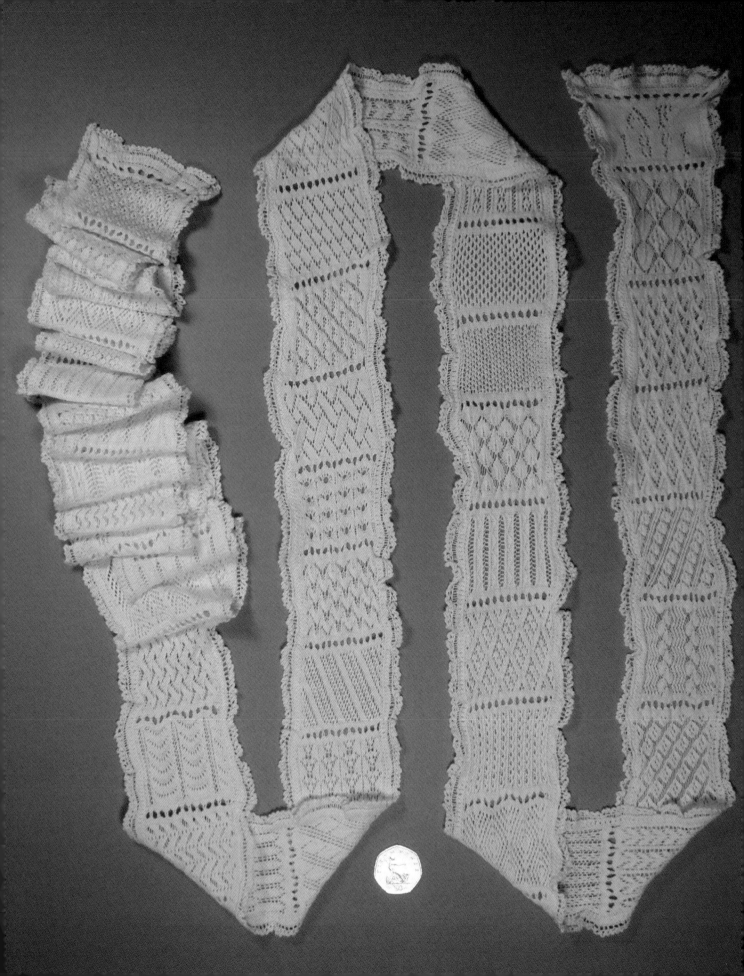

Part 1: Context

CHAPTER 1

HISTORICAL CONTEXT

Before beginning to explore new stitch patterns, a look back in time is essential. By gaining an understanding of the historical uses of twists and cables in knitting, we can appreciate the enormous range of techniques that have been in use over several hundred years.

Traditional knitting styles have used twist and cable patterns in many different ways, such as an embossed, raised line on a plain background or as a design feature within lace knitting. In gansey knitting, for example, cables are just one element of these garments containing multiple stitch combinations. In this style of knitting, the link between the twists and cables and the many ropes found on a fishing boat is clear. In Aran knitting, the individual twist and cable stitch patterns themselves have taken on meaning, with many complex combinations having their own specific names.

The review of historical examples in this chapter sets the context for the new designs in this book. So many beautiful cable patterns have been created already, and the aim of this book is to add to this body of design, not reproduce it. As well as referencing twist and cable designs that have been extensively used and are much loved for their specific stitch combinations, this chapter looks back to the time before Aran and gansey patterns became established. By considering early cable designs, the techniques and applications common to all twist and cable designs become apparent.

Although it would be exciting to find the very first example of a knitted twist or cable, this is not possible, for several reasons. Historical knitting research is restricted by the lack of actual examples that exist. Conservation of knitted items is a relatively recent development. Previously, knitted items of clothing were seen as functional objects for everyday wear. Many of the knitted garments and accessories would have been unravelled and reknitted as the wearer grew out of them or simply wore them out. Additionally, as an organic textile, knitted items made of wool decay over time, and, in many cases, only fragments of the original fabric remain. Examples of exceptional knitting do exist in museum collections; these include brocade silk jackets knitted in Italy and silk stockings knitted for wealthy landowners and royalty. Although these examples show texture, colourwork and surface decoration, there is limited evidence of the movement of stitches that we would call a twist or a cable.

Fig. 5 1891 knitted stitch sampler. (KCG Collection; photo: Angharad Thomas)

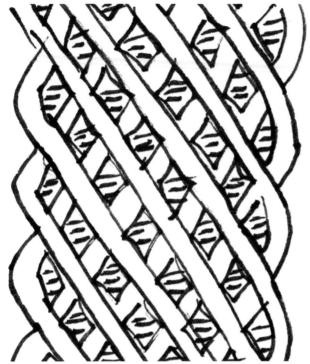

Fig. 6 Sketch of detail of the 1891 knitted stitch sampler.

Knitted samplers

Some of the earliest evidence of twist and cable knitting from the British Isles can be found within knitted samplers. These samplers were typically knitted by students either learning from a teacher or knitting at home. The samplers exist in several different forms, with some containing individual swatches stitched into a fabric book and others consisting of a long, narrow strip of multiple stitch patterns. Several beautiful examples are held in textile collections, such as those of the Victoria and Albert (V&A) Museum Collection.

Many of these samplers do not have a specific date of making. Instead, a wide time period over which they may have been made is referenced in the catalogue descriptions, for example, 1750 to 1850. Although catalogue entries often describe the sampler stitch patterns as being of lace or openwork knitting, many of the samplers also contain twisted stitches and cables. The stitch gauge of the knitted samplers is very fine, making the cables prominent against the background stitch pattern. Cable and twist stitch patterns found on many of the long-strip samplers include textured lattice arrangements, such as the example represented in the sketch shown in Figure 6. Another example is the long lines of twisted stitches separated by con-

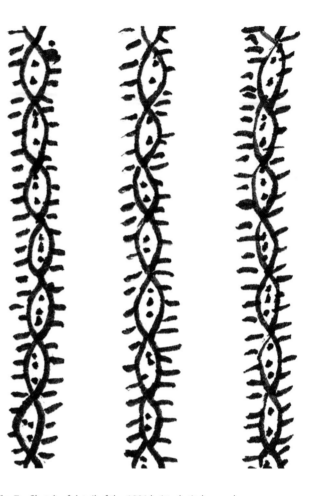

Fig. 7 Sketch of detail of the 1891 knitted stitch sampler.

trasting stocking stitch bands, represented in the sketch shown in Figure 7.

These types of stitch arrangements are also found within a late-nineteenth-century sampler held in the extensive collection of the Knitting & Crochet Guild (KCG) of Great Britain. This sampler, shown in Figure 5, is made up of sixty-three different knitting stitch patterns. One of the sections includes the initials of the maker and the year of the knitting: 'A.F. 1891'. Fine, white, cotton yarn has been used in this project, and the gauge has been measured at seventy-eight stitches by one hundred rows over ten centimetres (four inches). Working at this level of detail results in the beautiful stitch definition of the patterns. As shown in Figure 5, a fifty-pence piece has been placed next to the sampler, to reveal the scale of the stitch patterns. The majority of the stitch patterns in this sampler are of lace. However, as with other sampler examples, there are several knitted twist and cable sections in amongst the knitted

Fig. 8 Sketch of twisted stitches and eyelets from a section of the KCG 1891 knitted stitch sampler.

Fig. 9 Sketch of cables and lace lattice from a section of the KCG 1891 knitted stitch sampler.

lace panels. These sections are illustrated in the sketches shown in Figures 8, 9 and 10.

The sketch shown in Figure 8 represents a twisted stitch and eyelet design from the sampler. The twisted stitches move from side to side within a narrow panel. Each narrow panel is separated by a long line of eyelets, with the eyelets having been worked on every row.

The sketch shown in Figure 9 represents a cabled lattice-stitch pattern in the same sampler. The lattice includes eyelets on the lower part of each diamond shape and an eyelet pattern in the centre of each diamond. The cable stitch movements at the intersections of the diamonds are all worked in the same way. This detail is shown in Figure 10.

Fig. 10 Sketch of cable-crossing detail from a section of the KCG 1891 knitted stitch sampler.

Knitting publications

The knitting of samplers can be related to an explosion in publications about knitting, netting and crochet that occurred in Victorian times. These publications marked the change of knitting from a functional skill, for the production of everyday garments in continuous use, to a leisure activity for Victorian ladies. As a leisure activity, many delicate and detailed accessories were created, and new ideas and patterns were constantly sought by knitters. Before these publications became widely available, knitting was a skill that was mainly taught by word of mouth and by example. Patterns were passed on as children learned to knit by watching a family member or a teacher. Richard Rutt, in the historical glossary (p.226) of his 1987 book *A History of Hand Knitting*, lists the term 'cable' as first appearing in print in a knitting context in 1844. He points out that, although there are very few published references to knitting before 1837, terms used around that time will most probably already have been in use for a considerable period of time, even centuries.

Some of the earliest knitting publications are held in the National Art Library at the V&A Museum in London. A wide selection of Victorian knitting books, by several of the leading knitting figures of the day, are available for study. While references to cable patterns in any form are very limited, there are some interesting technique observations to be found in these delightful books.

Miss Lambert's needlework book of 1844 is one example that contains a cable pattern that is actually titled 'Cable Knitting' (p.54). Miss Lambert's cables are six-stitch cables worked with a left slant. The pattern instructions do not allow for any stitches to be worked between the cables. The cables are worked after seven rows of 'pearl' knitting and plain knitting. The pattern uses a third needle on which to slip the first three stitches. This stitch pattern sits amongst a variety of patterns for a great number of projects and stitch patterns. However, it is the only

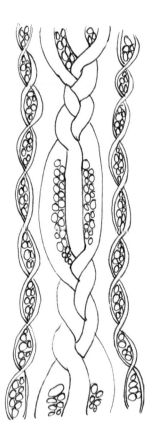

Fig. 11 Sketch of twists and cables similar to those of old Scotch stitch.

Most importantly, in an accompanying note to a pattern 'For Baby's Caps, Cuff, &c. &c.', Mrs Gaugain informs her readers of the stitch pattern's origin: 'This stitch is copied from a knit cap which was worked in Scotland more than 140 years since; I shall afterwards, in this Volume, produce it for a bed coverlet, &c. &c.' (p.45).

Mrs Gaugain's comment implies that cables had been in common use from the beginning of the eighteenth century. Although not conclusive evidence, this shows that there was already an assumption about the extensive use of cable-style knitting in the nineteenth century.

Bedcovers and counterpanes

As well as the many fine and detailed accessories created by Victorian knitters, other popular knitted items of the time were bedspreads, carriage blankets and counterpanes. The descriptions of knitted counterpanes in Mary Walker Phillips's 2013 book *Knitting Counterpanes* reveal that a cable was often used as a way of making a long, straight, vertical, raised line. Construction of the counterpanes was usually in separate pieces that were sewn together in the desired configuration after the knitting was complete. The cabled sections were often knitted in multiple long strips containing a mix of stitches.

In these patterns, the long lines of twisted columns are being used as part of the overall design of the knitted item. It is important to note the scale of the knitted item. A bedcover, counterpane or carriage blanket is a very large item that can have multiple decorative details on the same piece of work. Stockings and hats, the mainstay of earlier domestic knitting, have a smaller area available for decoration. Much of the detail would have been added afterwards through embroidery, and possibly with a contrasting shade of thread or yarn, rather than as a knitted-in twist or cable feature.

The KCG Collection includes the knitted bedspread that is shown in Figure 12. This item is quite unusual, as it can be dated and attributed to a specific maker. The name of the knitter and the date of the knitting have been recorded in purl stitches on a stocking stitch background within the bedspread itself. The panel reads 'Hannah Smith 1837'. The bedspread uses the long-strip technique and includes multiple cables, as well as sections of contrasting textural knitting. There is even a beautifully darned area, showing that the bedspread was well used and constantly maintained. A selection of intersecting stitch patterns are highlighted in the sketch shown in Figure 13. A textural basket-weave pattern contrasts with the bold cables

cable pattern in the entire book. It appears to be noted purely as an additional stitch pattern that is available for the knitter to use, as it does not form part of an accessory or garment pattern.

The cable patterns in these publications all specify a third needle or wire to work the cable. Each pattern gives directions as to where to place the stitches and the third needle, at either the front or the back of the work. Some patterns, such as the 'Cable Insertion' in Mdlle Rigolette de la Hamelin's *The Royal Magazine of Knitting, Netting, Crochet and Fancy Needlework*, No. 4, instruct the knitter to work the cable over two rows. The spare stitches remain on the third needle until the position of the cable is reached when knitting the second row.

'Beautiful Old Scotch Stitch' is referred to in the third edition of *The Lady's Assistant in Knitting, Netting and Crochet Work*, published in 1846, by Mrs Jane Gaugain. This stitch pattern is described in detail in the book and is used in knitting patterns designed by Mrs Gaugain. Old Scotch stitch consists of a combined twisted stitch, cable and lace pattern. There are several different types of twist and cable stitch movements, including two cables of different numbers of stitches. Figure 11 shows a sketch of combined twists and cables that are similar to those of old Scotch stitch, with eyelets forming an integral part of the pattern.

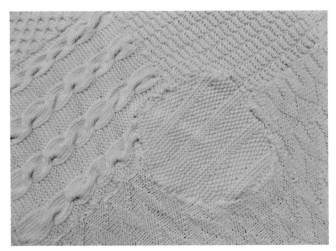

Fig. 12 Detail of knitted bedspread by Hannah Smith, 1837. (KCG Collection; photo: Angharad Thomas)

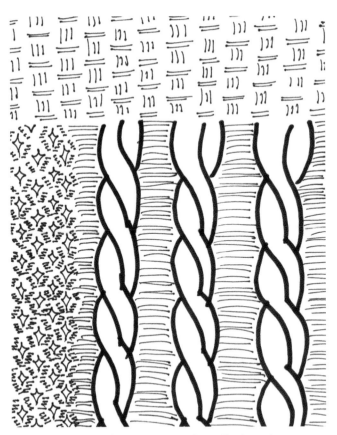

Fig. 13 Sketch of stitch patterns on 1837 knitted bedspread.

on a garter-stitch background and with the neighbouring honeycomb pattern.

A published example of this long-strip technique, also including the old-Scotch-stitch pattern referred to previously, can be found in the 1846 publication of *The Lady's Assistant in Knitting, Netting and Crochet Work* by Mrs Jane Gaugain, in a pattern for a 'Very Handsome Knit Bed-Cover', which is 'Composed of alternate stripes of the Old Scotch Stitch and a stripe of basketwork stitch. When knit to the length required, and as many stripes as are wished for the width of the counter-pane, sew or knit them together' (p.122).

The instruction for the basketwork stitch includes a precise description of the knitting technique required, as Mrs Gaugain had written a detailed footnote (p.125) to help the knitter:

Here lies my difficulty of description. – Take the right hand pin, and insert the point of it through to the front, between the first and second stitch on the left hand pin; work the second stitch in the common way, keep it on the left hand pin; you now have one stitch on the right hand pin; now work the first stitch from off the left hand pin, which is done in the common way. Now lift them both off the left hand pin. I gave this to a girl of 14 years of age to try, and she accomplished it, although I had my doubts concerning it. Both stitches in this bed-cover will not be found in the knowledge of many persons.

The description shows that the basketwork pattern comprises a two-stitch twisted stitch. The pattern instructions use the description for both right-side and wrong-side rows, revealing that the twists are worked as pearl stitches as well as plain. This bedcover pattern therefore contains both cables and twisted stitches, worked on both the right side and the wrong side of the knitting. It appears from the description that, despite her claim mentioned earlier, that the old-Scotch-stitch pattern has been in existence for the previous 140 years, Mrs Gaugain feels that the techniques required to achieve the stitch patterns are not well known. Clearly concerned that her readers would not be able to achieve either stitch pattern, Mrs Gaugain gives her knitters an alternative stitch pattern: 'Should the basket-stitch be found too difficult for comprehension, common garter stitch stripes may be substituted' (p.126).

Gansey and Aran knitting

The word 'traditional' implies a set knitting procedure that has been used again and again over many years and is instantly recognizable. Gansey and Aran knitting certainly fit this description. However recognizable these stitch patterns are, there is much evidence to show that they have evolved and changed over time, by either the deliberate or the accidental sharing of ideas.

The many ropes used on a fishing boat were an obvious inspiration source for early cable knitters. This link between ropes and knitted twists and cables is clear when reading the dictionary definitions of the words. The 1976 *Concise Oxford Dictionary of Current English* noun definition of 'twist' refers to a 'thread, rope, etc., made by winding two or more strands, etc., about one another', and the verb definition of 'twist' means 'the act of twisting, condition of being twisted' (p.1256). For 'cable', the noun is defined as a 'strong, thick rope of hemp or wire', and the definition of 'cable stitch' is a 'knitted pattern looking like twisted rope' (p.137).

As representations of different sizes of ropes, cable stitch patterns on a gansey sweater were worked on different scales, with different numbers of stitches and numbers of rows between twists. From fine, two-stitch lines to wide, eight-stitch braids, ropes provided knitters with a great inspiration source. Combinations of knitting stitches have been attributed to specific geographical areas and, in some cases, specific knitters. However, similar patterns can be found in very different geographical areas throughout the British Isles. The emergence of these related patterns in different parts of the country can be explained by the very nature of the fishing industry that inspired the patterns in the first place. As the fishing boats arrived in different ports, the patterning of a gansey from a far-away port was brought up close to a knitter who may in turn have been inspired to develop their own version. New stitch combinations emerged, but the similarity remained; hence, the evidence of the occurrence similar patterns at distant ports is accounted for.

Aran knitting emerged as a distinct style in the twentieth century. In Gladys Thompson's 1979 book, *Patterns for Guernseys, Jerseys & Arans*, the author makes some interesting comparisons between these different but closely related types of knitting. She notes that, while ganseys have always been knitted in the round with a very particular construction method, Aran sweaters were often knitted in pieces and then seamed. However, Thompson proposes that it is the use of travelling stitches across the surface of the knitting, along with cables in the design, that makes Aran patterns distinct from those of ganseys.

Later developments in Aran knitting in the early twentieth century have also resulted in many stitch combinations being named after the pattern that they resemble or the inspiration source that they came from. These clues to the knitters' thinking are important to recognize. The horseshoe cable, for example, actually resembles a horseshoe. The many versions of wave patterns are much more of an interpretation of the sea. Although the patterns all refer to waves, they are constructed in several different ways. A similar approach is taken throughout this book. The inspirational source material is the key component of the designs, and the stitch combinations chosen represent the essence of the pattern, shape or form from the source and the response to it. The naming of a pattern is helpful but does not always reveal the specific design behind it.

In her 1983 book, *The Complete Book of Traditional Knitting*, Rae Compton suggests that a great deal of experimentation was present in early Aran-style knitting before the designs became more commercialized. Compton suggests that early Aran garments were usually created for a specific wearer, with the knitter having complete control over the design. The pattern would often be different between the front and back of the garment, but the designs would always be linked. The set-in sleeves of these early Aran sweaters also functioned as the link between the front and back patterns. Knitters would add design elements while they were knitting and would experiment with different stitch combinations in different sweaters.

As the Aran industry became more commercialized, there was a need to standardize some of the stitch patterns. This was in part driven by the requirement to make multiple sizes of a similar design. The stitch-pattern panels were often bordered by a more simple design that could be widened or narrowed as needed. Raglan sleeves were introduced. Another change at this time was the need to write patterns down in order to share the instructions. Previously, patterns had been handed down by word of mouth, with no need for the instructions to be written line by line.

Alice Starmore, in her book *Aran Knitting*, defines an Aran sweater (p.46) as follows:

> ... a hand knitted garment of flat construction, composed of vertical panels of cabled geometric patterns and textured stitches. On each piece of the sweater there is a central panel flanked by symmetrically arranged side panels. The use of heavy undyed cream wool is a classic – though not essential – component of the style.

Fig. 14   Reconstructed 1936 Aran sweater. (KCG Collection; photo: Norman Taylor)

Fig. 15   Sketch of front stitch patterns of the reconstructed 1936 sweater.

Fig. 16   Sketch of sleeve stitch patterns of the reconstructed 1936 sweater.

This definition is an excellent way to consider the underlying structure of many of the historical Aran sweaters in museum collections. It also provides a framework with which to view the developments that occur within Aran-style knitting as consumer demand and fashion trends called for an expanding variety of styles and construction methods.

Barbara Smith, publications curator for the KCG, considers the development of these new twist and cable stitch patterns as an evolution of Aran style. Rather than there being a single definitive set of stitch patterns, or a definitive method of Aran garment construction, the many different cables, twists, bobbles and lace stitch patterns have continuously evolved and changed, to reflect the fashion trends of their times.

Three garments held in the KCG Collection are examples of some of the changes that occurred within Aran-style knitting during the twentieth century. The first example, shown in Figure 14, is a reconstruction of a sweater that was knitted in Dublin, Ireland, in the early twentieth century.

The original sweater was one of the first recorded examples of complex Aran patterning and was purchased in Dublin in 1936 by the historian Heinz Kiewe. The stitch patterns on this original sweater were recorded and illustrated by author Mary Thomas in her classic 1943 book, *Mary Thomas's Book of Knitting Patterns*.

This garment has a clearly defined central panel and symmetrically arranged side panels. The stitch patterning is complex, and there are at least eight different twist and cable

stitch variations on this sweater, as well as textural patterning. Looking at the stitch patterns on the garment in detail, with reference to Mary Thomas's descriptions, highlights the pattern variations and complex repeats found on this single garment. The sketches shown in Figures 15 and 16 represent some of the knitted lines in these patterns.

The patterns include two variations of a diamond lattice, one using a two-stitch twist and the other a four-stitch cable. The four-stitch cable lattice, or travelling rib, has moss-stitch texture within the outer diamonds and that of reverse stocking stitch within the centre diamonds. This texture beautifully echoes the moss-stitch diamonds that are visible on the outer sections of the front of the sweater. These diamond lattices form the

Fig. 17 1959 knitted cable sweater. (KCG Collection; photo: Barbara Smith)

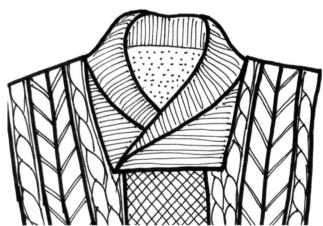

Fig. 18 Sketch of knitted detail on the 1959 sweater.

centre panels of the sweater's front and sleeves. The four-stitch cable lattice on the front is bordered by a five-stitch rope cable on each side. On the sleeves, the two-stitch-twist lattice is also bordered by a rope-style cable, but, in this case, it consists of two-stitch twists. Although the positioning of the rope cables on the front and sleeves is symmetrical, all of the twists have been worked in the same direction on each side of the centre panel, rather than as mirror images, with opposite twists.

Working outwards from the centre, the next pattern panels are combinations of twisted stitches. One combination forms a twisted stitch, diamond-column design with a twisted stitch rib pattern in the centre. This type of twisted stitch rib is made by knitting into the back of the stitch, making it appear more prominent. The column is placed on a stocking stitch background and has the same appearance on the front and the sleeves. The other combination forms zigzag lines of two sets of two-stitch twists on a reverse stocking stitch background. Again, the zigzags are worked in the same direction, rather than as mirror images. The welt comprises twisted stitches that are crossed on every eighth row. In Mary Thomas's description, the

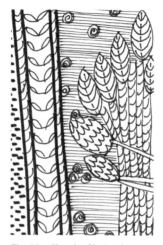

Fig. 20   Sketch of knitted
and embellished detail on the
wheatsheaf sweater.

stitches are slipped on to a match (rather than a wire or spare needle) and dropped to the front of the work to create the twist.

Aran-style knitting became less popular both during and after the years of the Second World War. One reason for this was that twist and cable knitting uses a considerable amount of yarn for a single garment. Wartime rationing meant that knitters had access to only extremely limited amounts of yarn. Knitters at that time devised many clever ways to make their limited supply of yarn go further. After this time, as yarn became more freely available again, twists and cables began to re-emerge as design features; nevertheless, the way that the stitch patterns were used began to change.

The sweater shown in Figure 17 was knitted from a pattern originally published in *Woman's Weekly* magazine in 1959. This sweater has a central panel, with symmetrical stitch-panel placement on each side of this panel, so it could be considered a traditional Aran sweater.

The knitting techniques used in this sweater, such as the bramble-stitch centre panel, the travelling, twisted stitch Vs and the double cable lines, were all commonly found on Aran-style garments. However, the square neckline and the shawl collar were not classic Aran constructions. These features, highlighted

in the sketch in Figure 18, show the influence of fashion at this time. The cable designs found on the 1959 sweater are in the style of Aran knitting, but the pattern is beginning to move into new design territories. Designers were using the Aran techniques in new ways and with different weights of yarn. For example, in 1957, the yarn company Patons had released a series of Aran-style patterns that were all designed for 4ply yarn.

By 1965, Patons had developed a heavier-weight knitting yarn called Capstan that was specifically for Patons Aran patterns. This yarn, initially available only in natural white, either oiled or scoured, proved so popular that by 1968 it was made available in several different colours. At around the same time, the *Patons Aran Book* was published. Although other ways of using twist and cable techniques in knitting had emerged, it was the huge popularity of Aran knitting in the late 1960s that set the style of what is now referred to as 'classic' Aran knitting.

The influence of fashion trends on all knitting is also seen from this point onwards. In the 1970s, bright neon colours made their way into hand-knitting patterns and, in the 1980s, oversized shoulders resulted in many cable sweaters being knitted with drop shoulders. A 1984 sweater from the KCG Collection, shown in Figure 19, demonstrates a clear inspiration source and the use of Aran techniques, but the result is very different when compared to the previous examples.

In the 1980s, picture knits were extremely popular, and the wheatsheaf sweater shown in Figure 19 is part of this fashion trend. The pattern is from a magazine supplement of *The Sunday Times* from 9 December 1984, also held in the KCG Collection. *The Sunday Times* describes the sweater as a 'wonderful modern interpretation of the traditional Aran'. The free pattern is one of two on offer to readers. The suggested yarn is Wendy Kintyre pure Aran wool. Interestingly, the second, much requested, pattern is a winter jacket designed by the Bishop of Leicestershire, Richard Rutt.

As with the previous sweater examples, the wheatsheaf sweater fulfils many of the requirements for it to be called Aran. The colour and weight of the yarn, the range of knitting techniques used and some of the garment construction methods can all be defined as Aran. However, this sweater is clearly different to a classic Aran sweater.

The wheatsheaf image itself is a very traditional symbol, and it is placed on the garment as the central panel, with additional symmetrical pattern panels on each side. The details are depicted in the sketch shown in Figure 20. However, the pictorial nature of the knitted wheatsheaf motif is very different to the Aran patterning of the previous example garments. Although knitted to include twisted stitch ropes, the design also incorporates additional surface-embroidery techniques. The cable patterning on each side of the central panel is worked in the style of a horseshoe or print-o'-the-hoof cable. The textured underside of the sleeves and the outer sides of the front are knitted in moss stitch, contrasting with the reverse stocking stitch background of the wheatsheaf motif. The cuffs, lower edging and neckband contain a combination of a zigzag travelling cable with bobbles and two-stitch twists worked as ropes.

The three garment examples from the KCG Collection highlight a few of the ways in which Aran style evolved during the twentieth century. The stitch-pattern combinations of classic Aran knitting originated with highly skilled, individual knitters experimenting with their knitting. Their ideas were shared, deliberately or accidentally, at a national and then international level throughout the twentieth century, with fishing boats taking gansey patterns to new destinations and design interpretations from other countries appearing in national newspaper supplements and magazines. Additional changes in the use of twist and cable patterns occurred in response to widening yarn availability, increased consumer demand for new knitting patterns and ever-changing fashion trends.

The continuing influence of twists and cables

This historical overview has included references to knitted samplers, garments and accessories that are held in several important textile collections. As well as forming the basis for research into historical knitting, these important items have themselves become the inspiration for new designs and directions in knitting. In recent years, knitted items containing twists and cables have been featured in several diverse exhibitions and within the collections of several renowned designers. In addition to being used as a reference point, these items have already generated and will continue to generate a multitude of new ideas when combined with other crafts and disciplines. This cross-fertilization into other areas of design reveals an exciting future for these most traditional of techniques.

In the exhibition Future Beauty: 30 Years of Japanese Fashion, held at the Barbican Art Gallery from October 2010 to February 2011, creative knitted garments featured alongside other examples of innovative Japanese fashion design. The impact of designers such as Rei Kawakubo and Tao Kurihara for the Tao Commes des Garçons label showed how, beginning in the 1980s and continuing until the present, Japanese designers have used traditional techniques in new and innovative ways. From Kawakubo's large-scale sweaters with loosely woven cable structures to Kurihara's use of underwear as outerwear, the approach of these influential designers was to deconstruct traditional ideas and construct a new style. Several knitted garments and accessories were featured in the exhibition, but one in particular showed this use of traditional techniques in a new way. An ivory, wool, knitted bodice and cable-knit shorts, designed by Kurihara for Tao Commes des Garçons for the Autumn–Winter 2005/06 season, were inspired by her detailed study of classic undergarments. The new designs had the appearance of delicate undergarments, but the features were completely reconfigured by using knitting techniques more usually associated with outerwear. The garments were knitted with bold, raised lines of twists and cables, as well as a travelling-stitch lattice filled with knitted bobbles. Crochet embellishment and laced ribbons completed the very delicate design that reflected the Japanese street style of the time.

Another Barbican exhibition, held in the summer of 2014, showed more examples of combinations of creative cables and twists and unexpected additional techniques. In The Fashion World of Jean Paul Gaultier: From the Sidewalk to the Catwalk, knitted twists and cables were displayed alongside high fashion.

The twists and cables were just one of the couture techniques used by the designer to create his visionary collections that featured on the catwalks throughout the world.

The importance of items in museum collections was highlighted in an exhibition at the Museum of Modern Art (MOMA) in New York, USA, from October 2017 to January 2018. This exhibition featured an iconic Aran sweater from the Country Life collection of the National Museum of Ireland. This 1942 sweater is one of several that have been studied by historians and researchers exploring the history and impact of Aran design. This example has similar design features to the reconstructed sweater from the KCG Collection looked at earlier in this chapter. In the MOMA exhibition, called Items: Is Fashion Modern?, the sweater is displayed as an example of a classic design with enduring popularity. It is one of 111 items of clothing and accessories, each selected to explore the notion of the past, present and future of world-renowned designs. This historically important Aran sweater, with its complex combinations of twists and cables, was displayed alongside other iconic designs such as Levi's® 501® jeans, the Breton shirt and the little black dress, clearly showing the enduring popularity of Aran style. The inclusion of this 1942 Aran sweater in the context of global design is a reminder of the endurance of twists and cables throughout fashion history.

These examples illustrate the nature of knitted twists and cables changing over time. The techniques used remain constant, but the way that they are applied has developed in many fascinating ways. This change of use and context reflects the skill and creativity of the designers involved. However, all of the twist and cable techniques owe their origin to the knitters and designers who developed the skills and ideas that form the link between all of these designs. Without the old Scotch stitch, the ganseys and the Arans, these new directions in the fashion world would not have been possible. As with the fishing boats transporting gansey-sweater patterns across the British Isles, the museum displays provide another means for the deliberate or accidental sharing of ideas to promote new design directions.

CHAPTER 2

TERMINOLOGY AND TECHNIQUES

This chapter looks at twisted stitches and cables in detail, beginning with the definitions, moving on to the knitting actions needed to create the stitch movements, then looking at the effect on the knitted fabric and concluding with how to work from a knitting chart.

Knitted lines

A knitter's sketchbook is all about the interpretation of pattern by using inspiration sources. Knitted lines and shapes are the building blocks for interpretative designs. The lines and shapes are formed by using a variety of widths of knitted lines. It is therefore essential to make a distinction between the fine lines of twisted stitches and the broader lines of cables, as the width of the line in the knitting is very important.

The twists and cables can be considered the equivalent of the strokes of pens, pencils or brushes. Narrow lines of twisted stitches can draw a delicate image similar to that achieved with fine pencil lines. A wide, chunky, multiple-stitch cable evokes a broad brushstroke. The knitted swatch shown in Figure 21 demonstrates how changing the number of foreground stitches changes the width of the knitted line, from the single twisted stitch on the right to the broad cable on the left. Although all

Fig. 21 Examples of widths of lines in knitting.

of the stitch movements could be called cables, this distinction between the fineness of the lines will be clearly defined in the following section.

The knitted lines in the swatch shown in Figure 21 have been worked on the foreground of the knitting, which in this example is the right side of the work. The background stitch pattern, again on the right side of the swatch, is also critical to the overall design. The background stitches are like the paper that is used for drawing on. In the same way that the choice of paper will change the look of a drawing, the choice of background stitch will affect how the foreground stitch pattern of the cables and twists will appear. Choosing to work on textured or smooth paper has a similar result to that of choosing to work on a moss-stitch or stocking stitch background.

Describing twists and cables

Before beginning a pattern, the most important advice for any knitter is to read the abbreviation definitions carefully. Never assume that any particular symbol means to perform the same action as that described in a context that you have previously encountered the symbol; different publications and patterns can use the same symbol to mean a completely different stitch movement. This book uses a consistent series of symbols and definitions throughout. The symbols are all part of the

Stitchmastery charting software. These symbols allow the knitter to 'see' the stitch movements, both in the format of charts and as the stitches appear within the knitted swatches. New symbols will be explained as they are used, and the terminology will be clearly explained. There is a full list of all of the symbols and definitions at the back of this book (*see* Abbreviations).

Twists

There are several definitions of a twist or twisted stitch, and all depend on the context of the stitches being worked. A twist can be a single stitch crossed over another single stitch or a group of stitches. This type of stitch movement can also be called a cross stitch or travelling stitch. The stitch movement can be a simple exchange of places between neighbouring stitches or a complex lattice worked over many rows. The twisting can be worked in the same position within the fabric, to create a vertical line, or can be linked over several rows across the fabric, to create diagonal lines. The twisting can be to the left or the right and be worked in a variety of different stitch textures. In many cases, this kind of stitch movement is referred to as a cable. The term 'twisted stitch' can also describe a stitch that results from the action of working into the back of that stitch, creating a twist in that particular stitch. Working this kind of twisted stitch throughout the knitting creates dense knitted fabric but without any crossing of stitches over each other.

There is a strong case to label all of the lines resulting from the movements of groups of stitches as cables. However, for this book, the distinction between the fine lines created by single-foreground-stitch movements, for delicate stitch patterning, and the broader lines created by moving larger groups of multiple stitches is very important. This book therefore defines a twisted stitch as a single foreground stitch that is moved or crossed over one or more background stitches. The knitted line on the right-hand side of the fabric shown in Figure 21 is an example of a twisted stitch.

Cables

A cable can be defined as a group of stitches that are crossed over another group of stitches. The group of foreground stitches can be worked over any number of background stitches and in a variety of textures. Cables are similar to twists, as they involve an exchange of position of the stitches. Cables are usually named after the number of stitches involved and the direction

of movement of the front stitches. In this book, the cable stitch movements supply a huge variety of width of foreground line.

Cables are also sometimes referred to as travelling stitches. A travelling stitch moves in a similar way to a cable, usually over several background stitches. In her 1979 book, *Patterns for Guernseys, Jerseys & Arans*, Gladys Thompson makes a distinction between cables and travelling stitches in the section about Aran knitting. Cables are described as being worked amongst the travelling stitches that run across the knitted-fabric surface. The stitch movements involved are the same movements as used in a vertical cable column; however, the effect is to create a moving line.

Cable stitch movements in this book therefore refer to two or more foreground stitches being moved over one or more background stitches. The stitch movement may be repeated in a vertical column or used to move the foreground stitches across the knitting. The knitted lines in the centre and on the left-hand side of the fabric shown in Figure 21 are examples of cables.

Front and back versus left and right

Knitting terminology varies between publication and country and certainly over time. There are multiple ways of describing the same movement of stitches. Wide variations in terminology are found in knitting stitch directories. Stitch directories can vary by the year of production, by country of origin and, of course, by the author's preferences. It is essential to be clear and consistent with whichever instructions are used throughout knitted samples. This book uses terminology from the Stitchmastery software, as it provides a clear, numerical guide to the stitch movements of each twist and cable. This section explains the way that I interpret the movements of twists and cables that are present throughout the book.

To understand the movement of twists and cables, each element in the movement needs to be looked at. Cable stitches have multiple variations in how they can be worked. These variations include the number of stitches in the whole cable, the number of stitches moved on to the cable needle, the direction of the cable, whether the cable is worked with or without a cable needle, the choices of stitch pattern worked in the foreground and the background of the cable, and the stitch pattern worked on the other stitches of the fabric while the slipped cable stitches are held on the cable needle. All of these elements influence the descriptions used in this book. Understanding how the individual elements work together

	Total no of stitches to be worked	No of foreground stitch(es)	No of background stitch(es)	Direction of foreground stitch	Abbreviation	Also known as
	2	1	1	R	1/1RC	C2B
	2	1	1	L	1/1LC	C2F
	3	1	2	R	½RC	C3B
	3	1	2	L	½LC	C3F
	3	2	1	R	2/1RC	C3B
	3	2	1	L	2/1LC	C3F
	4	1	3	R	1/3RC	C4B
	4	1	3	L	1/3LC	C4F
	4	2	2	R	2/2RC	C4B
	4	2	2	L	2/2LC	C4F
	4	3	1	R	3/1RC	C4B
	4	3	1	L	3/1LC	C4F

Fig. 22 Table describing two-, three- and four-stitch twist and cable variations worked in stocking stitch only.

is essential when techniques are combined to make complex shapes and designs.

To further illustrate the variations available, the table in Figure 22 describes examples of two-, three- and four-stitch twist and cable stitch movements worked in stocking stitch only. These stitch options are also shown later in this chapter, as a swatch photograph and accompanying chart (Figures 64 and 65, respectively). Each variable is considered in detail below. The final column, 'Also known as', demonstrates the difficulty of using only a direction and the total number of stitches as the description: the same description applies to many different combinations of cable stitches.

Total number of stitches

In this book, twists and cables are all categorized by the total number of stitches involved in the overall movement. The total comprises both the foreground stitches and the background stitches. The table clearly shows how the number of movement options available increases with the total number of stitches that we are working with. In this example, the table includes two-stitch twists, three-stitch twists and cables, and four-stitch cables. There is a total of twelve different movement combinations. There are two movements available for the two-stitch twists, four movements for the three-stitch twists and cables and six movements for the four-stitch cables.

Number of stitches moved to the cable needle

The number of stitches on the cable needle is a proportion of the total number of stitches involved in the twist or cable. There are only two options for twists with a total of two stitches. These two options are to move the foreground stitch either to the right or to the left. A total of three stitches results in four options. In this case, there can be either one or two stitches as the foreground stitches and as the background stitches (to the maximum of three stitches). With a total of four stitches, the options available increase again. In this case, one, two or three stitches can be used as the foreground stitches and background stitches (to the maximum of four stitches), giving six different combinations.

Direction of the cable and placement of the cable needle

The cable can move to the left or the right over a varying number of stitches. Abbreviations refer to this movement as L for left and R for right. Sometimes the instructions refer to B for back and F for front. In this case, the B and F refer to the placement of the cable needle. As a four-stitch-cable example, two stitches can be moved to the left by lifting the first two stitches on to a cable needle and holding these stitches, on the cable needle, at the front of the work. The next two stitches on the left-hand needle are then worked, followed by the stitches on the cable needle. The cable is moving to the left, and the cable needle was held at the front of the work, so both ways of describing the cable are correct. Typically, the detailed pattern instructions will refer to the lhn, rhn and cn (or similar alternative abbreviations), for the left-hand needle, right-hand needle and cable needle, respectively. As this book is concerned with design, it is more helpful to refer to the direction of the cable rather than the technical movement of the stitches. The terminology therefore will focus on the direction of movement of the cable stitches.

Working with or without a cable needle

Many twist and cable descriptions consider the direction of movement of the foreground stitches versus the position of the cable needle required to work the stitches. This can cause confusion when working without a cable needle. As long as the desired stitch manipulation is achieved, how the twist or cable is actually worked is up to the knitter. In this book, the terminology used to describe the cable will be consistent, however the knitter chooses to work it. Working without a cable needle can help to speed up the knitting process.

Using the stocking stitch, four-stitch cable as an example, a left-leaning cable can be worked without a cable needle by knitting into the stitches without taking them off of the left-hand needle. Knit into the back of the third and fourth stitches on the left-hand needle in turn, without taking the stitches off of the left-hand needle, then knit into the front of the first and second stitches on the left-hand needle in turn. Keeping the worked loops on the right-hand needle, slip all four worked stitches off of the left-hand needle. This will create the same cable effect as that achieved by using a cable needle.

Foreground and background of the work

Within the cables, there is a distinction between the stitches moved into the foreground of the knitting and the stitches worked in the background. This is different from the front and back of the work and from the right side and wrong side of the work. For example, when working a four-stitch-wide cable such as a 3/1 RC or 3/1 LC, three stitches are worked in the foreground of the knitting and one stitch is worked in the background. This stitch manipulation is worked with the right side of the work facing.

A further distinction is made between the stitch pattern worked in the foreground and background. The example twist and cable stitches shown in the table in Figure 22 all use stocking stitch. If the background stitch is reverse stocking stitch, the cable will be moved in the same way; however, the stitch pattern will be different. We will look at twists and cables that use both stocking stitch and reverse stocking stitch in detail further on in this chapter.

How to work twists

A twisted stitch is a stitch movement that usually involves two or three stitches in total. There is an exchange of stitch positions, with one foreground stitch moving over one or two background stitches. Whether the twist has a total of two or three stitches, the techniques needed to work the stitch movements are similar. The following examples have a total of two stitches. Each example shows the stitch movements required to move one foreground stitch to the right or the left, with options given for working with and without a cable needle. Working without a cable needle can help to speed up the knitting process and allows the pattern to flow. However, a cable needle is very helpful for stitch movements involving combinations of stitch patterns.

Two-stitch twists in stocking stitch

In the following examples, of 1/1 RC and 1/1 LC, one foreground stitch is being moved over one background stitch, either to the right or to the left, without using a cable needle. The stitches are all knitted in stocking stitch.

Fig. 23 1/1 RC step 1.

Fig. 24 1/1 RC step 2.

Fig. 25 1/1 RC step 3.

Fig. 26 1/1 LC step 1.

Fig. 27 1/1 LC step 2.

Fig. 28 1/1 LC step 3.

1/1 RC right-leaning, two-stitch twist
Pattern to the twist location.
Step 1 (Figure 23): Knit into the front of the second stitch on the lhn.
Step 2 (Figure 24): Without taking the stitch that was just knitted into off of the lhn, knit into the front the first stitch on the lhn.
Step 3 (Figure 25): Keeping the worked loops on the rhn, slip both worked stitches off of the lhn.

1/1 LC left-leaning, two-stitch twist
Pattern to the twist location.
Step 1 (Figure 26): Knit into the back of the second stitch on the lhn.
Step 2 (Figure 27): Without taking the stitch that was just knitted into off of the lhn, knit into the front of the first stitch on the lhn.
Step 3 (Figure 28): Keeping the worked loops on the rhn, slip both worked stitches off of the lhn.

Fig. 29 1/1 RPC (with a cn) step 1.

Fig. 30 1/1 RPC (with a cn) step 2.

Fig. 31 1/1 RPC (with a cn) step 3.

Two-stitch twists in stocking stitch and reverse stocking stitch

In the following examples, one foreground stitch is being moved over one background stitch, either to the right or to the left. The foreground stitch is always knitted in stocking stitch. The background stitch is worked in reverse stocking stitch for a 1/1 RPC and 1/1 LPC. Options are given for working with and without a cable needle.

1/1 RPC right-leaning, two-stitch twist worked with a cable needle

Pattern to the twist location.

Step 1 (Figure 29): Slip the next stitch on to the cn, and hold the cn at back of work.

Step 2 (Figure 30): Knit the next stitch.

Step 3 (Figure 31): Purl the stitch from the cn.

Fig. 32   1/1 RPC (without a cn) step 1.

Fig. 33   1/1 RPC (without a cn) step 2.

Fig. 34   1/1 RPC (without a cn) step 3.

Fig. 35   1/1 LPC (with a cn) step 1.

Fig. 36   1/1 LPC (with a cn) step 2.

Fig. 37   1/1 LPC (with a cn) step 3.

1/1 RPC right-leaning, two-stitch twist worked without a cable needle

Pattern to the twist location.

Step 1 (Figure 32): Knit into the front of the second stitch on the lhn.

Step 2 (Figure 33): Without taking the stitch that was just knitted into off of the lhn, purl into the front of the first stitch on the lhn.

Step 3 (Figure 34): Keeping the worked loops on the rhn, slip both worked stitches off of the lhn.

1/1 LPC left-leaning, two-stitch twist worked with a cable needle

Pattern to the twist location.

Step 1 (Figure 35): Slip the next stitch on to the cn, and hold the cn at front of work.

Step 2 (Figure 36): Purl the next stitch.

Step 3 (Figure 37): Knit the stitch from the cn.

Fig. 38 1/1 LPC (without a cn) step 1.

Fig. 39 1/1 LPC (without a cn) after step 1 has been completed.

Fig. 40 1/1 LPC (without a cn) step 2.

Fig. 41 1/1 LPC (without a cn) step 3.

1/1 LPC left-leaning, two-stitch twist worked without a cable needle

Pattern to the twist location.

Step 1 (Figure 38): Slip the first and second stitches from the lhn to the rhn together purlwise. After step 1 is completed, the stitches are in the same order (Figure 39).

Step 2 (Figure 40): From right to left, insert the tip of the lhn into both stitches from the front.

Step 3 (Figure 41): Slip both stitches back to the lhn; the order of the stitches is now reversed.

Step 4: To complete the stitch movement, purl the new first stitch, then knit the new second stitch.

Fig. 42 2/2 RC and 2/2 RPC (with a cn) step 1.   **Fig. 43** 2/2 RC (with a cn) step 3.   **Fig. 44** 2/2 RPC (with a cn) step 3.

How to work cables

A cable is a stitch movement that usually involves three or more stitches in total. There is an exchange of stitch positions, with two or more foreground stitches moving over one or more background stitches. Whether the cable has a total of three, four, five, six or more stitches, the techniques needed to work the stitch movements are similar. The following examples have a total of four stitches. Each example shows the stitch movements required to move two foreground stitches to the right or the left, with options given for working with and without a cable needle. Working without a cable needle can help to speed up the knitting process and allows the pattern to flow. However, a cable needle is very helpful for stitch movements involving larger numbers of stitches and combinations of stitch patterns.

Four-stitch, right-leaning cables

In the following examples, of 2/2 RC and 2/2 RPC, two fore-ground stitches are being moved over two background stitches to the right. The cables begin in the same way, with two stitches being placed on the cable needle that is then held at the back of the work. The next two stitches are knitted. There is a difference in the way that the stitches on the cable needle are worked. The stitches are knitted for a 2/2 RC and purled for a 2/2 RPC.

2/2 RC and 2/2 RPC worked with a cable needle
Pattern to the cable location.
Step 1 (Figure 42): Slip the next 2sts on to the cn, and hold the cn at back of work.
Step 2. Knit the next 2sts.
Note: Step 3 is different for 2/2 RC and 2/2 RPC.
Step 3 (2/2 RC only, Figure 43): Knit the 2sts from the cn.
Step 3 (2/2 RPC only, Figure 44): Purl the 2sts from the cn.

Fig. 45 2/2 RC and 2/2 RPC (without a cn) step 1.

Fig. 46 2/2 RC and 2/2 RPC (without a cn) step 2.

Fig. 47 2/2 RC (without a cn) step 3.

Fig. 48 2/2 RC (without a cn) step 4.

Fig. 49 2/2 RC (without a cn) step 5.

2/2 RC and 2/2 RPC worked without a cable needle
The 2/2 RC and 2/2 RPC cables begin in the same way, with two stitches being knitted at the front of the work. There is a difference in the way that the next two stitches are worked. In this example, the stitches are knitted for a 2/2 RC and purled for a 2/2 RPC.

Pattern to the cable location.
Note: 2/2 RC and 2/2 RPC begin with the same two steps.
Step 1 (Figure 45): Knit into the front of the third stitch on the lhn.

Step 2 (Figure 46): Knit into the front of the fourth stitch on the lhn.
Note: Steps 3–5 are different for a 2/2 RC and a 2/2 RPC.

2/2 RC only
Step 3 (Figure 47): Leaving the stitches that were just knitted into on the lhn, knit into the front of the first stitch on the lhn.
Step 4 (Figure 48): Knit into the front of the second stitch on the lhn.
Step 5 (Figure 49): Slip the worked stitches off of the lhn.

Fig. 50 2/2 RPC (without a cn) step 3.

Fig. 51 2/2 RPC (without a cn) step 4.

Fig. 52 2/2 RPC (without a cn) step 5.

Fig. 53 2/2 LC and 2/2 LPC (with a cn) step 1.

Fig. 54 2/2 LC (with a cn) step 2.

Fig. 55 2/2 LPC (with a cn) step 2.

2/2 RPC only

Step 3 (Figure 50): Leaving the stitches that were just knitted into on the lhn, purl into the front of the first stitch on the lhn.

Step 4 (Figure 51): Purl into the front of the second stitch on the lhn.

Step 5 (Figure 52): Slip the worked stitches off of the lhn.

Four-stitch, left-leaning cables

In the following examples, of 2/2 LC and 2/2 LPC, two fore-ground stitches are being moved over two background stitches to the left. The cable stitch movements begin and end in the same way. For both cables, two stitches are placed on to the cable needle that is then held at the front of the work. There is a difference in the way that the next two stitches are worked. The stitches are knitted for a 2/2 RC and purled for a 2/2 RPC. For both cables, the two stitches on the cable needle are knitted.

2/2 LC and 2/2 LPC worked with a cable needle
Pattern to the cable location.

Step 1 (Figure 53): Slip the next 2sts on to the cn, and hold the cn at front of work.

Note: Step 2 is different for a 2/2 LC and a 2/2 LPC.

Step 2 (2/2 LC only, Figure 54): Knit the next 2sts.

Step 2 (2/2 LPC only, Figure 55): Purl the next 2sts.

Step 3 (2/2 LC and 2/2 LPC): Knit the 2sts from the cn.

Fig. 56 2/2 LC (without a cn) step 1.

Fig. 57 2/2 LC (without a cn) step 2.

Fig. 58 2/2 LC (without a cn) step 3.

Fig. 59 2/2 LC (without a cn) step 4.

2/2 LC and 2/2 LPC worked without a cable needle

Although two foreground stitches are being moved over two background stitches to the left, different techniques are used for a 2/2 LC and a 2/2 LPC when working without a cable needle.

2/2 LC only

Pattern to the cable location.

Step 1 (Figure 56): Knit into the back of the third stitch on the lhn.

Step 2 (Figure 57): Knit into the back of the fourth stitch on the lhn.

Step 3 (Figure 58): Without taking the stitches that were just knitted into off of the lhn, knit into the front of the first stitch on the lhn.

Step 4 (Figure 59): Knit into the front of the second stitch on the lhn.

Step 5: Keeping the worked loops on the rhn, slip all four worked stitches off of the lhn.

Fig. 60 2/2 LPC (without a cn) step 1.

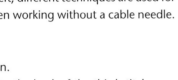

Fig. 61 2/2 LPC (without a cn) step 2.

Fig. 62 2/2 LPC (without a cn) step 3.

Fig. 63 2/2 LPC (without a cn) step 4.

2/2 LPC only

To work a mix of stocking stitch and reverse stocking stitch, the stitches on the needle need to be reordered before being worked. This method works best with a pure-wool yarn, for which the stitches hold their shape and do not unravel while temporarily off of the needle.

Pattern to the cable location.

Step 1 (Figure 60): Carefully slip the next 2sts off of the lhn, leaving them loose at front of work or holding them pinched between a thumb and forefinger.

Step 2 (Figure 61): Slip the next 2sts on the lhn on to the rhn purlwise.

Step 3 (Figure 62): Place the loose or pinched sts back on to the lhn.

Step 4 (Figure 63): Slip the first 2sts on the rhn back on to the lhn.

Step 5: Work the 4sts, which are now in the correct order, as p2, k2.

Stitch appearance

Twist-and-cable comparison

The appearance of the knitted twist or cable changes as the number of stitches changes. The knitted swatch shown in Figure 64 illustrates the stitches that are listed in the table shown in Figure 22. The chart shown in Figure 65 includes the symbols for the corresponding stitch abbreviations and indicates the position of the corresponding twist and cable stitch movements within the knitted swatch.

This sample of combined stitches is a line-by-line comparison of how single movements of groups of stitches affect the knitted fabric. Each paired set demonstrates a single option and direction. This comparison begins with twists of a total of two stitches on the right-hand side of the swatch and ends with twists and cables of a total of four stitches on the left-hand side. The stitch movements are shown as pairs of the stitches being worked in opposite directions.

The first set of stitch movements show the effect of using one foreground stitch, which results in a fine knitted line. The more stitches over which the foreground stitch is moved, the tighter the knitted fabric becomes. This is because stretching one stitch over multiple stitches pulls the background stitches together. Depending on the effect to be created, this property can be exploited. If the design is for a fine, lightly drawn line, it may be best to move the foreground stitch over fewer stitches and to use more rows between crosses. However, if a tight, gathered effect is to be created, multiple stitches can be pulled together in a single twist. These effects can be seen in the background stitches across the first row of twists in the swatch.

The second row of stitch movements uses two foreground stitches. This makes a wider knitted foreground line. As there is a total of only two stitches within the two lines at the right-hand side of the swatch, after the two single twists at the bottom of the swatch were worked, the rest of each of the two lines was worked without twists to provide a comparison between stitches worked with and without twists or cables. The three- and four-stitch examples can both be worked with two foreground stitches. In the three-stitch examples, the two foreground stitches are moved over one stitch. The stitch tension is looser than that resulting within the four-stitch example. In this case, the two stitches are moved over two background stitches, making a tighter-tensioned set of stitches.

Fig. 64 Knitted swatch of the twist-and-cable comparison.

For the final row of cable stitch movements, three foreground stitches have been used. This movement is possible only in the example that has a total of four stitches. The rest of each of the two- and three-stitch sections was worked in stocking stitch for comparison. Moving three stitches in the foreground over one stitch as the background results in a wide, loosely tensioned knitted line, as compared to the tension of the first row of stitch movements.

This terminology-and-techniques chapter has looked at ways of describing and working twists and cable stitches. By using a comparison to drawn and painted lines created with the strokes of a pen, pencil or brush, it can be seen how knitted lines can be formed by using twists and cables of different numbers of stitches. A consideration of the way that the stitches are moved reveals that there are several different techniques available to manipulate twists and cables. The use of precise abbreviations to describe these stitch movements illustrates that the number of options available increases as the number of stitches increases. These stitch options are usually communicated through a chart.

By building on the techniques from this chapter, further enhancements can be added to the knitted twists and cable lines. One of the ways to do this is by adding contrast to the stitch patterns. When sketching with a pen or pencil, the technique of mark-making can be used to add a variety of lines and textures, by drawing with different sizes of pens tips or adding dots, dashes and cross-hatching. In the knitted fabric, this process can be translated into stitch patterns. For example, different concentrations of drawn dots can be represented by changing from moss stitch to rice stitch over a number of rows, either within the cable stitches or in the background stitch pattern. These techniques will be considered in much more detail throughout the following chapters in the context of designing from inspirational images.

Twist-and-cable comparison

(32sts and 14 rows)

Row 1 (RS): P2, 1/1 RC, p2, 1/1 LC, p2, 1/2 RC, p2, 1/2 LC, p2, 1/3 RC, p2, 1/3 LC, p2.

Row 2 and all WS rows: (K2, p4) twice, (k2, p3) twice, (k2, p2) twice, k2.

Row 3: (P2, k2) twice, (p2, k3) twice, (p2, k4) twice, p2.

Row 5: As row 3.

Row 7: (P2, k2) twice, p2, 2/1 RC, p2, 2/1 LC, p2, 2/2 RC, p2, 2/2 LC, p2.

Rows 9 and 11: As row 3.

Row 13: (P2, k2) twice, (p2, k3) twice, p2, 3/1 RC, p2, 3/1 LC, p2.

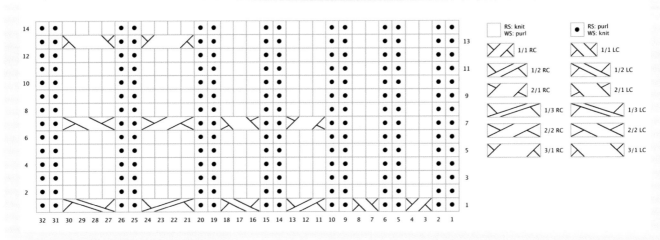

Fig. 65   Chart of the twist-and-cable comparison.

How to work from a chart

Throughout this book, designs are shown as a knitted swatch accompanied by a chart and written instructions for working one repeat of the pattern. The charted or written instructions describe how to recreate the knitted swatch.

Symbols
The symbol for a twist or cable will always fit across the total number of stitches that are worked within the twist or cable, so a four-stitch cable will always be worked over four stitches and the symbol therefore will be placed over four boxes of the chart. The way that the stitches are moved will vary. Before casting on, always check the symbol definitions, as there may be some special instructions. Variations will occur for the foreground stitches, the background stitches and what happens to the stitches on the cable needle.

Flat and circular knitting
The same chart can be used for flat knitting, in rows, and circular knitting, in the round. However, there are some differences in the way that the charts are read.

For flat knitting in rows, for this book, row 1 is always read from right to left, beginning with stitch number one. Row 2 is always read from left to right, beginning with the highest-number stitch; for example, that would be stitch number nine of a nine-stitch chart. Rows are always read from the bottom of the chart to the top, beginning with row 1. Odd-numbered rows are the right-side rows. Even-numbered rows are the wrong-side rows.

For circular knitting in rounds, round 1 is always read from right to left, beginning with stitch number one. Round 2 is also read from right to left. Rounds are always read from the bottom of the chart to the top, beginning with round 1. All of the rounds are right-side rows.

Chart repeats
Always check each chart for a highlighted box. This box indicates the pattern repeat. For the chart shown in Figure 66, this box is red and labelled 'Cornish-hedge repeat'. Working the stitches in this box two or more times across the row will link up the design horizontally over the given number of stitches. In this example, the box is stepped on row 3 and row 11. This is to accommodate the twisted stitch pattern in the design, as a repeat cannot run through the centre of a stitch movement. The box will also indicate the row repeat, and working the specified rows two or more times will link the design vertically. Additional stitches may be worked before and/or after the repeat box, to balance the pattern and create edgings.

A design may begin with additional rows that are worked once only. This is usually to set the pattern and will include a linking stitch pattern between any welt and the main design. The repeat box will follow this first section. The same transition may also be worked for the end of the design. If in doubt about how a pattern flows, cast on the minimum number of stitches with some spare yarn, and try out the pattern before casting on to work a tension swatch or a project.

Keeping track
Highlighting the current row of a chart that is being worked can help to keep track of your knitting. There are some great software packages that will do this for you when you are working from a digital chart, otherwise a ruler works very well for this purpose when you are working from printed charts. Individual cable charts can be enlarged, if preferred. Placing stitch markers on the needles between the end of each stitch repeat and the start of the next one is a great way of keeping track of the stitches until the pattern is established. Using a row counter can also help.

Keep looking at the worked stitches on both the right side and the wrong side of the knitting. The design will begin to emerge, and a point can be reached where there is no need to look at the instructions to recognize the pattern placement. This rhythm of a design is the perfect balance between a pattern that is straightforward to follow being combined with enough interest to keep the knitter engaged throughout the project.

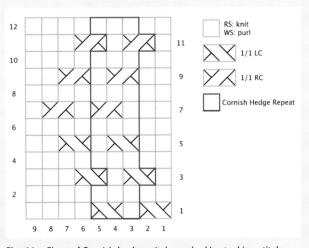

Fig. 66   Chart of Cornish-hedge stitch, worked in stocking stitch.

CHAPTER 3

YARN AND TOOLS

Yarn

'Yarn and pattern go hand in hand': as Montse Stanley's quote from *The Handknitter's Handbook* (1990, p.17) implies, yarn affects pattern, and pattern affects yarn. Experimenting with a wide variety of yarn fibres and weights increases the options available when designing with twists and cables. Although some general principles apply, for a knitter's sketchbook, the most important elements to consider are the effect on the knitted fabric and the link to the chosen inspirational source material.

There are several different elements to consider when deciding which yarn to choose for a design. For example, if clarity of the stitches is key to the design, a smooth yarn may be best. Using a highly textured yarn for the same stitch pattern may obscure the design and hide the detail. However, using the textured yarn for a larger cable may add interesting folds and structure to the knitted fabric. Using a fine yarn for a complex design can result in an extremely dense knitted fabric, with many repeats of the detailed pattern in a small area. Working fewer repeats of the same design in a heavier weight of yarn may create a bold, more distinctive pattern.

The best way to find out the effect of a particular yarn is to knit a test swatch. The knitting of experimental swatches is an important stage of developing any stitch-pattern design. The first swatches may involve only a small number of stitches and may just be a reminder of the elements of the design for later exploration. Next steps may include knitting a larger swatch, to show several repeats of the stitches and rows, to further refine ideas. These experimental swatches are different to a tension swatch. A tension swatch allows a designer to calculate the stitches and rows necessary for a final project. The fabric

Fig. 67 Swatches worked with different yarn weights.

Fig. 68 Comparison of different yarn weights.

Fig. 69 Comparison of yarn weight, with examples (from left to right) knitted in 2ply, 3ply, 4ply, DK, worsted, aran and chunky weights of wool yarn.

of an experimental swatch for the early exploration of a stitch pattern may neither be large enough nor be accurate enough for this purpose. Additionally, a stitch pattern designed with one weight and fibre type of yarn should always be retested if a different yarn is to be used in the project.

The ball band

Before casting on for any experimental swatch, a great deal of information can be gathered about a yarn and its suitability for a project from the band or label attached to the yarn.

The weight of the ball or skein is usually provided in both grams and ounces. Information about the specific fibre content will also be shown on the ball band. This is especially important for a blended yarn, where the actual proportion of the different fibres will have a big impact on the knitted fabric. The metreage or yardage given provides information about the length of the yarn in the ball or skein, to help determine how much yarn will be needed for a project.

The standard recommended tension, and the knitting-needle size to achieve this tension, will always be listed. You may need to adjust your needle size for several reasons. Tension is usually given for stocking stitch. To match this tension, you may need to go up or down a needle size or half size. Additionally, a different needle size may better suit the specific stitch pattern. A swatch knitted for a pattern with a high density of twists and cables may have a more even tension when worked on larger needles.

The international symbols for garment care will be listed on the ball band. This cleaning and pressing information is essential to consider when blocking any knitting, whether it is a swatch or a finished item. Many knitting patterns ask the knitter to refer to the ball-band information before blocking the final work.

The ball band will also have the shade name and/or number and the dye-lot code of the yarn. For a project involving multiple balls or skeins of yarn, it is important for all of the yarn to be of the same dye lot, as subtle colour variations between balls or skeins of yarn of different dye lots can otherwise show up in the finished knitting.

Yarn weight

Changing the weight of the yarn used to work a stitch pattern changes the scale of the design. For a knitter's sketchbook, experimenting with different yarns is an excellent way of exploring the knitted lines of a design. The fine lines created when knitting with a lace-weight yarn can then be compared to the broad brushstroke effects of knitting with a chunky yarn.

To illustrate the effect of different yarn weights, a series of swatches have been knitted by using the same stitch pattern but changing the yarn used for each swatch throughout the series. Each comparison swatch has been knitted separately with the comparison-cable stitch pattern. This pattern includes a wide cable braid and two twisted stitch ropes that are worked over two stitches.

Figure 69 shows these swatches knitted with the same stitch pattern over a range of different weights of yarn. In this case, the term 'weight' refers to the thickness of the fibre strand and not to the total weight of the yarn in the ball or skein.

There is a great deal of variation in the terminology used to describe yarn weight. Comparing yarns from different countries shows that similar yarns can fall into multiple categories. Many of the categories overlap, and, as new yarns are developed, the category definitions change. Additionally, many manufacturers

	Category name	Common label names (UK, USA, AUS and NZ)	Stocking stitch tension per 10cm/4in	Recommended needle size
Fig. 70 Table of yarn categories, showing common equivalent yarn weights.	Lace	Lace; Baby; Cobweb; Thread; 2ply; 3ply	33–40sts	1.5–2.25mm (000–1 US)
	4ply (Light)	Super Fine; Sock; Light Fingering; Baby; 3ply; 4ply	27–32sts	2.25–3.25mm (1–3 US)
	4ply	Fine; Sport; Fingering; Baby; Sock; 4ply; 5ply	23–26sts	3.25–3.75mm (3–5 US)
	DK	DK; Light Worsted; Sport; 8ply	21–24sts	3.75–4.5mm
	Aran	Aran; Medium; Worsted; 10ply	16–20sts	4.5–5.5mm (7–9 US)
	Chunky	Chunky; Bulky; 10–12ply	12–15sts	5.5–8mm (9–11 US)
	Super Chunky	Super Chunky; Super Bulky; Roving; 14–16ply	7–11sts	8–12.75mm (11–17 US)

Comparison cable

(24sts and 20 rows)

Row 1 (RS): K1, 1/1 RC, (p3, k3) twice, p6, 1/1 LC, k1.

Row 2 (WS): P3, k6, (p3, k3) twice, p3.

Row 3: K1, 1/1 RC, p3, 3/3 LC twice, p3, 1/1 LC, k1.

Row 4: P3, k2, p13, k3, p3.

Row 5: K1, 1/1 RC, p3, k12, p3, 1/1 LC, k1.

Row 6: P3, k3, p12, k3, p3.

Row 7: K1, 1/1 RC, p3, k3, 3/3 RC, k3, p3, 1/1 LC, k1.

Row 8: As row 6.

Rows 9–10: As rows 5–6.

Rows 11–19: As rows 3–11.

Row 20: (P3, k3) twice, p3, k6, p3.

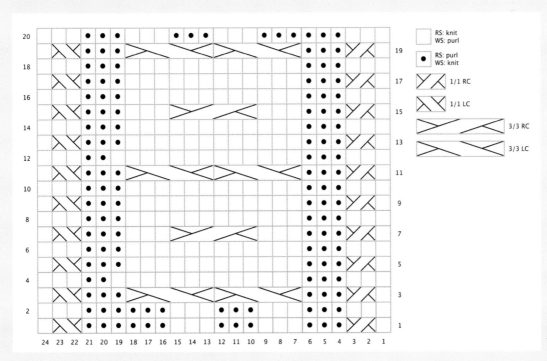

Fig. 71 Chart of comparison cable.

Fig. 72 Comparison of yarn fibre, with examples (from left to right) knitted in cotton, bamboo, alpaca, wool–silk blend, hemp–wool blend, mohair, superwash-merino and slub-wool yarns.

specify their own yarn categories and tension recommendations and produce specific stitch patterns for their yarns.

The table in Figure 70 shows the broad category names that cover the weights of yarn that were used for the series of comparison swatches. It includes label names commonly used in the UK, USA, Australia and New Zealand to describe yarns. This list highlights the overlapping categories and is intended as a guide, to help with design choices, rather than as a complete list of label names.

To illustrate the effect of using different yarn weights, each swatch shown in Figure 69 has been knitted in a different weight of a similar shade of cream, wool yarn. The swatches include 2ply, 3ply, 4ply, double-knit (DK), aran, worsted and chunky weights of yarn. Each swatch consists of the same number of stitches and rows and was worked from the chart for the comparison-cable stitch pattern shown in Figure 71. This is a very useful way to test an unfamiliar yarn when experimenting with designs.

There are several interesting differences between the swatches. The first concerns scale. The size of each knitted stitch changes throughout the series, with the lightest yarns having small stitches and the heavier weights of yarns having clearly defined, large stitch structures. The six-stitch cable braid is very distinctive in each sample; however, the width and length of the braid varies considerably, and the prominence of the braid also changes. In the chunky-yarn swatch, the braid appears as a wide, bold, raised pattern. In the swatches worked with 2ply and 3ply yarns, a more delicate design is evident. One bold cable would be sufficient to fill a large area on a design worked in chunky yarn, but the same design worked in the lighter-weight yarns will require several repeats or additional patterning to create a full design for a knitting pattern to cover that same area of fabric. This change of scale highlights the

Fig. 73 Detail of the comparison swatches (from top to bottom) knitted in pure-merino wool, alpaca, wool–silk blend and hemp–wool blend yarns.

difference between working a complex, detailed design over a large area, which requires many repeats, versus working a single repeat of a complex pattern in a heavier weight of yarn.

Yarn fibre

The choice of yarn for a project can be influenced by many diverse factors. The fibre content of the yarn has as big of an impact on the appearance of the stitch pattern as does the weight of the yarn. As well as to show each stitch pattern clearly, the yarn-fibre choices demonstrated in this book were made to aim to reflect the inspirational source material. The best way to test the suitability of a particular yarn fibre for a design is to knit a test swatch in the stitch pattern of that design.

Different yarn fibres will affect a knitted line by changing its appearance. For example, using a smooth, pure-merino yarn will increase the stitch definition, whereas a fluffy, mohair-based yarn will create a fluffy cable that can blend into the background of the knitted fabric. A cotton yarn will produce a cable with strong structure but minimal elasticity. Many yarns consist of combinations of different fibres and therefore can exhibit the best of different characteristics of the included fibres. A wool–silk blend, for example, has the sheen of silk and the elasticity of wool.

Wool is one of the most popular and versatile fibres. With excellent stitch definition, a pure-wool yarn is perfect for a wide variety of cables. However, within the category of wool, the yarns can appear very different. Working with a pure-merino-wool yarn will result in a smooth, regular set of cables; working with a yarn of wool blended with another fibre, such as hemp, will result in a more textured appearance. Additional variations can be due to the particular fleece used, the way that the yarn was spun and any treatments applied to the yarn after spinning.

In the comparison swatches, the pure-cotton yarn appears shiny, similar to the appearance of the bamboo and the wool–silk-blend yarns. The alpaca and mohair yarns have a brushed appearance, with some of the fibres forming a layer above the knitting. The yarn that includes hemp has a grainy, textured appearance. These examples illustrate the wide variety of commercially available yarns.

Fig. 74 Comparison of (from left to right) a slub yarn and a superwash, pure-merino-wool yarn.

Yarn style

The style of a yarn should be considered carefully, to achieve the desired effect of a design. Styles range from smooth yarns spun from filament fibres to those with more textured appearances. Some common examples include bouclé, brushed and slub yarns. Figure 74 shows how the appearance of the same cable braid varies between swatches knitted with a slub yarn, and a superwash, merino yarn.

Slub yarns have an uneven thickness, with alternating tight and loose spinning. The cable braid knitted in the slub yarn varies in thickness depending on which part of the yarn was being used while knitting the stitches of the cable. The cable is clearly visible, but the dimensions change throughout. The sizes of the individual stitches vary, even though the same needle size was used throughout the working of the swatch.

The superwash, merino yarn has a smooth appearance and is of the same diameter throughout the whole length of the

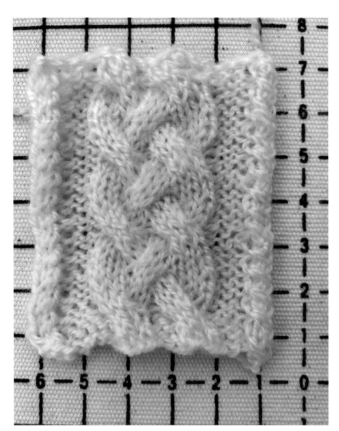

Fig. 75 Knitted swatch on a blocking board with marked measurements.

yarn within the ball. This results in an even texture throughout the whole cable braid. The sizes of the stitches and of the lines of knitting are completely consistent throughout the swatch.

These two swatches demonstrate the importance of experimenting with yarn choices. The same design can look completely different, depending on the style of the yarn used to knit the design. As with choices of yarn weight and fibre, the decision about which yarn style to use will depend on the inspiration for the design, the availability of yarn types and personal preferences.

Knitting tools

In this book's introduction, we looked at what is needed to create a knitter's sketchbook. As well as a notepad and pens and pencils for sketching, knitting tools are required to experiment with different designs. Let us take a closer look at some of the options available and how these might be used.

Knitting needles

Knitting-needle types

Straight needles are produced as pairs in a variety of lengths and can be used for only flat knitting. The preferable length is determined by how the knitter holds their work: for example, a longer length is needed if the needle is to be tucked under an arm; a shorter length is needed if the needle is to be held in a similar way to the holding of a pen.

Circular needles can be used for flat or circular knitting and consist of two very short needles connected by a strong, flexible cord or wire. The needles can be interchangeable so that different lengths of cord or wire can be used, depending on the requirements of the project.

Double-pointed needles (or simply dpns) are available in sets of four or five needles and are usually used for circular knitting. If used with a removable stopper at one end, they can also be used for flat knitting.

Knitting-needle materials

Knitting needles are manufactured in a wide variety of different materials. Examples of commonly available materials include bamboo, wood (such as birch, rosewood and olive), carbon fibre, aluminium, steel and plastic. Using the same size of needles but of a different material to knit with the same yarn and stitch pattern can result in different stitch tensions. It is therefore important to use needles of the same type of material throughout the working of each swatch, design and project.

The most important requirement from the perspective of a knitter's sketchbook is that, when experimenting with a design, the needles chosen, and whose details are recorded in your sketchbook, give you both freedom and control over the stitch pattern. This may sound contradictory. It is very important that the material of the needles allows the yarn to glide along the needle comfortably while at the same time allowing the manipulation of the stitches on to and off of the needle without the stitches being dropped.

Metric	UK	US
2mm	14	0
2.25mm	13	0
2.5mm	–	–
2.75mm	12	2
3mm	11	–
3.25mm	10	3
3.5mm	–	4
3.75mm	9	5
4mm	8	6
4.5mm	7	7
5mm	6	8
5.5mm	5	9
6mm	4	10
6.5mm	3	10 ½
7mm	2	–
7.5mm	1	–
8mm	0	11
9mm	00	13
10mm	000	15
12mm	–	17
16mm	–	19
19mm	–	35
25mm	–	50

Fig. 76 Table of common knitting-needle size equivalents.

Knitting accessories

Cable needles

Just as with knitting needles, cable needles are produced in a wide variety of materials and thicknesses. Again, the important part is that they are comfortable to work with, depending on the weight and fibre content of the yarn being used. A highly polished cable needle will be very helpful when working with a textured yarn, but it may be challenging to use to hold on to stitches being worked in a smooth, cotton yarn.

Cable needles have a point at each end so that stitches can be slipped off in either direction. A straight cable needle is similar to a double-pointed knitting needle. A notched cable needle has an indentation or bend at the centre that can help with holding on to the stitches. For large cable manipulations, a notched needle allows you to leave groups of stitches at the front or back of the knitting while you work on other parts of the knitting.

Stitch markers

Stitch markers are extremely useful for keeping track of pattern repeats, especially complex repeats that are worked multiple times. The markers can be used to set the pattern for the first few rows and then be removed when the rhythm of working the design and the placement of the pattern stitches are established. Markers are made in a variety of materials such as plastic and metal. A knotted loop of yarn of a contrasting shade or colour also works very well as a stitch marker. Markers that have an opening can be added or removed as needed at any point while knitting.

Stitch holders

Stitch holders are used to keep live stitches from unravelling while another part of the knitting is being worked. They can be made of metal or plastic. A spare needle can also be used to temporarily hold stitches.

Darning needles

A darning needle with a large eye and blunt point is used for sewing in the ends of yarn after blocking a finished piece of knitting. The blunt point helps to avoid splitting the yarn when you move the needle through the knitted fabric. For very chunky, thick or textured yarns, a plastic needle with a large looped eye is a useful alternative to an inflexible metal needle.

Tape measure

The type of tool used to measure your knitting can vary from a flexible tape to a hard plastic ruler. The most important consideration is to be consistent with measuring, working either in centimetres or in inches throughout the duration of a project.

Blocking board

All of the knitted samples in this book were blocked before being photographed. The blocking process is essential to relax the knitted stitches and show a design at its best. There are many different ways to make a blocking board, from using a spare piece of carpet covered with a clean cloth to using a custom-sized foam mat. There are some important elements to consider when constructing a blocking board. The board should enable the safe pinning out of the knitting, without any other surface being pierced or damaged unintentionally. The surface must be able to tolerate the heat and steam of an iron. If the knitting is to be wet blocked, by first soaking the knitting in water to fully saturate the yarn fibres, the blocking surface must be able to tolerate water, without any colour from the surface or the yarn running into the work or any damage such as buckling occurring to the underlying surface.

Part 2: Line and Shape

CHAPTER 4

STRAIGHT LINES

Chapter 2 looked in detail at the twists and cables that will be used throughout this book. These twisted stitches and cables, when used in stitch patterns in our knitting, can represent the fine, medium and broad lines that we use to draw with.

The straight and curved lines that will be explored in this chapter form the basis for all of the shapes and designs that follow. Working from inspirational source material, a series of stitch patterns have been designed to illustrate the versatility of line and shape that can be created in knitting. Textural elements are also included in the samples; in particular, these samples show how the changing of the background stitch pattern has a big impact on the appearance and characteristics of the foreground stitches. The use of texture in both the foreground and background will be considered in much more detail later in this book.

The first designs in this chapter are inspired by images and sketches from the North Cornwall coastline in south-west England. The designs include cable and twisted stitch straight lines. There is an abundance of inspiration to be found along the cliff tops and estuary banks and at the seashore. The photographs were taken during several spring walks around Padstow, the Camel Estuary and Trevone Bay.

There are many options to create straight lines in knitting. For example, Chapter 1 discussed how the Victorian knitters used long rope-like twists for the vertical straight lines in carriage blankets. The inspirational images provide ideas and encourage the addition of more and more ways to create lines to our range of techniques. Beginning with examples of twists and cables that are worked in stocking stitch and on a stocking stitch background, this section will then look at twists and cables with a reverse stocking stitch background. Moving on from the vertical lines of rope twists that were covered in Chapters 1 and 2, the straight lines covered in this chapter are going to move across the foreground of the knitted fabric in a variety of ways.

The Camel Estuary, shown in Figure 78, has some lovely inspiration for these twists and cables. The photograph shows many straight lines in several different combinations. In the foreground, there are some thorny bushes that are made up of multiple straight lines, including the tiny thorns on the angular branches. Beyond the thorns, there are small tributary streams flowing from the bank into the main flow of the Camel Estuary.

Fig. 77   Knitted swatch of individual diagonal lines (yarn: pure wool, worsted weight; needles: 4.5mm; total stitches: 18; total rows: 38).

Fig. 78   The Camel Estuary, Cornwall, UK.

Fig. 80   Sketch of river tributaries.

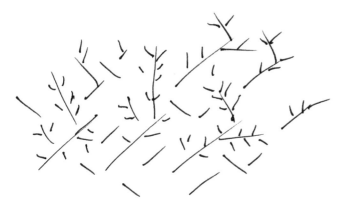

Fig. 79   Sketch of thorns.

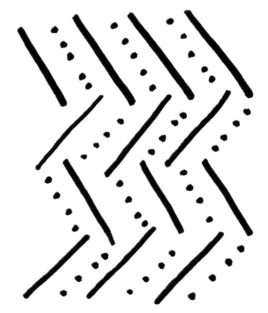

Fig. 81   Sketch of diagonal lines.

The streams have cut into the mud bank of the estuary. Because of the angle of the flow, the stream has created a beautiful zigzag pattern in the mud. The angular lines of the thorns and tributaries are captured in sketches shown in Figures 79 and 80. Starting with the representation of some individual straight lines by using twisted stitches and cables, the knitted twists and cables will be built up into patterns, and then these elements will be combined to make zigzag designs later in the chapter.

Diagonal lines

Before beginning to create complex patterns with straight lines, let us take a look at ways to create individual lines in knitting, to represent lines such as those in the sketch shown in Figure 81. There are several ways to do this. The choice of technique will

depend on the source material, on the number of lines that we wish to move across the fabric and on the overall look of the design that we wish to create. A single stitch knitted in stocking stitch on the foreground of a reverse stocking stitch background when worked over several rows makes a clear and distinct vertical line. This straight line can be made into a diagonal line by increasing on one side of the line and decreasing on the other. This is an ideal approach for creating a single line that progresses at a regular angle. For more complex diagonals that change direction, twists and cables give a greater amount of flexibility.

Having looked at individual twists and cables in Chapter 2, these stitch movements will be linked in this chapter, to create diagonal lines. The knitted swatch shown in Figure 77 and the corresponding chart shown in Figure 82 present three examples of straight lines that are made when we continue to move

Individual diagonal lines

(18sts and 38 rows)

Row 1 (RS): K3, 1/1 RC, k3, 2/1 RC, k3, 3/1 RC.

Row 2 (WS): Purl.

Row 3: K2, 1/1 RC, k3, 2/1 RC, k3, 3/1 RC, k1.

Row 4: Purl.

Row 5: K1, 1/1 RC, k3, 2/1 RC, k3, 3/1 RC, k2.

Row 6: Purl.

Row 7: 1/1 RC, k3, 2/1 RC, k3, 3/1 RC, k3.

Rows 8–9: Purl.

Row 10: Knit.

Row 11: 1/1 LC, k3, 2/1 LC, k3, 3/1 LC, k3.

Row 12: Purl.

Row 13: K1, 1/1 LC, k3, 2/1 LC, k3, 3/1 LC, k2.

Row 14: Purl.

Row 15: K2, 1/1 LC, k3, 2/1 LC, k3, 3/1 LC, k1.

Row 16: Purl.

Row 17: K3, 1/1 LC, k3, 2/1 LC, k3, 3/1 LC.

Rows 18–19: Purl.

Row 20: Knit.

Row 21: P3, 1/1 RPC, p3, 2/1 RPC, p3, 3/1 RPC.

Row 22: K1, p3, k4, p2, k4, p, k3.

Row 23: P2, 1/1 RPC, p3, 2/1 RPC, p3, 3/1 RPC, p1.

Row 24: K2, p3, k4, p2, k4, p, k2.

Row 25: P1, 1/1 RPC, p3, 2/1 RPC, p3, 3/1 RPC, p2.

Row 26: K3, p3, k4, p2, k4, p, k1.

Row 27: 1/1 RPC, p3, 2/1 RPC, p3, 3/1 RPC, p3.

Row 28: K4, p3, k4, p2, k4, p1.

Rows 29–30: Purl.

Row 31: 1/1 LPC, p3, 2/1 LPC, p3, 3/1 LPC, p3.

Row 32: As row 26.

Row 33: P1, 1/1 LPC, p3, 2/1 LPC, p3, 3/1 LPC, p2.

Row 34: As row 24.

Row 35: P2, 1/1 LPC, p3, 2/1 LPC, p3, 3/1 LPC, p1.

Row 36: As row 22.

Row 37: P3, 1/1 LPC, p3, 2/1 LPC, p3, 3/1 LPC.

Row 38: P3, k4, p2, k4, p1, k4.

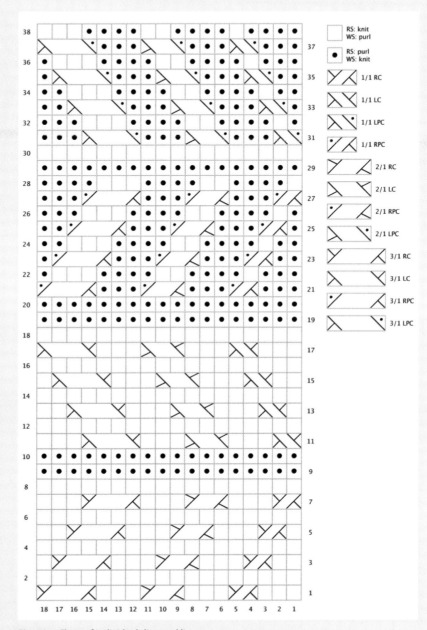

Fig. 82 Chart of individual diagonal lines.

foreground stitches in the same direction. These movements use the placement of the foreground stitches to determine the next step in the sequence. If the same cable stitch movement were to be worked exactly above the cable stitch movement below, a tight, vertical line would be formed: this is sometimes referred to as rope stitch. The vertical-rope-stitch technique is useful for creating a raised, vertical line and for edgings and borders with a design link to the main pattern. In this example,

Fig. 83   Detail of a Cornish hedge wall.

Fig. 84   Sketch of Cornish-hedge-wall diagonal lines.

the aim is to create a series of cabled diagonal lines that will move the stitches horizontally and vertically across the work.

Twists and cables can be worked on both stocking stitch and reverse stocking stitch backgrounds. The choice of background has a big effect on our foreground stitches. Working stocking stitch foreground stitches on a stocking stitch background creates a softer, less defined line than working the same stitches on a reverse stocking stitch background. In particular, in the knitted swatch, the two-stitch-twist line with one background stitch is much less defined than the lines of the three- and four-stitch cables. When these stitch movements are worked on a reverse stocking stitch background, they all become much more prominent.

In the knitted swatch, the lower two sections show two-, three- and four-stitch twists and cables with the foreground and background stitches worked in stocking stitch. Each section has been separated with a reverse stocking stitch ridge. The first section shows lines moving to the right, and the second section shows lines moving to the left. The upper two sections show the same foreground stitches worked on a reverse stocking stitch background. The lines are much more distinct. The twists and cables have been formed by the same actions as for the previous sections, with the exception of how the background stitch is worked. The abbreviations for these movements include a 'P', for purl, to indicate the difference. The symbols have a

small dot in the corner to visually indicate that reverse stocking stitch is to be worked. These new abbreviations have added to the total number of options for each type of movement. The stitch-movement table in Chapter 2 included only stocking stitch foreground- and background-stitch options (*see* Figure 22). If a reverse stocking stitch background is included, the number of options immediately doubles.

Diagonal patterns

Following on from the consideration of how to create individual lines, the same techniques of working with twists and cables will now be used to build patterns. I have chosen a constructed feature of the Cornish countryside to illustrate how to combine straight lines. Cornish hedge walls, such as the section shown in Figure 83, can be seen all over the landscape. They are made from stone slabs laid diagonally in layers. The edges of the layers are offset to give stability to the wall. A notable feature of some of these walls is the way that nature has taken them over. Many have only a small proportion of the original stone slabs showing through the vegetation that has grown throughout the wall. When the walls are built, a layer of soil is added to the top, and grasses and plants are placed along the top for their root networks to provide stability. The stone slabs

Fig. 85 Knitted swatch of Cornish-hedge stitch with stocking stitch background (yarn: alpaca and wool, DK weight; needles: 4mm; total stitches: 33, comprising nine 3-stitch repeats plus 6sts; total rows: 18, comprising one 12-row repeat, plus 6 additional rows).

also provide nooks and crannies for mosses and lichens to take hold. The result is a beautiful combination of man-made and natural elements that provides structured and unstructured features for design inspiration.

The construction of the wall perfectly illustrates the way that straight lines can be used to build up pattern. In Figure 84, showing a section of sketchbook work, the lines have been drawn by using a fine pen. Within each part of the wall, there are multiple fractures and lines. The lichen breaks up and blurs the lines and adds a softness to the hard stone.

Cornish-hedge stitch with stocking stitch background

The swatch shown in Figure 85 includes multiple diagonal, intersecting, straight lines. The pattern consists of a multiple of three stitches plus an additional six stitches and is worked over twelve rows. This means that, to knit this stitch pattern, it is necessary to have a minimum of nine stitches. Additional repeats can be added in multiples of three stitches.

Although a minimum of nine stitches is needed to create the interlocking effect, the Cornish-hedge-stitch pattern works best over a larger number of stitches. In the swatch, there are eight additional sets of three stitches. The swatch therefore has a total of thirty-three stitches.

The twists are worked on every right-side row over twelve rows. Each repeat starts one stitch position further over to the left for the first three right-side rows and one stitch position further over to the right for the following three right-side rows. This creates the multiple interlocking, diagonal, straight lines. If the twists were repeated directly in line over several rows, we would make a vertical line of twisted stitches, which is rope stitch. The accompanying charted and written instructions describe the same stitch pattern.

Cornish-hedge stitch with stocking stitch background
(3sts, plus 6sts, and 12 rows)

Note: the repeat box for this chart has a stepped appearance, as the repeat cannot run through the centre of a stitch movement.

Row 1 (RS): 1/1 LC, *k1, 1/1 LC; rep from * once, k4.
Row 2 and all WS rows: Purl.
Row 3: K1, *1/1 LC, k1; rep from * once, 1/1 LC, k3.
Row 5: K2, *1/1 LC, k1; rep from * once, 1/1 LC, k2.
Row 7: K2, *k1, 1/1 RC; rep from * once, k1, 1/1 RC, k1.
Row 9: K2, *1/1 RC, k1; rep from * once, 1/1 RC, k2.
Row 11: K1, *1/1 RC, k1; rep from * once, 1/1 RC, k3.

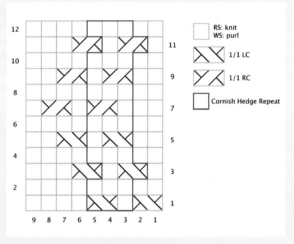

Fig. 86 Chart of Cornish-hedge stitch with stocking stitch background.

The short, fine, diagonal lines are represented by twisted stitches that are worked over two stitches. The abbreviation for these two movements are 1/1 LC and 1/1 RC. Using only these two twists, a pattern has been built up that is full of short, diagonal lines, with a stocking stitch foreground stitch on a stocking stitch background stitch. In the swatch, the lines intersect and are slightly offset where they change direction. This overlapping reflects the slab pattern in the hedge wall. Both of these twisted stitches can be worked with or without a cable needle, as described in the Chapter 2, about terminology and techniques. Both methods create the same result, with the foreground stitch moving in the desired direction. Although working without a cable needle can seem fiddly at first, with practice, this can significantly speed up the knitting process.

Fig. 87 Knitted swatch of Cornish-hedge stitch with stocking stitch and reverse stocking stitch background (yarn: alpaca and wool, DK weight; needles: 4mm; total stitches: 30, comprising five 6-stitch repeats; total rows: 44, comprising 28 chart rows plus one additional 8-row repeat per section).

Cornish-hedge stitch with stocking stitch and reverse stocking stitch background

The knitted swatch shown in Figure 87 is a second example of the Cornish-hedge stitch, inspired by Cornish hedge walls, and it explores the effects of changing the background stitch pattern. There are multiple diagonal, intersecting, straight lines in both the stocking stitch and reverse stocking stitch sections. These lines have been spaced out over the knitted fabric.

The stitch pattern is worked over a multiple of six stitches. This means that, to knit this stitch pattern, there needs to be a minimum of six stitches, as shown in the chart. If only six stitches were to be worked, this would produce only one column of the pattern repeat. The swatch was worked with five stitch repeats, with a total of thirty stitches.

Each different background section is worked over a multiple of eight rows plus six additional rows. Although the highlighted pattern repeat for each section contains eight rows, to make a complete pattern, an extra six rows must be worked. These extra six rows are made up of two rows at the start of each section and four rows at the end. These rows are necessary for

Cornish-hedge stitch with stocking stitch and reverse stocking stitch background

(6sts and 8 rows, plus an additional 6 rows for each different background section)

Row 1 (RS): 1/1 LC, k4.
Rows 2, 4, 6, 8, 10, 12 and 14 (WS): Purl.
Row 3: K1, 1/1 LC, k3.
Row 5: K2, 1/1 LC, 1/1 RC.
Row 7: K3, 1/1 RC, k1.
Row 9: 1/1 LC, 1/1 RC, k2.
Rep rows 3–10 to extend the pattern, then complete the section by working rows 11–14.
Row 11: K1, 1/1 LC, k3.
Row 13: K2, 1/1 LC, k2.
Row 15: 1/1 LPC, p4.
Row 16: K4, p1, k1.
Row 17: P1, 1/1 LPC, p3.
Row 18: K3, p1, k2.
Row 19: P2, 1/1 LPC, 1/1 RPC.
Row 20: K1, p2, k3.
Row 21: P3, 1/1 RPC, p1.
Row 22: K2, p1, k3.
Row 23: 1/1 LPC, 1/1 RPC, p2.
Row 24: K3, p2, k1.
Rep rows 17–24 to extend the pattern, then complete the section by working rows 25–28.
Row 25: P1, 1/1 LPC, p3.
Row 26: K3, p1, k2.
Row 27: P2, 1/1 LPC, p2.
Row 28: Knit.

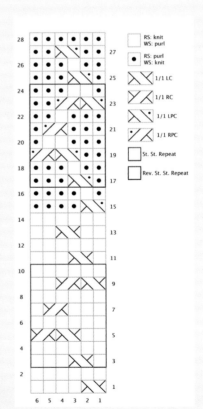

Fig. 88 Chart of Cornish-hedge stitch with stocking stitch and reverse stocking stitch background.

Fig. 89   Detail of a mud bank of the Camel Estuary.

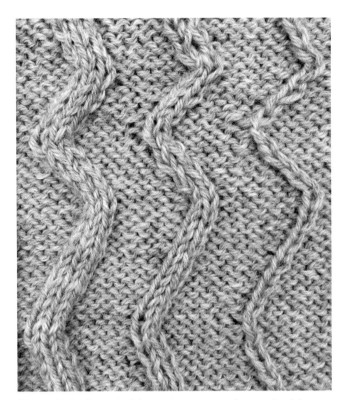

Fig. 90   Knitted swatch of zigzags (yarn: pure wool, worsted weight; needles: 4.5mm; total stitches: 24; total rows: 34).

two reasons. Firstly, the initial two rows begin the pattern and set the knitted line in the correct position within the repeat. Secondly, the final four rows of each section complete the knitted lines and avoid beginning a new set of repeats when you wish to conclude the pattern.

The knitted swatch is made up of two sets of row repeats, giving a total of twenty-two rows in each section. For chart rows 1–14, all of the background stitches are worked as stocking stitch. This repeat is shown within the red box on the chart, with the additional rows shown before and after it. For chart rows 15–28, the foreground stitch is worked in stocking stitch and the background stitches are reverse stocking stitch. This repeat is shown within the blue box on the chart, with the additional rows shown before and after it.

For the stitches worked on the reverse stocking stitch background, the twist movements are similar to those of the previous swatch. However, in this case, a reverse stocking stitch background stitch has been worked. This sample can be knitted either with or without a cable needle, as described in Chapter 2, about terminology and techniques. Both methods create the same result, with the foreground stitch moving in the desired direction.

Joining straight lines

Zigzags

Having looked at ways to move straight lines diagonally across the knitted fabric, we are now going to join up the lines to form zigzags. The images of the Camel Estuary show some amazing straight-line patterns in the muddy bank, such as those visible in the close-up shown in Figure 89. The tributary streams have made these patterns as the water flows from the bank into the main flow of the estuary. In the sketchbook illustrations of the river estuary shown at the beginning this chapter, the tributary-stream zigzags have been drawn with several different angles, representing the way that the stream has cut down into the mud.

This zigzag-pattern inspiration can be used to create movement in the stitch-pattern designs; this natural pattern can be represented in the knitting by joining up multiple combinations of left- and right-leaning diagonals. Instead of completing one diagonal line and then beginning a new line heading in the opposite direction, the lines can be linked together. By also combining a number of different twists while

Zigzags

(24sts and 34 rows)

Row 1 (RS): P3, 1/1 LPC, p5, 2/1 LPC, p5, 3/1 LPC, p2.

Row 2 (WS): K2, p3, k6, p2, k6, p1, k4.

Row 3: P4, 1/1 LPC, p5, 2/1 LPC, p5, 3/1 LPC, p1.

Row 4: K1, p3, k6, p2, k6, p1, k5.

Row 5: P5, 1/1 LPC, p5, 2/1 LPC, p5, 3/1 LPC.

Row 6: P3, k6, p2, k6, p1, k6.

Row 7: P5, 1/1 RPC, p5, 2/1 RPC, p5, 3/1 RPC.

Row 8: As row 4.

Row 9: P4, 1/1 RPC, p5, 2/1 RPC, p5, 3/1 RPC, p1.

Row 10: As row 2.

Row 11: P3, 1/1 RPC, p5, 2/1 RPC, p5, 3/1 RPC, p2.

Row 12: K3, p3, k6, p2, k6, p1, k3.

Row 13: P2, 1/1 RPC, p5, 2/1 RPC, p5, 3/1 RPC, p3.

Row 14: K4, p3, k6, p2, k6, p1, k2.

Row 15: P1, 1/1 RPC, p5, 2/1 RPC, p5, 3/1 RPC, p4.

Row 16: K5, p3, k6, p2, k6, p1, k1.

Row 17: 1/1 RPC, p5, 2/1 RPC, p5, 3/1 RPC, p5.

Row 18: K6, p3, k6, p2, k6, p1.

Row 19: 1/2 LPC, p4, 2/2 LPC, p4, 3/2 LPC, p4.

Row 20: As row 14.

Row 21: P2, 1/2 LPC, p4, 2/2 LPC, p4, 3/2 LPC, p2.

Row 22: As row 2.

Row 23: P4, 1/2 LPC, p4, 2/2 LPC, p4, 3/2 LPC.

Row 24: As row 6.

Row 25: P4, 1/2 RPC, p4, 2/2 RPC, p4, 3/2 RPC.

Row 26: As row 2.

Row 27: P2, 1/2 RPC, p4, 2/2 RPC, p4, 3/2 RPC, p2.

Row 28: As row 14.

Row 29: 1/2 RPC, p4, 2/2 RPC, p4, 3/2 RPC, p4.

Rows 30–31: As rows 18–19.

Row 32: As row 14.

Row 33: P2, 1/1 LPC, p5, 2/1 LPC, p5, 3/1 LPC, p3.

Row 34: As row 12.

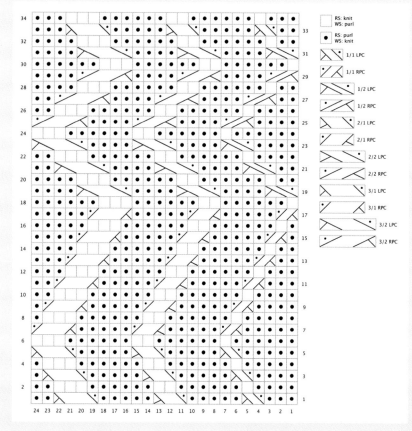

Fig. 91   Chart of zigzags.

continuing the same foreground line, the angles of the zigzags can also be varied.

In the knitted swatch shown in Figure 90, the foreground stitches move from side to side in straight lines on a reverse stocking stitch background. This sample shows how keeping the number of foreground stitches the same but varying the number of background stitches over which they move changes the angle of the lines. In the knitted swatch, there are examples of two- and three-stitch twists and three-, four- and five-stitch cables, demonstrating the different widths of lines that can be drawn. For a given row on which the stitch movements are worked, although the actual abbreviations and symbols for the three lines are different, the number of background stitches worked is the same. This means that the lines move in parallel across the knitted fabric.

A large number of symbols have been used in the corresponding chart for this swatch. As seen in Chapter 2, each different twist or cable requires its own abbreviation. In this chart, there are three different numbers of foreground stitches that are used to create three different widths of line. These three lines are moved over one and then two background stitches. For these moves, all of the foreground stitches are worked in stocking stitch and all of the background stitches are worked in reverse stocking stitch.

All three lines of knitting begin in the centre of a zigzag. The lines then move to the left over six rows. On each right-side row, the lines move over by one stitch, giving a total of a three stitch movements over the six rows. All three lines then move to the right over twelve rows, again moving over by one stitch on every right-side row, making a total of six stitch movements. This movement creates elongated diagonals that reflect only part of the inspiration source. The next part of the zigzag needs to change direction more sharply. To do this, the number of foreground stitches remains the same, but they are moved over two background stitches instead of one. The total number of stitches in the cables has now changed, but the foreground line retains the same appearance. In this part of the swatch, the lines are moving to the left over two stitches on every right-side row. This continues over six rows and a total of six stitches. The lines then change direction and move to the right by the same number of stitches and rows. The zigzag swatch is completed by moving the lines back towards the centre of their vertical sections. This means that working the whole thirty-four rows of the chart could be repeated, starting from row 1, should the knitter wish to work the whole chart again.

This swatch is the key to many of the stitch movements found throughout this book. To represent the lines from my knitter's sketchbook inspiration, the main focus is on the knitted line made on the foreground of the knitted fabric. By focusing on the foreground stitches, we can control the lines and draw the designs by our choice of stitch movements. The background stitches become the means by which the lines are moved. The total number of stitches in the movement will always be determined by how we wish to move the line, rather than the other way around.

Implied diamonds

Having looked at several different ways to create movement with straight lines in knitting, this section looks at the area surrounding the lines. In some of the previous swatches, several lines were placed next to each other, to compare lines or to create a repeated stitch pattern. This space between the lines is just as important as the lines themselves. When designing a new pattern, we must remember to consider this aspect along with any twists or cables that we knit.

This space between the distinct elements of a stitch patterns is sometimes referred to as negative space. It is the area where stitch movements are not actively being worked. This negative space can be used in many different ways. It may be the area where any decreases or increases required in our project are included. It may also be the area that contains any additional stitch patterns that are required to join different parts of the overall design.

By using the previous zigzag stitch patterns in alternative ways, negative space can be used in different ways to create an additional layer of design within the stitch patterns. In the zigzag swatch, the areas between the lines echoed the lines

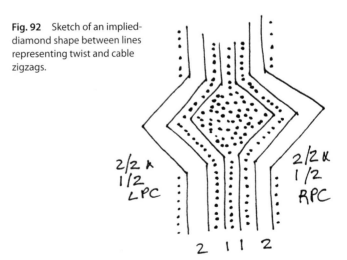

Fig. 92 Sketch of an implied-diamond shape between lines representing twist and cable zigzags.

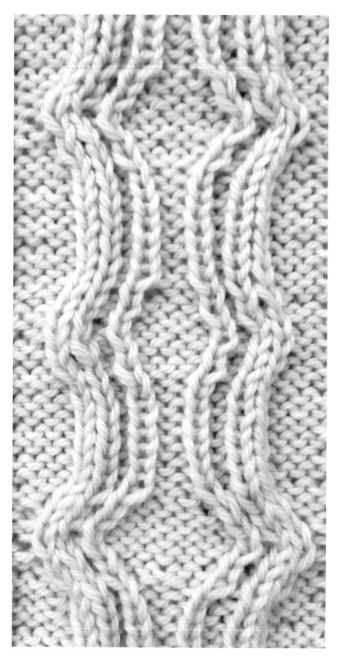

Fig. 93 Knitted swatch of implied diamonds (yarn: fine merino, DK weight; needles: 4mm; total stitches: 20; total rows: 34).

swatch, the mirror image can be created by working all of the same stitch movements in a second line but the opposite way round. When the original line moves to the right, the new line will move to the left by the same number of stitches, and so on.

Placing the two mirror-imaged zigzags next to each other begins to create new shapes between the lines of the knitting. In this case, as in the sketchbook drawing shown in Figure 93, a diamond shape is formed. Shapes can also be created within the knitted fabric in other ways, and in the coming chapters we are going to look at the steps needed to make shapes by using twist and cable stitch movements. As no stitch movements have been used to make the diamond, this shape is referred to as an implied diamond. In other words, there is the suggestion of a diamond shape resulting from the way that the lines of knitting have been moved. This is a powerful drawing tool for a knitter's sketchbook, as it allows layers of design to be added by implying a shape between lines. However, there needs to be an awareness of creating these implied shapes unintentionally. The space between the lines is as important as the actual lines and can dominate a design unintentionally.

Continuing with the example of the implied-diamond shape between the mirror-imaged zigzags, the size of the diamond can be manipulated by increasing or decreasing the number of stitch movements within the zigzag lines. Again, this should be a deliberate choice of design, rather than an unintended consequence.

In the knitted swatch of the implied diamond shown in Figure 93, the zigzags are made up of two different widths of line, which are worked opposite a mirror-imaged pair. The zigzag lines are knitted with two- and three-stitch twists and cables. The outer lines have two foreground stocking stitch stitches and the inner lines have one. The background stitch pattern is reverse stocking stitch throughout. All of the directional stitch movements are worked twice.

The first zigzags move over two background stitches. This wide movement outwards from and then inwards to the centre mirroring line between the two sets of zigzag lines forms a wide implied-diamond shape. The second set of zigzags move outwards then inwards over one background stitch, forming a centre space that implies a smaller, less defined diamond. The third zigzags combine these two sets of movements to create an angled bend in the lines that emphasizes the outer points where the zigzags change direction. This zigzag begins with an outward movement over one background stitch followed by an outward movement over two stitches, before the direction turns inwards over the same number of stitches and types of moves in reverse.

themselves. Although the zigzags were created by the shaped lines, the reverse stocking stitch sections between them also appear as zigzags. This dual aspect of the stitch pattern creates balance horizontally and vertically over the swatch.

Another way to exploit the negative space is to change the shape of this area by working two lines as a mirror image of each other. For example, by selecting one of the lines from the zigzag

Implied diamonds

(20sts and 34 rows)

Row 1 (RS): P4, k2, (p2, k1) twice, p2, k2, p4.
Row 2 (WS): K4, p2, (k2, p1) twice, k2, p2, k4.
Row 3: P2, 2/2 RPC, 1/2 RPC, p2, 1/2 LPC, 2/2 LPC, p2.
Row 4: K2, p2, k2, p, k6, p, k2, p2, k2.
Row 5: 2/2 RPC, 1/2 RPC, p6, 1/2 LPC, 2/2 LPC.
Row 6: P2, k2, p1, k10, p1, k2, p2.
Row 7: 2/2 LPC, 1/2 LPC, p6, 1/2 RPC, 2/2 RPC.
Row 8: K2, p2, k2, p1, k9, p2, k2.
Row 9: P2, 2/2 LPC, 1/2 LPC, p2, 1/2 RPC, 2/2 RPC, p2.
Row 10: As row 2.
Rows 11–14: Rep rows 1–2 twice.
Row 15: P3, 2/1 RPC, p1, 1/1 RPC, p2, 1/1 LPC, p1, 2/1 LPC, p3.
Row 16: K3, p2, k2, p1, k4, p1, k2, p2, k3.
Row 17: P2, 2/1 RPC, p1, 1/1 RPC, p4, 1/1 LPC, p1, 2/1 LPC, p2.
Row 18: As row 4.
Row 19: P2, 2/1 LPC, p1, 1/1 RPC, p4, 1/1 RPC, p1, 2/1 RPC, p2.
Row 20: As row 16.
Row 21: P3, 2/1 LPC, p1, 1/1 LPC, p2, 1/1 RPC, p1, 2/1 RPC, p3.
Row 22: As row 2.
Rows 23–26: Rep rows 1–2 twice.
Rows 27–28: As rows 15–16.
Row 29: P1, 2/2 RPC, 1/2 RPC, p4, 1/2 LPC, 2/2 LPC, p1.
Row 30: K1, p2, k2, p1, k8, p1, k2, p2, k1.
Row 31: P1, 2/2 LPC, 1/2 LPC, p4, 1/2 RPC, 2/2 RPC, p1.
Row 32: As row 16.
Row 33: As row 21.
Row 34: As row 2.

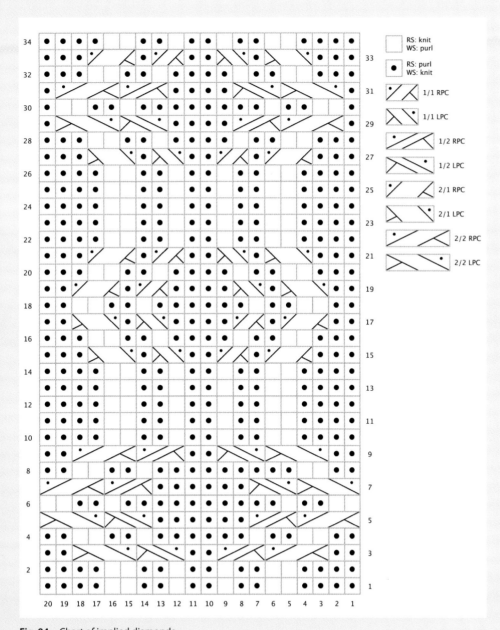

Fig. 94 Chart of implied diamonds.

Using a more angled line creates a more distinct implied diamond. The least angled lines of the centre diamond have a more curved appearance. The two outer stitch lines also have a curved appearance in places, especially between the stitch movements. This is because several straight rows with no stitch movements have been worked. The joining lines appear to bend. This property of the knitted line will be looked at in greater detail in the next chapter.

The implied-diamonds swatch is an excellent example of a symmetrical design. Symmetry can be described as the regularly spaced repetition of a figure, vertically and/or horizontally. This repetition can also include reflection, or mirror imagining, and rotation around a defined point. In this case, the design has been reflected down the centre line. If the design were to be folded in half, the lines and points would all match up.

Using the properties of symmetry can help to extend the designs. Including a change of scale adds a further dimension. Some of the design sources that we will consider already have an inbuilt symmetry. The shapes that make up the basic building blocks are generally symmetrical, such as the diamonds in the last example.

Once we have looked at symmetry, we will consider asymmetry, where we deliberately change the balance and scale of the design. Asymmetrical features add interest and direct attention to certain parts of the knitting. Overall balance needs to be maintained to keep the design in harmony. This is why looking at unconventional source material is so fascinating. Leaves are stunning in their regular growth pattern, but a decayed leaf reveals the interior structure in a way that a living leaf cannot.

Throughout this chapter, we have looked at a wide selection of cabled straight lines. From the individual diagonal lines of the Cornish-hedge stitch to the mirror-imaged lines that form the implied diamonds of the last swatch, we can see the versatility of a knitted straight line. In the next chapter, we are going to use all of these techniques of knitting straight lines to explore curved lines.

Fig. 95   Detail of a Cornish hedge wall.

Fig. 96   Sketch of detail of a Cornish hedge wall.

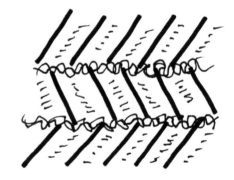

Straight-lines pattern: stepper wristwarmers

Using photographs and sketches of the Cornish hedge wall as inspiration, several related stitch patterns have been designed. These stitch patterns are shown in the previous sections as charts and swatches, which are also a record of design development as part of my knitter's sketchbook. Using the ideas from the swatches, the stitch patterns have been developed into an accessory project, to illustrate the design possibilities of a knitted straight line. Wristwarmers are an excellent way to use design swatches in a practical project. Seeing a design on hands brings it to life and makes it look different to when it is viewed as a flat

Fig. 97 Stepper wristwarmers. (Photo: Maxine Vining)

Fig. 98 Stepper wristwarmers.

rectangular swatch. With the addition of edges and borders, the pattern from the design swatch can be transformed into a wearable accessory.

For this project, the Cornish-hedge-stitch patterns have been used in a slightly different way, by taking many of the elements explored previously and creating a new pattern. The design is named Stepper as many of the photographs for this chapter were taken around Stepper Point, near Padstow. The name also refers to the construction of the wristwarmers, as they are knitted in steps of patterns from the cast-on border to the cast-off border.

The main stitch pattern for the Stepper wristwarmers draws on the previous straight-line swatches. Strong, diagonal lines appear, but this time they change direction twice. The ideas are captured in the sketch shown in Figure 96. To further emphasize the change of direction, there is a change of colour. The two shades of grey selected for the featured sample are inspired by the stone slabs that form the Cornish hedge walls. Between each different slab section of knitting, a third, contrasting, col-

our of yarn has been added to represent the moss and lichen growing on the walls. The three colours can be seen together in Figures 97 and 98. By working this contrasting yarn as a reverse stocking stitch ridge between the slab sections running in alternate directions, the contrasting yarn also acquires texture. As the colours within the wall vary a great deal, a second wristwarmer has been worked with the colours in reverse, by swapping the positions of the shades of grey.

When considering the design of the cast-on and cast-off borders of the wristwarmers, a stitch pattern that reflects the main stitch pattern was deliberately chosen. Design elements for borders and edges will be highlighted in the projects throughout this book. In this case, using a rib pattern that runs into the main design from the wrist border and then also continues on from the main pattern into the cast-off border at the fingers brings balance to the design.

The Stepper-wristwarmers rib sections are made up of two different ribs, which are both wide-rib designs. The cast-on border has two right-side knit stitches separated by a single purl stitch. The cast-off border has two right-side purl stitches separated by a single knit stitch. Using two different but related patterns in this way represents the different sizes of stone slabs that were used in the building of the Cornish hedge walls. The heavier, wider slabs form the wall foundation and are echoed in the cast-on border. The lighter, thinner slabs form the upper part of the hedge wall and are referenced in the cast-off border.

As there should be some elasticity in wristwarmers, so that they fit well, always include a selvedge at each side of the knitted fabric. These are the edges that will be visible at the gap left for the thumb in the side seam. In this case, the selvedges also help to ensure a snug fit around the thumb. For the Stepper wristwarmers, a two-stitch, stocking stitch selvedge has been included in the pattern. When each wristwarmer is seamed, the selvedges will help the seam to lie flat. At the thumb gap, the selvedges will curl slightly, providing a neat edge around the thumb hole.

The Stepper wristwarmers are knitted flat as rectangular shapes. After casting off, each rectangle is sewn up to make a cylinder, with a gap being left in the side seam for the thumb. The pattern is written for two sizes. The first size (size 1) will fit snugly on an average adult hand; the second size (size 2) is for a looser fit.

Stepper wristwarmers pattern

Size
Two sizes

Size 1
- 19.5cm (7¾in) circumference × 18.5cm (7¼in) deep

Size 2
- 22.5cm (9in) circumference × 19cm (7½in) deep

Yarn
- J. C. Rennie Chunky Aran, 100-per-cent wool, aran weight, 95m (104yd) per 50g ball
- 1 × 50g ball in Silver (shade A)
- 1 × 50g ball in Stonehenge (shade B: only a small amount of this shade is used)
- 1 × 50g ball in Medium Grey (shade C)

Fig. 99 Blocking diagram of Stepper wristwarmers.

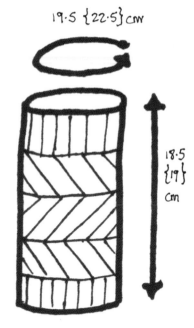

19.5 {22.5} cm

18.5 {19} cm

Needles and accessories
- A pair of 4.5mm (UK7, US7) straight needles
- A pair of 5mm (UK6, US8) straight needles
- Cable needle
- Darning needle

Tension
- 18sts and 26 rows to 10cm (4in) over Stepper pattern, using 5mm needles

Pattern notes
Figures for the size 2 instructions are shown in brackets following the size 1 figure instructions. Where only one figure is given, it applies to both sizes.

Pattern instructions

First wristwarmer

Cast on 35 {41} sts by using shade A and 4.5mm needles.

Row 1 (RS): *K2, p1; rep from * to last 2sts, k2.

Row 2 (WS): *P2, k1: rep from * to last 2sts, p2.

Rep rows 1–2 four times.

Using shade B, knit two rows.

Change to 5mm needles, and begin Stepper pattern as follows:

Row 1 (RS): Using shade C, k1, *1/1 LC, k1; rep from * to last st, k1.

Row 2 and all WS rows except rows 8 and 16: Purl.

Row 3: K2, *1/1 LC, k1; rep from * to end of row.

Row 5: K3, *1/1 LC, k1; rep from * to last 2sts, k2.

Row 7: Using shade B, k1, *1/1 LC, k1; rep from * to last st, k1.

Row 8: Knit.

Row 9: Using shade A, k1, *1/1 RC, k1; rep from * to last st, k1.

Row 11: K3, *1/1 RC, k1; rep from * to last 2sts, k2.

Row 13: K2, *1/1 RC, k1; rep from * to end of row.

Row 15: Using shade B, k1, *1/1 RC, k1; rep from * to last st, k1.

Row 16: Knit.

Rep rows 1–8 once.

Change to 4.5mm needles.

Row 1 (RS): Using shade A, knit.

Row 2 (WS): *K2, p1; rep from * to last 2sts, k2.

Row 3: *P2, k1; rep from * to last 2sts, p2.

Rep rows 2–3 three {four} times.

Cast off in patt with WS facing.

Second wristwarmer

Work as for first wristwarmer, but swapping shades A and C.

Block the work gently to the measurements given in Figure 99 and according to the yarn's ball-band instructions.

Sew each side seam, leaving a gap of approximately 4cm (1½in) to accommodate a thumb.

Sew in all loose ends.

CHAPTER 5

CURVED LINES

Chapter 4 looked at ways to create diagonal lines in designs by using straight lines of knitting. By changing the direction of the diagonals, complex patterns were built up from these lines. The last swatch of the chapter, of implied diamonds, shows a linked series of diagonals that also create a great deal of movement within the design. This chapter will look at how the same knitting techniques can be used to create curved lines.

It is important to remember that, as well as the choice of cable manipulations, the choice of yarn and fibre will affect how the knitted lines appear. Yarn weight and fibre were reviewed in Chapter 3. The importance of yarn weight and fibre is especially relevant to this chapter, as cabled lines of knitting can appear as soft lines, so even a sharp bend can sometimes appear as a curve. This effect can be emphasized by the particular fibre content of the yarn being used in the design. For example, a loosely twisted, wool yarn worked with a larger needle size will result in a gentle bend over the location of the cable manipulation. A tightly twisted yarn worked with a smaller needle size will give a firmer, more angled look for the same cable manipulation. These fibre properties can be used to great effect in knitting.

An example would be to create tight, cabled-rib patterns in a border that become looser when worked within the main set of cabled stitch repeats, by using a larger needle size.

This chapter begins by covering the creation of curves by working extra rows between stitch movements. The stitch movements use the techniques of working diagonal straight lines that we looked at previously. For the zigzag swatch, we began to combine different cable stitch movements to sharpen the angles of the cables' changes of direction. By working additional rows between these zigzag movements, the stitch pattern is elongated and forms a series of gentle or pronounced curves.

As with the zigzags, the curves can be worked by using a combination of different angles. Moving the foreground stitches across more background stitches before working rows without movements will create a wider curved bend. A long, narrow, flowing line will be formed with fewer stitches in the background and a greater number of rows being worked without cable stitch movements. As before, the width of our foreground line can be varied to enhance the effect. These choices will be determined by the inspirational source material.

Fig. 100 Aerial view of a meandering river.

Fig. 101 Sketch of meandering lines.

Fig. 102 Knitted swatch of meandering lines (yarn: pure wool, worsted weight; needles: 4.5mm; total stitches: 24; total rows: 38).

Meandering curves

As discussed in the previous section, the techniques to create the curves are all based on the same stitch manipulations that were used to create diagonal lines. To highlight how to move from a set of straight, diagonal, zigzag lines to a series of curved lines, an inspirational image will be referred to.

This inspiration for curved lines is an aerial shot, taken near Gatwick Airport, of a river meander, shown in Figure 100. In the centre of the photograph, many linked curves formed by a river cutting across the cultivated fields can be seen. These river meanders are formed through a natural process of deposition and erosion and do not have a static position within the field. The meander pattern will change over time as the river water finds the most efficient way to flow. If this image were to be taken again in a few years' time, the curves could look quite different. The widest meanders will eventually form oxbow lakes and eventually be cut off from the main river. The river will rejoin in a more straightened line of flow. This process could be seen in action at a smaller scale with the zigzag inspiration of the mud on the bank of the Camel Estuary. This time, the curved lines have been sketched as a series of linked bends, as shown in Figure 101. The angles of the bends vary, reflecting the river's path. This aspect of the pattern helps with inspiration to experiment with the effect of different cables.

The resulting knitted swatch, shown in Figure 102, has three distinct lines so that we can compare the effect of using a single foreground stitch, two foreground stitches and three foreground stitches. The lines created follow the same meander by using movements over the same number of background stitches. The foreground lines are all worked in stocking stitch, and the background remains as reverse stocking stitch throughout the swatch. Although there are just three lines of knitting, there are a large number of cable manipulations. This is because, for each line, there needs to be a set of separate cable instructions. There are four sets of movements for each number of foreground stitches. However, although the corresponding list of abbreviations looks like a long list, the number of background stitches that the foreground stitches move over is the same for each curved line for a given row on which stitch movements are worked. Working in this way allows a direct comparison of the effect of using the different numbers of foreground stitches.

Meandering lines

(24sts and 38 rows)

Row 1 (RS): P3, 1/1 RPC, p5, 2/1 RPC, p5, 3/1 RPC, p2.
Row 2 (WS): K3, p3, k6, p2, k6, p1, k3.
Row 3: P2, 1/1 RPC, p5, 2/1 RPC, p5, 3/1 RPC, p3.
Row 4: K4, p3, k6, p2, k6, p1, k2.
Row 5: P1, 1/1 RPC, p5, 2/1 RPC, p5, 3/1 RPC, p4.
Row 6: K5, p3, k6, p2, k6, p1, k1.
Row 7: 1/1 RPC, p5, 2/1 RPC, p5, 3/1 RPC, p5.
Row 8: K6, p3, k6, p2, k6, p1.
Row 9: K1, p6, k2, p6, k3, p6.
Row 10: As row 8.
Row 11: 1/2 LPC, p4, 2/2 LPC, p4, 3/2 LPC, p4.
Row 12: As row 4.
Row 13: P2, 1/2 LPC, p4, 2/2 LPC, p4, 3/2 LPC, p2.
Row 14: K2, p3, k6, p2, k6, p1, k4.
Row 15: P4, 1/2 LPC, p4, 2/2 LPC, p4, 3/2 LPC.
Row 16: P3, k6, p2, k6, p1, k6.
Row 17: P6, k1, p6, k2, p6, k3.
Row 18: As row 16.
Row 19: P4, 1/2 RPC, p4, 2/2 RPC, p4, 3/2 RPC.
Row 20: As row 14.
Row 21: P2, 1/2 RPC, p4, 2/2 RPC, p4, 3/2 RPC, p2.
Row 22: As row 4.
Row 23: 1/2 RPC, p4, 2/2 RPC, p4, 3/2 RPC, p4.
Rows 24–25: As rows 8–9.
Row 26: As row 8.
Row 27: As row 11.
Row 28: As row 4.
Rows 29–30: As rows 13–14.
Row 31: P4, k1, p6, k2, p6, k3, p2.
Row 32: As row 14.

Row 33:
As row 21.
Row 34: As row 4.
Row 35: P2, k1, p6, k2, p6, k3, p4.
Row 36: As row 4.
Rows 37–38: As rows 13–14.

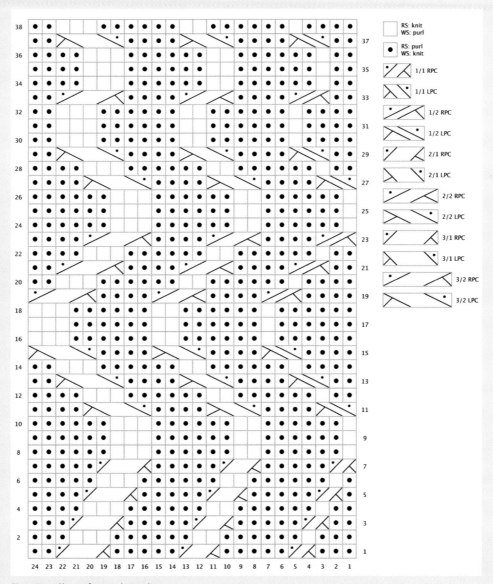

Fig. 103 Chart of meandering lines.

Fig. 104 Knitted swatch of outlined meander (yarn: Falkland wool, DK weight; needles: 4mm; total stitches: 12; total rows: 36).

Outlined meander

(12sts and 36 rows)

Row 1 (RS): P4, k1, p2, k2, p2, k1.

Row 2 (WS): P1, k2, p2, k2, p1, k4.

Row 3: P3, 1/1 RPC, p1, 2/1 RPC, p1, 1/1 RPC.

Row 4: K1, p1, k2, p2, k2, p1, k3.

Row 5: P2, 1/1 RPC, p1, 2/1 RPC, p1, 1/1 RPC, p1.

Row 6: K2, p1, k2, p2, k2, p1, k2.

Row 7: P2, k1, p2, k2, p2, k1, p2.

Row 8: As row 6.

Row 9: P2, 1/1 LPC, p1, 2/1 LPC, p1, 1/1 LPC, p1.

Row 10: As row 4.

Row 11: P3, 1/1 LPC, p1, 2/1 LPC, p1, 1/1 LPC.

Row 12: As row 2.

Rows 13–16: As rows 1–4.

Row 17: P1, 1/2 RPC, 2/2 RPC, 1/2 RPC, p1.

Row 18: K3, p1, k2, p2, k2, p1, k1.

Row 19: P1, k1, p2, k2, p2, k1, p3.

Row 20: As row 18.

Row 21: P1, 1/2 LPC, 2/2 LPC, 1/2 LPC, p1.

Row 22: As row 4.

Row 23: As row 11.

Row 24: As row 2.

Rows 25–26: As rows 1–2.

Row 27: P2, 1/2 RPC, 2/2 RPC, 1/2 RPC.

Row 28: As row 6.

Row 29: 1/2 RPC, 2/2 RPC, 1/2 RPC, p2.

Row 30: K4, p1, k2, p2, k2, p1.

Row 31: K1, p2, k2, p2, k1, p4.

Row 32: As row 30.

Row 33: 1/2 LPC, 2/2 LPC, 1/2 LPC, p2.

Row 34: K5, p2, k2, p1, k2.

Row 35: P2, 1/2 LPC, 2/2 LPC, 1/2 LPC.

Row 36: As row 2.

☐	RS: knit / WS: purl
●	RS: purl / WS: knit
╱╲	1/1 RPC
╲╱	1/1 LPC
╱	1/2 RPC
╲	1/2 LPC
╱	2/1 RPC
╲	2/1 LPC
╱	2/2 RPC
╲	2/2 LPC

Fig. 105 Chart of outlined meander.

The first point to note is that, at the lower part of the swatch, the line of three foreground stitches appears much more prominent and bold than the other two lines. However, at the top of the swatch, where the meanders are tighter and were worked closer together, this line is slightly distorted, and here it is the line with a single foreground stitch that creates the clearest curve.

The preferred choice of cabled line will always be determined by the effect that we wish to create in the knitting. If these meanders were to be worked over a large piece of knitting, the wider cable could be more effective and prominent. If the meanders were to be worked on a small scale, the single-foreground-stitch line will provide delicate stitch detail. Conversely, this detail could be lost, if it were to be used on the larger area of knitting.

Recognizing that the river meanders will change over time, the second swatch, shown in Figure 104, has been designed to include additional lines that echo the main meander in the centre of the pattern. This cable combination emphasizes the meander of the river with fine, twisted stitch lines resembling the river bank, mirroring the flow of the river. There are long, sweeping curves, as well as sharper bends, so the cable lines will bend both sharply and gently at different points. The number of foreground stitches will remain the same throughout, but they will move over different numbers of background stitches to achieve the various bends. The three lines always move over the same number of background stitches at the same time. The outer curves have been represented by using two lines of twists that follow the single centre cable line. The twists have one stocking stitch foreground stitch, and the cable has two stocking stitch foreground stitches. The background stitches are of reverse stocking stitch throughout.

A notable effect of this cable combination is to tighten up the knitted fabric in certain places. The upper part of the swatch has more concentrated cable stitch movements than does the lower part. This also affects the tension of the swatch and may result in a tightening of the upper part of fabric as compared to the tension of the lower part, with its less angled curves. If this group of cables were to be worked in only a narrow section of a larger piece of knitting, the pattern of the rest of the knitted fabric would need to be considered carefully, to achieve balance throughout the fabric.

Working evenly spaced bands of this tight meander pattern would create a balanced, rib-like effect. Separating the bands with textured, non-cabled sections would create contrast between the lines.

Implied circles

The implied-diamond example shown in Chapter 4, where two zigzag lines were worked next to each other as a mirror image, formed diamond shapes in the spaces between the lines. In this swatch, the implied shapes are ovals or circles. As with the zigzag lines that created the implied diamonds, when our curved design is mirror imaged, the same cable stitch movements are always worked on the same row but in the opposite direction. Complete curved shapes, with distinct beginnings and endings, will be considered in much more detail in the next chapter.

Continuing to use the river-meander image as inspiration, the design has been developed to include implied circular shapes, which are visible in the swatch shown in Figure 106.

Fig. 106 Knitted swatch of implied circles with texture (yarn: pure wool, DK weight; needles: 4mm; total stitches: 29, comprising two 14-stitch repeats plus 1st; total rows: 36, comprising three 12-row repeats).

Additional textural features have also been added to create contrast. Only one set of cable stitch movements has been used in this swatch. These are four-stitch cables, which have two foreground stocking stitch stitches that were moved over two background reverse stocking stitch stitches. For the lower and upper part of each pattern repeat, two sets of cable stitch movements were worked to the left opposite two sets that were worked to the right. The cable lines do not cross each other. To create a curve, two additional rows with no cable stitch movements have been worked between each set of cable stitch movements. In effect, long lines of curves have been formed. These lines are separated by a single stitch worked in reverse stocking stitch. Once again, this shows the versatility of lines of knitting in design.

The textural element of this swatch is inspired by the fields surrounding the river. These fields are very distinct in the image. In particular, the planted fields have a textured pattern. This has been included in the implied-circles design in two ways, firstly as reverse stocking stitch and secondly as moss stitch. Mixing the textures creates more contrast within the design. Although the background stitch pattern is different in each section, all of the cables are worked in the same way. This means that, for this example, the moss-stitch patterning begins on a wrong-side row.

Implied circles with texture

(14sts, plus 1st, and 12 rows)

Row 1 (RS): *P1, k3, (p1, k1) three times, p1, k3; rep from * once, p1.
Row 2 (WS): K1, *p2, (k1, p1) four times, k1, p2, k1; rep from * once.
Row 3: *P1, 2/2 LPC, (k1, p1) twice, k1, 2/2 RPC; rep from * once, p1.
Row 4: K1, *k2, p2, (k1, p1) twice, k1, p2, k3; rep from * once.
Row 5: *P3, 2/2 LPC, p1, 2/2 RPC, p2; rep from * once, p1.
Row 6: K1, *k4, p2, k1, p2, k5; rep from * once.
Row 7: *P5, k2, p1, k2, p4; rep from * once, p1.
Row 8: As row 6.
Row 9: *P3, 2/2 RPC, p1, 2/2 LPC, p2; rep from * once, p1.
Row 10: As row 4.
Row 11: *P1, 2/2 RPC, (k1, p1) twice, k1, 2/2 LPC; rep from * once, p1.
Row 12: As row 2.

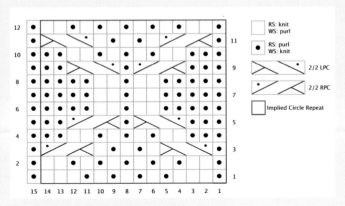

Fig. 107   Chart of implied circles with texture.

This stitch pattern is a multiple of fourteen stitches plus one additional stitch. The additional stitch is worked as reverse stocking stitch throughout and is used to balance the pattern across the rows. The swatch has been knitted to include two repeats of the charted pattern for the width, which is a total of twenty-nine stitches. Three sets of row repeats, which is a total of thirty-six rows, are worked for the length of the swatch.

Using a balanced, repetitive curve for the meanders creates a regular pattern over the swatch. This contrasts to our earlier swatches where we varied the curve angles. As the textured sections are also worked in a regular pattern, the tension of the whole swatch remains even and balanced. The meander lines are given additional emphasis by the textured background stitches. Again, as these lines are evenly placed throughout the knitted fabric, the tension remains even.

Arches

Knitted arches are made when two mirror-imaged curves bend towards each other. They can be pointed or rounded, depending on the angles of the bends. Somewhere between a straight and a curved line, this example brings together the principles of the previous two chapters.

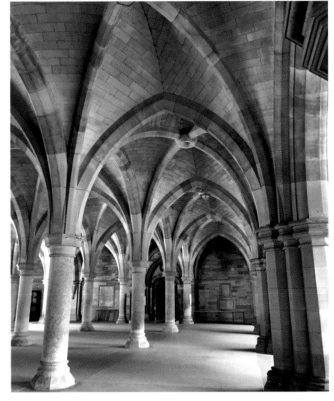

Fig. 108   The Undercroft of the University of Glasgow.

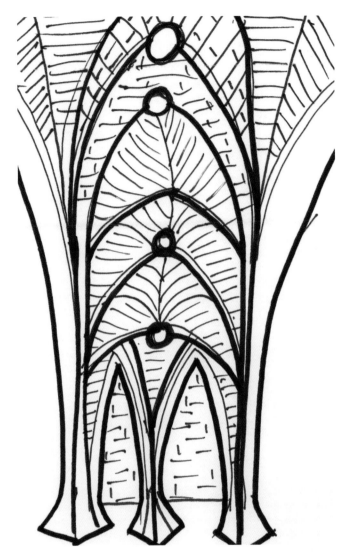

Fig. 109 Sketch of Undercroft arches.

Pointed arches

The inspiration for the swatch showing pointed arches contains a complex series of several arches. Figure 108 shows a photograph taken from within the cloisters, also known as the Undercroft, situated between the east and west quadrangles of the Gilbert Scott Building at the University of Glasgow. The Gilbert Scott Building was built in the Gothic style of architecture and was completed in 1891. The vaulted area shows several supported arches within the same covered area. The angles of the arches appear to change, depending on the viewer's precise location within the Undercroft. The pillars are linked by additional rounded, curved arches within the more pointed

Fig. 110 Knitted swatch of Undercroft arches (yarn: pure wool, DK weight; needles: 4mm; total stitches: 29, comprising two 14-stitch repeats plus 1st; total rows: 36).

arches. Within these sections, there is a circular decorative feature and, in some places, a light fixture. All of these elements are excellent inspiration for knitted pointed arches, and the sketch shown in Figure 109 includes the key design features that are subsequently used in the knitted swatch.

By using different widths of foreground lines and different angles of curves, a series of arches can be created within the same knitted swatch, as shown in Figure 110. A circular feature has also been introduced to the design so that the knitted

Undercroft arches
(14sts, plus 1st, and 36 rows)

Row 1 (RS): *P1, k1, 1/1 LC, p7, 1/1 RC, k1; rep from * once, p1.

Row 2 (WS): K1, *p3, k7, p3, k1; rep from * once.

Row 3: *P1, k2, 1/1 LPC, p5, 1/1 RPC, k2; rep from * once, p1.

Row 4: K1, *p2, k1, p1, k5, p1, k1, p2, k1; rep from * once.

Row 5: *P1, k2, p1, 1/2 LPC, p1, 1/2 RPC, p1, k2; rep from * once, p1.

Row 6: K1, *p2, k3, p1, k1, p1, k3, p2, k1; rep from * once.

Row 7: *P1, k2, p2, 1/1 RC, p1, 1/1 LC, p2, k2; rep from * once, p1.

Row 8: K1, *(p2, k2, p2, k1) twice; rep from * once.

Row 9: *P1, k2, p2, 1/1 LC, p1, 1/1 RC, p2, k2; rep from * once, p1.

Row 10: As row 6.

Row 11: *P1, 2/1 LPC, 1/2 RPC, p1, 1/2 LPC, 2/1 RPC; rep from * once, p1.

Row 12: K1, *k1, p3, k5, p3, k2; rep from * once.

Row 13: *P2, 2/1 LPC, p5, 2/1 RPC, p1; rep from * once, p1.

Row 14: K1, *k2, p2, k5, p2, k3; rep from * once.

Row 15: *P3, 2/2 LPC, p1, 2/2 RPC, p2; rep from * once, p1.

Row 16: K1, *k4, p2, k1, p2, k5; rep from * once.

Row 17: *P5, 1/1 LC, p1, 1/1 RC, p4; rep from * once, p1.

Row 18: As row 16.

Row 19: *P4, 1/1 RC, k1, p1, k1, 1/1 LC, p3; rep from * once, p1.

Row 20: K1, *k3, p3, k1, p3, k4; rep from * once.

Row 21: *P3, 1/1 RPC, k2, p1, k2, 1/1 LPC, p2; rep from * once, p1.

Row 22: K1, *k2, p1, (k1, p2) twice, k1, p1, k3; rep from * once.

Row 23: *P1, 1/2 RPC, (p1, k2) twice, p1, 1/2 LPC; rep from * once, p1.

Row 24: K1, *p1, k3, p2, k1, p2, k3, p1, k1; rep from * once.

Row 25: *P1, 1/1 LC, p2, k2, p1, k2, p2, 1/1 RC; rep from * once, p1.

Row 26: As row 8.

Row 27: *P1, 1/1 RC, p2, k2, p1, k2, p2, 1/1 LC; rep from * once, p1.

Row 28: As row 24.

Row 29: *P1, 1/2 LPC, 2/1 RPC, p1, 2/1 LPC, 1/2 RPC; rep from * once, p1.

Row 30: K1, *k2, p3, k2, p4, k3; rep from * once.

Row 31: *P3, 2/1 RPC, p3, 2/1 LPC, p2; rep from * once, p1.

Row 32: As row 14.

Row 33: *P1, 2/2 RPC, p5, 2/2 LPC; rep from * once, p1.

Row 34: K1, *p2, k9, p2, k1; rep from * once.

Row 35: *P1, 1/1 RC, p9, 1/1 LC; rep from * once, p1.

Row 36: As row 34.

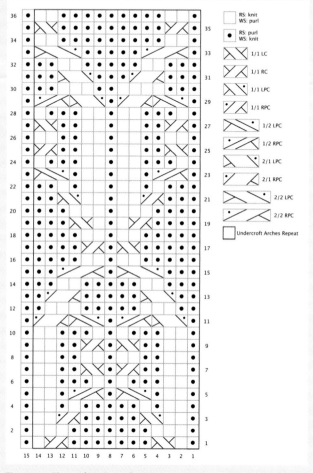

Fig. 111 Chart of Undercroft arches.

arches link vertically and horizontally across the knitted fabric. The arches have also been joined vertically as an integral part of the pattern repeat of the design. This reflects the multiple interlocking archways of the inspiration and creates an elongated honeycomb effect on the knitted fabric. The little arches have their own sub-pattern in the background of the larger honeycomb pattern.

The swatch consists of a stitch pattern that is a multiple of fourteen stitches plus one additional stitch. To show the arch repeat clearly, two repeats have been worked, making a total of twenty-nine stitches.

Rounded arches

An arch pattern can be a two-dimensional, flat design as well as a three-dimensional architectural feature of a building. For this design inspiration, a glance into a lane near one of the main

Fig. 112 Mosaic-tiled arches in Rome, Italy.

Fig. 115 Knitted swatch of mosaic-tiled arches (yarn: pure wool, aran weight; needles: 4.5mm; total stitches: 28, comprising two 14-stitch repeats; total rows: 48, comprising three 16-row repeats).

tourist areas in Rome revealed a pattern of work in progress. The arch pattern shown in Figure 112 was immediately apparent. The mosaic-tiled arches in the alleyway were still under construction. Not only the main fan-shaped arch pattern in the lighter tiles was visible but also an excellent background textured pattern was emerging. Both elements were captured in the sketches shown in Figures 113 and 114.

Although the mosaic pattern has different widths of arches, to fit the passageway and possibly the uneven ground, the knitted design of the swatch, shown in Figure 115, has a regular set of cabled movements. A similar set of cables to that used for the pointed-arches pattern have been used. In this case, each new arch grows out of the top of the arch below it. This layout creates a pattern that is reminiscent of joined semicircles. Once again, the design essentially uses lines of knitting to make the pattern.

Fig. 113 Sketch of tiled arches.

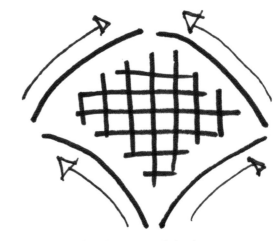

Fig. 114 Sketch of line directions in tiled arches.

Mosaic-tiled arches

(14sts and 16 rows)

Row 1 (RS): (K2, p2) three times, k2.
Row 2 (WS): (P2, k2) three times, p2.
Row 3: 2/1 LC, k1, p2, k2, p2, k1, 2/1 RC.
Row 4: P4, k2, p2, k2, p4.
Row 5: P1, 2/2 LC, k1, p2, k1, 2/2 RC, p1.
Row 6: K1, p5, k2, p5, k1.
Row 7: K1, p2, 2/2 LC, 2/2 RC, p2, k1.
Row 8: P1, k2, p8, k2, p1.
Row 9: P1, k2, p2, k4, p2, k2, p1.
Row 10: K1, p2, k2, p4, k2, p2, k1.
Row 11: K1, p2, k1, 2/1 RC, 2/1 LC, k1, p2, k1.
Row 12: As row 8.
Row 13: P1, k1, 2/2 RC, p2, 2/2 LC, k1, p1.
Row 14: As row 6.
Row 15: 2/2 RC, p2, k2, p2, 2/2 LC.
Row 16: As row 4.

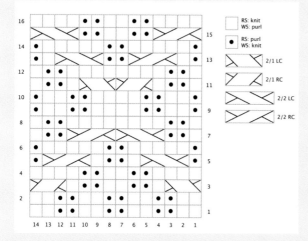

Fig. 116   Chart of mosaic-tiled arches.

Curved-lines pattern: meander cowl

The detail of the meander cowl shown in Figure 117 indicates that the pattern was developed from the exploration of curved lines that were inspired by the meandering river course featured earlier in this chapter. This development is illustrated in the sketch shown in Figure 118. Bending the foreground lines of knitting over different numbers of background stitches creates a varied flow pattern. The stitch pattern includes three- and four-stitch cables with the same number of foreground stitches. The four-stitch cables create more acute bends than do the three-stitch cables.

These cable stitch movements create a curved line with several different but balanced curves. It is by changing the angle of the bends throughout the line that creates the meandering curve rather than a series of regular bends. In the cowl pattern, two sets of row repeats of the stitch pattern are worked, adding more meanders and enhancing the asymmetrical element of the lines.

The meandering lines are worked in groups of three, separated by double-moss-stitch patterning. By repeating the groups of three lines around the cowl, the design acquires a great deal of horizontal and vertical movement. As the lines in each set contain the same bends, a rhythmic series of curves is created over the knitted fabric.

Working the double-moss-stitch pattern between each set of three lines softens the outer two lines and provides contrast to the centre line. This textural pattern links each set of three meanders and also appears to meander itself, as the pattern edges move along with the enclosed lines. The textural double-moss-stitch pattern also creates a flat section between the raised, ribbed lines of the meanders. The lines and texture of the main pattern have been extended into the cast-on and cast-off rib edgings of the cowl.

The cowl, shown in Figure 119, can be knitted in the round or flat. The flat version is knitted as a rectangle, with the side edges being sewn together after casting off. There is a two-stitch difference between the two patterns, as there is a selvedge stitch at each end of the rows of the flat version, to create a seam allowance for sewing up the cowl.

Fig. 117 Detail of the curved-line stitch pattern of the meander cowl.

Fig. 118 Sketch of meander lines.

Fig. 119 Meander cowl.

Meander cowl pattern

Size
One size
- 68cm (26¾in) circumference × 20cm (8in) deep

Yarn
- West Yorkshire Spinners Illustrious DK, 70-per-cent Falkland wool/30-per-cent British alpaca, DK weight, 225m (245yd) per 100g ball
- 1 × 100g ball in 331 Highland

Needles and accessories
- A pair of 3.25mm (UK10, US3) straight needles or an equivalent circular needle, as preferred
- A pair of 4mm (UK8, US6) straight needles or an equivalent circular needle, as preferred
- Cable needle
- Darning needle
- Stitch marker (if working in rounds)

Tension
- 29sts and 28 rows to 10cm (4in) over meander pattern (MP), using 4mm needles

Pattern notes
Refer to meander pattern (MP) written or charted instructions, as preferred.

Use the same MP chart for knitting flat or in the round. For working flat, read the chart from right to left for all right-side rows and left to right for all wrong-side rows. For working in the round, read the chart from right to left for all rounds. (The featured cowl was knitted flat.)

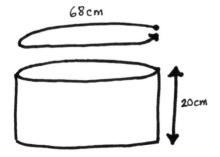

Fig. 120   Blocking diagram of meander cowl.

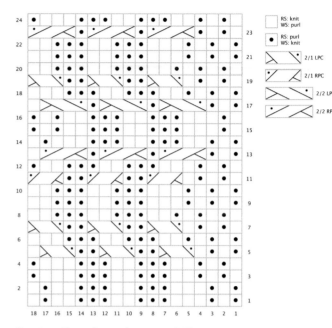

Fig. 121   Chart of meander pattern (MP).

Meander pattern (MP) written instructions for rows (multiple of 18sts and 24 rows)

Row 1 (RS): P1, k1, p1, k3, (p3, k2) twice, p1, k1.
Row 2 (WS): P1, k1, (p2, k3) twice, p3, k1, p1, k1.
Row 3: (K1, p1) twice, (k2, p3) twice, k3, p1.
Row 4: K1, p3, (k3, p2) twice, (k1, p1) twice.
Row 5: (P1, k1) twice, (2/1 LPC, p2) twice, 2/1 LPC, k1.
Row 6: P3, (k3, p2) twice, (k1, p1) twice, k1.
Row 7: (K1, p1) twice, k1, (2/1 LPC, p2) twice, 2/1 LPC.
Row 8: (P2, k3) twice, p2, (k1, p1) three times.
Row 9: (P1, k1) twice, p1, k3, (p3, k2) twice.
Row 10: (P2, k3) twice, p3, (k1, p1) twice, k1.
Row 11: (K1, p1) twice, k1, (2/1 RPC, p2) twice, 2/1 RPC.
Row 12: K1, (p2, k3) twice, p3, (k1, p1) twice.
Row 13: P1, k1, (p1, 2/2 RPC) three times, k1.
Row 14: P1, k1, p3, (k3, p2) twice, k1, p1, k1.
Row 15: K1, p1, k3, (p3, k2) twice, p1, k1, p1.
Row 16: K1, p1, k1, (p2, k3) twice, p3, k1, p1.
Row 17: P1, k1, (p1, 2/2 LPC) three times, k1.
Rows 18–22: As rows 6–10.
Row 23: K1, p1, k1, (p1, 2/2 RPC) three times.
Row 24: As row 4.

Meander pattern (MP) written instructions for rounds (multiple of 18sts and 24 rounds)

Round 1 (RS): P1, k1, p1, k3, (p3, k2) twice, p1, k1.

Round 2: As round 1.

Round 3: (K1, p1) twice, (k2, p3) twice, k3, p1.

Round 4: As round 3.

Round 5: (P1, k1) twice, (2/1 LPC, p2) twice, 2/1 LPC, k1.

Round 6: (P1, k1) twice, p1, (k2, p3) twice, k3.

Round 7: (K1, p1) twice, k1, (2/1 LPC, p2) twice, 2/1 LPC.

Round 8: (K1, p1) three times, (k2, p3) twice, k2.

Round 9: (P1, k1) twice, p1, k3, (p3, k2) twice.

Round 10: As round 9.

Round 11: (K1, p1) twice, k1, (2/1 RPC, p2) twice, 2/1 RPC.

Round 12: (K1, p1) twice, k3, (p3, k2) twice, p1.

Round 13: P1, k1, (p1, 2/2 RPC) three times, k1.

Round 14: P1, k1, p1, (k2, p3) twice, k3, p1, k1.

Round 15: K1, p1, k3, (p3, k2) twice, p1, k1, p1.

Round 16: As round 15.

Round 17: P1, k1, (p1, 2/2 LPC) three times, k1.

Rounds 18–22: As rounds 6–10.

Round 23: K1, p1, k1, (p1, 2/2 RPC) three times.

Round 24: As round 3.

Pattern instructions for working flat

Cast on 200sts by using a pair of 3.25mm straight needles.

Edge row 1 (RS): K1, *work MP row 1; rep from * to last st, k1.

Edge row 2 (WS): P1, *work MP row 2; rep from * to last st, p1.

Edge row 3: K1, *work MP row 3; rep from * to last st, k1.

Edge row 4: P1, *work MP row 4; rep from * to last st, p1.

These four edge rows set the selvedge stitches and the placement of MP.

Rep these four rows once, using MP rows 1–4 only.

Change to a pair of 4mm straight needles.

Continue as set, from MP row 5, working all twenty-four rows of MP twice.

Change to a pair of 3.25mm straight needles.

Work edge rows 1–3 once.

Cast off in patt as set by edge row 4, with WS facing.

Block the work gently to the measurements given in Figure 120 and according to the yarn's ball-band instructions.

Sew side seam.

Sew in all loose ends.

Pattern instructions for working in the round

Cast on 198sts by using a 3.25mm circular needle.

Place stitch marker, and join to work in the round.

Edge round 1: *Work MP round 1; rep from * to mrk, slm.

Edge round 2: *Work MP round 2; rep from * to mrk, slm.

Edge round 3: *Work MP round 3; rep from * to mrk, slm.

Edge round 4: *Work MP round 4; rep from * to mrk, slm.

Rep these four rounds once, using MP rows 1–4 only.

Change to a 4mm circular needle.

Continue as set, from MP round 5, and work all twenty-four rounds of MP twice.

Change to a 3.25mm circular needle.

Work edge rounds 1–3 once.

Cast off in patt as set by edge round 4.

Block the work gently to the measurements given in Figure 120 and according to the yarn's ball-band instructions.

Sew in all loose ends.

CHAPTER 6

STRAIGHT-SIDED SHAPES: DIAMONDS

One of the most versatile shapes in knitting, the diamond, can be applied in many different ways within the knitted fabric. Chapter 4 looked at the implied diamonds that can be formed between lines of moving stitches. This chapter will explore shapes that have a distinct opening and closure. Diamond shapes can be worked in separate, vertical columns and in horizontal, linked chains. The linked-diamond shapes can be used as a pattern that covers a large area of knitting, or they can be used as a means to enhance and draw attention to individual sections of knitting.

Inspiration for diamond shapes can be found in many diverse locations, from tiled plazas to tall buildings and from ironwork to architectural details. The photographs and sketches featured in this chapter reflect this mix of sources. Particular examples are from the cities of London, UK, and Lisbon, Portugal, and include the decorative detail on a porch in Bermondsey, London; tall buildings in the City of London, as shown in Figure 122; and ironwork patterning on a doorway and mosaic paving on the streets and in the plazas of Lisbon.

These sources provide ideal inspiration at several scales. Looking closely at the detail helps to reflect the key features with additional texture and line. This leads to a large number of design ideas and creates new and original patterns. Notes from my sketchbook have been included throughout this chapter,

Fig. 122 Diamond inspiration in the City of London.

to indicate the sorts of details to look out for.

In this section, which begins by considering a single diamond, the shapes are knitted by using twisted stitches. Ways to link the diamonds vertically to create a column will be looked at next, followed by the linking the shapes horizontally to make a diamond lattice or grid.

Single diamonds

The *Cambridge Dictionary* defines the noun 'diamond' as 'a shape with four straight sides of equal length, forming two opposite angles that are wide and two that are narrow'.

The single diamond shape has four knitting construction steps, as presented in the diagram shown in Figure 123. Step one is the start of the diamond, at the diamond's bottom point. The shape is formed by using a single twist or cable stitch movement. Step two is a symmetrical widening of the shape from that point. In this case, we move the foreground stitches outwards at the same time, with a series of repeated and mirror-imaged cable stitch movements. These movements continue until the desired width of the diamond is reached. Step three in the construction of the diamond occurs once the full width of the diamond is reached. At this point, a change of direction of the stitch movements occurs, bringing the foreground stitches back towards each other. This change of direction also creates

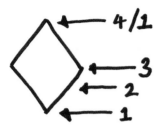

Fig. 123 Sketch of four steps to construct a single diamond shape.

Fig. 124 Mosaic-tiled diamond in Lisbon, Portugal.

Fig. 125 Knitted swatch of single-diamond shapes (yarn: pure wool, worsted weight; needles: 4.5mm; total stitches: 16; total rows: 26).

the side points of the diamond. The last step in the formation of the single diamond shape occurs at the top of the diamond. A final single twist or cable stitch movement is made to close the shape, at the diamond's top point. This is the final step, if the diamond is to be a single shape. If the diamond is to be a linked shape, steps one to three are repeated until the top of the column is reached, then the final step, step four, is used to end the column.

These four steps are the basis for creating diamonds of different sizes and components. There are many ways to work each step, and these will be considered throughout this section.

To illustrate the different ways that the four steps can be used, the first example is a group of four single-diamond shapes. These shapes have been inspired by a plaza full of mosaic diamond shapes in the city of Lisbon, shown in Figure 124. The knitted shapes are shown in Figure 125. There are differences in the foreground and background that will be looked at diamond by diamond.

All of the diamonds begin with a two-stitch twist as step one. The lower sides are then widened, for step two, by continuing to move the foreground stitches over the same number of background stitches. Once the diamond is of the correct width, for step three, each front stitch is then moved back over the same number of stitches as were worked for the lower half. The top of the diamond is completed by using a final two-stitch twist, for step four.

The diamonds have different centres and have been worked on different backgrounds. This is to highlight the difference in appearance that can be achieved by changing these two aspects only. Each diamond shown in Figure 125 will be looked at in detail, beginning with the diamonds on the bottom row and working from right to left.

The first diamond, on the right-hand side of the bottom row, has a stocking stitch foreground stitch on a stocking stitch background. The surrounding stitch pattern is also of stocking stitch, as is the diamond's centre. The main effect of working everything in stocking stitch is that the diamond blends into the background. The beginning and end of the shape blend into the background stitch pattern.

The second diamond, on the left-hand side of the bottom row, appears much more distinct, and the outline is emphasized. This is in part because of the way that the reverse stocking stitch background contrasts with the stocking stitch foreground stitches. The diamond's background surround is worked in reverse stocking stitch, which is also used to work the diamond's centre. When working step 4 of a single diamond shape on a reverse stocking stitch background, a tidy finish can be achieved: the final twist or cable is worked as set; however, when these stitches are reached on the following wrong-side row, they are worked in reverse stocking stitch.

The third diamond to be considered is on the right-hand side of the top row. This diamond has a stocking stitch foreground stitch. The centre of the diamond is worked in stocking stitch, and the background surround is of reverse stocking stitch. The

effect of this combination is that the whole diamond shape appears prominent and that the background recedes.

The fourth and final diamond in this set of diamond examples is on the left-hand side of the top row. This diamond has a stocking stitch foreground stitch. The background surround is worked in stocking stitch, and the centre is of reverse stocking stitch. In this case, the centre of the diamond appears to recede into the stocking stitch surround.

These four examples demonstrate how a small number of variations can have a big impact on the design. Although always guided by the source inspiration, there needs to be an awareness of the impact of choices and particularly their impact on the knitted fabric. Further variations can be made by changing the foreground and background stitch patterns to more textural patterns and having a different number of stitches

Single-diamond shapes
(16sts and 26 rows)

Row 1 (RS): K3, 1/1 RC, k3, p3, 1/1 RC, p3.

Row 2 (WS): K3, p2, k3, p8.

Row 3: K2, 1/1 RC, 1/1 LC, k2, p2, 1/1 RPC, 1/1 LPC, p2.

Row 4: (K2, p1) twice, k2, p8.

Row 5: K1, 1/1 RC, k2, 1/1 LC, k1, p1, 1/1 RPC, p2, 1/1 LPC, p1.

Row 6: K1, p1, k4, p1, k1, p8.

Row 7: K1, 1/1 LC, k2, 1/1 RC, k1, p1, 1/1 LPC, p2, 1/1 RPC, p1.

Row 8: As row 4.

Row 9: K2, 1/1 LC, 1/1 RC, k2, p2, 1/1 LPC, 1/1 RPC, p2.

Row 10: As row 2.

Row 11: K3, 1/1 RC, k3, p3, 1/1 RPC, p3.

Rows 12–13: K8, p8.

Row 14: P8, k8.

Row 15: P3, 1/1 RC, p3, k3, 1/1 RC, k3.

Row 16: P8, k3, p2, k3.

Row 17: P2, 1/1 RC, 1/1 LC, p2, k2, 1/1 RPC, 1/1 LPC, k2.

Row 18: (P3, k2) twice, p4, k2.

Row 19: P1, 1/1 RC, k2, 1/1 LC, p1, k1, 1/1 RPC, p2, 1/1 LPC, k1.

Row 20: P2, k4, p2, k1, p6, k1.

Row 21: P1, 1/1 LPC, k2, 1/1 RPC, p1, k1, 1/1 LC, p2, 1/1 RC, k1.

Row 22:
As row 18.

Row 23: P2, 1/1 LPC, 1/1 RPC, p2, k2, 1/1 LC, 1/1 RC, k2.

Row 24:
As row 16.

Row 25: P3, 1/1 RPC, p3, k3, 1/1 RC, k3.

Row 26: P8, k8.

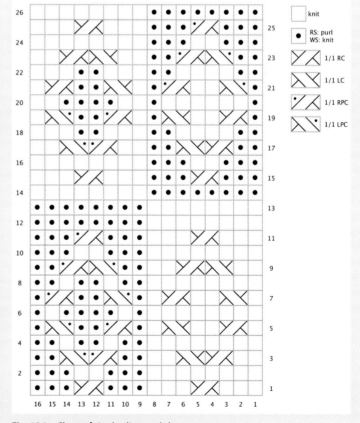

Fig. 126 Chart of single-diamond shapes.

Fig. 127 Knitted swatch of vertical diamonds (yarn: pure wool, 4ply weight; needles: 4.5mm; total stitches: 30, comprising three 10-stitch repeats; total rows: 44, comprising three 14-row repeats plus 2 rows).

Vertical diamonds

(10sts and 14 rows)

Row 1 (RS): P3, 2/2 RC, p3.
Row 2 (WS): K3, p4, k3.
Row 3: P2, 2/1 RC, 2/1 LC, p2.
Row 4: K2, p6, k2.
Row 5: P1, 2/1 RC, k2, 2/1 LC, p1.
Row 6: K1, p8, k1.
Row 7: 2/1 RC, k4, 2/1 LC.
Row 8: Purl.
Row 9: 2/1 LPC, k4, 2/1 RPC.
Row 10: As row 6.
Row 11: P1, 2/1 LPC, k2, 2/1 RPC, p1.
Row 12: As row 4.
Row 13: P2, 2/1 LPC, 2/1 RPC, p2.
Row 14: As row 2.

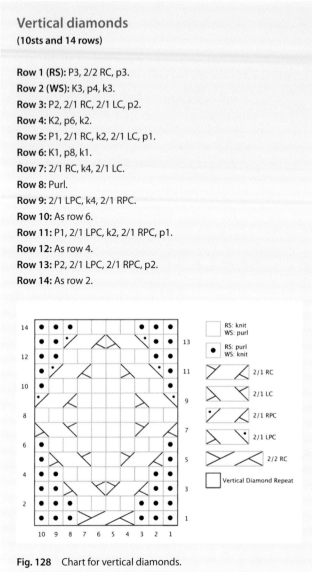

Fig. 128 Chart for vertical diamonds.

in the twist or cable. Using twists and cables that move over a large number of background stitches will create a variety of thick and thin lines that in turn make narrow or wide diamond shapes. Mixing these lines will achieve interesting asymmetrical variations. More of these variations will be discussed later in this chapter, in the context of additional inspirational images.

Multiple diamond shapes

Vertical diamond columns

Having considered the properties of single knitted diamonds, ways of linking the diamonds will be looked at next, beginning with vertical columns of diamonds, then moving on to horizontal linking techniques. From there, decorative effects will be added to the diamond stitch patterns, to reflect the inspiration source and create a complex, balanced design.

Columns of diamonds begin by being worked in the same way as for the single-diamond examples of the previous section. Once the first three steps have been worked, the first step is

repeated, to create the beginning of the next diamond of the column. The column can be extended to the desired length by repeating steps one to three. When the column is ready to be completed, it is finished by working step four, to close the twist or cable. Any one of the mosaic-tile-inspired single-diamond examples could be used in this way, to build up a variety of different columns. However, this example is inspired by a source on a different scale.

The inspiration source for the first set of knitted vertical columns of diamonds is the Leadenhall Building in the City of London, also known informally as the Cheesegrater, because of its distinctive shape. This prominent building, visible on the left-hand side of Figure 122, was designed by Rogers Stirk Harbour + Partners and opened in 2014. The reason for choosing this view of the building is that the architectural structure is clearly visible, even at a distance; in particular, three large diamond shapes can be seen across the front facade.

The glass frontage of the building creates a smooth surface. To reflect this characteristic in the knitted fabric, the first sample, shown in Figure 127, has been knitted as columns of diamonds with stocking stitch centres. Two stocking stitch stitches have been used for the foreground cables, to reflect the wide lines on the front of the building. The columns' background is knitted in reverse stocking stitch. This makes the diamond columns more prominent and gives good contrast between the foreground and background of the fabric.

This swatch was knitted in a fine, 4ply-weight yarn. This weight of yarn is used to achieve more detail in the pattern. The knitted sample has three 10-stitch repeats, making thirty stitches in total. The diamond columns were linked vertically by repeating the rows of the chart that correspond to the original construction steps one to three. There are three 14-row repeats, plus an extra two rows that correspond to step four were worked, to close the top of the diamond. In this case, the last two rows of the swatch are the same as the first two rows.

Horizontal diamond links

Having linked the diamond shapes vertically in the last section, in this section, the links will be horizontal. This kind of link can be achieved with several different techniques. In general, the diamonds to be linked begin with a twist or cable that is worked in the same way as for our previous diamonds. The horizontal link occurs when the diamonds reach their widest points and the individual diamonds almost touch each other. The links that we are going to look at will be worked in a similar way whether there are two, three or more diamonds next to each other.

Twisting the diamond links

The first technique to link our diamonds horizontally is to twist or cable the diamond points where they meet at the widest parts of the shapes. Considering the previous examples, it can be seen that the vertical diamond columns are worked as stand-alone patterns. Some adjustments to the stitch and row placement are necessary, to facilitate the formation of the horizontal links. To work additional twists, the columns will need to have some additional rows in order to fit in the linking twists.

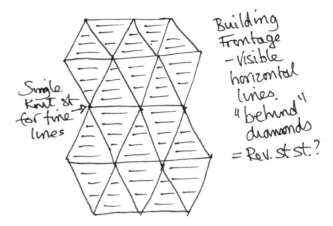

Fig. 129 Sketch of textured background detail of the inspiration source.

Fig. 130 Knitted swatch of ridged diamonds (yarn: pure wool, worsted weight; needles: 4.5mm; total stitches: 20, comprising three 6-stitch repeats plus 2sts; total rows: 38, comprising three 12-row repeats plus 2 rows).

Returning to the inspiration of the Leadenhall Building, the glass frontage of the building appears smooth. Additionally, upon looking closely at the building once more, each floor level shows through the glass as a visible horizontal line. This detail is noted in the sketch shown in Figure 129. To highlight this aspect, some background texture has been added to the design. In the knitted swatch shown in Figure 130, the linked-diamond columns also have reverse stocking stitch ridges on a stocking stitch background. These ridges contrast with the stocking stitch background and draw attention to the twisted links between the diamonds. In this example, fine, twisted stitches have been used to create thin, structural lines. Although the twists are fine lines, they are emphasized by the weight of the yarn chosen to work with, a worsted-weight yarn.

Looking at the swatch in detail, it can be seen that all of the inner diamonds are connected by twists. The outer diamonds also have twists at the edges of the lattice.

The swatch is made up of a stitch pattern that is a multiple of six stitches plus an additional two stitches. The chart's repeat box has six stitches within it. This means that, to add extra diamonds to this lattice, the necessary stitches would be added in a multiples of six. The additional two stitches are for the extra outer twist on the edge of the lattice. These extra stitches are represented on each side of the repeat box. This swatch includes twenty stitches, which correspond to three 6-stitch, linked diamonds and the two extra stitches for the additional outer twist.

The chart's repeat box has twelve rows within it, but two extra rows are required to close the tops of the diamonds. For this swatch, the row repeat was worked three times, then the last two rows were knitted, to finish the swatch. To add extra diamond row repeats, work a multiple of twelve extra rows, then work the final two rows afterwards.

Within the swatch, the twists that link the diamonds are all worked in the same direction. This can be varied, depending on the effect to be created. Working all of the twists in this way makes the diamonds look overlapping and adds to the effect of strong, diagonal lines. As more repeats are added, the lattice begins to build, and further diamonds form between the columns of the original diamonds.

Wrapping the diamond links

As well as by using a twist or cable to connect the horizontal diamonds, the link between the diamonds can be worked with different methods. The link can be made more prominent by 'wrapping' the stitches where they meet. In Figure 132, more of the mosaic diamond shapes from the plaza in Lisbon can

Ridged diamonds
(6sts, plus 2sts, and 12 rows)

Note: the repeat box for this chart has a stepped appearance, as the repeat cannot run through the centre of a stitch movement.

Row 1 (RS): P1, *p2, 1/1 RC, p2; rep from * once, p1.
Row 2 and all WS rows: Purl.
Row 3: K1, *k1, 1/1 RC, 1/1 LC, k1; rep from * once, k1.
Row 5: K1, *1/1 RC, k2, 1/1 LC; rep from * once, k1.
Row 7: 1/1 RC, *p4, 1/1 RC; rep from * once.
Row 9: K1, *1/1 LC, k2, 1/1 RC; rep from * once, k1.
Row 11: K1, *k1, 1/1 LC, 1/1 RC, k1; rep from * once, k1.

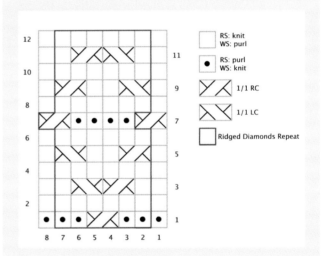

Fig. 131 Chart of ridged diamonds.

Fig. 132 Mosaic-tiled plaza in Lisbon, Portugal.

Fig. 133 Knitted swatch of wrapped diamonds (yarn: pure wool, worsted weight; needles: 4.5mm; total stitches: 18, comprising two 6-stitch repeats plus 6sts; total rows: 26, comprising three 8-row repeats plus 2 rows).

Wrapped diamonds
(6sts, plus 6sts, and 8 rows)

Note: the repeat box for this chart has a stepped appearance, as the repeat cannot run through the centre of a stitch manipulation.

Row 1 (RS): P2, *wrap 2sts, p4; rep from * once, wrap 2sts, p2.
Row 2 (WS): K2, p1, *p1, k4, p1; rep from * once, *p1, k2; rep from * once.
Row 3: 1/2 RPC, *1/2 LPC, 1/2 RPC; rep from * once, 1/2 LPC.
Row 4: P1, k2, *k2, p2, k2; rep from * once, *k2, p1; rep from * once.
Row 5: K1, p2, *p2, wrap 2sts, p2; rep from * once, p2, k1.
Row 6: As row 4.
Row 7: 1/2 LPC, *1/2 RPC, 1/2 LPC; rep from * once, 1/2 RPC.
Row 8: As row 2.

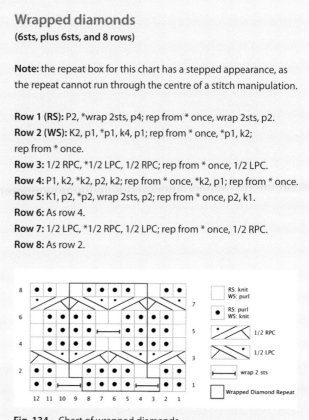

Fig. 134 Chart of wrapped diamonds.

be seen. The wider view shows how the diamonds appear to be linked together by a distinct join. In this case, using a wrapped-stitch link reflects this aspect really well.

The knitted swatch shown in Figure 133 has a diamond lattice made with mirror-imaged three-stitch twisted stitches. The twists all have a stocking stitch foreground stitch and a reverse stocking stitch background. The stitches are wrapped where the diamond shapes meet at their widest points. Combining the three-stitch twists and the wraps makes a raised pattern on the front of the work. The centres of the diamonds recede, and the wrapped links have a three-dimensional quality. When knitted in a pure-wool, aran-weight yarn, as for the featured swatch, this stitch pattern has a strong structure, even though there is only a single foreground stitch for each twist.

The wraps are all worked within the diamond lattice. Where two diamonds meet at their widest points, the stitches are wrapped instead of twisted. The edges of the knitted lattice do not have an extra wrap. Completing the end of the panel requires an additional set of wraps, so two extra rows are worked to complete the lattice. The stitch pattern has a multiple of six stitches plus six stitches.

This swatch was knitted with two sets of the stitch repeat. This means that the twelve stitches of the chart shown in Figure 134 have been used, plus an extra six stitches. Once the six stitches indicated within the red pattern-repeat box have been knitted, the working of those six stitches is repeated. The working of the full chart is completed by using the extra six stitches, which are represented on each side of the pattern-repeat box. Regarding the row repeats of the swatch, three repeats were worked. This means that the first eight rows are worked, then repeated twice, before the swatch is completed by working rows 1 and 2 of the chart once more.

How to work a wrapped stitch

A group of stitches can be pulled together by using a wrapped stitch. This method is a useful joining technique that can be combined with different twist and cable patterns. Any number of stitches can be wrapped. However, the greater the number of stitches pulled together in a wrap, the more the knitted fabric is tightened and distorted. In this example, two stitches are wrapped on a right-side row.

The stitches are wrapped by pulling a loop of yarn through from the back of the work. This yarn loop is placed on to the left-hand needle. The manner in which the yarn loop is placed on to the needle can vary according to personal preference: the loop may be partially twisted, as when working a cable cast-on, or, alternatively, the loop is not twisted, as when slipping a stitch purlwise. However, whichever option is selected, it should be used consistently throughout the working of the pattern. The loop is then knitted together with the first of the wrapped stitches (the stitch closest to the loop and the point of the left-hand needle).

Pattern to the stitches to be wrapped.

Step 1 (Figure 135): Insert the rhn point between the second and third stitches on the lhn.

Step 2 (Figure 136): Pull a yarn loop through from the back of the work to the front with the rhn point, and place this loop on to the lhn point, in front of the first stitch.

Step 3 (Figure 137): Knit the loop and the first stitch together.

Step 4 (Figure 138): Knit the second stitch.

Fig. 135   Step 1 of wrapping a stitch.

Fig. 136   Step 2 of wrapping a stitch.

Fig. 137   Step 3 of wrapping a stitch.

Fig. 138   Step 4 of wrapping a stitch.

Textured diamonds

As well as the strong, diagonal lines and the prominent links between the shapes, the Lisbon tiled plaza has additional features that make it ideal as further inspiration for more diamond designs. For instance, there are many tiny mosaic tiles within the outlined diamonds. The sketch shown in Figure 139 highlights this aspect of the inspiration. The separate tiles suggest a moss-stitch texture, so the next featured diamonds will use this contrasting stitch pattern.

Although the next swatch, shown in Figure 140, uses the same three-stitch twisted stitch movement as used for the pre-

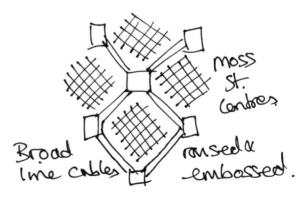

Fig. 139   Sketch of textured diamonds, inspired by the mosaic-tiled plaza in Lisbon.

Fig. 140 Knitted swatch of textured diamonds (yarn: pure wool, worsted weight; needles: 4.5mm; total stitches: 27, comprising three 8-stitch repeats plus 3sts; total rows: 26, comprising three 8-row repeats plus 2 rows).

vious swatch, you can see that the diamonds created are larger. This is because there are two movements before the diamond reaches its widest point, instead of one.

When considering how to actually work the stitch movement to connect the points of the diamonds, there are two choices: a twisted stitch option that immediately sets the moss-stitch pattern on the right-side row and a stocking stitch-only cable that requires the setting of the moss-stitch pattern on the next wrong-side row.

In general, on a large-scale diamond, there will be plenty of rows to set the moss-stitch pattern and see its full effect. In this case, the cables have been worked with knit stitches only. This allows cabling without a cable needle and helps the knitter to work much faster. Another effect of working a knit-stitch-only cable is to slightly emboss the centre of the diamond, as the edges of the diamond will be slightly smooth, with the centres being more textured. This stitch pattern is very textural, reflecting the character of the mosaic tiles really well. On a design with smaller diamonds, consider starting the moss stitch straight away within the twist, in order to get the full effect of the stitch pattern throughout the small area available.

The textured-diamonds design has a multiple of eight stitches plus three stitches. The knitted swatch contains three pattern repeats and therefore has a total of twenty-seven stitches.

1/1/1 RC abbreviation

In the accompanying textured-diamonds chart, there is a special abbreviation for a movement that forms a new twist with the stitches of the points of our diamonds: 1/1/1 RC. This twist allows the movement of the outer two foreground stitches across the middle stitch. The full description of this movement is as follows: slip the next two stitches to a cable needle, and hold the cable needle at the back of the work; k1, slip the left-most stitch from the cable needle to the left-hand needle, move the cable needle with the remaining stitch to the front of the work, k1 from the left-hand needle, then k1 from the cable needle.

It is also possible to work this stitch without a cable needle as follows: knit into the front of the third stitch on the left-hand needle; knit into the back of the second stitch on the left-hand needle; knit into the front of the first stitch on the left-hand needle; then, keeping the worked loops on the right-hand needle, carefully slip all three worked stitches off of the left-hand needle. As there are three manipulations in this movement, try to keep your stitches loose and avoid pulling the yarn too tight.

Textured diamonds
(8sts, plus 3sts, and 8 rows)

Note: the repeat box for this chart has a stepped appearance, as the repeat cannot run through the centre of a stitch movement.

Row 1 (RS): P1, k1, *p1, k1, 1/1/1 RC, k1, p1, k1; rep from * once, p1.
Row 2 and all WS rows: P1, *(k1, p1) four times; rep from * once, k1, p1.
Row 3: P1, k1, *1/2 RC, k1, 1/2 LC, k1; rep from * once, p1.
Row 5: 1/1/1 RC, *(k1, p1) twice, k1, 1/1/1 RC; rep from * once.
Row 7: P1, k1, *1/2 LC, k1, 1/2 RC, k1; rep from * once, p1.

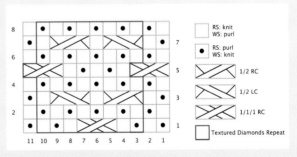

Fig. 141 Chart of textured diamonds.

Fig. 142 Stone-porch diamonds in Bermondsey, London, UK.

Patterned diamonds links

The diamonds shown in Figure 142 are located on a porch in Bermondsey, London. These decorative diamonds are an ideal inspiration source for the next diamond design. In particular, they inspire another variation of our diamond columns, to reflect the stonework design. This time, instead of joining the diamond columns, they will be once more worked as separate columns. In the sketch shown in Figure 143, you can see the emphasis on the intersections. Where the diamond points meet in the knitted fabric, a mini oval is made by using twisted stitches. In this example, the stitches within the mini oval are worked as reverse stocking stitch, to provide contrast with the larger stocking stitch-centred diamonds. This will make the centre of the joining ovals recede. The link between the diamonds in this design is a visual link rather than a knitted twisted stitch link. By working these long columns side by side, the joining ovals form within the knitted fabric.

This design has a repeat of six stitches and sixteen rows. The knitted swatch shown in Figure 144 has three repeats of the six stitches, making it a total of eighteen stitches wide. Two repeats of sixteen rows have been worked, then the swatch has been

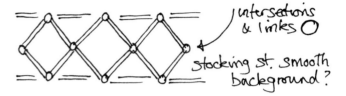

Fig. 143 Sketch of porch diamonds.

Fig. 144 Knitted swatch of porch diamonds (yarn: pure wool, worsted weight; needles: 4.5mm; total stitches: 18, comprising three 6-stitch repeats; total rows: 36, comprising two 16-row repeats plus 4 rows).

Porch diamonds

(6sts and 16 rows)

Row 1 (RS): K1, 1/1 RPC, 1/1 LPC, k1.
Row 2 (WS): P2, k2, p2.
Row 3: K1, 1/1 LC, 1/1 RC, k1.
Rows 4, 6 and 8: Purl.
Row 5: K1, 1/1 RC, 1/1 LC, k1.
Row 7: 1/1 RC, k2, 1/1 LC.
Row 9: 1/1 LPC, k2, 1/1 RPC.
Row 10: K1, p4, k1.
Row 11: As row 7.
Rows 12, 14 and 16: Purl.
Row 13: 1/1 LC, k2, 1/1 RC.
Row 15: As row 3.

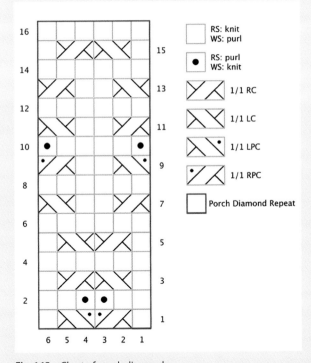

Fig. 145   Chart of porch diamonds.

completed by repeating the first four rows. This makes a total of thirty-six rows for the swatch. The last four rows complete the panel and balance the beginning and the end of the design.

The smooth-twist, pure-wool, worsted-weight yarn used for this swatch, along with the background stocking stitch pattern, reflects the smooth surface of the stone porch. The yarn also clearly shows the twisted stitch lines.

Diamonds pattern: Agora wrap

Cabled diamonds and their use in knitting were considered throughout the previous sections. The individual components of the diamond are extremely useful for a wide range of designs. A further manipulation of the diamond shape is to divide it into subsections. By knitting only selected sections of the diamond shape, we can create some interesting triangular shapes by using the same construction methods as used for diamonds. This approach was considered in the Leadenhall Building example, where ridges were added to the resulting smooth, cabled design (*see* the section 'Twisting the diamond links'). Bisecting the diamonds with the ridges split them into triangular subsections. The Agora-wrap design takes this subdivision a step further.

The triangle and diamond shapes are inspired by stunning architecture. The particular shot shown in Figure 146 was taken when looking straight up the outer glass facade covering the stairwell of one of the buildings of the European Parliament in Brussels. Important details of the stairwell design are included in the sketch shown in Figure 147. The building forms one of the sides of an open, public plaza known as the Agora. The ancient Greek word agora means meeting point. The definition has inspired this wrap's construction, where the centre section is the meeting point of the winged sides.

The Agora-wrap stitch pattern, part of which is shown in Figure 148, extends selected lines of the diamond shape and also splits the centre of the diamond with a long, cabled, vertical line. This new configuration creates sets of mirror-imaged triangles. The stitch pattern uses four-stitch cables throughout to create several different lines. Repeating the cables vertically over the same four stitches creates a bold rope pattern. Using the same cable manipulation to move the stitches across the foreground of the work creates the triangular shapes. This strong, architectural stitch pattern is further enhanced by using texture alongside the vertical and horizontal lines.

The wrap is constructed in three parts. The first part is a centre section, shown in Figure 148, that features a series of panels. The pattern uses all of the diamond-related techniques considered throughout this chapter, to build up a series of building blocks reminiscent of the featured stairwell. Looking carefully at the inspiration image, it can be seen that the shapes are divided then subdivided by the features of the stairwell. In the wrap's panels, these subdividing features are represented by reverse stocking stitch ridges.

All of the four-stitch cables are worked in stocking stitch. Reverse-stocking stitch sections are used to highlight the tri-

Fig. 146   Glass facade of a staircase within the Agora, Brussels.

Fig. 147   Sketch of staircase facade.

Fig. 148   Knitted detail of the Agora-wrap centre section.

angular staircase structure. This use of texture creates a contrast between the sections and a more interesting reverse side of the wrap, with the triangular shapes showing up clearly on both sides of the fabric.

The centre-section panels are all worked in a similar way but at different scales. The narrowing is achieved by gradually decreasing within the fourth and fifth panel repeats. Although the central, vertical cable line of the pattern remains the same throughout, the three accompanying charts show how the placement of the cable and reverse stocking stitch pattern changes as the panels narrow.

The second and third parts of the wrap comprise triangular wings, one of which is sketched in Figure 149 and both of which are shown in Figure 150. The stitches to start the wings are picked up along the sides on the centre section, to allow the wings to be knitted outwards, while decreases are worked along one side edge. Because the centre section is narrower towards the top, the wings are set at a slight angle to the centre section, giving the wrap a lovely drape around the shoulders. The wings have a cable border and are worked in stocking stitch, which was inspired by the smooth glass surfaces all around the area of the Agora. Reverse-stocking stitch ridges, highlighted in the images shown in Figures 150 and 151, echo the structure of the centre section.

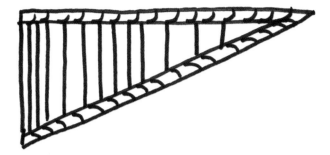

Fig. 149 Sketch of Agora-wrap triangular wing.

Fig. 150 Agora-wrap centre section and start of winged sides.

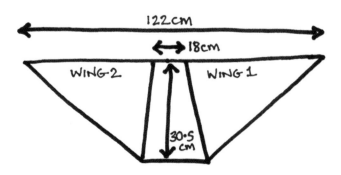

Fig. 152 Blocking diagram of Agora wrap.

Fig. 151 Agora wrap, showing ridged wing and its cabled edge. (Photo: Maxine Vining)

Agora wrap pattern

Size

One size
- 122cm (48in) wide (measured point to point) × 30.5cm (12in) deep (centre section)

Yarn

- Brooklyn Tweed Arbor, 100-per-cent American Targhee wool, DK weight, 133m (145yd) per 50g skein
- 3 × 50g skeins in Sashiko

Needles and accessories

- A pair of 4mm (UK8, US6) straight needles or an equivalent circular needle, as preferred
- A pair of 4.5mm (UK7, US7) straight needles or an equivalent circular needle, as preferred
- Cable needle
- Darning needle

Tension

- 26sts and 29 rows to 10cm (4in) over centre-section Agora patterns A–C, using 4.5mm needles
- 20sts and 26 rows to 10cm (4in) over wing ridge patterns 1–3, using 4.5mm needles

Pattern notes

The Agora wrap is knitted in three parts, beginning with the centre section, followed by the two side-wing sections. Each section uses just under one skein of the specified yarn.

Refer to written or charted instructions for each stitch pattern (Agora patterns A–C), as preferred.

Agora pattern A (worked over 40sts and 16 rows)

Row 1 (RS): P12, (k4, p2) twice, k4, p12.
Row 2 (WS): K12, (p4, k2) twice, p4, k12.
Row 3: K12, (2/2 RC, p2) twice, 2/2 LC, k12.
Row 4: P16, k2, p4, k2, p16.
Row 5: P10, 2/2 RC, k2, p2, k4, p2, k2, 2/2 LC, p10.
Row 6: K10, p6, k2, p4, k2, p6, k10.
Row 7: K8, 2/2 RC, k4, p2, 2/2 RC, p2, k4, 2/2 LC, k8.
Row 8: As row 4.
Row 9: P6, 2/2 RC, k6, p2, k4, p2, k6, 2/2 LC, p6.
Row 10: K6, p10, k2, p4, k2, p10, k6.
Row 11: K4, 2/2 RC, 2/2 LC, k4, p2, 2/2 RC, p2, k4, 2/2 RC, 2/2 LC, k4.
Row 12: As row 4.
Row 13: P2, 2/2 RC, k4, 2/2 LC, k2, p2, k4, p2, k2, 2/2 RC, k4, 2/2 LC, p2.
Row 14: K2, p14, k2, p4, k2, p14, k2.
Row 15: 2/2 RC, k8, 2/2 LC, (p2, 2/2 RC) twice, k8, 2/2 LC.
Row 16: As row 4.

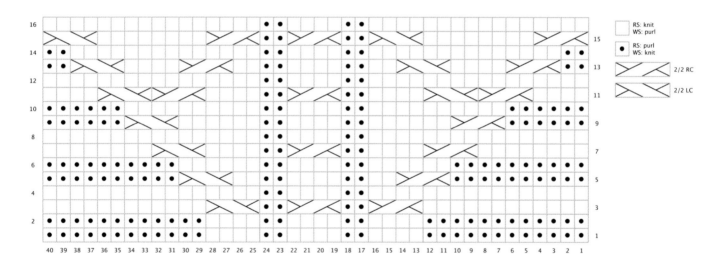

Fig. 153   Chart of Agora pattern A.

Agora pattern B (worked over 40sts and 16 rows)

Row 1 (RS): P12, 2/2 LC, p2, k4, p2, 2/2 RC, p12.

Row 2 (WS): K12, (p4, k2) twice, p4, k12.

Row 3: K12, 2/2 LC, (p2, 2/2 RC) twice, k12.

Row 4: P16, k2, p4, k2, p16.

Row 5: P10, 2/2 RC, k2, p2, k4, p2, k2, 2/2 LC, p10.

Row 6: K10, p6, k2, p4, k2, p6, k10.

Row 7: P8, 2/2 RC, k4, p2, 2/2 RC, p2, k4, 2/2 LC, p8.

Row 8: K8, p8, k2, p4, k2, p8, k8.

Row 9: P6, 2/2 RC, k6, p2, k4, p2, k6, 2/2 LC, p6.

Row 10: K6, p10, k2, p4, k2, p10, k6.

Row 11: P4, 2/2 RC, 2/2 LC, k4, p2, 2/2 RC, p2, k4, 2/2 RC, 2/2 LC, p4.

Row 12: K4, p12, k2, p4, k2, p12, k4.

Row 13: P2, 2/2 RC, k4, 2/2 LC, k2, p2, k4, p2, k2, 2/2 RC, k4, 2/2 LC, p2.

Row 14: K2, p14, k2, p4, k2, p14, k2.

Row 15: 2/2 RC, k8, 2/2 LC, (p2, 2/2 RC) twice, k8, 2/2 LC.

Row 16: As row 4.

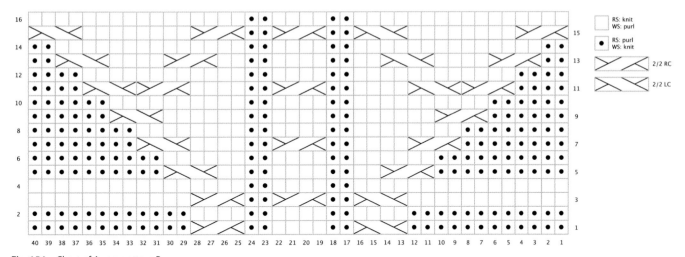

Fig. 154   Chart of Agora pattern B.

Agora pattern C (worked over 32sts and 12 rows)

Row 1 (RS): P8, 2/2 LC, (p2, 2/2 RC) twice, p8.

Row 2 (WS): K8, (p4, k2) twice, p4, k8.

Row 3: K8, 2/2 LC, p2, k4, p2, 2/2 RC, k8.

Row 4: P12, k2, p4, k2, p12.

Row 5: P6, 2/2 RC, k2, p2, 2/2 RC, p2, k2, 2/2 LC, p6.

Row 6: K6, p6, k2, p4, k2, p6, k6.

Row 7: P4, 2/2 RC, (k4, p2) twice, k4, 2/2 LC, p4.

Row 8: K4, p8, k2, p4, k2, p8, k4.

Row 9: P2, 2/2 RC, 2/2 LC, k2, p2, 2/2 RC, p2, k2, 2/2 RC, 2/2 LC, p2.

Row 10: K2, p10, k2, p4, k2, p10, k2.

Row 11: 2/2 RC, k4, 2/2 LC, p2, k4, p2, 2/2 RC, k4, 2/2 LC.

Row 12: As row 4.

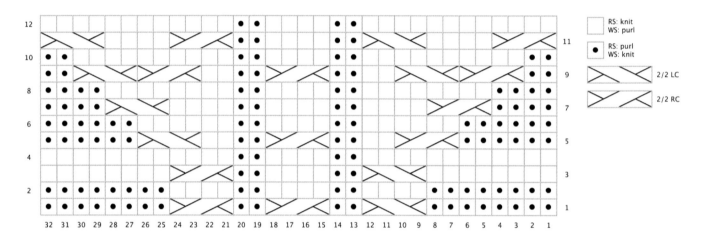

Fig. 155 Chart of Agora pattern C.

Pattern instructions

Centre section

Cast on 54sts by using 4mm needles.

Begin panel 1 lower-edge border by using written or charted instructions for pattern A, as preferred, as follows:

Edge row 1 (RS): K5, p2, work row 1 of pattern A, p2, k5.

Edge row 2 (WS): P5, k2, work row 2 of pattern A, k2, p5.

Edge row 3: K1, 2/2 RC, p2, work row 3 of pattern A, p2, 2/2 LC, k1.

Edge row 4: P5, k2, work row 4 of pattern A, k2, p5.

Keeping the four-row, cabled-edge pattern correct throughout the whole centre section, rep edge rows 1–4 two times, using pattern A rows 1–4 only.

Change to 4.5mm needles, and continue as set, from row 5 of pattern A, working all sixteen rows of pattern A once.

Work panels 2 and 3 by using written or charted instructions for pattern B, as preferred, as follows:

Row 1 (RS): K5, p2, work row 1 of pattern B, p2, k5.

Row 2 (WS): P5, k2, work row 2 of pattern B, k2, p5.

Row 3: K1, 2/2 RC, p2, work row 3 of pattern B, p2, 2/2 LC, k1.

Row 4: P5, k2, work row 4 of pattern B, k2, p5.

Continue as set, from row 5 of pattern B, working all sixteen rows of pattern B twice.

Note: Read ahead regarding panel 4 decreases.

Work panel 4 by continuing to use pattern B and, at the same time, beginning decreases on next row as follows:

Row 1 (decrease row): K5, p2tog, work row 1 of pattern B, p2togtbl, k5. (52sts)

Row 2: P5, k1, work row 2 of pattern B, k1, p5.

Row 3: K1, 2/2 RC, p1, work row 3 of pattern B, p1, 2/2 LC, k1.

Row 4: P5, k1, work row 4 of pattern B, k1, p5.

Rows 5–8: Continue as set, from row 5 of pattern B, working four more rows (without decreases), ending with row 8 of pattern B.

Row 9 (decrease row): K4, k2tog, work row 9 of pattern B, ssk, k4. (50sts)

Row 10: P5, work row 10 of pattern B, p5.

Row 11: K1, 2/2 RC, work row 11 of pattern B, 2/2 LC, k1.

Row 12: P5, work row 12 of pattern B, p5.

Rows 13–14: Continuing as set, by working from pattern B row 13, work two more rows (without decreases), ending with pattern B row 14.

Work panel 5 by using written or charted instructions for pattern C, as preferred, as follows:

Row 1 (decrease row): K1, 2/2 RC, p2tog, p2, work row 1 of pattern C, p2, p2togtbl, 2/2 LC, k1. (48sts)

Row 2: P5, k3, work row 2 of pattern C, k3, p5.

Row 3: K5, p2, k1, work row 3 of pattern C, k1, p2, k5.

Row 4: P5, k2, p1 work row 4 of pattern C, p1, k2, p5.

Row 5: K1, 2/2 RC, p3, work row 5 of pattern C, p3, 2/2 LC, k1.

Row 6: P5, k3, work row 6 of pattern C, k3, p5.

Row 7: K5, p3, work row 7 of pattern C, p3, k5.

Row 8: P5, k3 work row 8 of pattern C, k3, p5.

Row 9 (decrease row): K1, 2/2 RC, p2tog, p1, work row 9 of pattern C, p1, p2togtbl, 2/2 LC, k1. (46sts)

Row 10: P5, k2, work row 10 of pattern C, k2, p5.

Row 11: K5, p2, work row 11 of pattern C, p2, k5.

Row 12: P5, k2, work row 12 of pattern C, k2, p5.

Change to 4mm needles, and work upper edge as follows:

Row 1: K1, 2/2 RC, p2tog, p8, 2/2 LC, (p2, 2/2 RC) twice, p8, p2togtbl, 2/2 LC, k1. (44sts)

Row 2: P5, k9, (p4, k2) twice, p4, k9, p5.

Row 3: K5, p2, k11, p2, k4, p2, k11, p2, k5.

Row 4: P5, k2, p11, k2, p4, k2, p11, k2, p5.

Row 5: K1, 2/2 RC, p9, 2/2 LC, (p2, 2/2 RC) twice, p9, 2/2 LC, k1.

Cast off in patt as set by upper-edge row 2, with WS facing.

Wing 1

With RS of work facing and by using 4mm needles, pick up and knit 60sts evenly along the right-hand-side cabled edge of the centre section.

Set-up row (WS): P5, k2, p to last 7sts, k2, p5.

Change to 4.5mm needles.
Work ridge pattern 1 as follows:
Row 1 (RS): K1, 2/2 RC, p to last 5sts, 2/2 LC, k1.
Row 2 (WS): P5, k to last 5sts, p5.
Row 3: K5, p2, k to last 7sts, p2, k5.
Row 4: P5, k2, p to last 7sts, k2, p5.
Rep rows 1–4 once.
***

Begin ridge pattern 2, and, at the same time, decrease on the next and every following fourth row as follows:
Row 1 (decrease row): K1, 2/2 RC, p1, p2tog, p to last 5sts, 2/2 LC, k1. (59sts)
Row 2: P5, k to last 5sts, p5.
Row 3: K5, p2, k to last 7sts, p2, k5.
Row 4: P5, k2, p to last 7sts, k2, p5.
Row 5 (decrease row): K1, 2/2 RC, p1, p2tog, k to last 7sts, p2, 2/2 LC, k1. (58sts)
Row 6: As row 4.
Row 7: As row 3.
Row 8: As row 4.
Rep rows 1–8 eight times, until 42sts remain, ending with row 8.

Begin ridge pattern 3, and, at the same time, decrease on the next and every following RS row as follows:
Row 1 (decrease row): K1, 2/2 RC, p1, p2tog, p to last 5sts, 2/2 LC, k1. (41sts)
Row 2: P5, k to last 5sts, p5.
Row 3 (decrease row): K5, p1, p2tog, k to last 7sts, p2, k5. (40sts)
Row 4: P5, k2, p to last 7sts, k2, p5.
Row 5 (decrease row): K1, 2/2 RC, p1, p2tog, k to last 7sts, p2, 2/2 LC, k1. (39sts)
Row 6: As row 4.
Row 7 (decrease row): As row 3. (38sts)
Row 8: As row 4.
Row 9 (decrease row): As row 5. (37sts)
Row 10: As row 4.
Row 11 (decrease row): As row 3. (36sts)
Row 12: As row 4.
Rep rows 1–12 three times, then rows 1–8 once. (14sts)

Shape wing point as follows:
Row 1 (RS): K1, 2/2 RC, p1, p2togtbl, p1, 2/2 LC, k1. (13sts)
Row 2 (WS): P5, k2tog, k1, p5. (12sts)
Row 3: K5, p2togtbl, k5. (11sts)
Row 4: P4, p2tog, p5. (10sts)
Row 5: K3, k2tog, 2/2 LC, k1. (9sts)
Row 6: P5, p2tog, p2. (8sts)
Row 7: K1, k2tog, k5. (7sts)
Row 8: P4, p2tog, p1. (6sts)
Row 9: K1, k2tog, ssk, k1. (4sts)
Row 10: P2tog twice. (2sts)
K2tog, and fasten off.

Wing 2

With RS of work facing and by using 4mm needles, pick up and knit 60sts evenly along the left-hand-side cabled edge of the centre section.

Work as for wing 1 to ***.

Begin ridge pattern 2, and, at the same time, decrease on the next and every following fourth row as follows:

Row 1 (decrease row): K1, 2/2 RC, p2, p to last 8sts, p2togtbl, p1, 2/2 LC, k1. (59sts)

Row 2: P5, k to last 5sts, p5.

Row 3: K5, p2, k to last 7sts, p2, k5.

Row 4: P5, k2, p to last 7sts, k2, p5.

Row 5 (decrease row): K1, 2/2 RC, p2, k to last 8sts, p2togtbl, p1, 2/2 LC, k1. (58sts)

Row 6: As row 4.

Row 7: As row 3.

Row 8: As row 4.

Rep rows 1–8 eight times, until 42sts remain, ending with row 8.

Begin ridge pattern 3, and, at the same time, decrease on the next and every following RS row as follows:

Row 1 (decrease row): K1, 2/2 RC, p to last 8sts, p2togtbl, p1, 2/2 LC, k1. (41sts)

Row 2: P5, k to last 5sts, p5.

Row 3 (decrease row): K5, p2, k to last 8sts, p2togtbl, p1, k5. (40sts)

Row 4: P5, k2, p to last 7sts, k2, p5.

Row 5 (decrease row): K1, 2/2 RC, p2, k to last 8sts, p2togtbl, p1, 2/2 LC, k1. (39sts)

Row 6: As row 4.

Row 7 (decrease row): As row 3. (38sts)

Row 8: As row 4.

Row 9 (decrease row): As row 5. (37sts)

Row 10: As row 4.

Row 11 (decrease row): As row 3. (36sts)

Row 12: As row 4.

Rep rows 1–12 three times, then rows 1–8 once. (14sts)

Shape wing point as follows:

Row 1 (RS): K1, 2/2 RC, p1, p2tog, p1, 2/2 LC, k1. (13sts)

Row 2: P5, k1, k2tog, p5. (12sts)

Row 3: K5, p2tog, k5. (11sts)

Row 4: P5, p2tog, p4. (10sts)

Row 5: K1, 2/2 RC, k2tog, k3. (9sts)

Row 6: P2, p2tog, p5. (8sts)

Row 7: K5, k2tog, k1. (7sts)

Row 8: P1, p2tog, p4. (6sts)

Row 9: K1, k2tog, ssk, k1. (4sts)

Row 10: P2tog twice. (2sts)

K2tog, and fasten off.

Block the work gently to the measurements given in Figure 152 and according to the yarn's ball-band instructions.

Sew in all loose ends.

CHAPTER 7

STRAIGHT-SIDED SHAPES: HEXAGONS

A hexagon is an example of a polygon, a shape with many sides. In this case, 'hex' means six, and this polygon has six sides of equal length.

Hexagons can be found in both the natural and built environments. Well-known examples in the natural world include honeycomb made by bees in a hive and rock formations formed by cooling of molten rock after a volcanic eruption. Many hexagonal shapes can be found in urban areas too. These include ironwork grills on buildings, tiled surfaces and even car-park matting. The hexagon shape is an efficient way to build surfaces and structures with shared boundaries. The honeycomb structure made by bees, for example, uses the minimum amount of wax, for the most efficient form of honey storage.

In knitting, the hexagon enables the design of regular, geometric patterns of different scales, which can be filled with a variety of textures. Many traditional styles of knitting make use of the hexagon in combination with several kinds of twist and cabling techniques. For example, the honeycomb cable pattern is a very recognizable stitch pattern that is found in Aran-style knitting. By looking first at the construction steps and then moving on to ways to change individual elements,

this chapter will consider ways to use the extremely versatile hexagonal shape to design stitch patterns based on a variety of inspiration sources.

Single hexagons

The hexagon shape has five knitting construction steps, as presented in the diagram shown in Figure 157. The way that the beginning and the end of the hexagon shapes are formed is similar to that of the construction of diamond shapes.

Step one concerns the starting point of the hexagon, at its bottom point. The shape is formed from this central point, either with or without a single twist or cable stitch movement. Step two represents the symmetrical widening of the shape. For a regular, two-dimensional hexagon shape, all sides should be equal in length. In this case, the foreground stitches are moved outwards from the central point, with a series of repeated and mirror-imaged twist or cable stitch movements. These movements continue until the desired width of the hexagon is reached. This width sets the size of the hexagon. For a knitted shape, this means that the tension of the knitting also must be considered. This will determine the actual stitch movements and number of rows to be worked in order to balance the dimensions of the shape's sides.

Fig. 156 Knitted swatch of single-hexagon shapes (yarn: pure wool, worsted weight; needles: 4.5mm; total stitches: 16; total rows: 22).

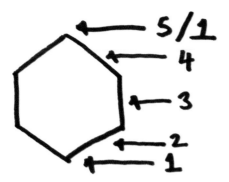

Fig. 157 Sketch of five steps to construct a single hexagon shape.

Step three of the construction of a hexagon is to form its straight, vertical edges. To do this, the foreground cable stitches are now worked as a straight, vertical line until the length of this line matches the length of the line formed by performing the stitch movements of step two.

Once the correct length has been reached, step four brings the foreground stitches back towards each other by the same number of movements as were performed for step two. Step five either extends the straight lines of the upper sides in an upward direction from the top, central point or involves a final twist or cable stitch movement to close the hexagon shape. If this is the final step of a single shape, a contrasting stitch pattern can be used to emphasize the top of the shape. If this is one of a series of linked shapes, steps one to four can be repeated until the desired length of column is reached, when the final step, step five, is used to end the column.

These five steps are the basis for creating hexagons of different sizes and components. To illustrate the differences in appearance that can be generated by small changes in the way that the five steps are performed, the first example, shown in Figure 156, is of four separate hexagon shapes.

In the swatch, all of the hexagons begin with a two-stitch twist as step one. The lower sides are then widened in step two by continuing to move the foreground stitches over the same number of background stitches. In this case, a single foreground stitch is moved over two background stitches. The hexagons are then at their full width. The sides are now formed in step

three with a knitted vertical line. Once the correct length is reached, in step four, the foreground stitches are then moved back over the same number of background stitches as were used in step two. The top of the hexagon is completed by using a final two-stitch twist, as step five.

The hexagons in the swatch have different stitch patterns in their centres and have been worked on different backgrounds. This is to highlight the difference in appearance that can be achieved by changing these two aspects only.

The first hexagon, on the right-hand side of the bottom row, has a stocking stitch foreground stitch on a stocking stitch background. The surrounding stitch pattern is also stocking stitch, as is the hexagon's centre. The main effect of working this whole section of the swatch in stocking stitch is that the shape blends into the background.

The second hexagon, on the left-hand side of the bottom row, appears much more distinct, with its outline emphasized. This is in part due to the reverse stocking stitch background stitches contrasting with the stocking stitch foreground stitch and the hexagon's background surround and centre both being worked in reverse stocking stitch. When working the final, closing step of a single hexagon on a reverse stocking stitch background, a tidy finish can be achieved by the final twist or cable being worked as set, followed by reverse stocking stitch being worked on the next row.

The third hexagon, on the right-hand side of the top row, has a stocking stitch foreground stitch and centre. The surrounding background is of reverse stocking stitch, making the shape appear more prominent and causing the background to recede.

The fourth and final hexagon in this set of hexagon examples is on the left-hand side on the top row and has a stocking stitch foreground stitch. The background surround is worked in stocking stitch, and the centre is of reverse stocking stitch. In this case, the centre of the hexagon appears to recede into the stocking stitch surround.

These small number of variations can have a big impact on a design's development. They are part of the decision-making process when choosing which knitted lines best represent the inspirational source material.

Single-hexagon shapes

(16sts and 22 rows)

Row 1 (RS): K3, 1/1 RC, k3, p3, 1/1 RC, p3.

Row 2 (WS): K3, p2, k3, p8.

Row 3: K1, 1/2 RC, 1/2 LC, k1, p1, 1/2 RPC, 1/2 LPC, p1.

Row 4: K1, p1, k4, p1, k1, p8.

Row 5: K8, p1, k1, p4, k1, p1.

Row 6: As row 4.

Row 7: K1, 1/2 LC, 1/2 RC, k1, p1, 1/2 LPC, 1/2 RPC, p1.

Row 8: As row 2.

Row 9: As row 1.

Rows 10–11: K8, p8.

Row 12: P8, k8.

Row 13: P3, 1/1 RC, p3, k3, 1/1 RC, k3.

Row 14: P8, k3, p2, k3.

Row 15: P1, 1/2 RC, 1/2 LC, p1, k1, 1/2 RPC, 1/2 LPC, k1.

Row 16: P2, k4, p2, k1, p6, k1.

Row 17: P1, k6, p1, k2, p4, k2.

Row 18: As row 16.

Row 19: P1, 1/2 LPC, 1/2 RPC, p1, k1, 1/2 LC, 1/2 RC, k1.

Row 20: As row 14.

Row 21: As row 13.

Row 22: P8, k8.

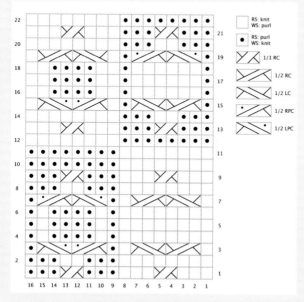

Fig. 158   Chart of single-hexagon shapes.

Multiple hexagons

Implied hexagons

The linked shapes in this example have been inspired by a very ordinary source of hexagonal shapes. Supportive matting in a car park, shown in Figure 159, located at Watts Gallery in Compton, Surrey, UK, provides the perfect starting point for this series of designs.

Often obscured by the plants that grow through the centres of the shapes, this matting is an example of an inflexible structure that has been altered by natural processes. Each visit to the car park shows that the composition of these hexagons changes as the vegetation growing through the rigid, geometric structure grows or is cut back.

Using the hexagonal matting as inspiration, individual lines are included in the sketch shown in Figure 160. Putting these lines together in a mirror image of each other forms a series of implied hexagons. The hexagons are implied because the shapes are formed between the lines rather than being formed by a series of joins or links.

The foreground lines of knitting in the swatch shown in Figure 161 have all been worked in stocking stitch. The background texture is of reverse stocking stitch, creating a contrast between the stitch patterns. The knitting tension requires working more rows than stitches to ensure that the sides of the hexagon are all of the same length. In this case, where the first foreground twists have been moved over two stitches, three further rows are required to make the lengths of the hexagon's sides equal.

Three repeats of the stitch pattern have been worked in the swatch, both horizontally and vertically. As the stitch pattern is six stitches wide and eight rows long, this means the swatch is eighteen stitches by twenty-four rows. Although only one hexagon is shown in the chart, the placement of the twisted stitch pattern means that additional hexagons form between the repeats. The resulting pattern forms a repeating pattern of multiple hexagons that has a honeycomb appearance. This tiling property is very useful in creating stitch patterns. A small, repeating pattern can create a complex design over a larger area.

Fig. 159   Hexagonal car-park matting, Watts Gallery, Compton, UK.

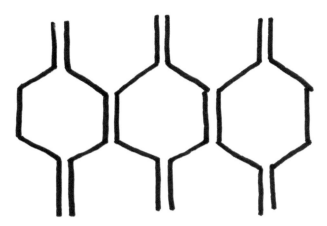

Fig. 160   Sketch of implied hexagons.

Implied hexagon
(6sts and 8 rows)

Row 1 (RS): P2, k2, p2.
Row 2 (WS): K2, p2, k2.
Row 3: 1/2 RPC, 1/2 LPC.
Row 4: P1, k4, p1.
Row 5: K1, p4, k1.
Row 6: P1, k4, p1.
Row 7: 1/2 LPC, 1/2 RPC.
Row 8: As row 2.

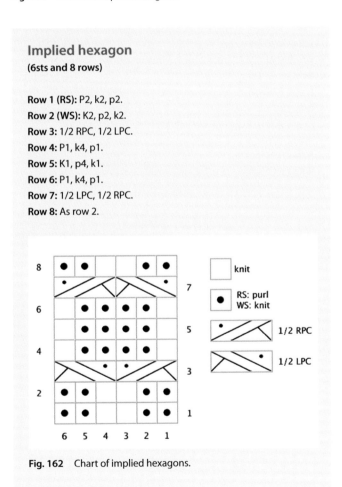

Fig. 162   Chart of implied hexagons.

Fig. 161   Knitted swatch of implied hexagons (yarn: pure wool, worsted weight; needles: 4.5mm; total stitches: 18, comprising three 6-stitch repeats; total rows: 24, comprising three 8-row repeats).

Double hexagons

A join between two sections of matting is visible in the centre of the image shown in Figure 159. The two sections of matting have been placed close together, with a double line occurring at the intersection. This double line is an interesting feature to explore in design development and is represented in the sketch shown in Figure 163.

The swatch shown in Figure 164 reproduces this feature in a knitted double-hexagon shape. A small, central hexagon is surrounded by an outer, larger hexagon shape. This pattern has been included twice within the swatch, both horizontally and vertically.

The four double hexagons have the appearance of flowing around the smaller shapes present within the swatch. The knitted lines that form the larger hexagons also create contrasting hexagons between them. In this case, an additional hexagonal shape with a contrasting centre of reverse stocking stitch is formed in the centre of the swatch. This example demonstrates the need to consider the patterns that are formed between the repeats of a design.

Fig. 164 Knitted swatch of double hexagons (yarn: pure wool, aran weight; needles: 4.5mm; total stitches: 20, comprising two 10-stitch repeats; total rows: 36, comprising two 18-row repeats).

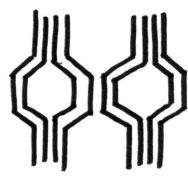

Fig. 163 Sketch of double hexagons.

Double hexagons
(10sts and 18 rows)

Row 1 (RS): P4, k2, p4.
Row 2 (WS): K4, p2, k4.
Row 3: P2, 1/2 RC, 1/2 LC, p2.
Row 4: K2, p1, k1, p2, k1, p1, k2.
Row 5: 1/2 RPC, p1, k2, p1, 1/2 LPC.
Row 6: P1, k3, p2, k3, p1.
Row 7: K1, p1, 1/2 RPC, 1/2 LPC, p1, k1.
Row 8: P1, k1, p1, k4, p1, k1, p1.
Row 9: K1, p1, k1, p4, k1, p1, k1.
Row 10: As row 8.
Row 11: K1, p1, 1/2 LPC, 1/2 RPC, p1, k1.
Row 12: As row 6.
Row 13: 1/2 LPC, p1, k2, p1, 1/2 RPC.
Row 14: As row 4.
Row 15: P2, 1/2 LPC, 1/2 RPC, p2.
Row 16: As row 2.
Rows 17–18: As rows 1–2.

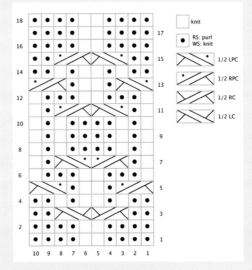

Fig. 165 Chart of double hexagons.

Linked textured hexagons

Having looked at knitting hexagonal shapes by using individual lines, in the following example, the shapes are formed by linking the edges of the hexagons where they meet. As more shapes are knitted and more joins are made, the shapes form a joined lattice with a honeycomb appearance, which is depicted in the sketch shown in Figure 166.

Textural stitch patterns have been added within the knitted shapes, reflecting the different areas of vegetation within the hexagonal car-park matting. The texture adds contrast to the shapes, making some of the them more prominent and some less so.

The swatch shown in Figure 167 includes a variety of textures, such as reverse stocking stitch, stocking stitch and moss stitch, within the hexagon shapes. All of the shapes' outlines and links are knitted by using four-stitch cables. The honeycomb-lattice effect is the dominant feature of this example, as the cable links define the joins. The outer edges of the lattice have a non-linked edge.

To soften the bold lines of the lattice, a yarn containing alpaca fibre has been used. The bloom of the alpaca fibre slightly blurs the cables.

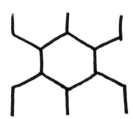

Fig. 166 Sketch of linked hexagons.

Fig. 167 Knitted swatch of textured hexagons (yarn: alpaca and wool, DK weight; needles: 4mm; total stitches: 24, comprising two 8-stitch repeats plus 8sts; total rows: 24).

Textured hexagons
(8sts, plus 8sts, and 24 rows)

Note: the repeat box for this chart has a stepped appearance, as the repeat cannot run through the centre of a stitch movement.

Row 1 (RS): K2, 2/2 RC, *k4, 2/2 RC; rep from * once, k2.
Row 2 (WS): Purl.
Row 3: 2/2 RC, *2/2 LC, 2/2 RC; rep from * once, 2/2 LC.
Row 4: P2, k2, *k2, p4, k2; rep from * once, k2, p2.
Row 5: K2, p2, *p2, 2/2 RC, p2; rep from * once, p2, k2.
Rows 6–7: As rows 4–5.
Row 8: As row 4.
Row 9: 2/2 LC, *2/2 RC, 2/2 LC; rep from * once, 2/2 RC.
Row 10: As row 2.
Rows 11–14: Rep rows 1–2 twice.
Row 15: As row 3.
Row 16: P3, k1, *p1, k1, p5, k1; rep from * once, p1, k1, p2.
Row 17: K3, p1, *k1, p1, 2/2 RC, k1, p1; rep from * once, k1, p1, k2.
Rows 18–19: As rows 16–17.
Row 20: As row 16.
Row 21: As row 9.
Row 22: As row 2.
Rows 23–24: As rows 1–2.

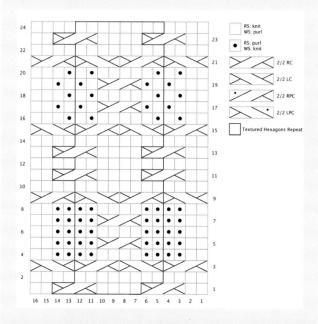

Fig. 168 Chart of textured hexagons.

Extended hexagons

Now that the single, implied and double hexagons have been explored, the next step is to elongate the hexagons and change the scale. The hexagon shapes shown in Figure 169 are on a metal grid near King's Cross St. Pancras Railway Station in London. Although all of the hexagons on the grid are of the same size, this image gives the impression of a change in their scale. For knitted hexagons, the change in scale can be explored by extending the sides of the shapes. The original shape, with sides of equal length, will be transformed into an elongated structure. A lattice can be formed with these new shapes that also includes this change of scale. In the sketch shown in Figure 170, the construction of the shapes follows the same principles as applicable for the single hexagons.

In the knitted swatch shown in Figure 171, additional twisted joins have been added between the sides of the hexagons. In this example, a two-stitch twist is knitted on all of the right-side rows of the vertical meeting edges. The background stitch pattern is reverse stocking stitch, to provide contrast to the stitch movements in the foreground of the swatch.

The stitch pattern is a multiple of six stitches, plus an additional six stitches. For the additional six stitches, there are three stitches at the beginning and three stitches at the end of each row. The swatch has three repeats of six stitches plus the additional six stitches, making a total of twenty-four stitches. There are twenty-four rows in the vertical pattern repeat, which have been worked once.

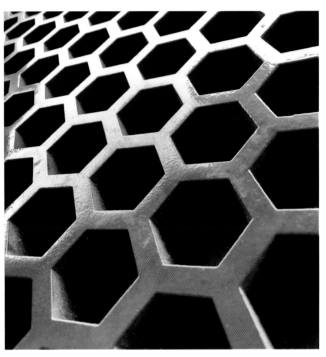

Fig. 169 Ironwork hexagonal grid at King's Cross St. Pancras Railway Station in London.

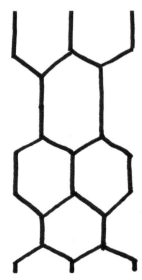

Fig. 170 Sketch of extended hexagons.

Fig. 171 Knitted swatch of extended hexagons (yarn: wool and silk, DK weight; needles: 4mm; total stitches: 18, comprising two 6-stitch repeats plus 6sts; total rows: 24).

Extended hexagons

(6sts, plus 6sts, and 24 rows)

Note: the repeat box for this chart has a stepped appearance, as the repeat cannot run through the centre of a stitch movement.

Row 1 (RS): K1, p2, *p2, 1/1 RC, p2; rep from * once, p2, k1.
Row 2 (WS): P1, k2, *k2, p2, k2; rep from * once, k2, p1.
Row 3: 1/2 LPC, *1/2 RPC, 1/2 LPC; rep from * once, 1/2 RPC.
Row 4: K2, p1, *p1, k4, p1; rep from * once, p1, k2.
Row 5: P2, 1/1 RC, *p4, 1/1 RC; rep from * once, p2.
Row 6: As row 4.
Row 7: 1/2 RPC, *1/2 LPC, 1/2 RPC; rep from * once, 1/2 LPC.
Row 8: As row 2.
Rows 9–12: Rep rows 1–2 twice.
Rows 13–14: As rows 3–4.
Rows 15–20: Rep rows 5–6 three times.
Row 21: As row 7.
Row 22: As row 2.
Rows 23–24: As rows 1–2.

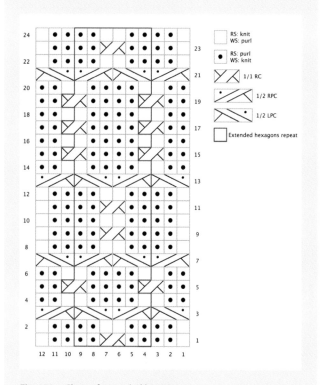

Fig. 172 Chart of extended hexagons.

Hexagons pattern: postpile wrap

The Devils Postpile National Monument is located within a beautiful area of California, USA, near the city of Mammoth Lakes. A walk along a beautiful forest trail brings visitors up close to the rock formations known collectively as the Devils Postpile, shown in Figure 173. These majestic, hexagonal columns of volcanic rock known as basalt had their origin deep in the earth's crust. Volcanic activity forced hot, molten magma to the surface, where it cooled and crystallized into columns of rock, as shown in Figure 174. The tops of the columns have been exposed in some areas, revealing their hexagonal patterning, as shown in Figure 175.

Fig. 173 Devil's Postpile National Monument, showing basalt columns.

Fig. 174 Devil's Postpile National Monument, showing basalt columns with a hexagonal structure.

In some sections, weathering of the tops of the columns has polished them to a smooth surface. In other areas, the columns have fractured much more unevenly. A variety of mosses and shrubs grow in the cracks between the basalt columns, creating a mix of textures, reflected in the sketch shown in Figure 176. These textures pick out the closely packed hexagon shapes, making the stunning natural features of the Devils Postpile excellent inspiration for this hexagon project.

Fig. 175 Devil's Postpile National Monument close-up, showing the hexagonal structure.

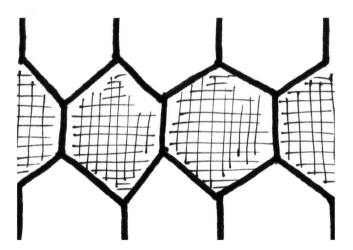

Fig. 176 Sketch of textured hexagons.

The Postpile-wrap pattern, shown in Figures 177 and 178, uses a regular hexagonal layout to create a geometric pattern. The hexagon shapes are all of the same dimensions throughout the wrap. The outline of each hexagon is enhanced by using contrasting stitch patterns of stocking stitch and reverse stocking stitch. Each shape is formed by using the same series of three-stitch twisted stitches.

The hexagonal shape is further emphasized by the yarn choice for the project. The fine, mercerized cotton accentuates the fine knitted lines that are repeated across the knitted fabric. The way that the sun is filtered through the forest canopy at the Devils Postpile National Monument gives the surface of the basalt columns a delicate sheen. Mercerized cotton yarn is perfect to represent this element of the inspiration and highlight the contrasting textures within the pattern. Although the colour of the basalt is black, the location of this natural wonder within a forest setting, combined with the moss and lichen, gives the surface a green–blue appearance, which is reflected in the chosen shade of this cotton yarn.

These contrasting textures have been inspired by the differential weathering of the basalt formations. In some areas of the national monument, the hexagonal structures appear as smooth tiles. In other areas, they form an uneven surface of multiple broken hexagonal shapes. The edges of the Postpile wrap are also textured: garter-stitch ridges widen and narrow along with the knitted hexagon formations.

The lower part of the wrap begins with a three-stitch-twist pattern that flows into the full hexagon shapes of the main pattern. The lower side edges of the wrap are shaped by increasing stitches on every right-side row until the full width of the wrap is reached. The upper side edges are decreased to match the shape of the lower side edges before the remaining stitches are cast off.

On the reverse side of the wrap, the different stitch patterns of the hexagons' centres show through, creating a subtle textured pattern that echoes the right side of the knitting.

Fig. 177 Stitch-pattern detail of the Postpile wrap.

Fig. 178 Postpile wrap. (Photo: Maxine Vining)

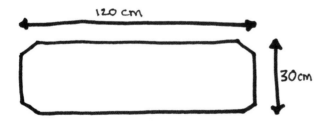

Fig. 179 Blocking diagram of Postpile wrap.

Postpile wrap pattern

Size
One size
- 30cm (12in) wide × 120cm (47in) long

Yarn
- Sirdar Cotton 4ply, 100-per-cent cotton, 4ply weight, 335m (366yd) per 100g ball
- 2 × 100g balls in 524 Mosaic

Needles and accessories
- A pair of 2.75mm (UK12, US2) straight needles or an equivalent circular needle, as preferred
- A pair of 3.25mm (UK10, US3) straight needles or an equivalent circular needle, as preferred
- Cable needle
- Darning needle

Tension

- 30sts and 36 rows to 10cm (4in) over Postpile pattern (PP), using 3.25mm needles

Pattern notes

Refer to written or charted instructions for each stitch pattern, as preferred.

Postpile border pattern (PBP) (multiple of 12sts and 4 rows)

Row 1 (RS): K2, 1/2 RC, p1, 1/2 LC, k3.
Row 2 (WS): P6, k1, p5.
Row 3: K2, 1/2 LC, p1, 1/2 RC, k3.
Row 4: K5, p1, k1, p1, k4.

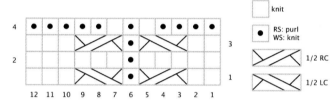

Fig. 180   Chart of Postpile border pattern (PBP).

Postpile pattern (PP) (multiple of 12sts and 16 rows)

Row 1 (RS): K1, p9, k1, p1.
Row 2 (WS): K1, p1, k9, p1.
Row 3: 1/2 LC, p5, 1/2 RC, p1.
Row 4: K1, p3, k5, p3.
Row 5: K2, 1/2 LC, p1, 1/2 RC, k2, p1.
Row 6: (K1, p5) twice.
Row 7: (K5, p1) twice.
Rows 8–9: As rows 6–7.
Row 10: As row 6.
Row 11: K2, 1/2 RPC, p1, 1/2 LPC, k2, p1.
Row 12: As row 4.
Row 13: 1/2 RPC, p5, 1/2 LPC, p1.
Rows 14: As row 2.
Rows 15–16: As rows 1–2.

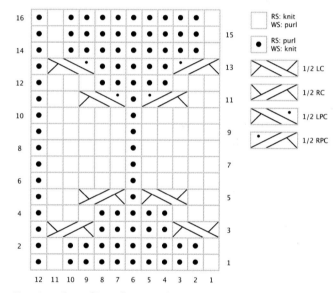

Fig. 181   Chart of Postpile pattern (PP).

Pattern instructions

Cast on 77sts by using 2.75mm needles.
Set up lower-border pattern as follows:
Row 1 (RS): K8, *p1, k11; rep from * to last 9sts, p1, k to end.
Row 2 (WS): K7, *p1, k1, p1, k9; rep from * to last 10sts, p1, k1, p1, k to end.

Using PBP written or charted instructions, as preferred, begin side increases at each end of the next seven RS rows as follows:
Row 3: K1, m1, k2, *work row 1 of PBP; rep from * to last 2sts, k1, m1, k1. (79sts)
Row 4: P3, *work row 2 of PBP; rep from * to last 4sts, p to end.
Row 5: K1, m1, k3, *work row 3 of PBP; rep from * to last 3sts, k2, m1, k1. (81sts)
Row 6: K4, *work row 4 of PBP; rep from * to last 5sts, k to end.
Row 7: K1, m1, k4, *work row 1 of PBP; rep from * to last 4sts, k3, m1, k1. (83sts)
Row 8: P5, *work row 2 of PBP; rep from * to last 6sts, p to end.
Row 9: K1, m1, k5, *work row 3 of PBP; rep from * to last 5sts, k4, m1, k1. (85sts)
Row 10: K6, *work row 4 of PBP; rep from * to last 7sts, k to end.
Row 11: K1, m1, k6, *work row 1 of PBP; rep from * to last 6sts, k5, m1, k1. (87sts)
Row 12: P7, *work row 2 of PBP; rep from * to last 8sts, p to end.
Row 13: K1, m1, k7, *work row 3 of PBP; rep from * to last 7sts, k6, m1, k1. (89sts)
Row 14: K8, *work row 4 of PBP; rep from * to last 9sts, k to end.
Row 15: K1, m1, k8, *work row 1 of PBP; rep from * to last 8sts, k7, m1, k1. (91sts)
Row 16: P9, *work row 2 of PBP; rep from * to last 10sts, p to end.

Extend border pattern without increasing as follows:
Row 17: K10, *work row 3 of PBP; rep from * to last 9sts, k to end.
Row 18: K9, *work row 4 of PBP; rep from * to last 10sts, k to end.
Row 19: K10, *work row 1 of PBP; rep from * to last 9sts, k to end.
Row 20: P9, *p4, k5, p3; rep from * to last 10sts, p to end.
Row 21: K10, *1/2 RPC, p5, 1/2 LPC, k1; rep from * to last 9sts, k to end.
Row 22: K9, *k1, p1, k9, p1; rep from * to last 10sts, k to end.
Row 23: K9, p1, *k1, p9, k1, p1; rep from * to last 9sts, k to end.
Row 24: P9, *k1, p1, k9, p1; rep from * to last 10sts, k1, p to end.

Change to 3.25mm needles, and begin main pattern by using PP written or charted instructions, as preferred, as follows:
Row 1 (RS): K9, p1, *work row 1 of PP; rep from * to last 9sts, k to end.
Row 2 (WS): K8, p1, *work row 2 of PP; rep from * to last 10sts, k1, p1, k to end.
Row 3: K6, 1/2 RC, p1, *work row 3 of PP; rep from * to last 9sts, 1/2 LC, k to end.
Row 4: P9, *work row 4 of PP; rep from * to last 10sts, k1, p to end.
Row 5: K4, 1/2 RC, k2, p1, *work row 5 of PP; rep from * to last 9sts, k2, 1/2 LC, k to end.
Row 6: K4, p5, *work row 6 of PP; rep from * to last 10sts, k1, p5, k to end.
Row 7: K9, p1, *work row 7 of PP; rep from * to last 9sts, k9.
Row 8: P9, *work row 8 of PP; rep from * to last 10sts, k1, p to end.
Row 9: As row 7.
Row 10: As row 6.
Row 11: K4, 1/2 LC, k2, p1, *work row 11 of PP; rep from * to last 9sts, k2, 1/2 RC, k to end.
Row 12: As row 4.
Row 13: K6, 1/2 LC, p1, *work row 13 of PP; rep from * to last 9sts, 1/2 RC, k to end.
Row 14: As row 2.
Row 15: As row 1.
Row 16: P9, *work row 16 of PP; rep from * to last 10sts, k1, p to end.

Rep rows 1–16 twenty-three times.

Change to 2.75mm needles, and begin upper-border pattern as follows:
Row 1 (RS): K11, *p9, k3; rep from * to last 8sts, k to end.
Row 2 (WS): K10, p1, *k9, p3; rep from * to last 20sts, k9, p1, k to end.
Row 3: K10, *1/2 LC, p5, 1/2 RC, p1; rep from * to last 21sts, 1/2 LC, p5, 1/2 RC, k to end.
Row 4: P13, *k5, p3, k1, p3; rep from * to last 18sts, k5, p to end.

Begin side decreases at each end of the next seven RS rows as follows:
Row 5: K1, ssk, k9, *1/2 LC, p1, 1/2 RC, k2, p1, k2; rep from * to last 19sts, 1/2 LC, p1, 1/2 RC, k9, k2tog, k1. (89sts)
Row 6: K13, *p1, k1, p1, k9; rep from * to last 4sts, k to end.
Row 7: K1, ssk, k6, *work row 1 of PBP; rep from * to last 8sts, k5, k2tog, k1. (87sts)
Row 8: P7, *work row 2 of PBP; rep from * to last 8sts, p to end.
Row 9: K1, ssk, k5, *work row 3 of PBP; rep from * to last 7sts, k4, k2tog, k1. (85sts)
Row 10: K6, *work row 4 of PBP; rep from * to last 7sts, k to end.

Row 11: K1, ssk, k4, *work row 1 of PBP; rep from * to last 6sts, k3, k2tog, k1. (83sts)
Row 12: P5, *work row 2 of PBP; rep from * to last 6sts, p to end.
Row 13: K1, ssk, k3, *work row 3 of PBP; rep from * to last 5sts, k2, k2tog, k1. (81sts)
Row 14: K4, *work row 4 of PBP; rep from * to last 5sts, k to end.
Row 15: K1, ssk, k2, *work row 1 of PBP; rep from * to last 4sts, k1, k2tog, k1. (79sts)
Row 16: P3, *work row 2 of PBP; rep from * to last 4sts, p to end.
Row 17: K1, ssk, k1, *work row 3 of PBP; rep from * to last 3sts, k2tog, k1. (77sts)
Row 18: K2, *work row 4 of PBP; rep from * to last 3sts, k to end.
Row 19: K8, *p1, k11; rep from * to last 9sts, p1, k to end. Cast off with WS facing.

Block the work gently to the measurements given in Figure 179 and according to the yarn's ball-band instructions.

Sew in all loose ends.

CHAPTER 8

CURVED SHAPES: CIRCLES AND OVALS

In the same way that straight lines were the basis of the diamond and hexagon shapes covered in Chapters 6 and 7, curved lines are the starting point for this chapter's exploration of circles and ovals. Using two curved lines together, as a mirror image of each other, will create implied shapes. The size of these shapes can be altered by changing the properties of the curved lines. Working stitch movements close together over a small number of rows will form a tight curve and result in a small shape. Conversely, spreading the stitch movements out over a greater number of rows will produce larger shapes with gently curving sides.

As there is a strong relationship between hexagonal and circular shapes, similar knitted construction techniques can be used. If a circular shape is placed inside a hexagonal shape, the outer circumference of the circle will touch each of the six straight edges of the hexagon at the same point on each edge. This property must be taken into consideration when deciding on the specific stitch pattern for a circular shape, as unintended shapes can emerge and dominate a design.

In this regard, yarn fibre has a large impact on the appearance of the stitch pattern. For example, a pure-wool yarn, with a great deal of elasticity, will produce a different effect to that of a pure-cotton yarn, with minimal elasticity. The line produced by the stitch movements worked in cotton yarn will appear to be straighter, whereas the equivalent line worked in wool yarn will take on a more curved appearance.

The width of the knitted line can also change the appearance of the shape. The line produced by a twist movement where a single foreground stitch is moved over two background stitches will appear finer than that produced by a cable stitch movement where two foreground stitches are moved over two background stitches. As with all of the developments of all designs, a test swatch is essential to check that the appearance of the stitch pattern reflects the inspiration and the intention of the designer.

Single circles and ovals

The construction steps for a circle are indicated in the sketch shown in Figure 183. These steps can also be applied to form ovals. Step one to start the formation of a circular shape is to work a single twist or cable stitch movement. Step two involves the widening of the shape, with the stitches being moved outwards in both directions with a series of mirror-imaged movements that continue until the full width of the shape is reached.

Fig. 182 Knitted swatch of circle and ovals (yarn: pure wool, 4ply weight; needles: 3.5mm; total stitches: 20; total rows: 30).

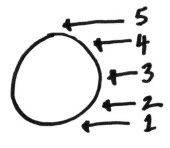

Fig. 183   Sketch of five steps to construct a single circle shape.

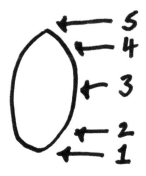

Fig. 184   Sketch of five steps to construct a single oval shape.

Before changing the direction of the stitch movements to narrow the top of the shape, additional rows are worked in step three. These rows create the sides of the circle or oval. The number of rows needed will vary depending on the number of cable stitch movements that were worked in step two. In general, the greater the number of cable stitch movements used to open the shape, the more rows will be needed to balance the shape.

Should the desired shape be an oval, more rows will be needed in step three, to create the elongated sides. The construction steps are shown in Figure 184. In step four, the top of the circle or oval is formed by moving the foreground stitches inwards towards each other. These movements will be over the same number of stitches as were involved in step two. The top of the shape is completed in step five. If a column of shapes is being worked, steps one to four are repeated. If a single circle or oval is being worked, step five will be a stitch movement that closes the shape. This is often followed by working a contrasting stitch-pattern row, to create a neat edge for the shape.

The swatch shown in Figure 182 features a series of single circles and ovals, knitted by using the five steps outlined above. All of the shapes begin with a four-stitch cable being worked as step one. As step two, the lower part of each shape is widened by continuing to move the foreground stitches over the same number of background stitches. In these shapes, two mirror-imaged, four-stitch cables are used to move the foreground stitches outwards by two stitches in each direction.

When the shape is at its full intended diameter, extra rows are worked for step three. For the circle examples on the lower right and left, five additional rows were worked. In the oval examples on the upper right and left, nine additional rows were worked. For step four, the foreground stitches are moved back over the same number of stitches as were worked in step two. The top curve of the shape is completed by using a final four-stitch cable as step five.

Although the principles of construction are similar for all four of these shapes, each one has a different centre and background stitch pattern, highlighting the differences in appearance that can be achieved by changing these elements.

The first circle, on the right-hand side of the bottom row, has a been worked completely in stocking stitch. This means that the cable stitches, the surrounding stitch pattern and the centre of the circle are all knitted in the same stitch pattern. The main effect of working everything in stocking stitch is to create a shape with a raised centre. This gives the circle a prominent appearance, even though the background stitch pattern matches the shape's stitch pattern.

The second circle, on the left-hand side of the bottom row, has an outline that appears much more distinct. This circle was knitted in two contrasting stitch patterns. Reverse stocking stitch has been used for the circle's centre and the surround and stocking stitch for the two foreground stitches. This circle has very prominent cable outlines, with a centre that recedes. Although the shape has been worked over the same number of stitches and rows as the first circle, its overall appearance is more oval.

The first oval, on the right-hand side of the top row, has a stocking stitch centre and foreground stitches. The surrounding stitch pattern is reverse stocking stitch. The effect of this combination is that the whole shape, not just the outline, appears prominent and that the background stitches recede. The second oval, on the left-hand side of the top row, has a stocking stitch background and foreground stitches. The centre is of reverse stocking stitch and appears to recede into the surrounding stocking stitch pattern.

These four examples and their stitch variations illustrate the many possibilities for design variation. In particular, shapes can be formed as an outline or a solid shape. The effect created by the centre's stitch pattern has a large impact on the shape itself. For example, a filled centre, made by using the same stitch pattern as that used for the cable foreground stitches, results in the most prominent shape.

Circles and ovals

(20sts and 30 rows)

Row 1 (RS): K3, 2/2 RC, k3, p3, 2/2 RC, p3.

Row 2 (WS): K3, p4, k3, p10.

Row 3: K1, 2/2 RC, 2/2 LC, k1, p1, 2/2 RPC, 2/2 LPC, p1.

Row 4: K1, p2, k4, p2, k1, p10.

Row 5: K10, p1, k2, p4, k2, p1.

Rows 6–7: As rows 4–5.

Row 8: As row 4.

Row 9: K1, 2/2 LC, 2/2 RC, k1, p1, 2/2 LPC, 2/2 RPC, p1.

Row 10: As row 2.

Row 11: As row 1.

Rows 12–13: K10, p10.

Row 14: P10, k10.

Row 15: P3, 2/2 RC, p3, k3, 2/2 RC, k3.

Row 16: P10, k4, p2, k4.

Row 17: P1, 2/2 RC, 2/2 LC, p1, k1, 2/2 RPC, 2/2 LPC, k1.

Row 18: P3, k4, p3, k1, p8, k1.

Row 19: P1, k8, p1, k3, p4, k3.

Rows 20–25: Rep rows 18–19 three times.

Row 26: As row 18.

Row 27: P1, 2/2 LPC, 2/2 RPC, p1, k1, 2/2 LC, 2/2 RC, k1.

Row 28: P10, k3, p4, k3.

Row 29: As row 15.

Row 30: P10, k10.

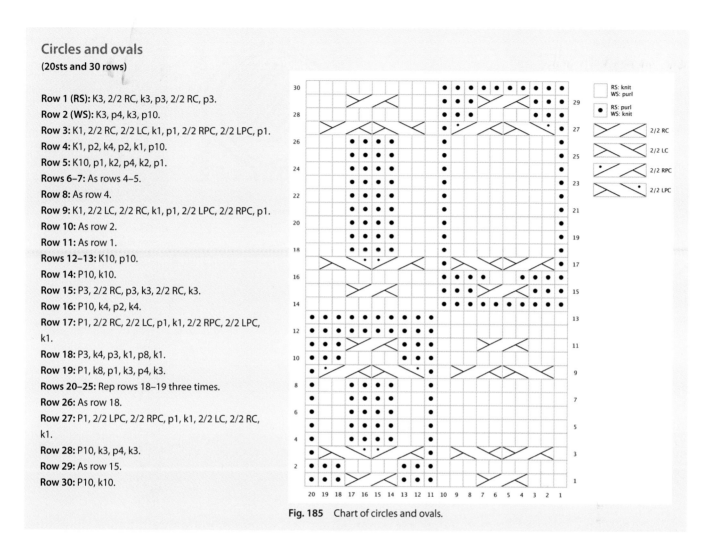

Fig. 185 Chart of circles and ovals.

Water-well circles

The image shown in Figure 186 is of a water-well cover in the German town of Mainz. Located in amongst the beautiful, traditional buildings of this lovely town, this well, with the combination of its ironwork cover, the water and the shadows cast on to the base of the well, incorporates many fascinating design elements. The large, central, circular shape and the small, curled branches that surround it provide excellent inspiration for circles and ovals of a knitting design. The horizontal lines of the metal grid enhance these details and can be used in designs in various ways.

These features have multiple interactions, with the ironwork and shadow lines crossing each other and several different sizes of shapes running along the central part of the cover. An extremely complex design can look beautiful when translated

Fig. 186 Water-well cover in Mainz, Germany.

into a knitted design, but it is very important to consider the enjoyment of knitting the stitch pattern. For designs inspired by a multilayered source such as this well cover, it is important to identify the key components that convey the essence of the original source. A great way to do this is through sketching the shapes and the layout of the elements. The following examples highlight several design options.

Shadow circle

Beginning with the large circular feature of the well cover, the following designs are all inspired by individual elements from the well cover. The sketched large circle shown in Figure 187 depicts the contrast between the curved lines of the ironwork circle and the straight lines created by the shadows that are cast below.

The pattern of the shadow-circle knitted swatch shown in Figure 188 was inspired by the shape of and the shadows seen below this circular feature. Diagonal lines of twisted stitches within a large, cabled circle are included in the swatch. The circle is a complete shape, formed from six-stitch cables that begin and end with a step-one, single cable stitch movement. These wide cable lines move outwards from this central cable stitch movement at the beginning of the shape. The lines move inwards at the top, creating the circle.

There is contrast between the wide, curved lines of the circular, cabled shape and the narrow, twisted stitch, diagonal lines in the centre of the shape. The diagonal lines have foreground stitches knitted in stocking stitch and a contrasting reverse stocking stitch background. The swatch was knitted with pure-wool yarn. The elasticity of the wool fibres enhances the circular shape that is formed by the cables.

Fig. 187 Sketch of central circle of the well cover, with shadow detail.

Fig. 188 Knitted swatch of shadow circle (yarn: pure wool, 4ply weight; needles: 3.5mm; total stitches: 18; total rows: 20, plus an additional 2 rows, of rows 1 and 2 repeated).

Shadow circle

(18sts and 20 rows)

Row 1 (RS): P6, 3/3 RC, p6.
Row 2 (WS): K6, p6, k6.
Row 3: P3, 3/3 RPC, 3/3 LPC, p3.
Row 4: K3, p3, k6, p3, k3.
Row 5: 3/3 RPC, p2, 1/1 LPC, p2, 3/3 LPC.
Row 6: P3, k5, p1, k6, p3.
Row 7: K3, (1/1 LPC, p1) four times, k3.
Row 8: P3, k1, (p1, k2) three times, p1, k1, p3.
Row 9: K3, (p1, 1/1 LPC) four times, k3.
Row 10: P4, (k2, p1) three times, k2, p3.
Row 11: K3, p2, (1/1 LPC, p1) twice, 1/1 LPC, p2, k3.
Row 12: P3, (k2, p1) three times, k3, p3.
Rows 13–16: As rows 7–10.
Row 17: 3/3 LPC, p2, 1/1 LPC, p2, 3/3 RPC.
Row 18: As row 4.
Row 19: P3, 3/3 LPC, 3/3 RPC, p3.
Row 20: As row 2.

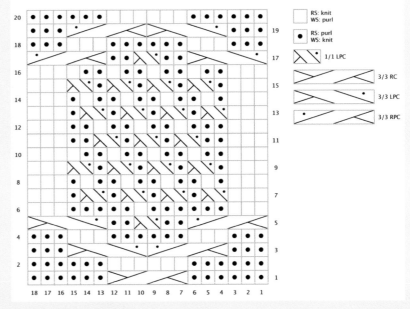

Fig. 189 Chart of shadow circle.

Linked well circles

The sketch of linked well circles shown in Figure 190 includes a series of shapes that represent the pattern at the centre of the well cover. There is a change in the scale of the circles across the well cover.

In the knitted swatch shown in Figure 191, the theme of using twisted stitches within a cabled shape is continued. The main circle shapes are knitted by using four-stitch cables. The shapes that are formed are implied, as they do not have a cable join at the beginning and end of each shape. The well cover has a series of smaller circles running up its centre line, and these shapes are represented in the swatch with two-stitch twists. These curved lines also resemble the ripples in the water and create a visual link between each vertical repeat of the stitch pattern.

Fig. 190 Sketch of linked well circles.

Fig. 191 Knitted swatch of linked well circles (yarn: pure wool, 4ply weight; needles: 3.5mm; total stitches: 13; total rows: 54, comprising three 18-row repeats).

Linked well circles
(13sts and 18 rows)

Row 1 (RS): P4, k2, p1, k2, p4.
Row 2 (WS): K4, p2, k1, p2, k4.
Row 3: P2, 2/2 RC, p1, 2/2 LC, p2.
Row 4: K2, p4, k1, p4, k2.
Row 5: 2/2 RPC, 1/1 RPC, p1, 1/1 LPC, 2/2 LPC.
Row 6: P2, k2, p1, k3, p1, k2, p2.
Row 7: K2, p2, 1/1 LPC, p1, 1/1 RPC, p2, k2.
Row 8: P2, k3, p1, k1, p1, k3, p2.
Row 9: K2, p2, 1/1 RPC, p1, 1/1 LPC, p2, k2.
Rows 10–12: As rows 6–8.
Row 13: 2/2 LPC, 1/1 RPC, p1, 1/1 LPC, 2/2 RC.
Row 14: K2, p3, k3, p3, k2.
Row 15: P2, 2/2 LPC, p1, 2/2 RPC, p2.
Row 16: As row 2.
Rows 17–18: As rows 1–2.

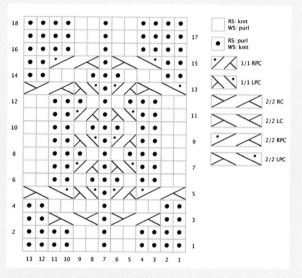

Fig. 192 Chart of linked well circles.

Ridged well circles

The smaller features of the well cover can also be captured in a knitted design. The previous swatches have taken inspiration from the large circle, using smaller shapes as background linking elements. The ridged-well-circles design uses the small shapes as vertical links, with a series of implied circles and ovals being knitted by using two-stitch twists. The shapes are joined horizontally by reverse stocking stitch ridges that were inspired by the ironwork bars across the well cover. When multiple repeats of the design are worked across a row of knitting, the ridges become a prominent feature, drawing the eye horizontally across the design.

Ridged well circles
(9sts and 10 rows)

Row 1 (RS): K2, 1/1 RPC, p1, 1/1 LPC, k2.
Row 2 (WS): P3, k3, p3.
Row 3: K2, 1/1 LC, p1, 1/1 RC, k2.
Row 4: K3, p1, k1, p1, k3.
Rows 5–6: As rows 1–2.
Row 7: K3, p3, k3.
Rows 8–10: As rows 2–4.

Fig. 194 Chart of ridged well circles.

Fig. 193 Knitted swatch of ridged well circles (yarn: pure wool, 4ply weight; needles: 3.5mm; total stitches: 27, comprising three 9-stitch repeats; total rows: 30, comprising three 10-row repeats).

Circles-and-ovals pattern: wishing-well wristwarmers

Inspired by the decorative detail visible on the ironwork well cover shown in Figure 195, this series of wristwarmer patterns explores circles, ovals and a combination of both shapes. The well cover has several different, intersecting straight and curved lines. The straight lines are joined to each other by a curved section of ironwork. These sections also have small circular pins at the joins. The sketch shown in Figure 196 picks out the transition between these shapes. There is a change from elongated, ovate curves at the bottom edge to tighter, more circular curves towards the top edge of the sketch.

In this project, the use of shapes and lines is extended to explore three different design variations of the same inspiration source, beginning with circles, moving on to ovals and then combining the two shapes. The placement of the design detail on the wristwarmer creates a beautiful decorative panel on the fabric covering the back of the hand.

The first design, pattern, A, explores circles interspersed along vertical lines. The two-stitch twists are arranged in a grid pattern. The movement of the stitches produces a ripple effect within the straight lines that is similar to the shape of the reflection of the well-cover circles on the water below.

Pattern B extends the first design, by rows being added to the circles, which creates oval shapes. A similar ripple effect is made, with the straight lines being distorted. The oval design is worked over more rows than the circle design, making the textured effect spread over a larger area of the wristwarmer.

Fig. 195 Detail of ironwork well cover.

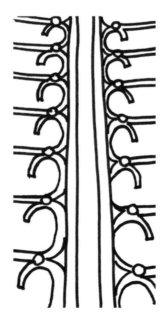

Fig. 196 Sketch of curved detail of the ironwork well cover.

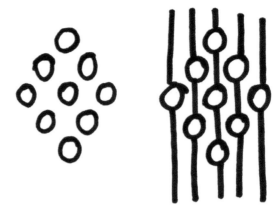

Fig. 197 Sketch of circles and lines for pattern A.

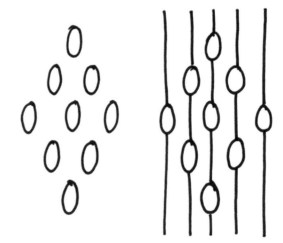

Fig. 198 Sketch of ovals and lines for pattern B.

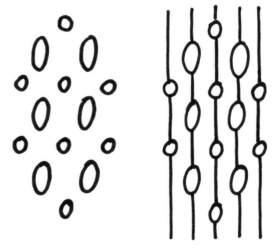

Fig. 199 Sketch of circles, ovals and lines for pattern C.

Fig. 200 Wishing-well wristwarmers worked with patterns A, B and C.

Fig. 201 Wishing-well wristwarmers, with the held wristwarmers (from left to right) worked with Birlinn Yarn Company 4 ply yarn in the shades Storm Grey, Reef, Storm Grey and Moor. (Photo: Maxine Vining)

Pattern C combines both circles and ovals. By putting both shapes together within the same grid, a linked effect is produced. The circles fit between the ovals and are positioned at the outer edges of the design panel.

Exploring these three designs within the wristwarmer pattern, it can be seen that small changes can have a large effect on overall patterning. This project also shows that several different, but related, patterns can be made by using the same inspiration source.

Each wristwarmer is knitted flat as a rectangle. After casting off, the rectangle is sewn up to make a cylinder, with a gap being left in the side seam for the thumb. The pattern is written for two sizes. The first size (size 1) will fit snugly on an average adult hand; the second size (size 2) is for a looser fit.

Using a twisted stitch, rope pattern creates raised lines, giving a three-dimensional effect to the stitch pattern. Separating each of the ropes by two stitches being worked in reverse stocking stitch results in a rib effect. This allows plenty of elasticity in the wristwarmer fabric so that it will fit snugly on the hand.

The length of the wristwarmers can be extended both before or after the patterned section, by working more rows within the beginning and end twisted-rib sections. This will require more yarn, so please ensure that a sufficient quantity is available before adding more rows of the pattern.

Wishing-well wristwarmers pattern

Size
Two sizes

Size 1
- 17.5cm (7in) circumference × 18.5cm (7¼in) deep

Size 2
- 20cm (8in) circumference ×18.5cm (7¼in) deep

Yarn
- Birlinn Yarn Company 4 ply, 100-per-cent wool, 4ply weight, 175m (191yd) per 50g ball
- Each pair of wristwarmers is knitted with 1 × 50g ball:
- Pattern A: wishing-well circles is used for the wristwarmers shown in Reef
- Pattern B: wishing-well ovals is used for the wristwarmers shown in Storm Grey
- Pattern C: wishing-well circles and ovals is used for the wristwarmers shown in Moor

Fig. 202 Blocking diagram of wishing-well wristwarmers.

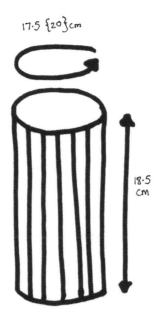

17.5 {20}cm

18.5 cm

Needles

- A pair of 3.25mm (UK10, US3) straight needles
- A pair of 3.5mm (UK9 or UK10, US4) straight needles
- Cable needle (optional)
- Darning needle
- Stitch markers

Tension

- 30sts and 31 rows to 10cm (4in) over twisted-rib pattern, using 3.5mm needles

Pattern notes

Figures for the size 2 instructions are shown in brackets following the size 1 figure instructions. Where only one figure is given, it applies to both sizes.

This wristwarmer pattern has three options for the decorative panel for the fabric on the back of the hand. Each option is worked over twenty stitches. The circles option, pattern A, has twenty rows, the ovals option, pattern B, has thirty rows, and the option for combined circles and ovals, pattern C, has thirty-four rows.

Stitch markers are used to set the placement of each decorative panel worked with pattern A, B or C. Slip the stitch markers from the lhn to the rhn as they are reached on subsequent rows.

Refer to written or charted instructions for each stitch pattern (A–C), as preferred.

Pattern A: wishing-well circles (worked over 20sts and 20 rows)
Row 1 (RS): (P1, 1/1 RC, p1) twice, 1/1 RPC, 1/1 LPC, (p1, 1/1 RC, p1) twice.
Row 2 (WS): (K1, p2, k1) twice, p4, (k1, p2, k1) twice.
Row 3: (P1, 1/1 RC, p1) twice, 1/1 LPC, 1/1 RPC, (p1, 1/1 RC, p1) twice.
Row 4: K1, (p2, k2) four times, p2, k1.
Row 5: (P1, 1/1 RC, p1, 1/1 RPC, 1/1 LPC) twice, p1, 1/1 RC, p1.
Row 6: (K1, p2, k1, p4) twice, k1, p2, k1.
Row 7: (P1, 1/1 RC, p1, 1/1 LPC, 1/1 RPC) twice, p1, 1/1 RC, p1.
Row 8: As row 4.
Row 9: (1/1 RPC, 1/1 LPC, p1, 1/1 RC, p1) twice, 1/1 RPC, 1/1 LPC.
Row 10: (P4, k1, p2, k1) twice, p4.
Row 11: (1/1 LPC, 1/1 RPC, p1, 1/1 RC, p1) twice, 1/1 LPC, 1/1 RPC.
Rows 12–15: As rows 4–7.
Row 16: As row 4.
Rows 17–20: As rows 1–4.

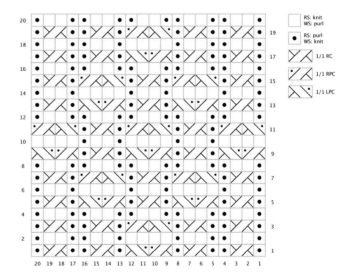

Fig. 203 Chart of wishing-well circles: pattern A.

Pattern B: wishing-well ovals (worked over 20sts and 30 rows)

Row 1 (RS): (P1, 1/1 RC, p1) twice, 1/1 RPC, 1/1 LPC, (p1, 1/1 RC, p1) twice.

Row 2 (WS): (K1, p2, k1) twice, p1, k2, p1, (k1, p2, k1) twice.

Row 3: (P1, 1/1 RC, p1) twice, k1, p2, k1, (p1, 1/1 RC, p1) twice.

Row 4: As row 2.

Row 5: (P1, 1/1 RC, p1) twice, 1/1 LPC, 1/1 RPC, (p1, 1/1 RC, p1) twice.

Row 6: K1, (p2, k2) four times, p2, k1.

Row 7: (P1, 1/1 RC, p1, 1/1 RPC, 1/1 LPC) twice, p1, 1/1 RC, p1.

Row 8: (K1, p2, k1, p1, k2, p1) twice, k1, p2, k1.

Row 9: (P1, 1/1 RC, p1, k1, p2, k1) twice, p1, 1/1 RC, p1.

Row 10: As row 8.

Row 11: (P1, 1/1 RC, p1, 1/1 LPC, 1/1 RPC) twice, p1, 1/1 RC, p1.

Row 12: As row 6.

Row 13: (1/1 RPC, 1/1 LPC, p1, 1/1 RC, p1) twice, 1/1 RPC, 1/1 LPC.

Row 14: (P1, k2, p1, k1, p2, k1) twice, p1, k2, p1.

Row 15: (K1, p2, k1, p1, 1/1 RC, p1) twice, k1, p2, k1.

Row 16: As row 14.

Row 17: (1/1 LPC, 1/1 RPC, p1, 1/1 RC, p1) twice, 1/1 LPC, 1/1 RPC.

Rows 18–21: As rows 6–9.

Row 22: As row 8.

Row 23: As row 11.

Row 24: As row 6.

Rows 25–27: As rows 1–3.

Row 28: As row 2.

Rows 29–30: As rows 5–6.

Pattern C: wishing-well circles and ovals (worked over 20sts and 34 rows)

Row 1 (RS): (P1, 1/1 RC, p1) twice, 1/1 RPC, 1/1 LPC, (p1, 1/1 RC, p1) twice.

Row 2 (WS): (K1, p2, k1) twice, p1, k2, p1, (k1, p2, k1) twice.

Row 3: (P1, 1/1 RC, p1) twice, 1/1 LPC, 1/1 RPC, (p1, 1/1 RC, p1) twice.

Row 4: K1, (p2, k2) four times, p2, k1.

Row 5: (P1, 1/1 RC, p1, 1/1 RPC, 1/1 LPC) twice, p1, 1/1 RC, p1.

Fig. 204 Chart of wishing-well ovals: pattern B.

Row 6: (K1, p2, k1, p1, k2, p1) twice, k1, p2, k1.

Row 7: (P1, 1/1 RC, p1, k1, p2, k1) twice, p1, 1/1 RC, p1.

Row 8: As row 6.

Row 9: (P1, 1/1 RC, p1, 1/1 LPC, 1/1 RPC) twice, p1, 1/1 RC, p1.

Row 10: As row 4.

Row 11: (1/1 RPC, 1/1 LPC, p1, 1/1 RC, p1) twice, 1/1 RPC, 1/1 LPC.

Row 12: (P1, k2, p1, k1, p2, k1) twice, p1, k2, p1.

Row 13: (1/1 LPC, 1/1 RPC, p1, 1/1 RC, p1) twice, 1/1 LPC, 1/1 RPC.

Rows 14–23: As rows 4–13.

Rows 24–27: As rows 4–7.

Row 28: As row 6.

Row 29: As row 9.

Row 30: As row 4.

Rows 31–34: As rows 1–4.

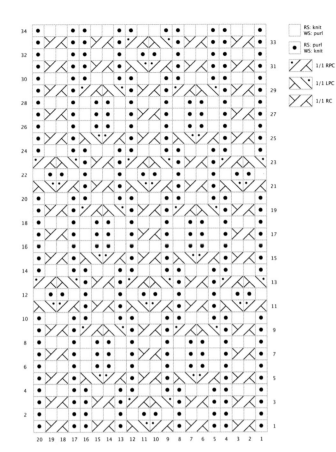

Legend:

☐ RS: knit / WS: purl
● RS: purl / WS: knit
1/1 RPC
1/1 LPC
1/1 RC

Fig. 205 Chart of wishing-well circles and ovals: pattern C.

Pattern instructions

Left wristwarmer

Cast on 52 {60}sts by using 3.25mm needles.

Row 1 (RS): K1, *1/1 RC, p2; rep from * to last 3sts, 1/1 RC, k1.

Row 2 (WS): P3, *k2, p2; rep from * to last st, p1.

Rows 1–2 set the twisted-rib pattern.

Continue in twisted-rib patt as follows:

If working pattern A for the decorative panel, rep rows 1–2 eleven times.

If working pattern B for the decorative panel, rep rows 1–2 eight times.

If working pattern C for the decorative panel, rep rows 1–2 six times.

***

Change to 3.5mm needles.

Keeping twisted-rib patt correct, place stitch markers on next row as follows:

Next row (RS): Patt 4 {8}sts, pm, patt 20sts, pm, patt to end of row.

Next row (WS): Patt 28 {32}sts, slm, patt 20sts, slm, patt to end of row.

Using charted or written instructions, as preferred, begin main pattern on next row.

Row 1: Patt to mrk, slm, work row 1 of pattern A, B or C, slm, patt to end.

Row 2: Patt to mrk, slm, work row 2 of pattern A, B or C, slm, patt to end.

Continuing as set, by working from row 3 of pattern A, B or C as established, work all rows of pattern A, B or C once.

Change to 3.25mm needles.

Continue in twisted-rib patt as follows:

If working pattern A for the decorative panel, work eleven more rows.

If working pattern B or C for the decorative panel, work seven more rows.

Cast off in patt with WS facing.

Right wristwarmer

Work as for left wristwarmer to ***.

Change to 3.5mm needles.

Keeping twisted-rib patt correct, place stitch markers on next row as follows:

Next row (RS): Patt 28 {32}sts, pm, patt 20sts, pm, patt to end of row.

Next row (WS): Patt 4 {8}sts, slm, patt 20sts, slm, patt to end of row.

Continue as for left wristwarmer.

Block the work gently to the measurements given in Figure 202 and according to the yarn's ball-band instructions.

Sew each side seam, leaving a gap of approximately 4cm (1½in) to accommodate a thumb.

Sew in all loose ends.

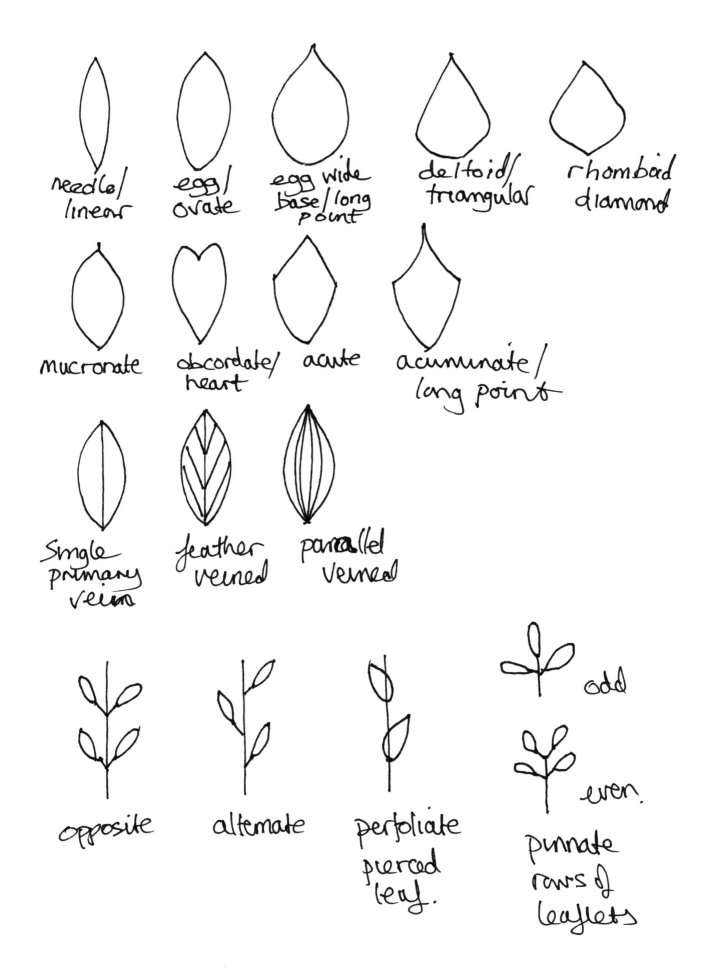

needle/ linear

egg/ ovate

egg wide base/ long point

deltoid/ triangular

rhomboid diamond

mucronate

obcordate/ heart

acute

acuminate/ long point

Single primary vein

feather veined

parallel veined

opposite

alternate

perfoliate pierced leaf.

odd

even.

pinnate rows of leaflets

Part 3: Enhanced Twists and Cables

CHAPTER 9

COMBINED CURVES

Single leaves

The techniques that were used to design and knit the regular shapes covered throughout the chapters of Part 2 can be combined in many different ways to make the complex angles and curves required to explore the shapes within the natural world. The complexity of these shapes can be represented by changing scale and using different widths of knitted lines.

Looking at examples of leaves, ranging from a single leaf to tree branches full of leaves, provides the inspiration for the following series of stitch patterns. There are a large number of design possibilities created by the different varieties of leaves. An individual leaf can provide inspiration from its outline shape or from an examination of its internal structure. As seasonal changes occur throughout the year, the transformation, from bud to leaf to autumn foliage to branch, can add an extra dimension to the resulting designs. Images and representations of leaves can also be found in textile designs, sculpture and architecture, and these depictions are also an excellent source of inspiration.

Although the structure of the whole plant or tree may be complex, a design can be simplified to preserve the structural elements yet be straightforward to knit. Start by looking at

the full, complex structure, then, keeping this in mind, reduce the complexity to a pattern of lines or shapes in a sketchbook.

Using these sketches, different twists or cables can be selected in order to convey the essence of the design. The following examples begin with single leaf shapes and then move on to combined leaves and linked leaves. To balance a larger-scale design, parts of the design can be worked as a mirror image. The stitch manipulations should be spread evenly across the knitted fabric to avoid unintentional changes in tension that could distort the fabric.

Fig. 207 Leaves of a *Cotinus coggygria* 'Royal Purple' smoke tree.

Fig. 206 Sketch of individual leaves and corresponding descriptive words.

Fig. 208 Knitted swatch of single leaves (yarn: pure wool, DK weight; needles: 4mm; total stitches: 22; total rows: 32).

Terminology can help to spark design ideas; For example, there are some useful descriptive terms that can be applied to leaves, such as egg-shaped (ovate), lance-shaped (lanceolate), heart-shaped (obcordate), simple leaf and compound leaf. The sketches shown in Figure 206 are labelled with appropriate terms.

The way that a leaf is attached to the stem that it grows from – for instance, alternate or opposite attachment – can also inspire ways of linking single knitted motifs.

In addition, reproducing the patterns of veins is an excellent way to include the structure of a leaf within a design. These patterns include parallel, pinnate and palmate vein arrangements.

Four different single leaf shapes are explored in the knitted swatch shown in Figure 208; these are acuminate or long point, obcordate or heart-shaped, acute and deltoid or triangular.

Single leaves
(22sts and 32 rows)

Rows 1–2: P11, k11.
Row 3: P5, 1/1 RC, p4, k4, 1/1 RC, k5.
Row 4: P11, k4, p2, k5.
Row 5: P3, 1/2 RPC, 1/2 LPC, p2, k3, 1/1 RC, 1/1 LC, k4.
Row 6: P11, k2, p1, k4, p1, k3.
Row 7: P2, 1/1 RPC, p4, 1/1 LPC, p1, k2, 1/1 RC, k2, 1/1 LC, k3.
Row 8: P11, k1, p1, k6, p1, k2.
Row 9: P2, k1, p6, k1, p1, k1, 1/1 RC, k4, 1/1 LC, k2.
Row 10: As row 8.
Row 11: P2, 1/2 LPC, p2, 1/2 RPC, p1, k4, 1/1 RC, k5.
Row 12: P11, k3, p1, k2, p1, k4.
Row 13: P4, 1/1 LPC, 1/1 RPC, p3, k1, (1/1 LC, 1/1 RC) twice, k2.
Row 14: As row 4.
Row 15: P5, 1/1 RC, p4, (k2, 1/1 RC) twice, k3.
Row 16: P11, k11.
Rows 17–18: K11, p11.
Row 19: K5, 1/1 RC, k4, p4, 1/1 RC, p5.
Row 20: K5, p2, k4, p11.
Row 21: K4, 1/1 RPC, 1/1 LPC, k3, p2, 1/2 RC, 1/2 LC, p3.
Row 22: K3, p6, k2, p4, k2, p5.
Row 23: K3, 1/1 RPC, p2, 1/1 LPC, k2, p2, k6, p3.
Row 24: K3, p6, k2, p3, k4, p4.
Row 25: K2, 1/1 RPC, p4, 1/1 LPC, k1, p2, k6, p3.
Row 26: K3, p6, k2, p2, k6, p3.
Row 27: K2, 1/2 LC, p2, 1/2 RC, k1, p2, 1/1 LPC, k2, 1/1 RPC, p3.
Row 28: K4, p4, k3, p4, k2, p5.

Row 29: K4, 1/1 LC, 1/1 RC, k3, p3, 1/1 LPC, 1/1 RPC, p4.
Row 30: As row 20.
Row 31: As row 19.
Row 32: K11, p11.

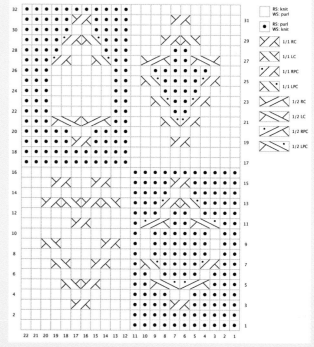

Fig. 209 Chart of single leaves.

These names already give inspiration for the basic shapes of the leaves. The necessary variety of twisted stitches to be used to knit these shapes can be built up from those covered in the chapters of Part 2: Line and Shape.

Each leaf shape of the swatch is made from a variety of twisted stitches. Each shape begins and ends with two-stitch twists. The foreground lines that make the shapes are all knitted as a single stitch worked in stocking stitch. The shapes are knitted on different background stitch patterns to demonstrate the effect that this has on the overall shape. The most prominent shapes are those on the reverse stocking stitch background.

Beginning with the long-point leaf shape, at the bottom right of the swatch, the wide base of the leaf shape is made by using a combination of two- and three-stitch twists. The same twists are worked in a different order to form the long point at the top of the leaf shape. The heart-shaped leaf, at the bottom left, has a narrow base, formed with a series of two-stitch twists. The two top points that create the heart shape are also formed by using two-stitch twists. The acute-point shape, at the top right has similar top shaping as for the long-point leaf positioned below it. The base of this leaf is triangular and is formed in almost the same way as for the base of the heart-shaped leaf. The triangular leaf, at top left, has a triangular top, which is similar to the tops of the long- and acute-point leaves, and a wide base, which is similar to the base of the long-point leaf. These four leaf shapes, each knitted with various two- and three-stitch twists, demonstrate how several different shapes can be constructed from the same stitch movements when they are combined in different orders.

Linked leaves

The single leaf shapes are individual stand-alone motifs. These beautiful shapes are flat, similar to pressed leaves in a book. Linking the leaves as if they were part of a branch or a trailing plant introduces movement into the design. Using combined straight lines and curves in different orders forms a leaf shape at an angle. Additional curved lines can be added between the shapes to join the individual motifs.

Whereas the single leaf shapes are symmetrical across the centre line, the linked leaves are asymmetrical. Forming shapes that are asymmetrical means that the beginning, end and two or more sides of the shape have several different stitch movements. The lines that form asymmetrical shapes move at different angles and are worked over different numbers of stitches and rows. As the complexity of the shape increases, the number

Fig. 210 Knitted swatch of linked leaves (yarn: pure wool, DK weight; needles: 4mm; total stitches: 22; total rows: 40, comprising two 20-row repeats).

of different twist and cable stitch movements that are used will also increase. To balance the overall design, mirror-imaged leaf shapes have been worked.

The leaves of the knitted swatch shown in Figure 210 are constructed in a similar way to that of the shapes throughout the chapters of Part 2, with opening, widening and closing steps. The leaf shapes can also be altered in several ways; for a longer leaf shape, the sides can be extended in the same way that circles were extended into ovals, or, for a broader leaf, additional two- or three-stitch twists can be added to widen the shape. If alterations are made, the tension of the knitting will change, as, for example, working more twists or cables closer together creates a tighter, denser knitted fabric.

Linked leaves
(22sts and 20 rows)

Row 1 (RS): 1/1 RC, p4, 1/1 LC, (p2, 1/1 RC) twice, p4, 1/1 RC.

Row 2 (WS): P2, k4, (p2, k2) twice, p2, k4, p2.

Row 3: 1/1 RC, p2, 1/2 RPC, 1/1 LPC, p1, 1/1 RC, p1, 1/1 RPC, 1/2 LPC, p2, 1/1 RC.

Row 4: P2, k2, p1, k3, p1, k1, p2, k1, p1, k3, p1, k2, p2.

Row 5: 1/1 RC, p1, 1/1 RPC, p2, 1/1 RPC, p1, 1/1 RC, p1, 1/1 LPC, p2, 1/1 LPC, p1, 1/1 RC.

Row 6: P2, k1, p1, k3, p1, k2, p2, k2, p1, k3, p1, k1, p2.

Row 7: 1/1 RC, p1, 1/1 LPC, 1/2 RPC, p2, 1/1 RC, p2, 1/2 LPC, 1/1 RPC, p1, 1/1 RC.

Row 8: P2, k2, (p2, k4) twice, p2, k2, p2.

Row 9: 1/1 RC, p2, (1/1 RC, p4) twice, 1/1 LC, p2, 1/1 RC.

Rows 10–11: As rows 8–9.

Row 12: As row 8.

Row 13: 1/1 RC, p1, 1/1 RPC, 1/2 LPC, p2, 1/1 RC, p2, 1/2 RPC, 1/1 LPC, p1, 1/1 RC.

Row 14: As row 6.

Row 15: 1/1 RC, p1, 1/1 LPC, p2, 1/1 LPC, p1, 1/1 RC, p1, 1/1 RPC, p2, 1/1 RPC, p1, 1/1 RC.

Row 16: As row 4.

Row 17: 1/1 RC, p2, 1/2 LPC, 1/1 RPC, p1, 1/1 RC, p1, 1/1 LPC, 1/2 RPC, p2, 1/1 RC.

Row 18: As row 2.

Rows 19–20: As rows 1–2.

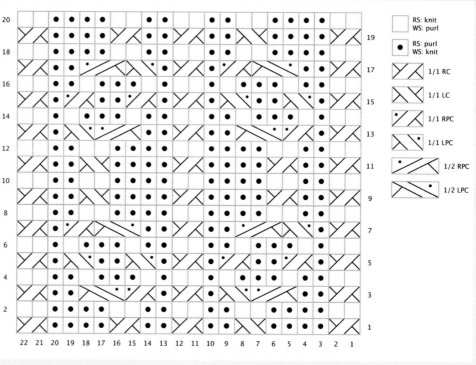

Fig. 211 Chart of linked leaves.

Legend:
- ☐ RS: knit / WS: purl
- • RS: purl / WS: knit
- ⤫ 1/1 RC
- ⤬ 1/1 LC
- 1/1 RPC
- 1/1 LPC
- 1/2 RPC
- 1/2 LPC

Leaf structure and symmetry

Fig. 212 A leaf carved in stone in Rome, Italy.

Examining the detail within a leaf can provide great inspiration for twists and cables. The layout of the leaf veins has a beautiful arrangement that can be represented in knitting. The inspiration-source leaf could be from a tree or plant but also could be a representation of a leaf in a different medium. In this example, the leaf inspiration is a stone carving of a single leaf, shown in Figure 212, that was present on a building in Rome, Italy. The stonemason has represented a curved leaf with pronounced veins. This structural carving is also ideal inspiration to illustrate symmetry within a stitch pattern.

In the sketch of this leaf, shown in Figure 213, design notes convey ideas about the direction of the stitch movements. The knitted leaf could begin at the narrow point or at the wide base. This will be determined by the ultimate use of the stitch pattern. In this case, the design has been developed from the point upwards, but it could have been designed the opposite way around.

In the knitted swatch shown in Figure 214, the pronounced structure of the leaf veins has been represented by using two

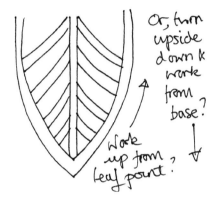

Fig. 213 Sketch of symmetrical leaf, with accompanying design notes.

Fig. 214 Knitted swatch of symmetrical leaf (yarn: pure wool, worsted weight; needles: 4.5mm; total stitches: 20; total rows: 30, comprising 22 rows plus 8 additional rows).

stocking stitch stitches as the foreground travelling stitches. Reverse stocking stitch in between the cables enhances these lines and makes them more prominent. The cabled veins converge at the centre of the stitch pattern. These converging lines have a further two-stitch twist worked at the centre of the leaf, to form a neat meeting point of the veins.

There are two distinct parts to this design, the point and the repeatable upper section of the leaf. The first fourteen rows of the chart correspond to the point. Rows 15–22 have been placed in a repeat, allowing the design to be extended to the desired length.

Combined-curves pattern: falling-leaves triangular shawl

Seasonal changes bring about beautiful variations in colour within the leaves on the trees. A bud bursting from a branch in spring is as captivating as a stunning autumn leaf that is about to fall to the ground. It is the leaf shapes and the autumnal hues that have inspired the project for this chapter. The falling-leaves triangular shawl is worked from its point to its wide edge, with an elegant, interlocking leaf pattern. Using a combination of

two- and three-stitch twists, the pattern builds up into multiple layers of leaves. The tips of the leaves are extended by using a picot cast-off along the edge.

The overlapping-leaf stitch pattern was inspired by the image shown in Figure 216. Looking up through the leaves of the tree from below reveals the arrangement of the leaves in multiple overlapping layers. The sketch shown in Figure 217 presents the layered and interlocking shapes, as does the stitch-pattern detail visible in Figures 218 and 219.

The leaf shapes cascade downwards from the tip of the shawl, building up from a single leaf. Using a lightweight yarn produces a beautiful drape of the shawl around the shoulders. Twisted stitches, worked in stocking stitch, show up clearly with this weight of yarn, producing fine lines on the surface of the knitting, resembling fine drawn lines. By using stocking stitch for both the foreground and background, the knitted lines become the focus, allowing the eye to perceive a bigger, linked pattern between all of the leaf layers.

The leaf shapes connect with the tips of the leaves of the previous layer and form the base of the leaves of the next layer.

Symmetrical leaf

(20sts and 22 rows)

Row 1 (RS): P8, 1/1 RC, 1/1 LC, p8.

Row 2 (WS): K8, p4, k8.

Row 3: P6, 2/2 RC, 2/2 LC, p6.

Row 4: K6, p8, k6.

Row 5: P4, 2/2 RC, k4, 2/2 LC, p4.

Row 6: K4, p12, k4.

Row 7: P4, k2, 2/1 LPC, k2, 2/1 RPC, k2, p4.

Row 8: K4, p2, k1, p6, k1, p2, k4.

Row 9: P2, 2/2 RC, p1, 2/1 LPC, 2/1 RPC, p1, 2/2 LC, p2.

Row 10: (K2, p4) three times, k2.

Row 11: P2, k2, 2/1 LPC, p1, 1/1 LPC, 1/1 RPC, p1, 2/1 RPC, k2, p2.

Row 12: K2, p2, k1, (p2, k2) twice, p2, k1, p2, k2.

Row 13: 2/2 RC, p1, 2/1 LPC, p1, k2, p1, 2/1 RPC, p1, 2/2 LC.

Row 14: P4, k2, (p2, k1) twice, p2, k2, p4.

Row 15: K2, 2/1 LPC, p1, 2/1 LPC, k2, 2/1 RPC, p1, 2/1 RPC, k2.

Row 16: P2, k1, p2, k2, p6, k2, p2, k1, p2.

Row 17: K2, (p1, 2/1 LPC) twice, (2/1 RPC, p1) twice, k2.

Row 18: (P2, k2) twice, p4, (k2, p2) twice.

Row 19: 2/1 LC, p1, 2/1 LPC, p1, 1/1 LPC, 1/1 RPC, p1, 2/1 RPC, p1, 2/1 RC.

Row 20: P3, (k2, p2) three times, k2, p3.

Row 21: K1, 2/1 LC, p1, 2/1 LPC, p1, k2, p1, 2/1 RPC, p1, 2/1 RC, k1.

Row 22: As row 14.

Rep rows 15–22 to extend upper leaf.

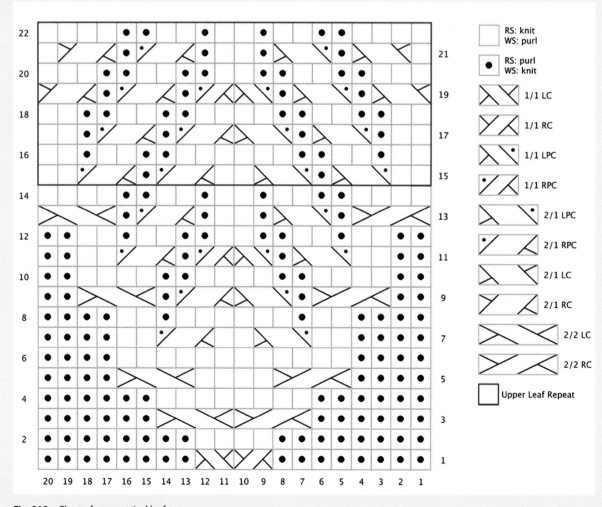

Fig. 215 Chart of symmetrical leaf.

Fig. 216 Autumn leaves on a *Cotinus coggygria* 'Royal Purple' smoke tree.

Fig. 217 Sketch of single leaf and linked leaves.

Falling-leaves triangular shawl pattern

Size
One size
- Length of side edge: 107cm (42in); length of longest edge: 126.5cm (50in)
- Width of cast-off edge: 67.5cm (26½in)

Yarn
- baa ram ewe Titus, 50-per-cent Wensleydale wool/20-per-cent Bluefaced Leicester wool/30-per-cent UK alpaca, 4ply weight, 320m (350yd) per 100g skein
- 1 × 100g skein in Brass Band (shade A)
- 1 × 100g skein in Bantam (shade B)

Needles and accessories
- A 3.25mm (UK10, US3) circular needle
- Darning needle
- Stitch marker (and optional additional stitch markers, as desired)

Tension
- 28sts and 35 rows to 10cm (4in) over falling-leaves pattern (FL), using 3.25mm needles

Pattern notes
Picot edging
The shawl is finished by using a two-row picot-edging technique, to create a rippled edge that emphasizes the points of the leaves of the last row. Stitches are cast on with the right side of the work facing and then cast off on the next wrong-side row. For the cast-on row, with the right side of the work facing, knit the number of stitches stated in the pattern, cast on three stitches by using the cable-cast-on method, knit ten stitches, including the three new stitches that were cast on,

Further leaf shapes are also formed between the layers. The edges of the shawl are worked in a pattern involving garter stitch and eyelets.

The cast-off picot edge gives the impression of the leaves falling outwards and away from the layered pattern. This cast-off helps to spread the lower edge of the shawl, to achieve a lovely drape of the fabric. The combined twisted stitch pattern is extremely effective when worked in this triangular shawl shape.

By beginning with just one repeat and building up to a large number of repeats as more rows are worked, the pattern takes on an extra layered dimension. In this case, there are twenty-five leaves along the long edge and twenty-five across the final row. For the featured shawl shown in Figures 218 and 219, the first eighteen rows of leaves were knitted in the Brass Band colourway and the final seven rows in a dark-red shade called Bantam.

Fig. 218 Detail of wide edge and picot cast-off of falling-leaves triangular shawl.

Fig. 219 Detail of point and picot cast-off of falling-leaves triangular shawl.

then continue as stated in the pattern.

Cable-cast-on method

*Insert the rhn point between the first and second sts on the lhn; wrap the yarn around the rhn point, as if to work a knit stitch; pull the yarn through between the first and second stitches on the lhn with the rhn point; and, with both needles pointing in the same direction, place the yarn loop on to the lhn point, to form a new st; rep from * twice (3sts cast on).

Stitch marker

A stitch marker is used to set the pattern placement. Slip the stitch marker from the lhn to the rhn as it is reached on subsequent rows. Reset the stitch marker every fourteen rows, as instructed in the written pattern, or after working row 14, if working from the chart. Once the pattern is established, the stitch marker can be removed, if preferred.

Refer to falling-leaves pattern (FL) written or charted instructions, as preferred.

Falling-leaves pattern (FL) (multiple of 7sts and 13 rows)

Row 1 (RS): K3, 1/1 RC, k2.

Row 2 and all WS rows: Purl.

Row 3: K1, 1/2 RC, 1/2 LC.

Rows 5 and 7: Knit.

Row 9: K1, 1/1 LC, k2, 1/1 RC.

Row 11: K2, 1/1 LC, 1/1 RC, k1.

Row 13: As row 1.

Pattern instructions

Cast on 3sts by using shade A and 3.25mm needles.

Knit two rows.

Set-up row 1 (RS): (K1, m1) twice, k1. (5sts)

Set-up rows 2 and 4 (WS): Knit.

Set-up row 3: K2, yo, k to end. (6sts)

Set-up row 5: K2, yo, k1, yo, k2tog, k1. (7sts)

Set-up row 6 and all following WS rows: K2, p to last 2sts, k2.

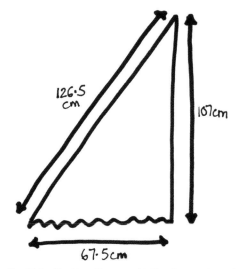

Fig. 220 Blocking diagram of falling-leaves triangular shawl.

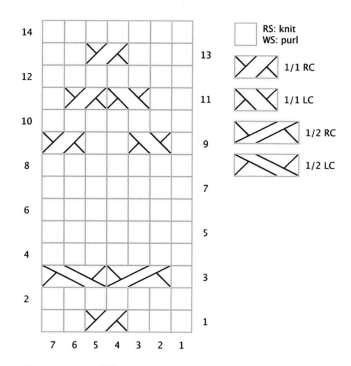

Fig. 221 Chart of falling-leaves pattern (FL).

Set-up row 7: K2, yo, k to last 3sts, yo, k2tog, k1. (8sts)

Rep rows 6–7 four times, until 12sts remain.

Rep row 6 once.

Begin working FL for first leaf, and place stitch marker on next row as follows:

Row 1 (RS): K2, yo, pm, work row 1 of FL, k to last 3sts, yo, k2tog, k1. (13sts)

Row 2 (WS) and all following WS rows: K2, p to last 2sts, k2.

Row 3: K2, yo, k to mrk, slm, work row 3 of FL, k to last 3sts, yo, k2tog, k1. (14sts)

Continue as set, from row 4 of FL, working all fourteen rows of FL once, and remove stitch marker when working row 14. (19sts)

Begin a new leaf as follows:

Row 1 (RS): K2, yo, pm, *work row 1 of FL; rep from * to last 3sts, yo, k2tog, k1. (1st increased)

Row 2 (WS) and all following WS rows: K2, p to last 2sts, k2.

Row 3: K2, yo, k to mrk, *work row 3 of FL; rep from * to last 3sts, yo, k2tog, k1. (1st increased)

Rows 4–14: Continue as set, from row 4 of FL, working all fourteen rows of FL once, and remove stitch marker when working row 14. (7sts increased over fourteen rows)

Rep rows 1–14 of FL as established, adding one new leaf every fourteen rows, until there are 131sts and seventeen leaf repeats across the row, ending with row 14.

Work rows 1–13 once. (138sts and eighteen leaf repeats across the row)

Change to using shade B, and work slip-stitch transition on the next row as follows:

Next row (WS): K2, p3, *sl2, p5; rep from * to last 7sts, p5, k2.

Continue in pattern, from row 1 of FL as established, until there are 187sts and twenty-five leaf repeats across the row, ending with row 14.

Work RS row of picot edging (*see* pattern notes) as follows: K6, *cast on 3sts with cable-cast-on method, k10; rep from * to last 6sts, slip last stitch on rhn back on to lhn and cast on 3sts, k to end. (265sts)

Cast off with WS facing.

Block the work gently to the measurements given in Figure 220 and according to the yarn's ball-band instructions.

Sew in all loose ends.

CHAPTER 10

OPENWORK

'Openwork' is a term used to describe decorative holes, piercings or gaps within a variety of materials, and it is often used in reference to architecture, metalwork and woven textiles. Using this term as a starting point provides a wide framework to consider for its application in knitting, by using lace techniques alongside twists and cables, especially as many of the inspirations for combined stitch patterns come from the sources just mentioned that have a connection with openwork. In knitting, openwork can also be referred to as lace knitting. However, whereas lace knitting implies a well-defined layout of stitches in patterns using yarn overs to create the holes, the term 'openwork' can suggest a wider use of holes or gaps, with less formal patterning.

Using a line of eyelets to emphasize a twisted stitch curve or to define a cabled zigzag will enhance the raised design. Similarly, including a flower-like pattern of eyelet holes in the centre of a twist or cable motif provides a beautiful contrast in knitting styles. The examples in this section use a variety of knitted eyelet techniques to complement and enhance twist and cable stitch patterns.

Lace stitch patterns have always been extremely popular in hand knitting. In nineteenth-century, Victorian knitting samplers and publications, the twist and cable stitch patterns were usually found as only a part of a lace pattern. The twist or cable provided a raised vertical line adjacent to the main lace openwork. For example, 'Old Scotch Stitch', identified by author Mrs Jane Gaugain in her 1846 work *The Lady's Assistant in Knitting, Netting and Crochet Work*, combines knitted lace, a cable braid and long lines of twisted stitches. In her description, Mrs Gaugain explained that this was an extremely versatile stitch pattern that could be used in many different ways. It is this versatility of openwork, twist and cable combinations that will be explored throughout this chapter.

Rivulets

Let us take a look at how one of the stitch patterns from Chapter 4 can be enhanced by the addition of eyelets. The original zigzag swatch was inspired by rivulet drainage into the Camel Estuary in Cornwall, UK. The design echoed the patterns made when the water cut down into the soft banks of the estuary. There are additional details that can be included in the design. A similar image, shown in Figure 222, reveals that the bank edges of these rivulets begin to erode away as the water level drops. This erosion has been interpreted in the sketch shown in Figure 223 as a pattern along one edge of each zigzag line. In the pattern inspired by these details, this erosion is represented by a line of eyelets. This provides

Fig. 222   Rivulet zigzags, with adjacent eroding bank edges.

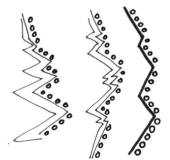

Fig. 223 Sketch of zigzags and edging detail.

Fig. 224 Knitted swatch of zigzags with eyelets (yarn: pure wool, worsted weight; needles: 4.5mm; total stitches: 26; total rows: 24).

Zigzags with eyelets
(26sts and 24 rows)

Row 1 (RS): P3, yo, p2tog, 1/1 RPC, p3, yo, p2tog, 2/1 RPC, p3, yo, p2tog, 3/1 RPC, p2.

Row 2 (WS): K3, p3, k6, p2, k6, p1, k5.

Row 3: P2, yo, p2tog, 1/1 RPC, p3, yo, p2tog, 2/1 RPC, p3, yo, p2tog, 3/1 RPC, p3.

Row 4: K4, p3, k6, p2, k6, p1, k4.

Row 5: P1, yo, p2tog, 1/1 RPC, p3, yo, p2tog, 2/1 RPC, p3, yo, p2tog, 3/1 RPC, p4.

Row 6: K5, p3, k6, p2, k6, p1, k3.

Row 7: Yo, p2tog, 1/1 RPC, p3, yo, p2tog, 2/1 RPC, p3, yo, p2tog, 3/1 RPC, p5.

Row 8: K6, p3, k6, p2, k6, p1, k2.

Row 9: Yo, p2tog, 1/2 LPC, p2, yo, p2tog, 2/2 LPC, p2, yo, p2tog, 3/2 LPC, p4.

Row 10: As row 4.

Row 11: P2, yo, p2tog, 1/2 LPC, p2, yo, p2tog, 2/2 LPC, p2, yo, p2tog, 3/2 LPC, p2.

Row 12: K2, p3, k6, p2, k6, p1, k6.

Row 13: P4, yo, p2tog, 1/2 LPC, p2, yo, p2tog, 2/2 LPC, p2, yo, p2tog, 3/2 LPC.

Row 14: P3, k6, p2, k6, p1, k8.

Row 15: P4, yo, p2tog, 1/2 RPC, p2, yo, p2tog, 2/2 RPC, p2, yo, p2tog, 3/2 RPC.

Row 16: As row 12.

Row 17: P2, yo, p2tog, 1/2 RPC, p2, yo, p2tog, 2/2 RPC, p2, yo, p2tog, 3/2 RPC, p2.

Row 18: As row 4.

Row 19: Yo, p2tog, 1/2 RPC, p2, yo, p2tog, 2/2 RPC, p2, yo, p2tog, 3/2 RPC, p4.

Rows 20–21: As rows 8–9.

Row 22: As row 4.

Row 23: P2, yo, p2tog, 1/1 LPC, p3, yo, p2tog, 2/1 LPC, p3, yo, p2tog, 3/1 LPC, p3.

Row 24: As row 2.

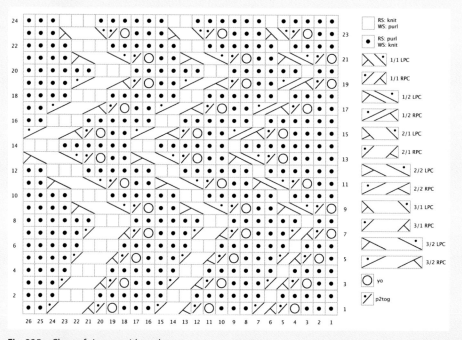

Fig. 225 Chart of zigzags with eyelets.

a decorative openwork detail in the knitting, with the lines of eyelets shadowing the zigzags as they move across the surface of the knitted fabric.

The swatch shown in Figure 224 includes these lines of eyelets on one side of each of the zigzag lines. As the lines change direction, the direction of the eyelet lines also change.

Although the eyelets follow each of the twist and cable lines, they also form a sub-pattern of their own. The emphasis of the eyelet lines changes depending on the length of the continuous twist, cable or eyelet line and the change in direction of the line. Towards the top of the swatch, where the changes in direction are more frequent and at a greater angle, the twist and cable lines are more prominent and the eyelet lines are more diffuse.

The eyelets have all been formed by using a yarn over and a decrease worked with two stitches being purled together, denoted as 'yo, p2tog' in the pattern instructions. The knitted fabric becomes tighter where the stitches are worked together. The decrease is worked immediately before the twist and cable stitch movements, providing further emphasis to the lines and contrast to the open eyelets.

Choice of yarn is also important when adding elements to the design. The swatch for this example was knitted in a worsted-weight yarn that consists of pure wool. This creates a bold series of lines from the twists, cables and eyelets. The same stitch pattern worked in a lighter weight of yarn, such as 4ply or lace, would appear more delicate, with smaller eyelet holes. Conversely, the same pattern knitted in a chunky-weight yarn would have much larger eyelet holes and bolder raised lines.

Ironwork diamonds

Ironwork ventilation or security grids on buildings frequently have an openwork element, allowing the passage of air. The beautiful grid shown in Figure 226 is from a low window on a building in Lisbon, Portugal.

The diamond grid is very dominant in the pattern, with large spaces between the floral joining motifs. Eyelets, especially those made by using a double yarn over, are an excellent way of adding this kind of openwork detail to a grid-like twist or cable design. Using a diamond-shaped framework, similar to that of an example looked at in Chapter 6, a large eyelet has been added to the centre of the wrapped-diamond stitch pattern in the sketch shown in Figure 227. The placement of the double eyelet echoes that of the wrapped stitches, by also having a regular grid-like pattern within the swatch.

Fig. 226   Ironwork diamond grid in Lisbon, Portugal.

Fig. 227   Sketch of diamonds and eyelets.

Fig. 228   Knitted swatch of wrapped diamonds with eyelets (yarn: pure wool, worsted weight; needles: 4.5mm; total stitches: 24, comprising three 6-stitch repeats plus 6sts; total rows: 24, comprising three 8-row repeats).

The double eyelets visible in the swatch shown in Figure 228 are made by working two yarn overs between two decreases. On the next row, the two loops around the needle are worked as a knit stitch and a purl stitch, forming two complete stitches. The advantage of this type of eyelet is the large size of the hole that it creates. By placing the large eyelet in the centre of the diamond shape, the structure of the grid becomes more prominent.

Wrapped diamonds with eyelets

(6sts, plus 6sts, and 8 rows)

Note: the repeat box for this chart has a stepped appearance, as the repeat cannot run through the centre of a stitch manipulation.

Note: For instructions on how to work wrapped stitches, see the feature box 'How to work a wrapped stitch' in the section 'Horizontal diamond links' in Chapter 6.

Row 1 (RS): P2, *wrap 2sts, p2tog, yo twice, p2tog; rep from * once, wrap 2sts, p2.
Row 2 (WS): K2, p1, *p1, k2, p1, k1, p1; rep from * once, p1, k2.
Row 3: 1/2 RPC, *1/2 LPC, 1/2 RPC; rep from * once, 1/2 LPC.
Row 4: P1, k2, *k2, p2, k2; rep from * once, k2, p1.
Row 5: K1, p2tog, yo, *yo, p2tog, wrap 2sts, p2tog, yo; rep from * once, yo, p2tog, k1.
Row 6: P1, k2, *p1, k1, p2, k2; rep from * once, p1, k1, p1.
Row 7: 1/2 LPC, *1/2 RPC, 1/2 LPC; rep from * once, 1/2 RPC.
Row 8: K2, p1, *p1, k4, p1; rep from * once, p1, k2.

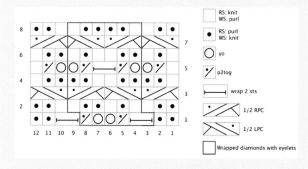

Fig. 229 Chart of wrapped diamonds with eyelets.

Ironwork circles

The inspiration for this stitch pattern, shown in Figure 230, was found within a metal grid that is located outside of a building in central London, UK. This grid provides cover for a series of low-level windows. In the grid structure, each intersection of the crossbars is fixed in place with a circular join.

The sketch shown in Figure 231 demonstrates how the different sizes of circles are regularly spaced within the grid, representing the openwork element. For the design, the addition of eyelets between the linking lines draws on this openwork inspiration, as is evident in the knitted swatch shown in Figure 232. Combinations of single and double yarn-over eyelets are used to highlight the grid structure.

Fig. 230 Ironwork grid with circles in London, UK.

Although they are knitted as long columns of shapes, the circles in this cabled grid have the appearance of being linked by the placement of the eyelets. The background eyelets are worked on each side of the linking cables. The large double eyelet in the centre of each circle creates a distinctive feature, inspired by the joins in the ironwork grid.

The type of decrease chosen will have a significant effect on the appearance of the knitted fabric. In the same way that a twist or cable may be worked as a mirror image to create balance in a design, the decreases are similarly balanced in this swatch. The purled decrease stitches are worked as a pair of p2tog and p2togtbl decreases. One decrease of the pair is worked on one side of each double yarn-over eyelet, and the other decrease of the pair is worked on the other side; the same approach is used on each side of the linking cables. Working into the back of stitches with the p2togtbl decrease causes the stitches to lean in the opposite direction to those worked with the p2tog decrease. This is most evident on the reverse side of the swatch and on each side of the cable links.

Although the inspiration source is made of a hard, metallic material, the swatch has been knitted in a soft, DK-weight yarn that is a blend of alpaca and wool fibres. This provides a contrast in texture between the source and the resulting swatch.

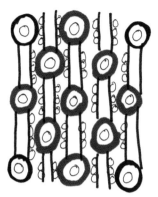

Fig. 231 Sketch of circles placed in a grid pattern, inspired by the ironwork grid.

Fig. 232 Knitted swatch of double-eyelet circles (yarn: pure wool, worsted weight; needles: 4.5mm; total stitches: 28, comprising one 18-stitch repeat plus 10sts; total rows: 24, comprising two 12-row repeats).

Double-eyelet circles
(18sts, plus 10sts, and 12 rows)

Row 1 (RS): *P1, yo, p2tog, k4, p2togtbl, yo, p1, k2, p2togtbl, yo twice, p2tog, k2; rep from * once, p1, yo, p2tog, k4, p2togtbl, yo, p1.

Row 2 (WS): K3, p4, k3, *p2, k2, p1, k1, p2, k3, p4, k3; rep from * once.

Row 3: *P1, yo, p2tog, 2/2 RC, p2togtbl, yo, p1, 2/2 LPC, 2/2 RPC; rep from * once, p1, yo, p2tog, 2/2 RC, p2togtbl, yo, p1.

Row 4: K3, p4, k3, *k2, p4, k5, p4, k3; rep from * once.

Row 5: *P1, 2/2 RPC, 2/2 LPC, p1, yo, p2tog, 2/2 RC, p2togtbl, yo; rep from * once, p1, 2/2 RPC, 2/2 LPC, p1.

Row 6: K1, p2, k4, p2, k1, *k2, p4, k3, p2, k4, p2, k1; rep from * once.

Row 7: *P1, k2, p2togtbl, yo twice, p2tog, k2, p1, yo, p2tog, k4, p2togtbl, yo; rep from * once, p1, k2, p2togtbl, yo twice, p2tog, k2, p1.

Row 8: K1, p2, k2, p1, k1, p2, k1, *k2, p4, k3, p2, k2, p1, k1, p2, k1; rep from * once.

Row 9: *P1, 2/2 LPC, 2/2 RPC, p1, yo, p2tog, 2/2 RC, p2togtbl, yo; rep from * once, p1, 2/2 LPC, 2/2 RPC, p1.

Row 10: As row 4.

Row 11: *P1, yo, p2tog, 2/2 RC, p2togtbl, yo, p1, 2/2 RPC, 2/2 LPC; rep from * once, p1, yo, p2tog, 2/2 RC, p2togtbl, yo, p1.

Row 12: K3, p4, k3, *p2, k4, p2, k3, p4, k3; rep from * once.

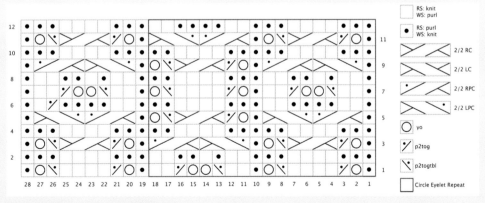

Fig. 233 Chart of double-eyelet circles.

Legend:
- RS: knit / WS: purl
- RS: purl / WS: knit (●)
- 2/2 RC
- 2/2 LC
- 2/2 RPC
- 2/2 LPC
- yo (○)
- p2tog
- p2togtbl
- Circle Eyelet Repeat

Fig. 234 Daisies.

Fig. 236 Knitted swatch of daisy twists (yarn: pure wool, 4ply weight; needles: 3.25mm; total stitches: 33, comprising two 12-stitch repeats plus 9sts; total rows: 36, comprising three 12-row repeats).

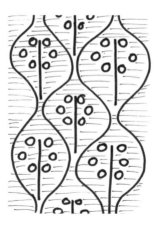

Fig. 235 Sketch of linked daisies.

Daisies

The ironwork-grid structures that have been explored so far have a very formal, grid-pattern style. Less formal pattern structures can be found in the natural world. The daisies of this example, shown in Figure 234, could be found in any grassy area. When the sun shines, these beautiful, little flowers explode into bloom. The image shows how the daisies overlap each other as they compete for sunshine.

In the sketch inspired by these daisies, shown in Figure 235, the curved lines that will be worked with twisted stitches imply the flower-outline shapes. In the swatch shown in Figure 236, the eyelet pattern has been used to suggest the petal detail in the centre of each curved section. The same decrease stitch is used for each of the three sets of petals. However, the placement of the yarn over is different in the centre, to represent the open petals. Each eyelet flower has a little stem that begins as the curve widens. The stem creates a mini-rib pattern where the curved lines are closest, which also helps to enhance the circular shapes. The combination of all of these stitch patterns transforms the individual flower elements of the design into a longer, flowing series of linked daisy chains.

The yarn chosen for this swatch was a 4ply, pure-wool yarn. This lightweight yarn gives the twists good stitch definition, which provides contrast to the eyelet flowers. The delicate pink shade picks up the hint of pink on the tips of the daisy petals.

Daisy twists

(12sts, plus 9sts, and 12 rows)

Row 1 (RS): K1, p1, yo, *p1, sl1, k2tog, psso, p1, yo, (p1, k1) three times, p1, yo; rep from * twice, p1, sl1, k2tog, psso, p1, yo, p1, k1.

Row 2 (WS): P1, k3, p1, k1, *k2, (p1, k1) twice, p1, k3, p1, k1; rep from * twice, k2, p1.

Row 3: 1/1 LPC, p1, *yo, sl1, k2tog, psso, yo, p1, 1/1 RPC, p1, k1, p1, 1/1 LPC, p1; rep from * twice, yo, sl1, k2tog, psso, yo, p1, 1/1 RPC.

Row 4: K1, p1, k4, *k1, (p1, k2) twice, p1, k4; rep from * twice, k1, p1, k1.

Row 5: P1, 1/1 LPC, *p3, 1/1 RPC, p1, yo, sl1, k2tog, psso, yo, p1, 1/1 LPC; rep from * twice, p3, 1/1 RPC, p1.

Row 6: K2, p1, k3, *(p1, k3) three times; rep from * twice, p1, k2.

Row 7: P2, k1, *(p1, k1) twice, p1, yo, p1, sl1, k2tog, psso, p1, yo, p1, k1; rep from * twice, (p1, k1) twice, p2.

Row 8: K2, (p1, k1) twice, *(p1, k3) twice, (p1, k1) twice; rep from * twice, p1, k2.

Row 9: P1, 1/1 RPC, *p1, k1, p1, 1/1 LPC, p1, yo, sl1, k2tog, psso, yo, p1, 1/1 RPC; rep from * twice, p1, k1, p1, 1/1 LPC, p1.

Row 10: K1, p1, k2, p1, k1, *k1, p1, k5, p1, k2, p1, k1; rep from * twice, k1, p1, k1.

Row 11: 1/1 RPC, p1, *yo, sl1, k2tog, psso, yo, p1, 1/1 LPC, p3, 1/1 RPC, p1; rep from * twice, yo, sl1, k2tog, psso, yo, p1, 1/1 LPC.

Row 12: P1, k3, p1, k1, *k2, (p1, k3) twice, p1, k1; rep from * twice, k2, p1.

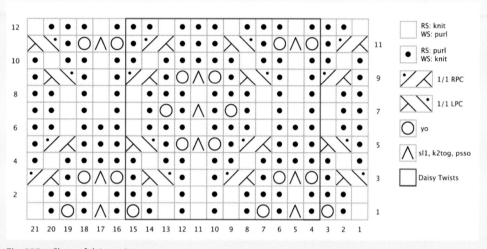

Fig. 237   Chart of daisy twists.

Openwork pattern: Sierra Nevada wrap

Sequoia and Kings Canyon National Parks in California, USA, are world-famous for their giant sequoia trees. The parks are located next to each other in the Sierra Nevada mountains of California. The enormous range of elevation in the parks has resulted in an incredible variety of plants growing there. Driving along the Generals Highway that links the General Sherman and General Grant giant sequoia trees reveals stunning ever-changing views. Further into Kings Canyon, the landscape changes to that of steep mountainsides and narrow gorges.

Appearing as giant candlesticks on the steep mountain-sides, the flowering yucca plants of the High Sierras have a very dramatic look, as captured in the image shown in Figure 238. The spiky leaves at the base of each plant contrast with the incredibly delicate individual flowers at the end of the long stem. This stunning, architectural plant is the inspiration for this lace-and-twisted stitch project.

The majestic yucca family plants of Kings Canyon manage to thrive amongst the rocks on the very steep slopes that tower high above the winding road and river beds. A closer look at an individual plant growing near the road reveals its true scale. Some of the stems are well above three metres (ten feet) in height, with the flower heads reaching towards the sky.

The flowers appear to have opened first at the lower edges, with the upper flower point still being in the bud stage. The open flowers hang with a beautiful elegance that is enhanced by the sheer number of individual flowers on the same small branch.

The branching structure of the upper flower stem can be seen as the flowers move in the breeze. The weight of the individual flowers pulls the multiple stems to a diagonal angle in relation to the central stalk. An almost abrupt change in direction occurs where the weight of the flowers pulls the lower stems away from the upper buds, which are much lighter.

Fig. 238 Yucca flower stalk in Kings Canyon National Park, California, USA.

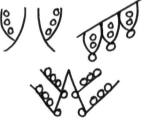

Fig. 239 Sketch of yucca plant detail.

Fig. 240 Sketch of yucca plant structure.

Fig. 241 Sierra Nevada wrap. (Photo: Maxine Vining)

The stunning colour of this High Sierras yucca plant has also influenced the pattern. The creamy-white colour of the petals has a very slight tint of green that is related to the green, spiky leaves at the base of the plant. 'Sierra Nevada' translates from Spanish as meaning snowy mountains. The beautiful white flowers of the yucca are reminiscent of those high, snowy peaks, and it is possible to see snow on the High Sierras at the same time as seeing the yucca flowers on the lower slopes. The choice of yarn reflects this soft creaminess and balances it with the need for clear stitch definition in the design. The sketches shown in Figures 239 and 240 highlight the change in direction of the diagonals and the way that the flowers change from bud stage to when they are fully open. The whole flower head is the perfect shape for a wrap accessory, with a wide base and a narrow point.

The knitting pattern uses both eyelets and twisted stitches to set the direction of the individual flower heads, visible in the featured sample shown in Figures 241 and 242. By using different types of twisted stitches and different ways of creating eyelets, the direction of the lines of knitting can be altered. This allows the yucca flower shapes to be drawn in different ways on the knitted fabric. On the reverse side of the wrap, the eyelets and textural changes are visible, creating an embossed pattern.

The flowers are worked in sets of two that mirror image each other. The direction changes between the two sets, reflecting the movement of the flower heads in the gentle breeze of the mountains. The same principle applies to the upper section. The diagonal lines of twisted stitches have eyelets to represent yucca flower buds. The bud pattern is also worked as a mirror image. This part of the wrap is decreased at the outer edges, forming a point. The techniques used are the same within the two sections, but they are used in a different way, to reflect the different growth stage. The whole wrap has a great deal of movement within it, as the diagonals change with every set of flowers. The rhythm is linked horizontally and vertically throughout. The edges and central stem patterns are worked in a pattern of garter stitch and eyelets throughout.

Sierra Nevada wrap pattern

Size

One size
- 28cm (11in) wide × 130cm (51in) long

Yarn

- Malabrigo Arroyo, 100-per-cent pure, superwash, merino wool, sport to DK weight, 305m (335yd) per 100g hank
- 2 × 100g hanks in 063 Natural

Needles and accessories

- A pair of 3.25mm (UK10, US3) straight needles or an equivalent circular needle, as preferred
- A pair of 4mm (UK8, US6) straight needles or an equivalent circular needle, as preferred
- Cable needle
- Darning needle
- Stitch markers

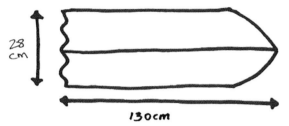

Fig. 243 Blocking diagram of Sierra Nevada wrap.

Tension

- 26sts and 31 rows to 10cm (4in) over flower pattern, using 4mm needles
- 26sts and 42 rows to 10cm (4in) over point garter-stitch-based diagonals pattern, using 3.25mm needles

Pattern notes

Stitch markers are used to set the pattern placements. Slip the markers from the lhn to the rhn as they are reached on subsequent rows.

Refer to written or charted instructions for each stitch pattern (A–D), as preferred.

Sierra Nevada pattern A (multiple of 8sts and 12 rows)
Row 1 (RS): P3, 1/1 LC, p3.
Row 2 (WS): K3, p2, k3.
Row 3: P2, k2tog, yo, 1/1 LC, p2.
Row 4: K2, p4, k2.
Row 5: P1, k2tog, yo, k2, 1/1 LC, p1.
Row 6: K1, p6, k1.
Row 7: P1, ssk, yo, k4, p1.
Rows 8–9: As rows 6–7.
Row 10: As row 6.
Row 11: Purl.
Row 12: Knit.

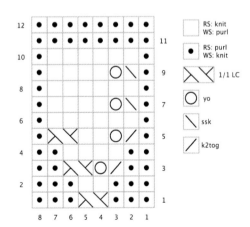

Fig. 244 Chart of Sierra Nevada pattern A.

Sierra Nevada pattern B (multiple of 8sts and 12 rows)
Row 1 (RS): P3, 1/1 RC, p3.
Row 2 (WS): K3, p2, k3.
Row 3: P2, 1/1 RC, yo, ssk, p2.
Row 4: K2, p4, k2.
Row 5: P1, 1/1 RC, k2, yo, ssk, p1.
Row 6: K1, p6, k1.
Row 7: P1, k4, yo, k2tog, p1.
Rows 8–9: As rows 6–7.
Row 10: As row 6.
Row 11: Purl.
Row 12: Knit.

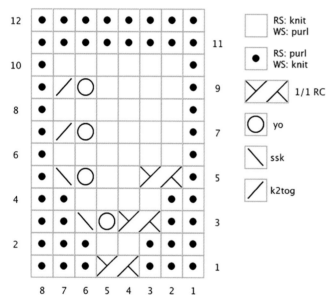
Fig. 245   Chart of Sierra Nevada pattern B.

Sierra Nevada pattern C (multiple of 8sts and 8 rows)
Row 1 (RS): K3, k2tog, yo, k1, 1/1 RC.
Row 2 (WS): K1, p4, k3.
Row 3: K2, k2tog, yo, k1, 1/1 RC, k1.
Row 4: K2, p4, k2.
Row 5: K1, k2tog, yo, k1, 1/1 RC, k2.
Row 6: K3, p4, k1.
Row 7: K2tog, yo, k1, 1/1 RC, k3.
Row 8: K4, p4.

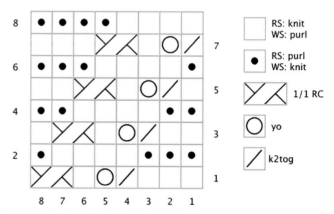
Fig. 246   Chart of Sierra Nevada pattern C.

Sierra Nevada pattern D (multiple of 8sts and 8 rows)
Row 1 (RS): 1/1 LC, k1, yo, ssk, k3.
Row 2 (WS): K3, p4, k1.
Row 3: K1, 1/1 LC, k1, yo, ssk, k2.
Row 4: K2, p4, k2.
Row 5: K2, 1/1 LC, k1, yo, ssk, k1.
Row 6: K1, p4, k3.
Row 7: K3, 1/1 LC, k1, yo, ssk.
Row 8: P4, k4.

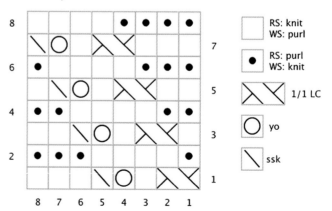
Fig. 247   Chart for Sierra Nevada pattern D.

Pattern instructions

Border

Cast on 74sts by using 3.25mm needles.

Border row 1 (RS): K1, ssk, yo, (k3, 1/1 LC, k3) four times, yo, k2tog, ssk, yo, (k3, 1/1 RC, k3) four times, yo, k2tog, k1.

Border row 2 (WS): (K6, p2) four times, k10, (p2, k6) four times.

Rep border rows 1–2 three times.

Border row 9: K1, ssk, yo, (k3, 1/1 LC, k3) four times, pm, yo, k2tog, ssk, yo, pm, (k3, 1/1 RC, k3) four times, yo, k2tog, k1.

Border row 10: As border row 2, slipping stitch markers as they are reached.

Change to 4mm needles, and begin main flower pattern.

Refer to written or charted instructions for each stitch pattern (A–D), as preferred, as needed.

Flower-section 1

Row 1 (RS): K1, ssk, yo, *work pattern A row 1; rep from * to mrk, yo, k2tog, ssk, yo, *work pattern B row 1; rep from * to last 3sts, yo, k2tog, k1.

Row 2 (WS): K3, *work pattern B row 2; rep from * to mrk, k4, *work pattern A row 2; rep from * to last 3sts, k3.

Continue as set, from row 3 of patterns A and B, working all twelve rows of patterns A and B once.

Flower-section 2

Row 1 (RS): K1, ssk, yo, *work pattern B row 1; rep from * to mrk, yo, k2tog, ssk, yo, *work pattern A row 1; rep from * to last 3sts, yo, k2tog, k1.

Row 2 (WS): K3, *work pattern A row 1; rep from * to mrk, k4, *work pattern B row 1; rep from * to last 3sts, k3.

Continue as set, from row 3 of patterns B and A, working all twelve rows of patterns B and A once.

Rep flower-section 1 and then flower-section 2 (twenty-four rows) fourteen times.

Point

Change to 3.25mm needles, and begin diagonals pattern.

Row 1 (RS): K1, ssk, yo, *work pattern C row 1; rep from * to mrk, yo, k2tog, ssk, yo, *work pattern D row 1; rep from * to last 3sts, yo, k2tog, k1.

Row 2 (WS): K3, *work pattern D row 2; rep from * to mrk, k4, *work pattern C row 2; rep from * to last 3sts, k3.

Rows 3–8: Continue as set, from row 3 of patterns C and D, working all eight rows of patterns C and D once.

Row 9: K1, ssk, yo, k to mrk, yo, k2tog, ssk, yo, k to last 3sts, yo, k2tog, k1.

Row 10: Knit.

Begin decreasing for point as follows:

Row 11 (RS): K1, ssk, yo, ssk, k6, pm, *work pattern C row 1; rep from * to mrk, yo, k2tog, ssk, yo, *work pattern D row 1; rep from * to last 11sts, k6, k2tog, yo, k2tog, k1. (72sts)

Row 12 (WS): K3, ssk, k5, *work pattern D row 2; rep from * to mrk, k4, *work pattern C row 2; rep from * to last 10sts, k5, k2tog, k3. (70sts)

Row 13: K1, ssk, yo, ssk, k4, *work pattern C row 3; rep from * to mrk, yo, k2tog, ssk, yo, *work pattern D row 3; rep from * to last 9sts, k4, k2tog, yo, k2tog, k1. (68sts)

Row 14: K3, ssk, k3, *work pattern D row 4; rep from * to mrk, k4, *work pattern C row 4; rep from * to last 8sts, k3, k2tog, k3. (66sts)

Rows 15–17: Continue from row 5 of patterns C and D, decreasing 2sts as set on next and every following row, until seven rows of patterns C and D each have been completed. (60sts)

Row 18: K3, p2togtbl, p3, k4, *work pattern D row 8; rep from * to mrk, k4, *work pattern C row 8; rep from * to last 12sts, k4, p3, p2tog, k3. (58sts)

Row 19: K1, ssk, yo, k to mrk, yo, k2tog, ssk, yo, k to last 3sts, yo, k2tog, k1.

Row 20: Knit.

Rep rows 11–20 two times. (26sts)

Row 41: K1, ssk, yo, ssk, k to mrk, yo, k2tog, ssk, yo, k to last 5sts, k2tog, yo, k2tog, k1. (24sts)

Row 42: K3, ssk, k to last 5sts, k2tog, k3. (22sts)

Rows 41–42 set the placement of the decreases. Continuing as set, rep rows 41–42 two times (14sts)

Rep row 41 once. (12sts)

Next row (WS): Knit.

Complete point as follows:

Next row (RS): K1, ssk, yo, ssk, k2, k2tog, yo, k2tog, k1. (10sts)

Next row (WS): K3, ssk, k2tog, k3. (8sts)

Next row: K1, ssk, k2, k2tog, k1. (6sts)

Cast off knitwise.

Block the work gently to the measurements given in Figure 243 and according to the yarn's ball-band instructions.

Sew in all loose ends.

CHAPTER 11

TEXTURE

Textured zigzag lines

Changing the texture of a twist or cable is an interesting way to change the appearance of a knitted line. Textural elements have been added to several of the stitch patterns throughout this book. However, in those designs, all of the knitted lines had foreground stitches worked in stocking stitch. In the following examples, we shall take a look at what happens to the knitted fabric when the foreground stitch is knitted in reverse stocking stitch.

A large number of beautiful mosaic paving areas can be found throughout the city of Lisbon. These vary from extensive plazas to short sections of pavement. The small section shown in Figure 248 is a narrow strip at the base of a high wall alongside a twisting lane. The design in this paving provides excellent textural inspiration for a comparison of textured cables. The zigzag design of mosaic tiles suggest a series of moving lines. As the whole paved area is a mosaic, the textured stitches will be used for both the foreground and background of the knitted swatch.

To allow a direct comparison of textures, the swatch shown in Figure 249 has three sections. The cables in each section are all four-stitch cables with three foreground stitches being moved over one background stitch. The foreground stitches are

Fig. 248 Mosaic paving in Lisbon, Portugal.

Fig. 249 Knitted swatch of textured cable lines (yarn: wool and hemp, aran weight; needles: 4.5mm; total stitches: 37; total rows: 32, comprising two 16-row repeats).

all knitted in reverse stocking stitch. The single background stitch is worked in either stocking stitch or reverse stocking stitch. There are three different background stitch patterns in the swatch: stocking stitch, reverse stocking stitch and moss stitch. Each section is divided by a two-stitch-twist rope pattern. This helps to provide contrast to the textured cables and backgrounds on the swatch and to clearly separate each of the three textured sections.

The different effects created by changing the background stitch pattern are evident. In section one, on the right-hand side of the swatch, the four-stitch cable has been worked on a stocking stitch background pattern. The three foreground stitches of the cable are in reverse stocking stitch, and the single background stitch is worked in stocking stitch. The cables have been worked from edge to edge, creating a difference in tension between the cable in the foreground and the stocking stitch in the background. As a result, the areas of stocking stitch background appear to bend between the cables.

In sections two and three, in the centre and on the left-hand side of the swatch, respectively, the four stitches of the cable are all knitted in reverse stocking stitch. The background in sec-tion two is worked in reverse stocking stitch. This combination results in a raised cable line that blends into the background. In section three, the background is worked as moss stitch on each side of the cable. The reverse stocking stitch cable forms a distinct knitted line on this background. However, a blurring of the edges of the cable occurs where the two stitch patterns meet.

This swatch provides an opportunity to review the effect of reverse stocking stitch cables on backgrounds with different textures. As these experiments all came from the same inspiration, of the Lisbon mosaic paving, the result is a series of related stitch patterns. Each of the three stitch patterns could be used on its own or in combination. Having these options can be very useful when choosing borders and edges in a final pattern. For

Textured cable lines
(37sts and 16 rows)

Row 1 (RS): K1, 1/1 RC, p1, 3/1 LCP, k3, p1, 1/1 RC, p1, 3/1 LPCP, p4, 1/1 RC, p1, 3/1 LPCP, (k1, p1) twice, 1/1 RC, k1.
Row 2 (WS): P3, k2, p1, k6, p2, k9, p2, k1, p3, k3, p1, k1, p3.
Row 3: K1, 1/1 RC, p1, k1, 3/1 LCP, k2, p1, 1/1 RC, p2, 3/1 LPCP, p3, 1/1 RC, p1, k1, 3/1 LPCP, p1, k1, p1, 1/1 RC, k1.
Row 4: P3, k2, p1, k3, p1, k2, p2, k9, p2, k1, p2, k3, p2, k1, p3.
Row 5: K1, 1/1 RC, p1, k2, 3/1 LCP, k1, p1, 1/1 RC, p3, 3/1 LPCP, p2, 1/1 RC, p1, k1, p1, 3/1 LPCP, k1, p1, 1/1 RC, k1.
Row 6: P4, k5, p1, k2, p2, k9, p2, k1, p1, k3, p3, k1, p3.
Row 7: K1, 1/1 RC, p1, k3, 3/1 LCP, p1, 1/1 RC, p4, 3/1 LPCP, p1, 1/1 RC, (p1, k1) twice, 3/1 LPCP, p1, 1/1 RC, k1.
Row 8: P4, k5, p1, k2, p2, k9, p2, k4, p4, k1, p3.

Row 9: K1, 1/1 RC, p1, k3, 3/1 RCP, p1, 1/1 RC, p4, 3/1 RPCP, p1, 1/1 RC, (p1, k1) twice, 3/1 RPCP, p1, 1/1 RC, k1.
Row 10: As row 6.
Row 11: K1, 1/1 RC, p1, k2, 3/1 RCP, k1, p1, 1/1 RC, p3, 3/1 RPCP, p2, 1/1 RC, p1, k1, p1, 3/1 RPCP, k1, p1, 1/1 RC, k1.
Row 12: P4, k1, p1, k3, p1, k2, p2, k9, p2, k1, p2, k3, p2, k1, p3.
Row 13: K1, 1/1 RC, p1, k1, 3/1 RCP, k2, p1, 1/1 RC, p2, 3/1 RPCP, p3, 1/1 RC, p1, k1, 3/1 RPCP, p1, k1, p1, 1/1 RC, k1.
Row 14: P4, k1, p1, k6, p2, k9, p2, k1, p3, k3, p1, k1, p3.
Row 15: K1, 1/1 RC, p1, 3/1 RCP, k3, p1, 1/1 RC, p1, 3/1 RPCP, p4, 1/1 RC, p1, 3/1 RPCP, (k1, p1) twice, 1/1 RC, k1.
Row 16: P4, (k1, p1) twice, k4, p2, k9, p2, k1, p4, k4, p3.

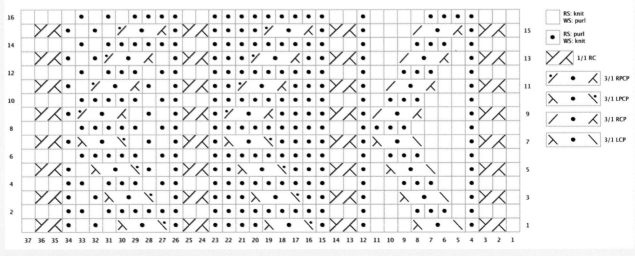

Fig. 250   Chart of textured cable lines.

How to work reverse stocking stitch cables

These four-stitch, reverse stocking stitch cables have three foreground stitches that are moved over one background stitch, either to the right or to the left, by using a cable needle. The three foreground stitches are always worked in reverse stocking stitch. The background stitch is either worked in stocking stitch, as a 3/1 RPC or 3/1 LPC, or in reverse stocking stitch, as a 3/1 RPCP or 3/1 LPCP.

3/1 RPC and 3/1 RPCP right-leaning, reverse stocking stitch cables
Pattern to the cable location.

Step 1 (Figure 251): Slip the next stitch on to the cn, and hold the cn at back of work.
Step 2 (Figure 252): Purl the next 3sts.
Note: Step 3 is different for 3/1 RPC and 3/1 RPCP.
Step 3 (3/1 RPC only): Knit the stitch from the cn.
Step 3 (3/1 RPCP only): Purl the stitch from the cn.

3/1 LPC and 3/1 LPCP left-leaning, reverse stocking stitch cables
Pattern to the cable location.

Step 1 (Figure 253): Slip the next 3sts on to the cn, and hold the cn at front of work.
Note: Step 2 is different for 3/1 LPC and 3/1 LPCP.
Step 2 (3/1 LPC only, Figure 254): Knit the next stitch.
Step 2 (3/1 LPCP only, Figure 255): Purl the next stitch.
Step 3: Purl the 3sts from the cn.

Fig. 251   3/1 RPC and 3/1 RPCP step 1.

Fig. 252   3/1 RPC and 3/1 RPCP step 2.

Fig. 253   3/1 LPC and 3/1 LPCP step 1.

Fig. 254   3/1 LPC step 2.

Fig. 255   3/1 LPCP step 2.

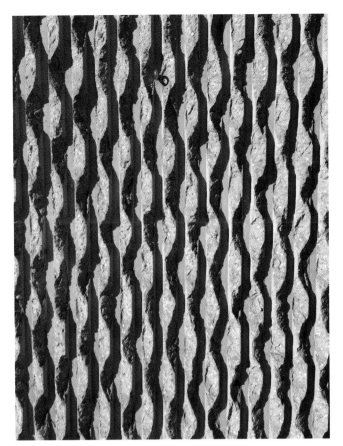

Fig. 256   Building wall with ridged-concrete texture.

Fig. 257   Sketch of curved line and texture.

Fig. 258   Sketch of curved line and two different textures.

example, the lower edge of a scarf could begin with a cable on the moss-stitch background. Keeping the cable the same, the pattern could then change to a stocking stitch background for the main section of the pattern.

Textured ovals

As well as textured lines, cables can be used to represent textured shapes within a design. The photo shown in Figure 256 is of a textured concrete wall on a building in the centre of Guildford, UK. The concrete has been cast in a series of ridges, some with straight edges and some with curves. This pattern is fascinating on many levels. There is a mix of straight and curved lines and a series of implied shapes. The pattern on the wall is further enhanced by the way that the sun casts shadows across the raised areas. Depending on where the shadow falls, the implied-oval shapes appear aligned or offset. In other parts of the wall, only the straight lines are visible.

To translate these elements into a knitted design, many of the techniques looked at in the chapters of Part 2: Line and Shape can be applied. For example, curved-line techniques will help to create the basic structure of the lines and implied-oval shapes.

The sketches shown in Figures 257 and 258 highlight the line and textural details of the concrete wall. There are two main textural elements, which are represented in the sketches by the cross-hatching and the horizontal lines. Placing these curved lines and the textural surround together forms a series of implied-oval shapes between these elements. The shapes imply different edge and centre textures. In order to recreate this varied, textural effect, different types of knitted lines can be used in combination. This is explored in the following three examples. Using the shape and line from these sketches, all three of the following stitch patterns have the same number of stitches and rows, as well as the same layout. Within this framework, the stitch patterns have been changed one at a time. Three stitch repeats of each pattern have been worked horizontally and two row repeats vertically.

Texture and stocking stitch

The pattern for the first swatch, shown in Figure 259, considers texture and stocking stitch. It combines twists and cables worked with a stocking stitch foreground stitch with sections of reverse stocking stitch as the background pattern. With this combination, one half of the implied oval is also knitted in stocking stitch. The other half is filled with reverse stocking stitch and is outlined by a two-stitch twist. The result is a contrasting pattern of half-ovals with smooth, raised surfaces. These shapes appear prominent on the reverse stocking stitch background.

Fig. 259 Knitted swatch of texture and stocking stitch (yarn: pure wool, DK weight; needles: 4mm; total stitches: 30, comprising three 10-stitch repeats; total rows: 24, comprising two 12-row repeats).

Fig. 261 Knitted swatch of texture and reverse stocking stitch (yarn: pure wool, DK weight; needles: 4mm; total stitches: 30, comprising three 10-stitch repeats; total rows: 24, comprising two 12-row repeats).

Texture and stocking stitch

(10sts and 12 rows)

Row 1 (RS): K3, p1, k3, p3.
Row 2 (WS): K3, p3, k1, p3.
Row 3: K1, 1/1 RPC, p1, k1, 2/1 LC, p2.
Row 4: K2, p4, k2, p2.
Row 5: 1/1 RPC, p2, k2, 2/1 LC, p1.
Row 6: K1, p5, k3, p1.
Row 7: K1, p3, k5, p1.
Row 8: As row 6.
Row 9: 1/1 LC, p2, k2, 2/1 RPC, p1.
Row 10: As row 4.
Row 11: K1, 1/1 LC, p1, k1, 2/1 RPC, p2.
Row 12: As row 2.

Fig. 260 Chart of texture and stocking stitch.

Texture and reverse stocking stitch

The pattern for the second swatch, shown in Figure 261, is also inspired by the concrete wall and considers texture and reverse stocking stitch. This pattern has been produced by changing one of the elements of the stitch pattern used for the first swatch. The stitch and row counts remain the same; however, for this stitch pattern, the three-stitch cable is worked in reverse stocking stitch. This immediately changes the knitted line into a textured line. This texture contrasts with the stocking stitch half-ovals bordered by the two-stitch twists. The cabled line worked in reverse stocking stitch is a more subtle feature than that when it is worked in stocking stitch. It appears more as a shadow of the prominent stocking stitch part of the knitting and forms an indentation in the knitted fabric.

Texture and reverse stocking stitch

(10sts and 12 rows)

Row 1 (RS): P2, k2, p6.
Row 2 (WS): K6, p2, k2.
Row 3: P, 1/1 RC, k1, p1, 2/1 LPCP, p2.
Row 4: K6, p3, k1.
Row 5: 1/1 RC, k2, p2, 2/1 LPCP, p1.
Row 6: K6, p4.
Row 7: K4, p6.
Row 8: K6, p4.
Row 9: 1/1 LPC, k2, p2, 2/1 RPCP, p1.
Row 10: K6, p3, k1.
Row 11: P1, 1/1 LPC, k1, p1, 2/1 RPCP, p2.
Row 12: As row 2.

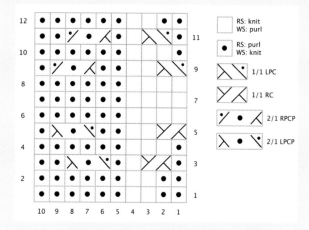

Fig. 262   Chart of texture and reverse stocking stitch.

Texture and moss stitch

The pattern for the third swatch, shown in Figure 263, explores texture and moss stitch. For this pattern, the three-stitch cable continues to be worked in reverse stocking stitch. This time, the stocking stitch half-oval has a moss-stitch background instead of one of stocking stitch. The twisted stitch outline continues to be worked as a two-stitch twist. The appearance of the swatch has changed again. In this swatch, the two-stitch twist with the single foreground stitch forms the most distinct knitted line. The three-stitch, reverse stocking stitch cable has blended into the background moss-stitch texture. The change of stitch pattern from moss stitch to reverse stocking stitch forms a pleated line, giving the swatch a three-dimensional effect. Although the knitted lines are less prominent, the contours formed on this swatch reflect the depth of the concrete ridges on the building wall.

All three swatches in this series of textured examples, shown in Figure 265, clearly represent elements of the original inspiration source. All three have textural stitch patterns that change the properties and tension of the stitch pattern. The designs are a progression of related stitch patterns that work both when used separately and when combined together.

Fig. 263   Knitted swatch of texture and moss stitch (yarn: pure wool, DK weight; needles: 4mm; total stitches: 30, comprising three 10-stitch repeats; total rows: 24, comprising two 12-row repeats).

Texture and moss stitch

(10sts and 12 rows)

Row 1 (RS): K1, p1, k1, p5, k1, p1.
Row 2 (WS): P1, k1, p1, k3, p3, k1.
Row 3: K1, 1/1 RC, p2, 2/1 LPCP, k1, p1.
Row 4: P1, k5, (p1, k1) twice.
Row 5: 1/1 RC, k1, p3, 2/1 LPCP, p1.
Row 6: P1, k5, p1, k1, p2.
Row 7: K1, p1, k1, p7.
Row 8: As row 6.
Row 9: 1/1 LPC, k1, p3, 2/1 RPCP, p1.
Row 10: As row 4.
Row 11: K1, 1/1 LPC, p2, 2/1 RPCP, k1, p1.
Row 12: As row 2.

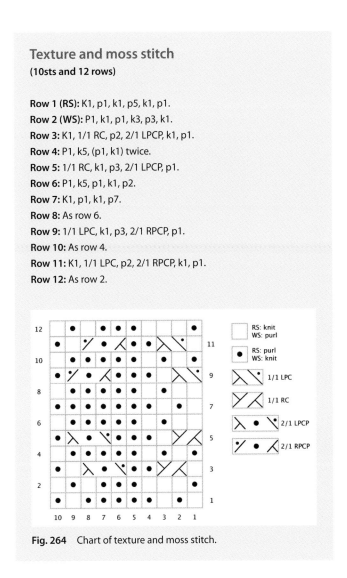

Fig. 264 Chart of texture and moss stitch.

Fig. 265 Comparison of three textured stitch patterns.

Texture pattern: concrete scarf

The curved lines and textured shapes of the concrete scarf are inspired by the section of the concrete-clad wall explored earlier in this chapter. This wall has a series of ridges with textured outer surfaces and smooth inner sections. Each vertical ridge is curved on one side and straight on the other. In the image shown in Figure 266, shadows have extended the curved lines and increased the three-dimensional effect of the ridges. Knitted in a soft, aran-weight yarn, the concrete scarf represents the appearance of the hard and inflexible wall; however, as a knitted structure, this concrete-inspired scarf can be folded and wrapped.

The scarf pattern is knitted by using three-stitch cables, moss stitch and reverse stocking stitch, as can be seen in Figures 267 and 268. One set of cables is worked in stocking stitch and the other set in reverse stocking stitch. These two different textures change the way that the knitted lines appear as they move across the knitted surface. In the detail of the concrete wall, the sun casts a distinct shadow between the concrete ridges on the wall. On the scarf, the clear, raised lines of the cables worked in stocking stitch are shadowed by the less prominent cables worked in reverse stocking stitch. The shadow effect is further enhanced by using moss stitch between certain sections of the cables, to contrast with smaller sections of reverse stocking stitch.

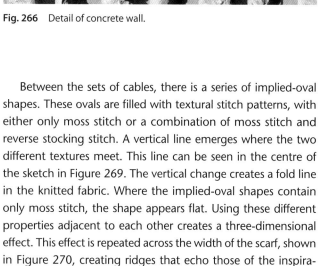

Fig. 266   Detail of concrete wall.

Fig. 267   Full length of concrete scarf.

Between the sets of cables, there is a series of implied-oval shapes. These ovals are filled with textural stitch patterns, with either only moss stitch or a combination of moss stitch and reverse stocking stitch. A vertical line emerges where the two different textures meet. This line can be seen in the centre of the sketch in Figure 269. The vertical change creates a fold line in the knitted fabric. Where the implied-oval shapes contain only moss stitch, the shape appears flat. Using these different properties adjacent to each other creates a three-dimensional effect. This effect is repeated across the width of the scarf, shown in Figure 270, creating ridges that echo those of the inspiration-source wall.

The reverse side, or wrong side, of the scarf, shown in Figure 271, also has a distinct design that is inspired by the same source. The central moss-stitch pattern of the right-side implied-oval shapes shows up as linked oval shapes on the wrong side of the scarf. The right-side reverse stocking stitch cables appear here as stocking stitch, linking the moss-stitch ovals. The vertical lines where the stitch patterns change are also distinct on this side of the scarf, helping to emphasize the folds in the knitting that create the ridges.

Fig. 268   Concrete scarf. (Photo: Maxine Vining)

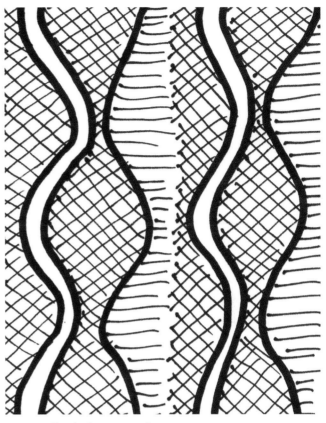

Fig. 269   Sketch of concrete-wall texture.

Fig. 270   Detail of concrete scarf.

Fig. 271   Detail of reverse side of concrete scarf.

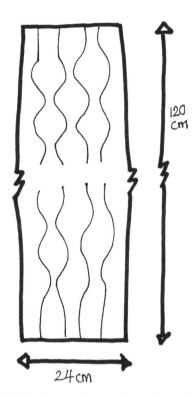

Fig. 272 Blocking diagram of concrete scarf (not to scale).

Concrete scarf pattern

Size
One size
- 25cm (10in) wide × 136cm (53½in) long

Yarn
- West Yorkshire Spinners Fleece Aran, 100-per-cent Bluefaced Leicester wool, aran weight, 166m (182yd) per 100g skein
- 3 × 100g skeins in 2 Light Brown

Needles and accessories
- A pair of 4.5mm (UK7, US7) straight needles or an equivalent circular needle, as preferred
- A pair of 5mm (UK6, US8) straight needles or an equivalent circular needle, as preferred
- Cable needle
- Darning needle

Tension
- 22sts and 27 rows to 10cm (4in) over concrete-cable pattern (CCP), using 5mm needles

Pattern notes
Refer to concrete-cable pattern (CCP) written or charted instructions, as preferred.

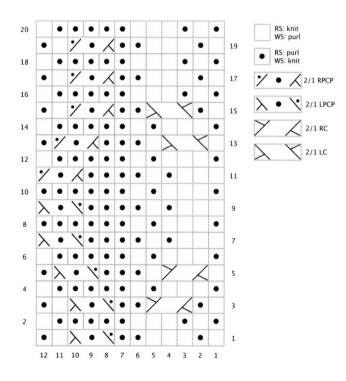

Fig. 273 Chart of concrete-cable pattern (CCP).

Concrete-cable pattern (CCP) (multiple of 12sts and 20 rows)
Row 1 (RS): K1, p1, k3, p2, 2/1 LPCP, k1, p1.
Row 2 (WS): P1, k5, p3, k1, p1, k1.
Row 3: K1, p1, 2/1 RC, p2, 2/1 LPCP, k1, p1.
Row 4: P1, k5, p1, k1, p3, k1.
Row 5: K1, 2/1 RC, k1, p3, 2/1 LPCP, p1.
Row 6: As row 4.
Row 7: K3, p1, k1, p4, 2/1 LPCP.
Row 8: K6, p1, k1, p3, k1.
Rows 9–10: As rows 7–8.
Row 11: K3, p1, k1, p4, 2/1 RPCP.
Row 12: As row 4.
Row 13: K1, 2/1 LC, k1, p3, 2/1 RPCP, p1.
Row 14: As row 4.
Row 15: K1, p1, 2/1 LC, p2, 2/1 RPCP, k1, p1.
Row 16: As row 2.
Row 17: K1, p1, k3, p2, 2/1 RPCP, k1, p1.
Row 18: As row 2.
Row 19: As row 17.
Row 20: As row 2.

Pattern instructions
Cast on 54sts by using 4.5mm needles.

Work cast-on-edge pattern as follows:
Cast-on-edge row 1 (RS): (P1, k1) twice, p1, *2/1 RC, p2, 2/1 LPCP, (k1, p1) twice; rep from * to last st, k1.
Cast-on-edge row 2 (WS): (K1, p1) twice, *k5, p5, k1, p1; rep from * to last 2sts, k1, p1.
  Rep cast-on-edge rows 1–2 six times.

Change to 5mm needles, and begin main pattern by using CCP, as follows:
Row 1 (RS): P1, k1, p1, *work row 1 of CCP; rep from * to last 3sts, k1, p1, k1.
Row 2 (WS): K1, p1, k1, *work row 2 of CCP; rep from * to last 3sts, p1, k1, p1.
Rows 1–2 set the moss-stitch edges and the CCP placement.
  Continue as set by these two rows, working all twenty rows of CCP a total of sixteen times, then work rows 1–15 once, ending with a RS row.

Change to 4.5mm needles, and work cast-off-edge pattern as follows:
Cast-off-edge row 1 (WS): (K1, p1) twice, *k5, p5, k1, p1; rep from * to last 2sts, k1, p1.
Cast-off-edge row 2 (RS): (P1, k1) twice, p1, *2/1 LC, p2, 2/1 RPCP, (k1, p1) twice; rep from * to last st, k1.
  Rep cast-off-edge rows 1–2 six times.
  Cast off in patt with WS facing.

Block the work gently to the measurements given in Figure 272 and according to the yarn's ball-band instructions.
  Sew in all loose ends.

CHAPTER 12

SHORT ROWS

Short-row-shaping techniques allow the selective addition of colour and depth. *Vogue Knitting: The Ultimate Knitting Book* defines 'short rows' as 'partial rows of knitting that are used to shape or curve sections or to compensate for patterns with different row gauges. The result is that one side or section has more rows than the other, but no stitches are decreased' (p.186).

This technique allows the alteration of knitted shapes and the inclusion of additional rows of knitting in specific areas of the fabric. The knitted fabric remains as a single layer throughout. The depth and dimensions of a shape and the placement of twist and cable stitch movements can be changed by using short rows.

Additional rows can be added to the knitting either as a wedge of extra, partial rows, which add depth to one area at a time, or as a distinctive 'pop' of extra, partial rows in the centre of a cabled shape. Each short-row section is worked within one row of the main knitting. The short row is begun by working a certain number of stitches on the right side of the knitting, followed by wrapping the next stitch, turning the knitting and working some stitches on the wrong side of the work, then turning the work back to the right side. This is repeated until the desired depth of the short-row section is reached. The row is then completed, by knitting to the end of the row.

Fig. 274 Seaside daisies in Falmouth, Cornwall, UK.

The bright and beautiful seaside daisies shown in Figure 274 have inspired the following short-row patterns that explore shape, size and depth. This member of the aster plant family grows all along the seafront in Falmouth, Cornwall, UK. On a bright day, the flowers burst open to catch the sunlight, revealing their brightly coloured centres. The different sizes of flower heads and the central pops of colour inspired the patterns of the next two knitted swatches.

Short-row wedges

It is possible to change the dimensions of several shapes at once by using the short-row-shaping technique. As shown in the inspiration-source image for this example, the seaside daisies consist of many different sizes of flower heads. As the daisies grow and compete for sunlight, they are all at different stages of flowering. These different sizes of flowers could be represented by manipulating the stitch pattern, by balancing a number of different twist or cable stitch movements across the whole area of the knitting. Depending on the size of the repeat, this would be an extremely complex pattern to design and to knit.

A more straightforward way of changing the size of the shapes in a stitch pattern is to use short-row shaping. By adding extra rows to the daisy shapes on the outer edges, the size of selected circles can be altered. The centre daisies will remain

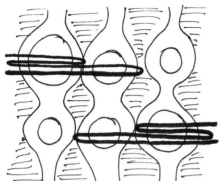

Fig. 275 Sketch of balanced short-row wedges.

Fig. 276 Knitted swatch of seaside daisies with short-row wedges (yarn: pure wool, DK weight; needles: 4mm; total stitches: 36; total rows: 24, not including short rows).

Fig. 277 Short-rows section 1 (SRS1), with wrapped-stitch locations indicated by green stitch markers.

Fig. 278 Angled knitted swatch after the working of SRS1 and several rows of knitting without short rows.

Fig. 279 Short-rows section 2 (SRS2), with wrapped-stitch locations indicated by green stitch markers.

Fig. 280 Reverse side of knitted swatch of seaside daisies with short-row wedges (yarn: pure wool, DK weight; needles: 4mm; total stitches: 36; total rows: 24, not including short rows).

the same size throughout the pattern, but the outer daisies will alternate between the largest size and the smallest size. For the following example, short rows are added in a wedge shape across the row in two sections.

The sketch shown in Figure 275 illustrates how this change of the size of a shape is achieved. Two sets of balanced short-row wedges are indicated by the two bold zigzag lines. The two wedge-shaped areas covered by the zigzag lines represent the extra depth that is added to only the middle area and the outer area on one side of the full width of the fabric for each short-row section. The larger shapes are formed where the most rows have been added.

The circle shapes of the knitted swatch shown in Figure 276 are all worked in the same way, by using four-stitch cables. It is the addition of short-row wedges that changes the size of selected shapes. There are two sections of short rows within the swatch. The first section of short rows, short-rows section 1 (SRS1), is worked within a right-side row. This wedge elongates the shapes on the right-hand side of the swatch. For the second section, short-rows section 2 (SRS2), the short rows are worked

Seaside daisies with short-row wedges
(36sts and 24 rows)

Pattern notes

SRS1 is worked on row 7 (RS). Remember to work each wrap loop and its wrapped stitch together as they are reached on the following rows (*see* the feature box 'Short-row wrapped stitches' for 'w&t' instructions and further information about wrapped stitches).

Work SRS1 as follows:

SR1 (RS): K24, w&t;

SR2 (WS): Purl to the end of the row;

SR3: K12, w&t;

SR4: Purl to the end of the row;

SR5: Knit one row.

Continue in patt from row 8.

SRS2 is worked on row 18 (WS). Remember to work each wrap loop and its wrapped stitch together as they are reached on the following rows.

Work SRS2 as follows:

SR1 (WS): P24, w&t;

SR2 (RS): Knit to the end of the row;

SR3: P12, w&t;

SR4: Knit to the end of the row;

SR5: Purl one row.

Continue in patt from row 19.

Row 1 (RS): P4, (k4, p8) twice, k4, p4.

Row 2 (WS): K4, (p4, k8) twice, p4, k4.

Row 3: P2, (2/2 RC, 2/2 LC, p4) twice, 2/2 RC, 2/2 LC, p2.

Row 4: K2, (p8, k4) twice, p8, k2.

Row 5: (2/2 RC, k4, 2/2 LC) three times.

Row 6: Purl.

Row 7 (*see* pattern notes): SRS1.

Row 8 (WS): Purl.

Row 9: (2/2 LPC, k4, 2/2 RPC) three times.

Row 10: As row 4.

Row 11: P2, (2/2 LPC, 2/2 RPC, p4) twice, 2/2 LPC, 2/2 RPC, p2.

Row 12: As row 2.

Rows 13–17: As rows 1–5.

Row 18 (*see* pattern notes): SRS2.

Row 19 (RS): Knit.

Rows 20–24: As rows 8–12.

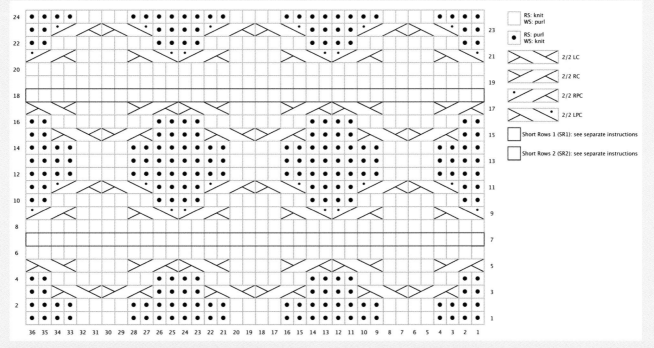

Fig. 281   Chart of seaside daisies with short-row wedges.

Short-row wrapped stitches

To avoid gaps in knitted fabric worked with short-row shaping, a stitch is 'wrapped' before the work is turned, which is usually abbreviated to 'w&t'.

Knit rows

To wrap a stitch on a knit row, knit the number of stitches stated in the pattern, to reach the location of the stitch to be wrapped.

Step 1: Bring yarn to front of work.
Step 2: Slip the next stitch purlwise from the lhn to the rhn.
Step 3: Take yarn to back of work.
Step 4: Return the slipped stitch to the lhn without working it (that is, slip it again purlwise).
Step 5: Turn the work.

Purl rows

To wrap a stitch on a purl row, purl the number of stitches stated in the pattern, to reach the location of the stitch to be wrapped, and leave the yarn at front of work.

Step 1: Slip the next stitch purlwise from the lhn to the rhn.
Step 2: Take yarn to back of work.
Step 3: Return the slipped stitch to the lhn without working it (that is, slip it again purlwise).
Step 4: Take yarn to front of work.
Step 5: Turn the work.

On the following rows, when a wrapped stitch is reached, work the wrap loop together with the stitch that it is wrapping. This closes the gap in the knitted fabric.

For a knit row, this action is shown in Figures 282 and 283.
For a purl row, this action is shown in Figures 284 and 285.

Fig. 282 Wrapped stitch on a knit row.

Fig. 283 Wrap loop and the stitch that it wrapped being knitted together.

Fig. 284 Wrapped stitch on a purl row.

Fig. 285 Wrap loop and the stitch that it wrapped being purled together.

within a wrong-side row. This second set balances the swatch by adding the same number of additional rows on the left-hand side of the knitting. Let us take a look at the short rows in detail and how the wedges change the knitted swatch.

The green stitch markers visible in Figure 277 indicate the location of the wrapped stitches within SRS1. After working the short rows, the swatch has an angled appearance, resulting from the presence of the additional rows that have been worked on the right-hand side of the fabric. The circular shapes are of different sizes, with the smallest circle being on the left-hand side and the largest on the right-hand side.

After working more rows of the swatch without short rows, the different sizes of the shapes are more obvious. The angled appearance is also more evident, as can clearly be seen in Figure 278. In some cases, an angled section of knitting is the desired result, for example, for an asymmetrical edge. However, it is possible to balance the overall appearance of the knitted fabric by working short rows on the opposite side of the swatch.

The green stitch markers visible in Figure 279 indicate the location of the wrapped stitches within the second short-row section, SRS2. The angled appearance of the swatch is no longer evident, as the swatch has now been balanced by working the same number of additional short rows on the left-hand side of the swatch as were worked for SRS1, on the right-hand side. The smallest circle formed by this set of short rows is on the right-hand side of the swatch and the largest circle on the left-hand side. The central circles remain the same size, as the same number of short rows have been worked in this part of the swatch in both of the short-row sections.

As shown in Figure 280, the wrong side of the swatch clearly shows the effect of the two balanced short-row wedges. Different sizes of circular shapes appear in both stocking stitch and reverse stocking stitch.

Short-row pops

In the inspiration image of the seaside daisies, the centre of each flower is very distinctive. Using short-row shaping over a small number of stitches in the centre of the circular shape will add depth to only this part of the knitting. By also using a contrasting shade of yarn, a three-dimensional pop of colour is formed.

The sketch shown in Figure 286 indicates the placement of the short rows inside the circular shape. In the knitted swatch shown in Figure 287, the corresponding daisy-outline shapes have been worked by using a four-stitch cable. Only the centre of each shape has short rows, which are worked in the contrasting shade of yarn (or 'CC', as indicated on the accompanying chart). These central rows are knitted in stocking stitch, with reverse stocking stitch being worked between the shapes in the main-colour yarn (or 'MC', as indicated on the accompanying chart).

Although the short rows are worked only in each shape's centre, the contrast-colour yarn has been used across the whole row. This avoids multiple loose ends of yarn being present on the wrong side of the stitch pattern. To maintain the shape and colour of the cables, two stitches are slipped on the rows that are worked in the contrasting shade of yarn. The use of slipped stitches also helps to create a three-dimensional effect in the centre of the daisy shapes, as fewer rows are worked on each shape's sides. The image shown in Figure 288 is of the wrong side of the swatch fabric, with the concave centres of each pop contrasting with the flatter areas between the shapes.

Fig. 286 Sketch of short-row placement for seaside-daisies stitch pattern.

Fig. 287 Knitted swatch of seaside daisies with short-row pops (yarn: pure wool, DK weight; needles: 4mm; total stitches: 24, comprising two 12-stitch repeats; total rows: 24, comprising two 12-row repeats, not including short rows).

Fig. 288 Reverse side of knitted swatch of seaside daisies with short-row pops.

Seaside daisies with short-row pops
(12sts and 12 rows)

Pattern notes

A contrasting shade of yarn is used for the short rows, and this is indicated by the light-grey squares on the chart. Although the short rows are worked on one row, an additional row is worked in the contrasting shade so that the yarn can be carried up one side of the knitting only.

Short rows (SR1–7) are all worked on row 6 (WS). Remember to work each wrap loop and its wrapped stitch together as they are reached on the following rows.
Work SR1–7 as follows:
SR1 (WS): P6, w&t;
SR2 (RS): K4, w&t;
SR3: P5, w&t;
SR4: K6, w&t;
SR5: P5, w&t;
SR6: K4, w&t;
SR7: P6, continue in patt from row 7.

Row 1 (RS): Using MC, p4, sl4, p4.
Row 2 (WS): K4, p4, k4.
Row 3: P2, 2/2 RC, 2/2 LC, p2.
Row 4: K2, p8, k2.
Row 5: 2/2 RC, k4, 2/2 LC.

Row 6 (see pattern notes): Using CC, sl2 wyif, SR, sl2 wyif.
Row 7: Sl2, k8, sl2.
Row 8: Using MC, purl.
Row 9: 2/2 LPC, k4, 2/2 RPC.
Row 10: As row 4.
Row 11: P2, 2/2 LPC, 2/2 RPC, p2.
Row 12: K4, sl4, k4.

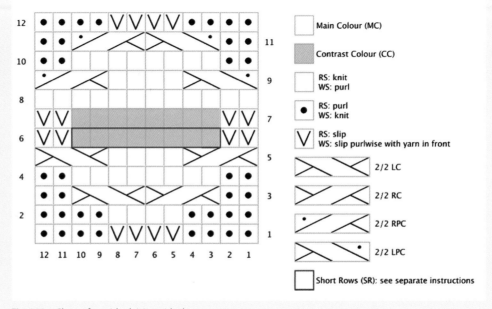

Fig. 289 Chart of seaside daisies with short-row pops.

Short-rows pattern: Yare scarf

The Yare scarf project uses short-row shaping along with combined curve techniques covered in earlier chapters to create the scarf shape and pattern. Short-row shaping is used to add depth to one side of the scarf. The twisted stitch pattern details have been inspired by a combination of a well-known textile pattern and a prominent modern building.

The intertwined floral motifs of paisley patterning are extremely well known, and the sketch shown in Figure 290 depicts aspects of this patterning. However, the origin of this instantly recognizable pattern is complex. One of the most widespread early uses for this style of pattern was on large-scale shawl designs. Throughout the nineteenth century, Norwich,

Edinburgh and Paisley were all major British centres for the production of woven and printed shawls. Each city had its own distinctive style, and the high-quality shawls were extremely sought after.

These British shawl designs were originally inspired by shawls imported from Kashmir. The distinctive designs found on the shawls have been and still are known by many different names. The terms used include 'tree of life', 'teardrop' and 'pine cone'. The shawls produced in the early nineteenth century were labour-intensive, high-quality, luxury items, owned by a few wealthy individuals. Ladies' fashions at the time were perfect to allow the showing off of the huge shawls over wide crinoline skirts.

Fig. 290 Sketch of a Norwich-, Edinburgh- and Paisley-style pattern.

Fig. 291 The seating at the Forum building, Norwich, UK.

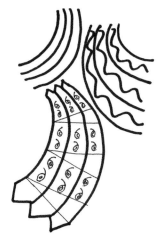

Fig. 292 Sketch of pattern development.

Fig. 293 Detail of Yare scarf.

Towards the end of the nineteenth century, innovations in technology, such as the invention of the jacquard loom and the use of large printing blocks, meant that everyone could own a shawl. These mass-market, woven and printed shawls cost much less to produce and to buy than the handmade, luxury shawls from the earlier part of the century. Fashion had also moved on to narrower dresses and skirts that did not lend themselves to displaying the shawls. The change from luxury to mass-market production meant that the Norwich and Edinburgh centres of production could not compete with Paisley. Paisley became the main centre of shawl production and gave its name to the distinctive design still recognized today.

The original designs were created for woven or printed shawls. However, the patterning is an excellent inspiration for knitting design. The intertwined pinecones inspire the use of complex twisted stitches and cables. The incredibly delicate design details encourage the use of texture and tiny pattern details. These details are explored in the Yare scarf.

The Yare-scarf design is inspired by the small-scale, intertwined pinecone motifs in the style of an original Norwich shawl, which are combined with elements inspired by the large-scale architecture of the Forum building in Norwich. The Forum building, designed by Sir Michael Hopkins of Michael Hopkins and Partners, is a prominent, modern feature of the Norwich city centre. The whole building was made by using curves, and in front of the building is distinctive, stepped seating, shown in Figure 291 and interpreted in the sketches in Figure 292. The scarf pattern is named Yare after the major river that flows through the city of Norwich.

The Yare scarf is knitted in a Rowan silk–wool mix, DK-weight yarn. The yarn offers excellent stitch definition along with the elegant sheen of silk. This combination means that the detailed twisted stitch sections stand out clearly and that the long, curved lines inspired by the Forum building look smooth and ribbon-like, as can be seen from the image shown in Figure 293. The long, smooth lines are made by using eyelets to raise a band of knitting. The yarn's steely shade of grey also reflects a characteristic of the seating at the Forum. The scarf begins and ends with three discrete knitted points, which are shown

Fig. 294 Yare scarf. (Photo: Maxine Vining)

in Figure 294. The pinecone design is worked with twisted stitches and flows from these points and changes in scale as the scarf narrows. A gentle curve is created by working more fabric on one side of the scarf. The curves are created with short rows, such that the motifs at the centre of the scarf are closer together than those at the outer edge. The width of the scarf narrows as the twisted stitch pinecone motifs change from large- to small-scale over the three sections of the scarf pattern.

Yare scarf pattern

Size
One size
- Length of inner edge: 100cm (39¼in); length of outer edge: 121cm (47¾in)
- Width after joining points: 21cm (8¼in); width before casting off edge stitches and points: 17.5cm (6¾in)

Yarn
- Rowan Baby Merino Silk DK, 34-per-cent tussah silk/66-per-cent merino superwash wool, DK weight, 135m (148yd) per 50g ball
- 3 × 50g balls in 672 Dawn

Needles and accessories
- A pair of 3.5mm (UK9 or UK10, US4) straight needles
- A pair of 4mm (UK8, US6) straight needles
- Cable needle
- Darning needle

Tension
- 31sts and 30 rows to 10cm (4in) over pinecone pattern 1 (PCP1), using 4mm needles.

Pattern notes
The pinecone twisted stitch pattern is worked as three variations, one for each of the three sections of the scarf. All twisted stitches are worked on RS rows.

Refer to written or charted instructions for each stitch pattern (PCP1–3), as preferred.

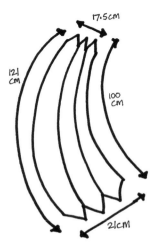

Fig. 295 Blocking diagram of Yare scarf.

Pinecone pattern 1 (PCP1) (multiple of 10sts and 40 rows)

Row 1 (RS): K4, 1/1 LC, k4.

Row 2 and every following WS row, except rows 8 and 28: Purl.

Row 3: K2, 1/2 RC, 1/2 LC, k2.

Row 5: 1/2 RC, 1/1 RC, 1/1 LC, 1/2 LC.

Row 7: Sl1, k2, ssk, yo twice, k2tog, k2, sl1.

Row 8: P4, k1, p5.

Row 9: Sl1, k2, 1/1 LC, 1/1 RC, k2, sl1.

Row 11: (1/2 LC, k1) twice, 1/1 RC.

Row 13: K2, 1/2 LC, k2, 1/1 RC, k1.

Row 15: K4, 1/2 LC, 1/1 LC, k1.

Row 17: K6, 1/2 LC, k1.

Row 19: K10.

Row 21: K4, 1/1 RC, k4.

Rows 23–30: As rows 3–10.

Row 31: 1/1 LC, (k1, 1/2 RC) twice.

Row 33: K1, 1/1 LC, k2, 1/2 RC, k2.

Row 35: K1, 1/1 RC, 1/2 RC, k4.

Row 37: K1, 1/2 RC, k6.

Row 39: K10.

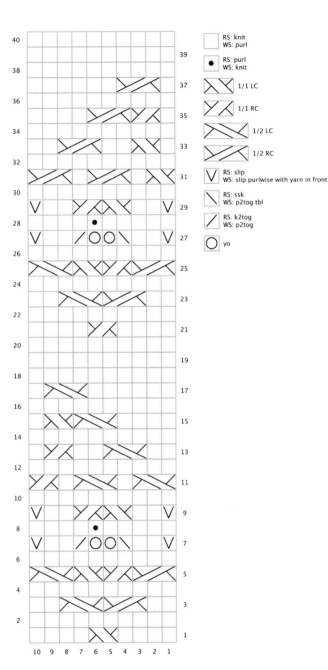

Fig. 296 Chart of pinecone pattern 1 (PCP1).

Pinecone pattern 2 (PCP2) (multiple of 8sts and 36 rows)

Row 1 (RS): K3, 1/1 LC, k3.

Row 2 and every following WS row, except rows 8 and 26: Purl.

Row 3: K1, 1/2 RC, 1/2 LC, k1.

Row 5: 1/1 RC twice, 1/1 LC twice.

Row 7: Sl1, k1, ssk, yo twice, k2tog, k1, sl1.

Row 8: P3, k1, p4.

Row 9: Sl1, k1, 1/1 LC, 1/1 RC, k1, sl1.

Row 11: 1/2 LC, 1/1 LC, 1/2 RC.

Row 13: K2, 1/2 LC, 1/1 LC, k1.

Row 15: K4, 1/2 LC, k1.

Row 17: K8.

Row 19: K3, 1/1 RC, k3.

Rows 21–28: As rows 3–10.

Row 29: 1/2 LC, 1/1 RC, 1/2 RC.

Row 31: K1, 1/1 RC, 1/2 RC, k2.

Row 33: K1, 1/2 RC, k4.

Row 35: K8.

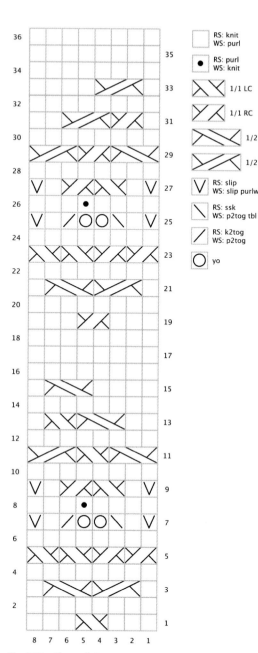

Fig. 297 Chart of pinecone pattern 2 (PCP2).

Pinecone pattern 3 (PCP3) (multiple of 6sts and 32 rows)

Row 1 (RS): K2, 1/1 LC, k2.

Row 2 and all WS rows: Purl.

Row 3: 1/2 RC, 1/2 LC.

Row 5: Sl1, 1/1 RC, 1/1 LC, sl1.

Row 7: Sl1, 1/1 LC, 1/1 RC, sl1.

Row 9: 1/1 LC twice, 1/1 RC.

Row 11: K, 1/2 LC, 1/1 LC.

Row 13: K3, 1/2 LC.

Row 15: K6.

Row 17: K2, 1/1 RC, k2.

Rows 19, 21 and 23: As rows 3, 5 and 7, respectively.

Row 25: 1/1 LC, 1/1 RC twice.

Row 27: 1/1 RC, 1/2 RC, k1.

Row 29: 1/2 RC, k3.

Row 31: K6.

Short-row shaping

The curved shape of the scarf is produced by using short-row shaping. To avoid gaps in the knitted fabric, a stitch is wrapped before the work is turned when using the short-row technique. On the following rows, when a wrapped stitch is reached, work the wrap loop together with its wrapped stitch to close the gap.

Stitches are wrapped as follows on RS rows: work the number of stitches stated in the instructions; bring the yarn to front of work (RS rows only; for WS rows, the yarn is already at front of work); slip the next stitch purlwise from the lhn to the rhn; take the yarn to back of work; return the slipped stitch to the lhn without working it; turn work; work to the end of the row.

For additional information and instructions about working short rows, see the feature box 'Short-row wrapped stitches' in the section 'Short-row wedges'.

Because of the different number of rows in the two outer sections of the scarf, resulting from the working of short rows, the rows are always counted along the inner, shortest edge.

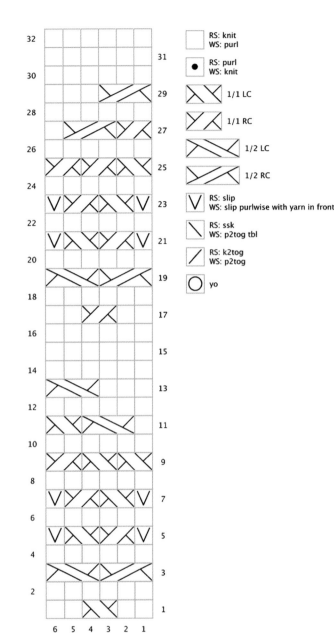

	RS: knit WS: purl
●	RS: purl WS: knit
⤬	1/1 LC
⤬	1/1 RC
⟍	1/2 LC
⟍	1/2 RC
V	RS: slip WS: slip purlwise with yarn in front
⟍	RS: ssk WS: p2tog tbl
╱	RS: k2tog WS: p2tog
O	yo

Fig. 298 Chart of pinecone pattern 3 (PCP3).

Pattern instructions

Points

Cast on 6sts by using 3.5mm needles.

Row 1 (RS): K2, p2, k2.

Row 2 (WS): P2, k2, p2.

Row 3: K2, yo, p2, yo, k2. (8sts)

Row 4: P2, k4, p2.

Row 5: K2, yo, p1, k2, p1, yo, k2. (10sts)

Row 6: P2, (k2, p2) twice.

Row 7: K2, yo, p1, k4, p1, yo, k2. (12sts)

Row 8: P2, k2, p4, k2, p2.

Row 9: K2, yo, p1, k6, p1, yo, k2. (14sts)

Row 10: P2, k2, p6, k2, p2.

Row 11: K2, yo, p1, k8, p1, yo, k2. (16sts)

Row 12: P2, k2, p8, k2, p2.

Row 13: K2, yo, p1, k10, p1, yo, k2. (18sts)

Row 14: P2, k2, p10, k2, p2.

Break the yarn. Leave the 18sts of the point on the lhn.

Work two more points as set, but do not break the yarn after working the third point.

To join the points, with the stitches of all three points on the lhn, with each point with RS facing and with the yarn to the right-hand side (closest to the point of the lhn), cast on edge stitches and work across all stitches as follows:

Row 15 (RS): Cast on 3sts at the beg of this row, then knit these 3sts, *k2, yo, p2, k10, p2, yo, k2; rep from * across the next two points. (63sts)

Row 16 (WS): Cast on 3sts at beg of this row, then purl these 3sts, *p3, k2, p10, k2, p3; rep from * to last 3sts, p3. (66sts)

Row 17: K4, *ssk, yo, p2, k10, p2, yo, k2tog, k2; rep from * to last 2sts, k2.

Scarf body

To begin working the body of the scarf, work short rows on next row as follows:

Row 18 (WS): P6, k2, p10, k2, p6, k2, p10, w&t; k10, p2, yo, k2tog, k2, ssk, yo, p2, k10, p2, yo, k2tog, k4, turn work; p6, k2, p10, w&t; k10, p2, yo, k2tog, k4, turn work; p6, *k2, p10, k2, p6; rep from * to end of row.

Change to 4mm needles, and begin first section of main pattern by using PCP1 written or charted instructions, as preferred, as follows:

Row 1 (RS): K4, *ssk, yo, p2, work row 1 of PCP1, p2, yo, k2tog, k2; rep from * to last 2sts, k2.

Row 2 (WS): P6, *k2, work row 2 of PCP1, k2, p6; rep from * to end of row.

Continue as set by last two rows, until the first nineteen rows of PCP1 have been completed.

Keeping patt correct as set by PCP1 rows 18 and 19, work short rows on next row as follows:

Row 20 (WS): Patt 38sts, w&t, patt to end of row; patt 18sts, w&t, patt to end of row; patt one full row.

Continue from row 21 of PCP1 as set, until the first thirty-nine rows of PCP1 have been completed.

Keeping patt correct as set by PCP1 rows 38 and 39, work short rows on next row as follows:

Row 40 (WS): Patt 38sts, w&t, patt to end of row; patt 18sts, w&t, patt to end of row; patt one full row.

Rep rows 1–40, including the short-row sections, once.

Begin second section of main pattern by using PCP2 written or charted instructions, as preferred, and, at the same time, decrease on next row as follows:

Row 81 (RS): K4, *ssk, yo, p2, ssk, k2, 1/1 LC, k2, k2tog, p2, yo, k2tog, k2; rep from * to last 2sts, k2. (60sts)

Row 82 (WS): P6, *k2, p8, k2, p6; rep from * to end of row.

Row 83: K4, *ssk, yo, p2, work row 3 of PCP2, p2, yo, k2tog, k2; rep from * to last 2sts, k2.

Continue from row 4 of PCP2 as set, until the first seventeen rows of PCP2 have been completed.

Keeping patt correct as set by PCP2 rows 16 and 17, work short rows on next row as follows:

Row 98 (WS): Patt 34sts, w&t, patt to end of row; patt 16sts, w&t, patt to end of row; patt one full row.

Continue from row 19 of PCP2 as set, until the first thirty-five rows of PCP2 have been completed.

Keeping patt correct as set by rows 34 and 35, work short rows on next row as follows:

Row 116 (WS): Patt 34sts, w&t, patt to end of row; patt 16sts, w&t, patt to end of row; patt one full row.

Work two more repeats of PCP2 as follows:

Row 117 (RS): K4, *ssk, yo, p2, k3, 1/1 LC, k2, k2tog, p2, yo, k3; rep from * to last 2sts, k2.

Rows 118–152: As rows 82–116 (including short-row sections).

Row 153: As row 117.

Rows 154–188: As rows 82–116 (including short-row sections).

Begin third section of main pattern by using PCP3 written or charted instructions, as preferred, and, at the same time, decrease on next row as follows:

Row 189 (RS): K4, *ssk, yo, p2, ssk, k1, 1/1 LC, k1, k2tog, p2, yo, k2tog, k2; rep from * to last 2sts, k2. (54sts)

Row 190 (WS): P6, *k2, p6; rep from * to end of row.

Row 191: K4, *ssk, yo, p2, work row 3 of PCP3, p2, yo, k2tog, k2; rep from * to last 2sts, k2.

Continue from row 4 of PCP3 as set, until the first fifteen rows of PCP3 have been completed.

Keeping patt correct as set by PCP3 rows 14 and 15, work short rows on next row as follows:

Row 204 (WS): Patt 30sts, w&t, patt to end of row; patt 14sts, w&t, patt to end of row; patt one full row.

Continue from row 17 of PCP3 as set, until the first thirty-one rows of PCP3 have been completed.

Keeping patt correct as set by PCP3 rows 30 and 31, work short rows on next row as follows:

Row 220 (WS): Patt 30sts, w&t, patt to end of row; patt 14sts, w&t, patt to end of row; patt one full row.

Work one more repeat of PCP3 as follows:

Row 221 (RS): K4, *ssk, yo, p2, k2, 1/1 LC, k2, p2, yo, k2tog, k2; rep from * to last 2sts, k2.

Rows 222–252: As rows 190–220 (including short-row sections).

Work the first sixteen rows of PCP2 as follows:

Row 253: As row 221.

Rows 254–268: As rows 190–204 (including short-row section).

Change to 3.5mm needles, and begin shaping the end of the scarf.

Next row: Cast off 3sts at beg of row, k1 *ssk, yo, p2, k6, p2, yo, k2tog, k2; rep from * to last 2sts, k2. (51sts)

Next row: Cast off 3sts at beg of row, p3 *k2, p6; rep from * to last 5sts, k2, p3. (48sts)

Points

Work three points separately as follows:

    ***

Row 1 (RS): K1, ssk, yo, p2, ssk, k2, k2tog, p2, yo, k2tog, k1, turn work. (14sts)

Leaving any rem stitches on lhn, and work on the 14sts as follows:

Row 2 (WS): P3, k2, p4, k2, p3.

Row 3: K1, ssk, yo, p2, ssk, k2tog, p2, yo, k2tog, k1. (12sts)

Row 4: P3, k2, p2, k2, p3.

Row 5: K1, ssk, yo, p1, p2tog twice, p1, yo, k2tog, k1. (10sts)

Row 6: P3, k4, p3.

Row 7: K1, ssk, yo, p2tog twice, yo, k2tog, k1. (8sts)

Row 8: P3, k2, p3.

Row 9: K1, ssk, p2tog, k2tog, k1. (5sts)

Row 10: P2, k1, p2.

Row 11: K1, sl1, k2tog, psso, k1. (3sts)

    Cast off purlwise.

Rejoin yarn to rem stitches on lhn, and rep from *** to complete second and then third points.

Block the work gently to the measurements given in Figure 295 and according to the yarn's ball-band instructions.

    Sew in all loose ends.

CHAPTER 13

LAYERS

Adding detail to a twist or cable design in separate layers is a great way of increasing the complexity of a stitch pattern. The layers in the following examples are shown in contrasting colours and as wrong-side stitch patterns. The colours and stitch placements are all inspired by tulip buds and flowers in my garden and the Guildford Castle grounds.

Tulip is the common name for the Tulipa bulbous perennials. These beautiful flowers usually bloom between March and May and are one of the best indicators that the season of spring has arrived. According to the Royal Horticultural Society, there are fifteen different types of tulip flower. The descriptions of the flowers include single or double, cup, bowl or goblet, fringed, parrot or lily, long, slender and star-shaped.

These descriptions provide a starting point for the design of a wide variety of knitted shapes that explore the wide range of tulip flowers, such as those shown in Figures 299 and 300. As well as of shapes, these flowers have a wide variety of colours and characteristics that can be reflected in a knitted design. Elements such as the fringed edges of the petals, the varying amounts of multiple colours and the points of the petals provide excellent inspiration.

For the following examples of layering, it is the goblet shape of a single tulip flower at an early stage of opening that is used to illustrate the addition of colour layers. The fringed petals of

Fig. 299 Tulip flower in the grounds of Guildford Castle.

Fig. 300 Parrot-tulip flower in my garden.

a parrot tulip are used as a design basis to demonstrate the addition of wrong-side cable layers.

Beginning with an outline-shape design, the layers of colour and cables are added to represent the distinctive petals of these beautiful flowers. Combinations of three- and four-stitch cables form the outline shape of the tulip. The first two examples look at the process of layering with colour, either during or after knitting. The project for this chapter features a layer of cables to the wrong side of the knitting, to enhance and extend the outline shapes.

Adding colour during knitting

In this example, colour is added during knitting by a combination of stranded-knitting and intarsia techniques. Stranded knitting is the technique of working with two shades of yarn within the same row. The shade not in use is loosely stranded across the back of the work while the other shade is being used to knit with. Intarsia is the technique of using a second shade of yarn in only specific areas of the knitting.

These two techniques have been combined in the tulip knitted swatch shown in Figure 301. The additional, contrasting shade is used only within the cabled tulip shapes. This means that, instead of having a single layer of knitting, there is a double layer, drawing attention to the flower shape and enhancing the design.

In the swatch, all of the tulip shapes are knitted by using the same set of cables on a reverse stocking stitch background. Each of the three tulip shapes shows a different way to add colour during knitting. Before beginning the knitting of this swatch, separate lengths of the contrasting shade of yarn were wound into mini balls. Each shape uses one mini ball. The main-colour yarn is stranded across the back of the work while the contrast-colour yarn is being used. It is important to ensure that the strands are loose enough to allow the knitted fabric to lie flat, by not pulling the strands too tightly across the back of the tulip shape. If you are working a larger shape and

Fig. 301 Knitted swatch of tulip shapes with colourwork layers that were added during knitting (yarn: pure wool, DK weight; needles: 4mm; total stitches: 26; total rows: 58).

Tulip buds with colourwork layers
(26sts and 58 rows)

Note: Use short lengths of the contrast-colour yarn (CC) for each area indicated. Strand the main-colour yarn (MC) loosely across the back of the work to create the double layer.

Use MC throughout, unless CC is indicated to be used.

Row 1 (RS): K1, (2/2 RC, p6) twice, 2/2 LC, k1.
Row 2 (WS): P5, k6, p4, k6, p5.
Row 3: K5, p4, 2/2 RC, 2/2 LC, p4, k5.
Row 4: P5, k4, p2, p4 in CC, p2, k4, p5.
Row 5: K1, 2/2 RC, p2, 2/2 RC, k4 in CC, 2/2 LC, p2, 2/2 LC, k1.
Row 6: P5, k2, p2, p8 in CC, p2, k2, p5.
Row 7: K5, p2, k2, k8 in CC, k2, p2, k5.
Row 8: As row 6.
Row 9: K1, 2/2 RC, p2, k2, k8 in CC, k2, p2, 2/2 LC, k1.
Row 10: P5, k2, p3, p6 in CC, p3, k2, p5.
Row 11: K5, p2, 2/1 LPC, k6 in CC, 2/1 RPC, p2, k5.
Row 12: P5, k3, p3, p4 in CC, p3, k3, p5.
Row 13: K1, 2/2 RC, p3, 2/1 LPC, k4 in CC, 2/1 RPC, p3, 2/2 LC, k1.
Row 14: P5, k4, p2, p4, p2, k4, p5.
Row 15: K5, p4, 2/2 LPC, 2/2 RPC, p4, k5.
Row 16: As row 2.
Rows 17–18: As rows 1–2.
Row 19: K5, p6, k4, p6, k5.
Row 20: As row 2.
Rows 21–23: As rows 1–3.
Row 24: P5, k4, p2, k4 in CC, p2, k4, p5.
Row 25: K1, 2/2 RC, p2, 2/2 RC, (p1, k1) twice in CC, 2/2 LC, p2, 2/2 LC, k1.
Row 26: P5, k2, p2, (k1, p1) four times in CC, p2, k2, p5.
Row 27: K5, p2, k2, (p1, k1) four times in CC, k2, p2, k5.
Row 28: As row 26.
Row 29: K1, 2/2 RC, p2, k2, (p1, k1) four times in CC, k2, p2, 2/2 LC, k1.
Row 30: P5, k2, p3, (p1, k1) three times in CC, p3, k2, p5.
Row 31: K5, p2, 2/1 LPC, (k1, p1) three times in CC, 2/1 RPC, p2, k5.
Row 32: P5, k3, p3, (k1, p1) twice in CC, p3, k3, p5.
Row 33: K1, 2/2 RC, p3, 2/1 LPC, (p1, k1) twice in CC, 2/1 RPC, p3, 2/2 LC, k1.
Rows 34–43: As rows 14–23.
Row 44: P5, k4, p3, p1 in CC, p1, p1 in CC, p2, k4, p5.
Row 45: K1, 2/2 RC, p2, 2/2 RC, (k1, k1 in CC) twice, 2/2 LC, p2, 2/2 LC, k1.
Row 46: P5, k2, p3, (p1 in CC, p1) four times, p1, k2, p5.

Row 47: K5, p2, k3, (k1 in CC, k1) four times in CC, k1, p2, k5.

Row 48: As row 46.

Row 49: K1, 2/2 RC, p2, k3, (k1 in CC, k1) four times, k1, p2, 2/2 LC, k1.

Row 50: P5, k2, p3, (p1 in CC, p1) three times, p3, k2, p5.

Row 51: K5, p2, 2/1 LPC, (k1 in CC, k1) three times, 2/1 RPC, p2, k5.

Row 52: P5, k3, p4, (p1 in CC, p1) twice, p3, k3, p5.

Row 53: K1, 2/2 RC, p3, 2/1 LPC, (k1, k1 in CC) twice, 2/1 RPC, p3, 2/2 LC, k1.

Rows 54–58: As rows 14–18.

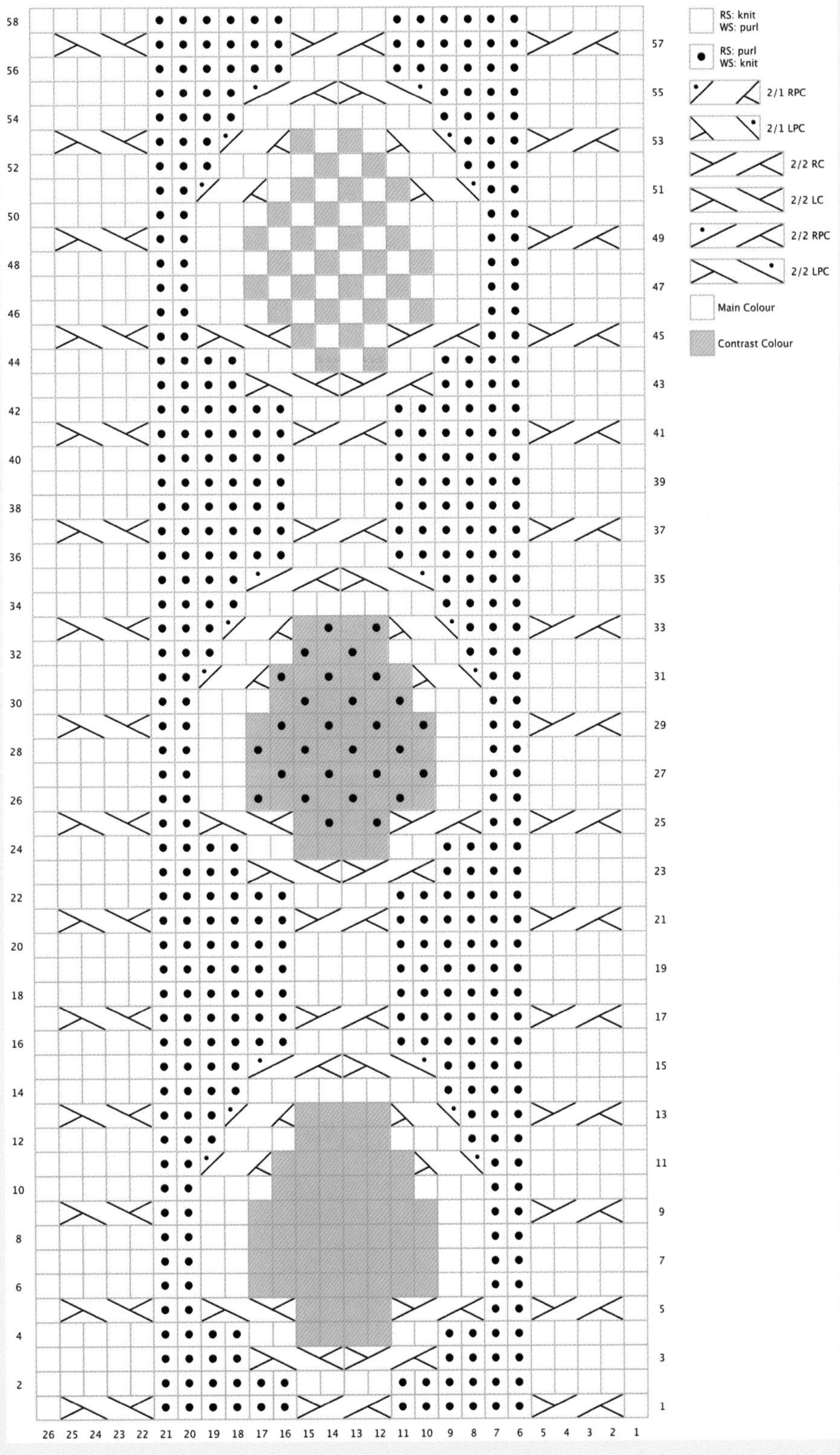

Fig. 302 Chart of tulip buds with colourwork layers.

Legend:
- RS: knit / WS: purl
- • RS: purl / WS: knit
- 2/1 RPC
- 2/1 LPC
- 2/2 RC
- 2/2 LC
- 2/2 RPC
- 2/2 LPC
- Main Colour
- Contrast Colour

the strands would be too long if they were to stretch from one side of the shape to the other, across the back of the work, you should catch each strand by every so often twisting the main-colour yarn and the contrast-colour yarn once around each other at the back of the work.

The first tulip shape, at the bottom of the swatch, is an example of stocking stitch, stranded intarsia. The contrasting shade has been worked in stocking stitch only. The same stranded-intarsia technique can also be used to produce a textured pattern. The second tulip shape, in the centre of the swatch, has a moss-stitch pattern instead of a stocking stitch pattern. The third tulip shape, at the top of the swatch, is an example of stranded knitting being worked to produce a two-colour pattern. By knitting one stitch alternately with each yarn shade horizontally across the part of the row within the tulip shape and vertically over the parts of subsequent rows within the shape, a checked pattern is formed.

Fig. 303 Front of shape knitted in a contrast-colour yarn by using stranded intarsia.

Fig. 304 Back of shape knitted in a contrast-colour yarn by using stranded intarsia.

Fig. 305 Start of knitting a shape in a contrast-colour yarn, on the wrong side of the fabric.

Fig. 306 Start of knitting a shape in a contrast-colour yarn, on the right side of the fabric.

In all three examples, the double layer of yarn that occurs within each tulip shape adds to the depth of the shape. These areas of the knitting will be thicker than the areas with one layer of main-colour yarn. In a larger design, these areas should be balanced so that there is an overall even tension to the knitted fabric.

How to add colour during knitting by using a combination of intarsia and stranded knitting (stranded intarsia)

To add colour during knitting by using stranded intarsia, work with a separate length of yarn of a contrast colour to fill in the centre of a knitted shape, as is shown in Figure 303. For textural contrast, place the shape outline on a reverse stocking stitch background. When working with the contrast-colour yarn, strand the main-colour yarn across the back of the work, as is visible in Figure 304. This technique adds a layer of colour to specific areas and forms a double layer of fabric, resulting in a three-dimensional effect. In the row below a stitch movement, make sure that the stitch that will be moved at the back of the work is knitted in the same colour of yarn as the cable outline. This will ensure that the contrast-colour yarn does not show through at the outer edges of the shape.

Work to the contrast-colour area as given in the pattern. Using a separate length of contrast-colour yarn, work the number of stitches stated, stranding the main-colour yarn across the back of the work, as shown in Figures 303–306. Continue working in main-colour yarn only. Where the yarn colour being used changes, twist the yarns around each other to close the gap that would otherwise occur between the adjacent stitches worked with the different yarn colours. Continue as given in the pattern. Sew in the loose yarn ends after blocking.

Adding colour after knitting

A layer of colour can be added to a completed knitted swatch by using a decorative weave-darning technique. This technique allows the centre of a knitted shape to be filled with a contrast-colour yarn, to create a dramatic feature. Weave darning is where a tapestry or darning needle is used to set up a base framework of wide, horizontal strands across the area to be worked over. The needle is then used to weave the yarn vertically up and down the ladder of wide strands, moving above and below alternate rungs. The result is a woven patch.

Fig. 307 Knitted swatch before darning, showing tulip-bud-inspired shapes.

Fig. 308 Knitted swatch with colour added by using the weave-darning technique.

By using one or two additional shades of yarn, a variety of different effects can be achieved.

The biggest advantage of adding colour after the knitting has been worked is that it allows the precise placement of the additional colour layer to be decided after knitting of the whole project is completed. Additionally, an asymmetrical layout can be achieved, as not all of the shapes have to be darned. Adding colour in this way creates an additional layer on the knitted fabric, requiring its balanced placement for an overall even tension.

In the following example, the surround and centres of the shapes have been worked in reverse stocking stitch to provide a strong contrast to the shapes' outlines. The pattern repeat for the tulip-bud shape has been worked twice over forty rows, creating two complete bud shapes. Blocking the knitting before weave darning is important, as this helps the stitches to lie evenly, which in turn helps when setting up the base ladder of contrast-colour strands. A separate length of yarn in the contrasting shade is used for each area of darning.

Tulip-bud shape
(26sts and 20 rows)

Row 1 (RS): K1, (2/2 RC, p6) twice, 2/2 LC, k1.

Row 2 (WS): P5, k6, p4, k6, p5.

Row 3: K5, p4, 2/2 RPC, 2/2 LPC, p4, k5.

Row 4: P5, (k4, p2) twice, k4, p5.

Row 5: K1, 2/2 RC, p2, 2/2 RPC, p4, 2/2 LPC, p2, 2/2 LC, k1.

Row 6: P5, k2, p2, k8, p2, k2, p5.

Row 7: K5, p2, k2, p8, k2, p2, k5.

Row 8: As row 6.

Row 9: K1, 2/2 RC, p2, k2, p8, k2, p2, 2/2 LC, k1.

Row 10: As row 6.

Row 11: K5, p2, 2/1 LPC, p6, 2/1 RPC, p2, k5.

Row 12: P5, k3, p2, k6, p2, k3, p5.

Row 13: K1, 2/2 RC, p3, 2/1 LPC, p4, 2/1 RPC, p3, 2/2 LC, k1.

Row 14: As row 4.

Row 15: K5, p4, 2/2 LPC, 2/2 RPC, p4, k5.

Row 16: As row 2.

Rows 17–18: As rows 1–2.

Row 19: K5, p6, k4, p6, k5.

Row 20: As row 2.

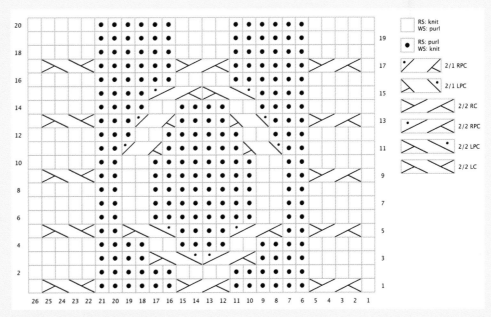

Fig. 309 Chart of tulip-bud shape.

How to add colour after knitting by using weave darning

Begin by threading a tapestry needle with the contrast-colour yarn, and secure one end of the yarn on the wrong side of the shape to be darned.

Step 1 (Figure 310): Bring the needle through the knitted fabric to the right side of the work so that the yarn emerges within the outlined shape, near the bottom of the shape and close to its outline.

Fig. 310 Weave-darning step 1.

Step 2 (Figure 311): Within the outlined shape, pass the needle under a loop of one knitted stitch at one side of the shape, and, keeping the tension of the knitted fabric even, pass the needle under a second loop of one knitted stitch on the opposite side of the shape. Gently pull on the yarn until a straight strand of yarn runs between these two loops, without excess yarn being present in the strand and without puckering the underlying fabric.

Fig. 311 Weave-darning step 2.

Fig. 312 Weave-darning step 3.

Step 3 (Figure 312): Close to and slightly above the last loop that the needle was passed under, again pass the needle under a loop of one knitted stitch on the side of the shape and then pass the needle under a second loop of one knitted stitch on the opposite side of the shape. Continue working back and forth from side to side, by passing the needle under loops of knitted stitches on opposite sides of the shape, as established, until there is a ladder of parallel, horizontal strands of yarn filling the outlined shape, from the bottom to the top of the shape.

Step 4 (Figure 313): Beginning at one side of the shape, from the top to the bottom of the ladder, weave the needle and yarn alternately under then over the strands of the ladder, filling the outlined shape, including filling in the sides of the shape as needed.

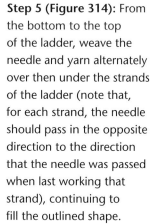

Fig. 313 Weave-darning step 4.

Step 5 (Figure 314): From the bottom to the top of the ladder, weave the needle and yarn alternately over then under the strands of the ladder (note that, for each strand, the needle should pass in the opposite direction to the direction that the needle was passed when last working that strand), continuing to fill the outlined shape.

Fig. 314 Weave-darning step 5.

Continue to weave up and down the ladder, until the shape is filled, keeping the vertical, woven lines close together.

Fasten off the yarn on the back of the work.

Fig. 315 Knitted swatch on which a weave-darning diagonal ladder is being worked.

Fig. 316 Knitted swatch on which a second yarn colour is being added to the weave-darning diagonal ladder.

Variations of the decorative weave-darning technique include setting up the ladder base at an angle and using two shades of contrast yarn. In step 1, bring the needle through to the right side of the fabric on one side of the shape, within its outline, near the top of the shape, and make the ladder diagonally across the shape (Figure 315). When the ladder is complete, fasten off, and then complete the weaving by working steps 4–5 in a third shade of yarn (Figure 316).

Layers pattern: tulip-bud scarf, with wrong-side cable layers

Parrot tulips have distinctive feathered edges along the petals of the flower heads. As the tulip bud opens, the feathered edges unfurl and the large petals expand to create a dramatic flower head. The image shown in Figure 317 and the corresponding sketches shown in Figure 318 are of tightly folded buds, where the petals are just beginning to unfurl. The feathered edges seem to peel away from the centre before it opens up into the flower head.

This scarf design is inspired by the different stages of bud opening. A series of cable stitch movements are used to make bud shapes on both the right and wrong sides of the knitting. Each bud has a patterned centre that represents the feathered edges of the petals. The cables are used for different effects on each side of the scarf, creating two complementary designs that have the same inspiration source.

In the majority of knitting patterns, the stitch movements are all worked on the right side of the knitting. As a consequence of these stitch movements, a pattern will emerge on the wrong side. For example, the concrete-scarf project of Chapter 11 has a stitch pattern for which all of the cables were worked on the right side of the work. Moss stitch and reverse stocking stitch provide textural elements to this design on both the front and reverse side of the scarf. Although the deliberate choice of stitch movements gave rise to this pattern, all of the stitch movements that are required to create the pattern are worked on the right side of the scarf. In the tulip-bud scarf, the cable pattern is worked on both sides of the scarf. Each part of the pattern therefore impacts the other, as the background stitch movements become as important as the foreground stitch movements. Carefully planned stitch movements create additional lines and textures to enhance the design. In this case, the feathered look of the petals on the right side is made by using a three-stitch cable. The single background stitch that is moved behind the two foreground stitches creates the effect, on

Fig. 317   Parrot-tulip bud, with feathered-edge petals.

Fig. 318   Sketch of parrot-tulip buds, with feathered-edge petals.

the other side of the knitting, that is reminiscent of the delicate, feathered petal edges. At the same time, these cables move the bud outlines into place on the reverse side of the work. It is the interaction between both parts of the pattern that sets the two-sided design as a whole. Figures 319 and 320 show both sides of the work. Together they add depth and complexity that would not otherwise be present.

Fig. 319 Detail of the tulip-bud scarf, with the right-side pattern shown in dark pink and the wrong-side pattern in light pink.

Fig. 320 Detail of the tulip-bud scarf, with the right-side pattern shown in light pink and the wrong-side pattern in dark pink.

Knitting a two-sided cable design can initially look complex, but, once the pattern is established and the bud patterns emerge on both sides, the stitch and row repeats become clear. The wrong-side cables are all combinations of three-stitch cables worked in stocking stitch. The right-side pattern has a combination of three- and four-stitch cables.

The yarn shades chosen for this project are also inspired by the beautiful colours found on tulip buds. As can be seen from Figures 321 and 322, using three tonally related shades of pink over the full length of the scarf changes the prominence of the design within each section. The pure-wool, DK-weight yarn shows the stitch structure perfectly on both sides of the scarf, allowing the delicate details to show through within the buds.

Tulip-bud scarf pattern, with wrong-side cable layers

Size

One size

- 18cm (7in) wide × 172cm (68in) long

Yarn

- John Arbon Textiles Knit By Numbers DK, 100-percent pure Falklands merino wool, 250m (273yd) per 100g skein
- 1 × 100g skein in KBN64 Dark Pink (shade A)
- 1 × 100g skein in KBN67 Light Pink (shade B)
- 1 × 100g skein in KBN66 Medium Pink (shade C)

Fig. 321   Tulip-bud scarf. (Photo: Maxine Vining)

Fig. 322   Tulip-bud-scarf stitch-pattern and colour detail.

Needles and accessories

- A pair of 3.5mm (UK9 or UK10, US4) straight needles
- A pair of 4mm (UK8, US6) straight needles
- Cable needle
- Darning needle

Tension

- 36sts and 29 rows to 10cm (4in) over bud pattern (BP), using 4mm needles

Pattern notes

Cables are worked on both the right side and the wrong side of the work.

The buds are worked in a repeating sequence in two sections over thirty-two rows, by using bud pattern (BP) throughout but changing its placement.

Refer to BP written or charted instructions, as preferred.

Fig. 323   Blocking diagram of tulip-bud scarf (not to scale).

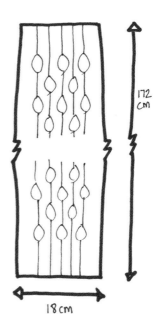

172 cm

18cm

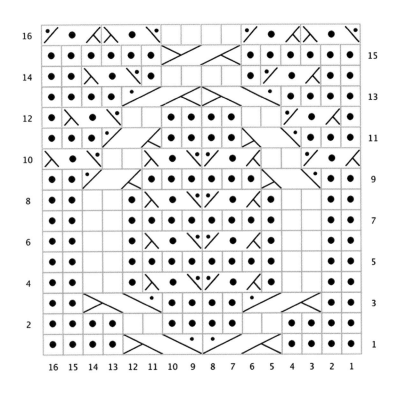

Fig. 324 Chart of bud pattern (BP): note the WS cables.

☐	RS: knit / WS: purl
●	RS: purl / WS: knit
⟋	2/1 RPC
⟍	2/1 LPC
	2/2 RC
	2/2 RPC
	2/2 LPC
	WS: 2/1 RC
	WS: 2/1 LC

Bud pattern (BP) (multiple of 16sts and 16 rows): note the WS cables

Row 1 (RS): P4, 2/2 RPC, 2/2 LPC, p4.

Row 2 (WS): (K4, p2) twice, k4.

Row 3: P2, 2/2 RPC, p4, 2/2 LPC, p2.

Row 4: K2, p2, k1, 2/1 LC, 2/1 RC, k1, p2, k2.

Row 5: P2, k2, p8, k2, p2.

Rows 6–7: As rows 4–5.

Row 8: As row 4.

Row 9: P2, 2/1 LPC, p6, 2/1 RPC, p2.

Row 10: 2/1 LC, p2, 2/1 LC, 2/1 RC, p2, 2/1 RC.

Row 11: P3, 2/1 LPC, p4, 2/1 RPC, p3.

Row 12: K1, 2/1 LC, p2, k4, p2, 2/1 RC, k1.

Row 13: P4, 2/2 LPC, 2/2 RPC, p4.

Row 14: K2, 2/1 LC, k1, p4, k1, 2/1 RC, k2.

Row 15: P6, 2/2 RC, p6.

Row 16: 2/1 RC, 2/1 LC, p4, 2/1 RC, 2/1 LC.

Pattern instructions

Cast on 66sts by using shade A and 3.5mm needles.

Edge row 1 (RS): K5, *p6, k4; rep from * to last st, k1.

Edge row 2 (WS): P5, *k6, p4; rep from * to last st, p1.

Edge row 3: K1, *2/2 RC, p6; rep from * to last 5sts, 2/2 LC, k1.

Edge row 4: P5, *2/1 RC, 2/1 LC, p4; rep from * to last st, p1.

These four edge rows set the placement of the two-sided cable pattern.

Rep edge rows 1–4 four times.

Change to 4mm needles, and begin main pattern by using BP, as follows:

Row 1 (RS): K5, *work BP row 1, k4; rep from * to last st, k1.

Row 2 (WS): P5, *work BP row 2, p4; rep from * to last st, p1.

Row 3: K1, *2/2 RC, work BP row 3; rep from * to last 5sts, 2/2 LC, k1.

Row 4: P5, *work BP row 4, p4; rep from * to last st, p1.

These four rows set the pattern placement for the first bud section.

Rows 5–16: Keeping four-row cable-column patt correct, continue as set, from BP row 5, working all sixteen rows of BP once.

Row 17: K5, p6, k4, *work BP row 1, k4; rep from * to last 11sts, p6, k5.

Row 18: P5, k6, p4, *work BP row 2, p4; rep from * to last 11sts, k6, p5.

Row 19: K1, 2/2 RC, p6, 2/2 RC, *work BP row 3, 2/2 RC; rep from * to last 11sts, p6, 2/2 LC. k1.

Row 20: P5, 2/1 RC, 2/1 LC, p4, *work BP row 4, p4; rep from * to last 11sts, 2/1 RC, 2/1 LC, p5.

These four rows set the pattern placement for the second bud section.

Rows 21–32: Keeping four-row cable-column patt correct, continue as set, from BP row 5, working all sixteen rows of BP once.

Rep rows 1–32 four times.

Change to shade B, and work rows 1–32 four times, then rep rows 1–16 once.

Change to shade C, and work rows 17–32.

Rep rows 1–32 four times, then rep rows 1–16 once.

Change to 3.5mm needles.

Work edge rows 1–4 four times, then rep edge row 1 once.

Cast off in patt with WS facing.

Block the work gently to the measurements given in Figure 323 and according to the yarn's ball-band instructions.

Sew in all loose ends.

Glossary of Terms

Cable: A stitch movement usually involving three or more stitches in total, where the foreground stitches are two or more in number.

Offset: A set of stitch movements that are worked over multiple rows, in which the stitch movement(s) of one row are out of line with the stitch movement(s) of a previous rows or rows.

Openwork: A term used to describe decorative holes, piercings or gaps within a variety of materials, and it is often used in references to architecture, metalwork and woven textiles. In this book, openwork refers to knitted stitch patterns that contain eyelets.

Mirror image: A paired sets of two or more stitch movements and/or stitch patterns that are worked in the opposite direction to each other.

Row repeat: The group of rows that form a repeating pattern when worked more than once.

Stitch movements: Groups of stitches that are knitted in a twist or cable pattern, by moving a foreground stitch or stitches over a background stitch or stitches.

Stitch repeat: The group of stitches that form a repeating pattern when worked more than once.

Swatch: A knitted sample showing a stitch pattern.

Twist: A stitch movement usually involving two or more stitches in total, where the foreground stitch is a single stitch.

Abbreviations

General knitting abbreviations

alt: alternate

approx: approximately

beg: beginning

CC: contrast-colour yarn

cn: cable needle

cont: continue

dec: decrease

DK: double-knit (yarn weight)

dpn: double-pointed needle

foll: following

g: gram(s)

in: inch(es)

inc: increase

k: knit

k2tog: knit the next two stitches together

k3tog: knit the next three stitches together

lhn: left-hand needle

m1: make one stitch knitwise. By moving the lhn point from the front of the work to the back, pick up the strand of yarn running between the stitch closest to the lhn point and the stitch that was just worked (that is, the stitch below the stitch that is closest to the rhn point). With the rhn point, knit into the back of the picked-up loop, making one new stitch and twisting the strand of yarn that ran between the two stitches.

m1p: make one stitch purlwise. By moving the lhn point from the back of the work to the front, pick up the strand of yarn running between the stitch closest to the lhn point and the stitch that was just worked (that is, the stitch below the stitch that is closest to the rhn point). With the rhn point, purl into the front of the picked-up loop, making one new stitch and twisting the strand of yarn that ran between the stitches.

MC: main-colour yarn

mrk: stitch marker

no.: number

p: purl

p2tog: purl the next two stitches together

p2togtbl: purl the next two stitches together through the back of the loops

p3tog: purl the next three stitches together

patt: pattern

pm: place stitch marker

psso: pass the slipped stitch over

rem: remaining

rep: repeat(s)

rev st st: reverse stocking stitch

rhn: right-hand needle

RS: right side of work

sk2po: slip one stitch knitwise, knit two stitches together, pass the slipped stitch over

sl: slip

slm: slip stitch marker

ssk: slip two stitches knitwise one at a time, knit the two slipped stitches together through the back of the loops

st(s): stitch(es)

st st: stocking stitch

tbl: through the back of the loop(s)

tog: together

WS: wrong side of work

wyif: with the yarn in front (that is, with the yarn held towards the knitter)

w&t: wrap and turn (*see* the feature box 'Short-row wrapped stitches' in Chapter 12 for a full description of this technique)

yb: yarn back

yf: yarn forward

yo: yarn over needle, to make a new stitch

yo twice: yarn over needle twice, to make two new stitches. The two resulting loops are worked as k1, p1 on the following row.

Chart abbreviations

General Chart Abbreviations

Symbol	Abbreviation	Description
	k	knit on RS; purl on WS
●	p	purl on RS; knit on WS
/	k2tog	knit the next two stitches together
⋏	k3tog	knit the next three stitches together
ᴆ	m1	make one stitch by picking up and twisting the loop between the stitches, then knitting into the back of this loop
ᴆ	m1p	make one stitch by picking up and twisting the loop between the stitches, then purling into the front of this loop
⑪	mb	make bobble by knitting into the next stitch as specified in the pattern
⋅/	p2tog	purl the next two stitches together
⋅\	p2togtbl	purl the next two stitches together through back of loops
⋋	p3tog	purl the next three stitches together
∨	sl	slip
\	ssk	slip two stitches knitwise one at a time, knit the two slipped stitches together through the back of the loops
∧	sk2po	slip one stitch knitwise, knit two stitches together, pass slipped stitch over
⊢	wrap	wrap the number of stitches shown in the chart as follows: insert rhn through gap between stitches to be wrapped and following stitch; pull a loop of yarn through the gap from back of work to front; place loop onto lhn; knit loop and next stitch together.
○	yo	yarn over needle to make a new stitch
∘∘	yo twice	yarn over needle twice to make two new stitches. These loops are worked as k1, p1 on the following row.

Fig. 325 Table of general chart abbreviations.

Twists and Cables: Symbols and Abbreviations

Abbreviations of two-stitch movements

All of the twist stitch movements shown in Figure 326 involve a total of two stitches, with one foreground stitch being moved over one background stitch.

Symbol	Abbreviation	Also known as	Description
 ⟩⟨	1/1 RC	C2B; C2R; T2R	knit into front of 2nd stitch on needle, then into front of 1st stitch.
 ⟩⟨	1/1 LC	C2F; C2B; T2L	knit into back of 2nd stitch on needle, then into front of 1st stitch.
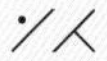 ⟩⟨	1/1 RPC	T2B; T2R	slip nxt st onto cn and hold at back of work, k1, p1 from cn.
 ⟩⟨	1/1 LPC	T2F; T2L	slip nxt st onto cn and hold at front of work, p1, k1 from cn.

Fig. 326 Table of abbreviations of two-stitch movements.

Abbreviations of three-stitch movements

All of the stitch movements shown in Figure 327 involve a total of three stitches, with one or two foreground stitch(es) being moved over two or one background stitch(es), respectively.

Symbol	Abbreviation	Also known as	Description
	1/1/1 RC		sl nxt 2sts onto cn and hold at back of work, k1, sl left-most stitch from cable needle to lhn, move cable needle with rem stitch to front of work, k1 from lhn, then k1 from cn.
			Alternatively, working without a cable needle: K into the front of the third stitch on the lhn; k into the back of the second stitch on the lhn; k into the front of the first stitch on the lhn; carefully slip the loops off the lhn.
	1/2 RC	C3B	sl nxt 2sts onto cn and hold at back of work, k1, k2 from cn.
			Alternatively, working without a cable needle: knit into the front of the third stitch on the lhn, then into the front of the first st on the lhn, then into the front of the second stitch on the lhn; slip the three stitches off the lhn.
	1/2 LC	C3F	sl nxt st onto cn and hold at front of work, k2, k1 from cn.
			Alternatively, working without a cable needle: knit into the back of the second stitch on the lhn, then into the back of the third st on the lhn; knit into the front of the first stitch on the lhn; slip the three stitches off the lhn.
	1/2 RPC	Tw1B	sl nxt 2sts onto cn and hold at back of work, k1, p2 from cn.
	1/2 LPC	Tw1F	sl nxt st onto cn and hold at front of work, p2, k1 from cn.
	2/1 RC	C3B	sl nxt st onto cn and hold at back of work, k2, k1 from cn.
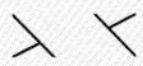	2/1 LC	C3F	sl nxt 2sts onto cn and hold at front of work, k1, k2 from cn.
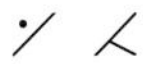	2/1 RPC	T3B	sl nxt st onto cn and hold at back of work, k2, p1 from cn.
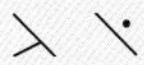	2/1 LPC	T3F	sl nxt 2sts onto cn and hold at front of work, p1, k2 from cn.
	2/1 RCP		sl nxt st onto cn and hold at back of work, p2, k1 from cn.
	2/1 LCP		sl nxt 2sts onto cn and hold at front of work, k1, p2 from cn.
	2/1 RPCP		sl nxt st onto cn and hold at back of work, p2, p1 from cn.
	2/1 LPCP		sl nxt 2sts onto cn and hold at front of work, p1, p2 from cn.

Fig. 327 Table of abbreviations of three-stitch movements.

Abbreviations of four-stitch movements

All of the stitch movements shown in Figure 328 involve a total of four stitches, with one, two or three foreground stitch(es) being moved over three, two or one background stitch(es), respectively.

Symbol	Abbreviation	Also known as	Description
	1/3 RC		sl nxt 3sts onto cn and hold at back of work, k1, k3 from cn.
	1/3 LC		sl nxt st onto cn and hold at front of work, k3, k1 from cn.
	1/3 RPC		sl nxt 3sts onto cn and hold at back of work, k1, p3 from cn.
	1/3 LPC		sl nxt st onto cn and hold at front of work, p3, k1 from cn.
	2/2 RC	C4B; C4R	sl nxt 2sts onto cn and hold at back of work, k2, k2 from cn.
	2/2 LC	C4F; C4L	sl nxt 2sts onto cn and hold at front of work, k2, k2 from cn.
	2/2 RPC	C4R	sl nxt 2sts onto cn and hold at back of work, k2, p2 from cn.
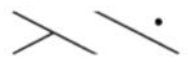	2/2 LPC	C4L	sl nxt 2sts onto cn and hold at front of work, p2, k2 from cn.
	3/1 RC		sl nxt st onto cn and hold at back of work, k3, k1 from cn.
	3/1 LC		sl nxt 3sts onto cn and hold at front of work, k1, k3 from cn.
	3/1 RPC		sl nxt st onto cn and hold at back of work, k3, p1 from cn.
	3/1 LPC		sl nxt 3sts onto cn and hold at front of work, p1, k3 from cn.
	3/1 RCP		Slip next st onto cn and hold at back of work, p3, then k1 from cn.
	3/1 LCP		Slip next 3sts onto cn and hold at front of work, k1, then p3 from cn.
	3/1 RPCP		Slip next st onto cn and hold at back of work, p3, then p1 from cn.
	3/1 LPCP		Slip next 3sts onto cn and hold at front of work, p1, then p3 from cn.

Fig. 328 Table of abbreviations of four-stitch movements.

Abbreviations of five-stitch movements

All of the stitch movements shown in Figure 329 involve a total of five stitches, with two, three or four foreground stitches being moved over three, two or one background stitch(es), respectively.

Symbol	Abbreviation	Description
	2/3 RC	sl nxt 3sts onto cn and hold at back of work, k2, k3 from cn.
	2/3 LC	sl nxt 2sts onto cn and hold at front of work, k3, k2 from cn.
	2/3 RPC	sl nxt 3sts onto cn and hold at back of work, k2, p3 from cn.
	2/3 LPC	sl nxt 2sts onto cn and hold at front of work, p3, k2 from cn.
	3/2 RC	sl nxt 2sts onto cn and hold at back of work, k3, k2 from cn.
	3/2 LC	sl nxt 3sts onto cn and hold at front of work, k2, k3 from cn.
	3/2 RPC	sl nxt 2sts onto cn and hold at back of work, k3, p2 from cn.
	3/2 LPC	sl nxt 3sts onto cn and hold at front of work, p2, k3 from cn.
	4/1 RC	sl nxt st onto cn and hold at back of work, k4, k1 from cn.
	4/1 LC	sl nxt 4sts onto cn and hold at front of work, k1, k4 from cn.
	4/1 RPC	sl nxt st onto cn and hold at back of work, k4, p1 from cn.
	4/1 LPC	sl nxt 4sts onto cn and hold at front of work, p1, k4 from cn.

Fig. 329 Table of abbreviations of five-stitch movements.

Abbreviations of six-stitch movements

All of the stitch movements shown in Figure 330 involve a total of six stitches, with two, three or four foreground stitches being moved over four, three or two background stitches, respectively.

Symbol	Abbreviation	Also known as	Description
	2/4 RC		sl nxt 4sts onto cn and hold at back of work, k2, k4 from cn.
	2/4 LC		sl nxt 2sts onto cn and hold at front of work, k4, k2 from cn.
	2/4 RPC		sl nxt 4sts onto cn and hold at back of work, k2, p4 from cn.
	2/4 LPC		sl nxt 2sts onto cn and hold at front of work, p4, k2 from cn.
	3/3 RC	C6B	sl nxt 3sts onto cn and hold at back of work, k3, k3 from cn.
	3/3 LC	C6F	sl nxt 3sts onto cn and hold at front of work, k3, k3 from cn.
	3/3 RPC	T6B	sl nxt 3sts onto cn and hold at back of work, k3, p3 from cn.
	3/3 LPC	T6F	sl nxt 3sts onto cn and hold at front of work, p3, k3 from cn.
	4/2 RC		sl nxt 2sts onto cn and hold at back of work, k4, k2 from cn.
	4/2 LC		sl nxt 4sts onto cn and hold at front of work, k2, k4 from cn.
	4/2 RPC		sl nxt 2sts onto cn and hold at back of work, k4, p2 from cn.
	4/2 LPC		sl nxt 4sts onto cn and hold at front of work, p2, k4 from cn.

Fig. 330 Table of abbreviations of six-stitch movements.

Bibliography

Black, S., *Knitting: Fashion, Industry, Craft* (V&A Publishing, 2012)

Cambridge Dictionary website, 'diamond' definition: https://dictionary.cambridge.org/dictionary/english/diamond (accessed June 2018)

Compton, R., *The Complete Book of Traditional Knitting* (Batsford Ltd, 1983)

Editors of *Vogue Knitting* magazine, *Vogue Knitting: The Ultimate Knitting Book* (SOHO Publishing Company, 2002)

Ellen, A., *Knitting: Colour, structure and design* (The Crowood Press, 2011)

Ellen, A., *Knitting: Stitch-led design* (The Crowood Press, 2015)

Foster, V. (ed.), *Knitting Handbook: An instructional guide to knitting* (Oceana Books, 2004)

Gaugain, Mrs J., *Mrs Gaugain's Miniature Knitting, Netting, and Crochet Book* (I.J. Gaugain and Ackermann and Co., 1845)

Gaugain, Mrs J., *The Lady's Assistant in Knitting, Netting and Crochet Work* (I.J. Gaugain and Ackermann and Co., 1846)

Ince, C. and Nii, R. (eds), *Future Beauty: 30 Years of Japanese Fashion*, (Merrell Publishers Limited, 2010)

Lambert, Miss F., *My Knitting Book*; seventh edition (J. Murray, 1844); a digital version is available from the University of Southampton's collection of Victorian knitting manuals: https://archive.org/details/krl00394035 (accessed June 2018)

Lambert, Miss F., *The Handbook of Needlework* (J. Murray, 1842)

Paden, S., *Knitwear Design Workshop: A Comprehensive Guide to Handknits* (Interweave Press, 2009)

Patons, *Patons Aran Book* (Patons, circa 1968)

Rigolette de la Hamelin, Mdlle., *The Royal Magazine of Knitting, Netting, Crochet, and Fancy Needlework, No.4* (Sherwood & Co., November 1848)

Rutt, R., *A History of Hand Knitting* (Batsford Ltd, 1987)

Stanley, M., *The Handknitter's Handbook* (David & Charles plc, 1990)

Stanley, M., *Knitting Plus: Simple, stunning techniques for embroidered knitting* (Batsford Ltd, 1989)

Stanley, M., *Knitting your own designs for a perfect fit* (David & Charles plc, 1983)

Starmore, A., *Aran Knitting: New and Expanded Edition* (Dover Publications, Inc., 2010)

Sykes, J.B. (ed.), *Concise Oxford Dictionary of Current English*; sixth edition (Oxford University Press, 1976)

The Sunday Times, 'Born-again Knitting/The Bishop in Sheep's Clothing', *The Sunday Times*; magazine supplement (9 December 1984, p.60); the two offered patterns were provided to readers who sent self-addressed envelopes to the addresses stated in the article.

Thomas, M., *Mary Thomas's Book of Knitting Patterns* (Dover Publications, Inc., 2015); this book is a reproduction of the original 1943 edition.

Thompson, G., *Patterns for Guernseys, Jerseys & Arans* (Dover Publications, Inc., 1979)

Walker Phillips, M., *Knitting Counterpanes* (Dover Publications, Inc., 2013)

Woman's Weekly, 'Aran style', *Woman's Weekly* (12 September 1959)

Wright, M., *Cornish Guernseys & Knit-frocks* (Polperro Heritage Press, 2008)

Further Information

Websites

The Knitting & Crochet Guild (KCG): http://kcguild.org.uk/

The Victoria and Albert (V&A) Museum Collections: https://collections.vam.ac.uk/

Victorian knitting manuals, University of Southampton: https://archive.org/details/victorianknittingmanuals

Yarn Stockists

baa ram ewe: https://baaramewe.co.uk/

Birlinn Yarn Company: https://www.birlinnyarn.co.uk/

Brooklyn Tweed: https://www.brooklyntweed.com/

J. C. Rennie: https://www.knitrennie.com/

John Arbon Textiles: https://www.jarbon.com/

LoveKnitting: https://www.loveknitting.com/

West Yorkshire Spinners: https://www.wyspinners.com/

Acknowledgements

My sincere thanks to everyone who has helped me with this book.

In particular, my thanks and appreciation to my husband, Bernie, for his excellent insights; my daughter, Maxine, for styling and photographing the accessory patterns; my son, Alexander, for his technical support; and my mum, Rosemarie, for encouraging me to experiment with knitting from an early age.

I would like to thank Loraine McClean, for continually inspiring me to find new ways of looking at the design of the natural and built environments.

I am extremely grateful to Teresa MacLeod and Sue Mogridge, for all of their help and advice.

Technical editing of the accessory patterns was by Heather Murray, whose constructive comments I very much appreciated.

Thank you to the Knitting & Crochet Guild (KCG), for the use of several photographs from the KCG Collection, and in particular to Barbara Smith and Angharad Thomas, for all of their help and assistance.

Yarn for several of the patterns and swatches was generously provided by West Yorkshire Spinners and the Birlinn Yarn Company.

The excellent Stitchmastery software by Cathy Scott was used to translate my designs into charted knitting patterns.

There are many other people who have helped me throughout writing this book, by generously sharing their experience and expertise, for which I am very grateful.

Index

Other Knitting Titles from Crowood

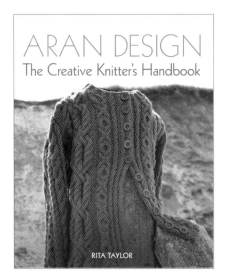

978 1 78500 407 0

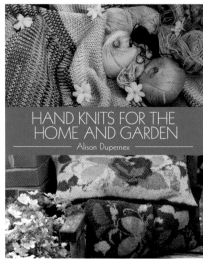

978 1 78500 455 1

978 1 78500 507 7

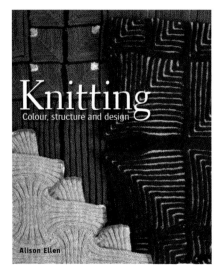

978 1 84797 284 2

987 1 78500 029 4

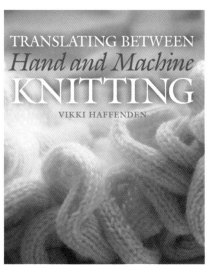

978 1 78500 431 5

The Jeanne Montez

Latin American Dancing in the Australian 1

as told to MARNIE WALTERS-BURGESS

The Jeanne Montez Story

Marnie Walters-Burgess

ISBN   1-876245-84-0

Cataloguing-in-publication Data

     The Jeanne Montez Story
     Publisher: Marnie Walters-Burgess

     Paperback

Cover Design by Marnie Walters-Burgess
Printed at 40 Bymount Road, Kilkivan 4600

For my Mum

Dorothy

Who never doubted.

ACKNOWLEDGEMENTS.

The process of writing Jeanne's story, from the first interview through to publication, seems to have taken forever and many people have helped me along the way. The story is all the richer for the input from Jeanne's friends, some of whom appear in the photographs. I am grateful also for the support from several people of Kilkivan.

Special thanks must go to Michael and Lee Allen and John Stapleton who so kindly loaned me Jeanne's photographs for such a long time, Nola Orchard for her foreword, The John Turner Dance Library for information and photographs from its unique collection, Jack Gow and Arch Watson for photos and memorabilia, Bill and Judy Bandidt and Toowoomba Education Centre for publishing assistance, and also to my friend Rosie Fitzgerald for her much-needed professional editing advice, and finally to Dallas Williams for her digital editing and wizardry.

Such generosity of spirit is always reassuring.

Contents

FOREWORD

With thanks to Jeanne Connelly (Montez) for giving my husband – Dick – and myself a great feeling of professionalism and understanding in the field of Exhibition Dancing.

We spent many years dancing as professional Ballroom Dancers all over Australia and when Jeanne settled in Brisbane, she commenced teaching and choreographing routines for floor shows, many of which were presented at Cloudland Ballroom.

Jeanne became a very close friend of mine for which I am sincerely grateful. She will be forever in my thoughts – yesterday, today and tomorrow.

Noela Orchard.
16th January, 2001

My Grandfather – William Butler Davis   Circa 1910

Chapter One: The Lonely Child.

My mother used to romance a bit so I don't know if this is true - but she used to tell me about a butler called Davis from Buckingham Palace who married one of the Royal Ladies-In-Waiting. Her name was Delysia Montez. I think Queen Victoria reigned then and Edward VII was her eldest son.

When Delysia married the butler Davis, she was pregnant but not to him and the palace officials were supposed to have sent the new couple off to Australia - the Colonies - somewhere in the south of Victoria. Delysia had a baby boy who was named William Butler Davis. Even though her husband wasn't the child's father, Delysia honoured him by including Butler in the name. They went on to have another son who they called Harry. William and Harry, see. Traditional royal names. On William's birth certificate, though, where the names of his parents should have been, there was nothing - only blank. Now, as I say, it was probably only one of Mum's stories but it's a funny thing that when people used to see the picture of my grandfather hanging up, they'd say to me - 'Gee you must be patriotic - having a picture of King George on the wall.' And I'd just laugh and say, 'No, that's my grandfather.' But there was a likeness.

William and Harry were very different. They both played piano well but William was.... fastidious. Everything had to be just right. He was exceptionally talented with architecture and building. As he grew up, William became the 'gentleman's gentleman'. He belonged to all the exclusive clubs in Sydney and Melbourne. He moved in all the social circles. He even had his own wharf where he used to import timber because he was a builder. His wife, Jane Eastway, came from New Zealand. She was of Scottish and Irish descent. I don't remember anyone calling her Jane. As far as I knew, her name was Marnie. At least, that's what she was known as. Must have got changed somewhere. Their son was my father, Ernest Davis.

My mother's mother was married to a Cronin. They had three children. The second one died at eighteen months and within about twelve months of that, my grandfather died. He was only about twenty-eight. So my grandmother lost her husband and her kiddy at the same time and was left with two children. I don't know if this is correct but my mother told me that when she remarried, she did so at the same church on the same date as she did her first husband. Her second husband was John Stapleton. Evidently he was best man at the first wedding. Now whether that's all true I couldn't say, but she went on to have five more children. Asking for punishment, wasn't she? My mother was the youngest of the first family who were all musical and loved life, then there were John's children - four boys and Nell. They were all brainy.

I was born at Essendon, Victoria in 1916, then we moved to Arthur's Creek. It was war years of course. Very shortly after my birth, my grandparents - Dad's parents - bought this farm at Arthur's Creek and my father managed it. It was a mixed farm - horses, cows, pigs, chooks, and fruit trees. It was right on top of a mountain. No neighbours within miles. Arthur's Creek is just out of Whittlesea and Yan Yean and I put my shyness back then down to the fact that I was so isolated. There were no other children around - just animals. So I used to play with animals - pigs, cats, dogs, anything. I used to walk under the legs of the draught horses. I slept in a cot at the back of the house and Mum reckoned there was often a possum in there sleeping with me! That's where I got my love of animals, I s'pose. I was with 'em all the time then.

The big excitement for the week was when my grandparents came to visit. My grandmother was a music teacher and my grandfather was a musician so when they came up on Saturdays and Sundays, that was big time for me. Even from that young age I can remember. I was only about three or four. They spent the weekend with me more than anyone else, playing tunes. That's where I first became aware of music. It was such a big treat! Even though I was only a little kid I can still remember - as clear as anything. I can even remember what the furniture was like! Rosewood was the in thing in those days. The lounge was rosewood and there were special cushions on the chairs - there was a beautiful table and chairs. I'd hide behind those chairs while they were playing the piano and they'd call 'Peek-a-boo! Come out from behind that chair!' And out I'd pop. Used all the chairs to hide. Sounds silly, doesn't it?

Most weeks Mum and Dad would go to the Arthur's Creek dance in the jinker. They'd take me along and wrap me up in blankets behind the stage curtain. One night I must have heard the music and thought it was the same game I played with my grandparents. I got up and danced across the stage. Apparently I was a big hit with all the dancers. Would have been my first public performance!

There's only one family from Arthur's Creek whose name I can remember. When my father remarried years later, he said, 'I'd love to go and see the farm.' So we drove him up and when we got there, there was nothing left but the chimney. It was burnt to the ground. Dad said, "Would you mind taking me over the next hill?" There used to be people there by the name of Murphy. So over we go and sure enough - there was still the same family. I think Dad must've had a bit of a crush on one of the girls. She was the only one he kind of remembered. She and her people had all gone of course, but it was still the same family.

Dad rode racehorses when we were at Arthur's Creek. He'd ride in the Whittlesea Stakes or at Yan Yean. They were hurdle races. He and his brother had this special horse called Lady Craig. They used to gamble and drink a bit. It was in their blood, you know. My mother was a different type. That life didn't suit her. She hated it. So every time they had a tiff, she'd pack up and take me and off we'd go down to her mother in Abbotsford. My grandmother was married to a fireman and in those days, all the firemen lived around the station. Then within a few days Dad'd be down to see why she'd gone. So it was a sort of series of being at the farm then being down with my grandmother at the fire station. After a few of these episodes, they finally decided to sell the farm and move into Melbourne. My father bought a billiard room in Glenhuntly, then one in Auburn. My mother thought because the billiard room was upstairs from where we lived, he'd just come down and be home. But it didn't work out that way.

There was a pastry shop just along from us. People who owned it were Germans. They made beautiful pastries. When Dad'd close upstairs about eleven, he'd always come home with a pasty. He came past my room and I'd be awake. First of my bad habits started then! I'd stay awake for the pasty he'd bring me.

Auburn was the first place I can recall going to school. The Auburn State School. About the same time I was sent to the Raynor School of Dancing. Those days there were dancing schools everywhere. Tap dancing was a big thing then. I thought it was great – being able to live in the city, go and learn dancing. My father, however, was very keen that I should sing. We had school concerts and my first big performance was at one of them. I sang 'Ain't She Sweet' and 'In You Green Hat'. Ever heard of them? *'In your green hat - the best dressed girl in town....* 'Funny how things stick in your mind. I put my memory down to being an only child with no one to play with. I was with adults all the time. That might have a lot to do with it.

SCHEDULE E.

(19 Victoria No. 30.)

(COPY OF) CERTIFICATE OF MARRIAGE.

Insert Christian and Surname at full length.

I, *James Woodward Winspear* being

Insert Designation.

Wesleyan Minister

do hereby Certify, that I have this day, at *Forbes Street*

Woolloomooloo Sydney duly celebrated Marriage between

Insert Christian and Surname of the Husband at full length.

William Butler Davis

Insert Designation, Residence, and Condition of Husband.

Architect, Rose bank Street Darlinghurst, Sydney, Bachelor and

Insert Christian and Surname of the Wife at full length.

Jane Eastway

Insert Designation, Residence, and Condition of Wife.

King Street Sydney Spinster

after Declaration duly made as by law required.

DATED this *25th* day of *January* 188*8*.

James W Winspear { Signature of Minister

William Butler Davis.

Signatures of Parties to the Marriage {

Jane Eastway

J. B. Milner.

Signatures of Witnesses {

Mary Maynes

14

Me as a child

1916

1918

Mum and I   1918

Mum (left) and Miss Devett
Kalgoorlie 1926

Mum and my Grandmother – Totty

My girlfriend was Roma Pegram. We used to play 'statues' in the garden. Take it in turns to strike a pose and hold it. We both went to the Raynor School of Dancing. Mrs. Raynor used to teach in a converted garage at her house. She wore really thick glasses and her eyes used to roll back and forth all the time. But she was a good teacher.

They also opened up a gymnastic school at the top of Auburn Road - around at the hall. They had tumbling mats, rings and that type of thing. It was just coming in - physical culture. A few years after that they started the South Street competitions at Ballarat. If you won there, that was really something. This teacher I was going to must have had the feeling that this was going to become popular so she started teaching the kids back bends and tumbling. Gymnastics. The beginning of what they do in the Olympics today. I used to go there one night a week between six and eight. Because I was double jointed I could get on the rings and twist my arms and go over a second time. So the teacher was very interested that I should keep going because she thought I had an advantage. But I was more interested in dancing.

They put me into a dancing competition when I was about ten. Saint Patrick's Day was the big event - the championships for highland dancing, Irish jigs and all that sort of thing. All the girls in the Raynor School were going to be in it. I couldn't go because I didn't have an outfit. They all had their own. However my mother came to light and she hired a costume. When I saw it I nearly died. I thought - I'm not going to wear that! I finally did and went into the competition for experience. Everyone thought Iris and Melba Lord from the other school would win. They had previously. Lo and behold, I won it! Was the first time I'd ever won anything in my life! It must have been because I thought I never had a chance, so I didn't care - wasn't nervous. Big surprise for everyone - especially me!

Another thing that happened back then - I was sent by the Raynor School to do a pantomime over at Box Hill. Someone in the cast had got sick, so I went to fill in. It was Cinderella and I was supposed to be the fairy godmother. No rehearsal - nothing. I just turned up on the night and the woman in charge said, 'When I go like this with my hand you've got to come on with your wand.... 'You know the bit with the two ugly sisters? Because I'd never rehearsed, I wasn't interested in the dialogue. I was looking for the lady with her hand up. She actually did do that with her hand - but not for me. It was for somebody else! I saw the hand go and I danced out onto the stage. Everybody - Cinderella, the rats, the sisters, everything - came to a standstill! You know that kind of feeling? Everybody was stunned. Including me! I just backed off. Anyway, the second time she cued me, *she* got it right.

Mum got a job as a governess with a family who travelled a lot. She loved the travelling and looking after the kiddies. She went with them over to Western Australia. Things got very sort of topsy-turvy. Mum'd be with us for three months, gone for six. When she'd go, I'd live with one of my grandmothers. When she'd come back, she and Dad would set up house somewhere and I'd go back with them. It made me a loner in every possible way.

My grandmother, the one they called Marnie, was a very spiritual woman. After her husband died, she used to go to this place and communicate with him through a medium. He advised her as to what to do with their properties and things like that. Something must've happened because she was always successful! She was a woman who would give everything to everyone and keep nothing for herself. A real giver. She and I both had a birth mark on our legs. She used to call it 'our potato'. It was as big as a potato and it used to be our big bond. Sort of a standing joke. We were very special because we both had these identical marks. I was the only other one in the family that had it, see? It was horrible. Like an identical mark passed on from one generation to the other. She always joked about it.

Sometimes I'd live with her at Carrum and sometimes with Totty, my mother's mother. I changed schools all the time. I went to Carrum, Aspendale, Mordialloc, Elwood, Glenhuntly, Auburn and Our Lady of Victories in Camberwell.... Funny thing happened to me there.

I had a long walk from my grandmother's home in Allenby Road on the border of Camberwell and Canterbury near Kew. I used to walk all the way down Bourke Road, past the station, then up the hill to Our Lady of Victories. Often I'd dawdle and I was late so I'd go to my uncle and get a note. If you were late for school you had to produce a reason. He and my Aunty Shelley lived in Havloc Road which was on the way. I'd get to school and sit in the back of the church until it was playtime then I'd walk in with the rest of 'em with my note and give it to Sister Theclar.

I was sitting in the back of the church this day and there was a nun praying right down in the front row. It was a beautiful church. They'd paid over a hundred pounds each for the Stations that were brought out from Italy - the Stations of the Cross. There were fourteen of them, all marble. Beautiful. Father Robinson had built the church by getting the parishioners to buy a brick at a time at a pound per brick. When he died, they buried him in a vault, inside the church.

As I was sitting there I saw this.... just like net.... something black moving across the front of the altar. It moved across then back to the side where the vault was and just disappeared. The nun jumped up and scurried over to the main building to where Sister Theclar's office was and I dawdled over after her because it was time for me to front up with my note. I could tell there was something wrong because there was such a scurry. When I got to the classroom, the kiddies had been all left sitting while the nun and Sister Theclar had gone downstairs to the office. So I waited for a while and when I saw them come up again I realised there was something wrong. I wondered if it was to do with what happened in the church. So I marched up with my note and said to Sister Theclar, 'I was in the church and I saw something funny.'

She took me outside with the nun and she said, 'Now both calm down and tell me what you saw.' Our stories coincided. She said, 'Are you sure it wasn't a reflection from a car hitting the windows?'

I said, 'No, it was just like black mesh and it moved from the front of the altar over to the side.... 'So she was convinced and the nun was very happy - the fact that we'd both seen it. It was never brought up again - just forgotten. Just one of those things. It was the first time I'd ever seen anything like it. I've seen a few since.

Being in the billiard and snooker rooms, Dad got to know a lot of racing people. He got to know a man called Wallace Mitchell who was a bookmaker and we used to get invited down to his weekender at Mordialloc. They had big parties just about every weekend. I would only have been about nine or ten and to me those weekends were marvellous. Mum used to come too. She loved company. She enjoyed it. Anything but farms. Dad used to join in with the rest and they all drank pretty heavily. Talked races. But it opened up a new area for me. It's where I first met Minnie and May Mitchell and Graeme Fitzgibbon. Smacka. They didn't call him that back then. I thought it was marvellous. Minnie Mitchell played piano and May would dance. She took me under her wing and taught me a few things - tapping, stuff like that. We went to those parties for quite a few years.

My father decided, since I'd had so many dancing lessons, it was time for me to start teaching. So he hired an old drill hall off Auburn Road - one of those round, corrugated things - and put on a pianist. Every Saturday morning I used to teach little kids but I didn't like it much. I only did it for him.

William Butler Davis and his wife Jane (nee Eastway)

I had a short career as a pianist too. I started taking lessons from a Miss Dand but we didn't have our own piano. Miss Dand would let me practice on hers for half an hour after I'd had the lesson but it wasn't really enough. She told me she didn't think I'd make a good pianist because I'd memorize it all. When she put the music in front of me, I never even looked at it. I'd just play the tune. It was all in the head. She said that wasn't a good sign. My grandmother - who was a music teacher - kind of backed her up. She said I didn't have the right hands for playing either. Too small. So my career as a pianist was finished. That was fast, wasn't it?

Another thing that happened at school that stands out in my memory was when some French nuns came asking for volunteers to go back to France and help the poor people. I was first up on the dais to put my name down. I had to go home and get permission and my grandmother was all for it because they were strict Catholics. Thought it would be marvellous - a nun in the family. My mother was in Western Australia and when she found out, she was straight back to stop it. So that went by the board.

I must have been fourteen I suppose, when I left school. Then I went to Zerchos Business College. See, when you got through your eighth grade in a Catholic school, you'd go for exams at the state school. Catholics didn't have their own exams. State schools set them. I was at the Nicholson Street Convent and I sat for a scholarship. In those days you could win a half scholarship or a third and you had to pay the balance. I got a half scholarship and my grandmother Marnie said she'd pay the rest. To put money out of any sort back then was a big deal because there wasn't that much around. It was in the depression. I had no ambitions. I was just going to be a shorthand typist. I thought, well, that's going to be my life by the look of it - you know - nothing else had happened. So every day I'd go into the city - Zerchos was up the top of Collins Street right opposite Scotts Church - and learn how to type.

One day we were all told to line the roads for a special funeral procession. Every school had to be there. Dame Nellie Melba had died. They had the ceremony at Scotts Church and there were huge crowds of people outside. Women were crying.... My grandmother loved her singing. She had her records - real old records. 'No Place Like Home', stuff like that. I used to think it was real old hat so I was amazed when I saw the procession coming up Collins Street. I didn't realise what a famous person she was. The procession was enormous and it went right out to Lilydale or somewhere where she was buried. Apparently the roads all the way were just lined with people and that'd have to be twenty miles or so. She was really very famous.

Circa 1932

Chapter Two: First Dances

When I lived with my grandmother Totty, Dad came and boarded with us. On Saturday nights he used to take me to the movies, then we'd go to the Palais de Danse next door. They'd give free pass outs for the last half hour so the people in the picture theatre could go and watch the dancing. Mr. Kerwin, the man who owned both places, was a pretty smart fella. He built up one place from the other. A real shrewd head. Dad and I would sit up the back as spectators. There were rows of seats - not a lot but enough for the mothers and fathers. Sunday we'd go to the vaudeville show at Richmond. Those were my outings. It was Dad's way of taking me out and at the same time checking on me. You know, making sure I wasn't gallivanting around. He loved the entertainment business but he couldn't do anything for himself. Funny, isn't it?

It's a strange thing, but at the Palais with my father, that's where I saw my husband in 1934 win an Exhibition Championship. I wasn't married to him then. I was just a kid with my father watching the dancing.

After a while it got to the stage when Dad thought I was old enough for him to move away. Live his own life. He had a lot of good points. When Mum came back she'd stay with my grandmother and sometimes we'd all go down to Wallace Mitchell's. Mum and Dad got back together a few times but it didn't work out. You couldn't change him and you couldn't change her. They were both opposites. So they separated and went their own ways to remarry later on.

Mum was born in December - a Sagittarian. She had the happy knack of getting on with anyone. Had a wonderful personality. Her sister - Aunty Irene - was a Scorpio and they both thought they knew it all. They both had their own ideas and you couldn't move either of them. And yet they thought the world of each other. I lived with Aunty Irene and her three kids for a while during one of Mum's disappearing tricks and she got very attached to me. Anyhow, this time Mum and I went down to St Kilda to stay with her and she was going to the Artist's Ball. She wanted to take Mum with her because she thought Mum was out of things a bit. All the kids stayed home and Mum and Aunty Irene went to the ball with this chappy called Bill Barnes. Bill was Aunty Irene's escort but Mum finished up pinchin' him! And she stayed with him right through from when I was a kid until I was in Sydney.

He was a very clever man. Well spoken. He came from Queensland. His people had a property up there somewhere. He was very well educated and had studied for all these special things over in London. He was an accountant and if a business was run down, his job was to get it back on its feet. He worked all over the place - Western Australia, New Guinea - and Mum loved it because she went everywhere with him. They'd come back and they'd be home, say, for a month then they'd be off again. As I got older they started taking me with them.

One of the times Mum was in Melbourne, they were living up at the top of Swanston Street, opposite the University. You go up past the cemetery, around a corner and almost into Carlton. On one side of the road was all guest houses and on the other side was the Uni. They lived in one of those guest houses and I went and stayed there with them. I could have been about sixteen then. One day Mum took me to this fortune teller. She loved to go and get her cards read and all that. It was somewhere in Russell Street. That's all I can tell you. One of those old two storey places. We went downstairs and she had her fortune done, then she had mine read too. This woman told me that she could see me working in a place where there was lots and lots of machinery. I thought, that's pretty uninteresting. But see I finished up getting a job at the Herald Office and all the machinery was down below - the paper machinery. All underneath. Then she told me that wasn't the type of work I particularly liked. I knew that because I'd been to Zerchos and I hated it. She said, 'No, don't worry. I can see lots of clapping. People clapping everywhere. Whatever you're doing, you're absolutely loving it and you keep getting applause.' Well, I thought, she's not so bad after all - that sounds a bit more interesting.

I'd left Zerchos by then and I'd tried a few jobs. My first job might have been the Hawaiian Club. That's where I met Tex Morton and old Buddy Waikara. They used to have this Hawaiian Club and you could pay for your lessons on the steel guitar by the half hour. I used to sit there in the office taking the bookings.

I had my Dad behind me all the time - giving me a push. We used to meet every day between three and three-thirty at either the Robur Tea Rooms or Tate's Coffee Shop. I'd have to tell him what I'd done for the day. Even though we weren't living together, he always checked up - gave me encouragement.

He'd say to me, 'Go into Woolworths.... ', or 'Go into Edments and ask if they've got any jobs.' Then he'd wait out the front while I went in. I got a job in Edments for a very short time, then I went to Woolworths. They must have got sick of seeing me so they told me one day - yes, I could start behind the handbags. No sooner had I started there than Dad would say to me, 'Be sure and tell 'em you can do shorthand and typing. If any jobs become vacant up in the office could you put your name down to be first?' Whatever he told me I'd do - like a puppet. I finished up being the secretary to the buyer who was a Mr. Merrilees. And that was probably the first Woolworths ever in Melbourne. That was about 1934.

The place where my father used to take me to the vaudeville shows on Sundays held a dance on Saturday nights. It was on top of a hill before you get to Bridge Road. It had to do with the church next door, I think. I'd go to this dance with my girlfriend Dorothy and we thought it was marvellous - going to Richmond on the bus and going up to the dance. Then coming home at night. I didn't dare tell my grandmother because I wasn't allowed to go that far on my own. That's where I think I met Zarf Rivers. Must have been playing there one night. I don't know how I'd got to be talking to him. He had this big fat man with him who played the piano - Barney Marsh. At this particular time they were also playing at St Kilda. At the end of St Kilda pier there used to be a cafe. Big cafe. Like a night club. Not dancing - just music. Palm Grove, where Bobby Gibson played, was over the other side and you walked down onto the pier and there was the shop right along there. It was just starting off.

I got to talking to this Zarf Rivers and Barney Marsh about dancing and music in general and they asked me if I'd be interested in an audition. I had to ask my father first and he said sure, I could go. So I went down to this place - a coffee shop or something - somewhere in Bridge Road.

They said, 'What type of singing do you do?'

I said, 'I only know a few songs - mostly blues.' My father always had me on blues. He loved that type of number. So I sang a couple of numbers and you wouldn't believe it.... They asked me to sing at the Orama Ballroom in Footscray.

I think Dad came with me that night. I suppose I was nervous. I don't remember. Zarf and Barney were there. This old Barney Marsh was so fat he couldn't see the keyboard. His hands just kind of fitted over and he'd play. He was a very good musician. The resident singer was a lady called Alice Smith, she was big and fat too! She wasn't a pop singer but she wasn't classical. She had an excellent voice though. She'd had good training and she could sing anything....all the new numbers....anything. The stuff I was doing was real kind of low down compared with what she did. Blues. Blues were just sort of coming in at that stage. I was just a change of sound from Alice Smith. I did two songs. I suppose they were accepted alright. They were songs you've probably never heard of. One was 'The Man I Love' because my father was mad on those types of songs and the other was called 'Shanghai Lil'. Ever heard of that? The public were a bit sort of taken with it. They'd never heard it either. All about some bloke who goes back to Shanghai looking for his Shanghai Lil. My father thought it was marvellous. He just loved it. The music was in him but he couldn't do anything.

At the Orama, the stage and the band were upstairs and the dancers were downstairs. I thought, well there's one good thing. At least I'm up high. Nobody can see much of me. If anything goes wrong, it doesn't matter. My two songs were such an extreme contrast with Alice Smith, I was a big hit. I'd given it a try for my father's sake and I'd realised singing wasn't really for me. Zarf thought I should have a larger selection of music - to sing different songs. Singing different stuff all the time - I thought to heck with that. I'm not going to be studying to sing different songs. That was a full time job! But at least I'd tried.

1932

25

There were no cabarets, nothing in those days. The coffee shops and things were just starting up. There were dances everywhere and bands were getting together. One day Dad said, 'Jean, why don't you go over to the Botanic Gardens kiosk. I've spoken to the man there and said my daughter's a good singer. When you go over, just ask for this Mr. Rosen and tell him who you are.' God I must have been a good kid! I did exactly what I was told and went over and asked for the man in charge of the band. They were all Jewish. Sunday was their night out. They don't go to church on Sunday. He took me up and introduced me to the rest of the chaps in the band. Got out a couple of numbers. They thought it was alright. When it was all over I had to get in touch with my father and tell him how it went. I rang him up and said I'd sung four or five numbers. They were all nice people. He said, 'Did you meet Mr. Rosen?'

'Yes.'

'Well I'll be seeing him tomorrow and find out what he thought.... '

You know, I worked in that kiosk years later with my husband Tom - but I'll tell you about that further on.

My girlfriend Dorothy and I started getting about to dances. They had 'em in funny places sometimes, like the Richmond Baths. Sometimes we didn't have enough money for the train fare so we'd have to jump off the end of the platform before the ticket collector saw us! They were running a dancing competition for amateurs at the Ziegfeld Palais at Hawthorn. It was just starting up at the time and this young chap asked me if I'd be allowed to dance with him. His name was Sid Watson. He had three brothers who were all good, established dancers - Archie, Bert and Wally. Wally Watson turned professional and went over to London later on. They were all quite good. I thought I'd better ask my grandmother - let her know what I was doing because she was pretty strict. She OK'd it because these Watson boys lived very close to Dorothy. Everyone knew everyone then. So we went in this championship - no practise or anything. We just met at the hall and went on the floor and that was it. They played three dances. No Tango. Just the Waltz, the Quickstep and the Foxtrot. Of course, we didn't win.

There was another competitor there - Bernie Glennon - who came from way over the other side of town. It was quite usual in those days to travel for miles to go to dancing competitions. It was the in thing. Sometimes, at the big competitions, there'd be busloads of people - just like at a football match. Buses supplied free. See, they'd always have a judge's decision and a public vote so the more people you took, the more chance you had of winning. That's how dancing competitions started. After it was all over, Bernie came up and asked me for a dance. When I'd danced with him, he said he'd like to take me out one night and would I go to a dance out his way. The Thornbury Palais. I said I'd think about it.

I let it go for a week or two 'cause I had to ask my grandmother if I could go that far away from home. About the third week I got a bit daring and I thought, well I might as well take a chance. So it was all arranged and he was to meet me at the Thornbury Station because I didn't even know where the Palais was. I travelled all the way into town then out again in a strange direction for me. When I got off the train he was waiting. Took me out to the Thornbury Palais and it was quite a nice place. Big. During the course of the evening he introduced me to his brother Bill. Never realised he was the same person I'd seen winning the titles at the Palais!

After I'd had a couple of dances with the both of them, his brother decided, being the elder of the two, he'd walk me to the station. So off they went - out the front and 'round the corner. Had a few words and a few fisticuffs! I finally finished up going back to the station with Bill! Then as a follow on from there, I started going out with him. But I was always friendly with both of them.

Then it was the big trip back. I had to get the train back to Princes Bridge Station, then cross the road and get my train from Flinders Street. You had to make sure you timed it right so you'd be certain of catching the last train for the night. Used to be so funny. You'd see all the couples standing there, holding hands 'cause their trains went in different directions. There was no such thing as taking you home.

With the dancing of course, I had to have the right clothes. My grandmother Totty was a dressmaker and she soon showed me how to use the old treadle machine. See, I couldn't afford to buy them. She had the machine and I used to buy the material. I'd just run 'em through and hope for the best. Stick on sequins by the million. Those days, to dance in local competitions you didn't have to have elaborate clothes - just a nice dress. I was always borrowing safety pins to hold 'em together!

Wally and Dilyss Watson   Circa 1936

Lorna and Jack Gow   1936

Dancing had a whole different meaning than it does today. With dancing in those days, if you were a top dancer people looked up to you. You were looked on like you'd really accomplished something. Every teacher in Melbourne would aim for one thing - the championships. Professional and amateur. Everyone'd compete and then go on with a series of eliminations until they finally got the best amateur and the best professional. Once you'd achieved that - that was the peak. Just ballroom though. Latin American was not part of the main competitions at that time and exhibition was handled one hundred percent by two men. Mickey Powell was one. He did all the exhibition stuff with his sister Mascotte. And the other man's name was Gerry Hales. They always used to refer to Jerry Hale as the man who really kicked exhibition off.

I often danced with the Watson boys and there were a whole lot of us who followed the circuit. Another chappy I remember was Jack Gow. I think he used to work on the railway stations servicing the Nestles chocolate machines where you put a penny in a little slot and a chocolate would come out.

Before I married him, my husband Bill danced in team competitions with his brothers. Anywhere he was dancing he'd have his mother and two brothers with him. Ruby Barton was the girl he danced with. They won the championships in '34. Sometimes the Watsons would challenge him and his brothers. It used to make for a big night at the Ziegfeld or over their way. It was all just publicity - one team against another. That sort of created a bit of interest. Then after I was married we used to challenge Sydney. That's how it all started. It was to hold me in good stead for when I went up there eight years later.

GERALD HALES and Miss RENE NICHOLSON, the inventors of the "Haleston," the sensational new Old Time Dance for 1941

Chapter Three: The Playhouse

Helen McMahon (nee Stapleton) is the one who got me the job at the Herald. She belonged to my grandmother's second marriage. When she first started at the Herald, she worked for a man called Mr. Pacini. Then she transferred over to work with Sir Keith Murdoch where the chance came up for a woman correspondent to be sent away for the first time. They chose her. Old Sir Keith finished up employing the first male secretary and Aunt Nell went up to report on MacArthur during the war. See, I told you that side of the family was all brainy.

For some reason I was up in Mildura with Mum and Bill Barnes. We'd been to Sydney a couple of times then we were coming back and he was applying for a job in New Guinea with Guinea Airways. All of a sudden Mum wanted me to go with them to New Guinea. I wasn't interested in that. I was just getting to the stage where I was allowed to go out to dances and things like that and I thought -I don't want to go to New Guinea. That'd be terrible!

Thank goodness, my Aunt Nell rang to say, 'We've got a position for Jean at the Herald. Could you put her on a train and send her straight back.' So that's what they did - put me on the train and I went back to Melbourne. And that's where I got the job with Corinella. My big position was sitting in the huge library they had there, opening up all the letters and arranging all the drawings and things from the kids to get them ready for Corinella - the kid's page in the newspaper. Very interesting! I used to get paid thirty shillings a week!

All up I worked at the Herald three or four different times. The pay master, Mr. Tupper, always used to say, 'If you ever want a job relieving or whatever, always come back.' I'd go and work there for three or four months - just relieving. It was very handy. The outcome of working at the Herald the first time was the fact that they decided to put on a musical show - a live show - at a place called the Playhouse, just over Princes Bridge. You turn right and you go back down towards the river and there's the YMCA right in front of you. There used to be this big two storey theatre - I'm sure it was called the Playhouse. And that's where they put the show on. They just called on any talent in the Herald Office and there was this man called Ivan Menzies. I don't know what he did at the Herald. Maybe writing. They put him in charge. Then they approached Jennie and Eileen Brenan who were the society dancing teachers and who had a studio that later became a nightclub at the back of the Herald. They came round to sort of put the show together.

The first half was to be for the younger ones and the other half was for the older people. "Blue Moon" and all that type of stuff. Menzies had control of it and I was part of the ballet. Part way through rehearsals, one of the Brenans got sick or something and they asked me if I'd keep the girls in trim by rehearsing them. Rehearsals went on for quite a while because it was a big show. Then I got a couple of parts. I danced apache - you know, the old French apache dance? There's Adagio and Apache. Apache dance - you know those old tunes? Brisk four-four. The bloke's got a cap on and a black shirt and he swaggers along with the girl and he spins her out and spins her in and throws her on the floor. Like he's beating her up. A real tough guy. I can't remember the chap's name that I danced with but, after the routine, the song I sang was 'Oh You Nasty Man'. Very appropriate. That made my father very happy. And at that stage the 'Continental' had just hit. So I got very game. I was getting confidence by now. I put a whole routine together on the 'Continental' - a Fred Astaire and Ginger Rogers routine - and had all the young girls doing the steps. I used the people from the dancing school in the stage production.

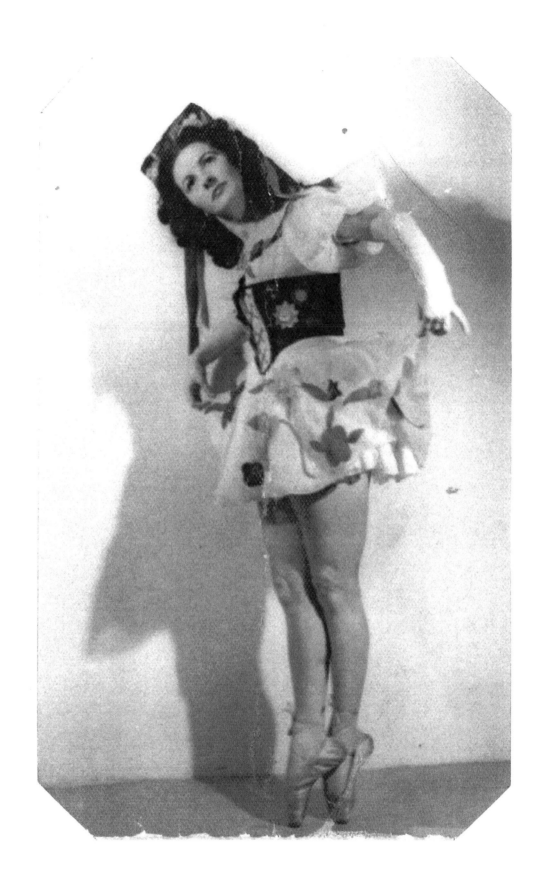

Publicity shot for a show

Ivan Menzies sang this 'Funinculi Funincula' and he wanted a chorus behind him so I asked my friend Bernie could he round up a few young lads who would come around on the night in their dinner suits just to sing. Through that chance happening I met my future husband again.

Funny part about this show - they tried to please everybody. They put a sketch in - 'Lady Chatterley's Lover'. It was just straight out talk for almost thirty minutes. The young girl who was doing the part - I don't know if she was Lady Chatterley or the lover! One of the two! She got trouble with her throat. Couldn't do it. And there was miles of it - back chat between the two of them. Because I had a good memory, never guess who got the part! That was the only reason. I had to remember that as well as all my other bits and pieces. It was the most boring thing I'd ever been stuck with in all my life! I learnt it in less than a week and I had to make sure I answered at the right time. I'd never be an actress! I'd hate it! Learning all those lines. I got through it but it was the worst half hour I've ever put in. She sat on the lounge and I had to stand up. Wouldn't have a clue how the audience reacted on the night. I was just glad to get off! I suppose the people who liked that sort of thing thought it was alright. The other girl was quite good but for me there was no feeling or anything. Just memorising.

So we put the show on and it turned out to be very successful. It was all amateur. All but Ivan Menzies and a few like that who were professional. It was only supposed to be on for one night but they extended it for a bit longer because it was a success. I had some publicity photos done for it too. The one they used was a terrible looking thing with my hands around my cheeks like the old time dance girls. And the poster read - 'This is Jean Davis'. It mentioned the show and all that sort of thing. I suppose those posters might still be around - I don't know.

Meanwhile, Bill Barnes got his job with Guinea Airways and next thing, he and Mum are off to New Guinea. Mum wanted me to go with her but I got married instead! They went on the Neptunia. That radio announcer Eric Welsh was on board too; years later, he finished up driving his car into the Yarra. So I'm down on the wharf waiting for Mum to come and say goodbye. She comes down just minutes before the gangway went up and all I had time to do was walk half way up the gangway with her, kiss her goodbye and off she went! They pulled the gangway up! She and Bill stayed in New Guinea for a long time. Mum loved it. Big social life up there.

My Aunty Irene, Mum's sister, used to be very generous towards me because she felt I didn't have much home life. When I mentioned to her I was going out with this young chap and I was going to be married, she insisted on doing everything. She sort of took me over. She was quite wealthy. Nothing was too good for her. I had three girls from the Herald Office as bridesmaids and the lass who was matron of honour was a cousin. Irene arranged the church - St. Joseph's in South Yarra - had all the frocks made and gave me the reception at the Playhouse, the same place we'd done the show. See, upstairs was a big reception room. She was very good. She arranged everything. She paid for everything. But because she was the black sheep of the family she wouldn't invite any of the others. There was just herself and her kids - who were all older than I - then myself and my husband. She wouldn't invite any of the second marriage ones. Nell wasn't invited. Mum wasn't there because she was in New Guinea.... We had quite a nice wedding but there was no one there I knew apart from my husband Bill Glennon and his people. Can't remember who gave me away. Somebody must have! Everything happened so quickly. I wasn't madly in love but I finally had a place where I could say well, this is my home. See, I was tossed around for many years. Funny way to be, isn't it?

We didn't have a honeymoon. We just went and lived with my husband's family in Thornbury for a while. It was dancing as usual. Bill kept dancing with his regular partner Ruby Barton and they were very good together. I didn't want anything to change. That was fair enough. You can't break things up just because you get married. Besides, ballroom didn't appeal to me that much. It was - to me - too restrictive.

It's doing the same steps.... everyone's doing the same thing. You don't sort of express yourself. Good grounding though. It gives you balance and poise.

Chapter Four: Catch Me and Spin

One night I was at the Casino Ballroom watching Bill dance with Ruby for a championship over there. I was sitting on the sidelines when Mickey Powell, who was the judge that night, came over to me and touched me on the shoulder. 'Excuse me,' he said, 'are you married to Bill Glennon?'

I said, 'Yes.'

He said, 'You've done some dancing, no doubt?'

I said, 'Yes - but not this kind though.'

He said, 'Well, I'm looking for a partner. My sister is giving it up because she's getting married and I wondered if you'd be prepared to come in for an audition?' I was stunned! Mickey Powell was the best dancer on the circuit. He was a real trick dancer. He and his sister used to do the 'Skater's Waltz' and you'd swear they were on ice. He was famous for his work.

After the championship was over, I told my husband and his mother what had happened and they thought I was having myself on! They all laughed. The more they thought it was a big joke, the more I was determined I was going to go. The next Tuesday I went into the Trocadero in Melbourne. I think it might have been the Green Mill then. Then it became the 40 Club which burnt down, then the foyer of that became the Trocadero. There were a few others there to audition as well so I lined up. When it was my turn, Mickey gave me a rough idea of the type of thing he'd be doing and he must have been happy with what I did because he decided that I was going to be his partner. That changed the smiles on their faces at home!

The first exhibition he ever taught me was the 'Skater's Waltz'. He was a wonderful dancer. His feet were just like lightning. Only a slim man but he had such perfect control that when he was spinning he did it so fast you could almost see it linking up. He was nimble and clever and he could go right around the floor like a skater. He was very good on explaining what I had to do. He said I had to sort of stiffen the body and once I got up into position I was not to move an inch. Then he showed me how the entrance into it would be. As I'd walk towards him I'd throw my leg and he'd grab me round the waist and he'd throw me straight up and around his neck. Once I got up there, he said, 'Don't even ask me a question. Hold your breath.' That's what I used to do. If I could do that for the full spin he was able to flick me around and catch me in the front again without any weight. It was scary the first few times but I was too busy letting it all sink in.

I danced ballroom with him which I didn't like doing much. The Quickstep was the only one he'd touch. He didn't do Waltz or any of the others. But if he was doing a Quickstep he could flicker his feet so quickly that it just dumbfounded the audience. I used to grab him and, holding his hand, I could slide him from one end of the floor to the other. He'd just position himself in, like, a splits movement and my body could take him right to the other end of the floor. I'd keep moving and he'd just stay in the one position. He was a real trick dancer. The 'Skater's Waltz' was, of course, his favourite. The whole tune, right through, you'd swear he was on ice. He'd diddle his feet and we'd be holding hands, cross-over, like they do on the ice. We'd be skating along like that and he'd throw me out and throw me up in the air, catch me and spin, bring me down and we'd skate off again. Very clever. His sister Mascotte gave me a pair of silver shoes when I started dancing with him. For luck, she said.

They used to put sawdust on the floor to make it easier to dance but just before Mickey would go on, they'd take it all off because it's dangerous for that overhead stuff. I know, because he had me on the back of his neck spinning at the end of the 'Skater's Waltz' routine and, to make it that little bit better, he'd take his hands down, put them behind his back and keep spinning. There was a tiny bit of sawdust on the floor and he was spinning so fast his foot slipped slightly and I went sailing straight through the air. Landed on my

Mickey Powell and Dorothy St. John.

side. Broke all my ribs! You can just imagine. The crowd thought it was wonderful! Thought it was all part of the act!

I stayed where I was. I couldn't move. I was stunned. Mickey came rushing over to help me up. I actually got up and bowed to everybody. When I got outside, they took me straight up to the hospital and taped me all up. Mickey said to me, 'Jean, I hate to say this, but if you don't appear on Saturday night, you'll lose your nerve.' He was a pretty shrewd man. He said, 'We'll still do the routine but we'll cut out the hard spins. The easy ones won't hurt.'

So I backed up on the Saturday night to dance with him. We did the easier lifts that didn't affect my side. It was quite true, I suppose. I would have lost my nerve. Mickey had enough sense to realise I had to go back and do it again as soon as possible. When I finished, my left side was swollen because I'd kept dancing. But I got over it quick enough.

One night we danced at the Ziegfeld Palais and Ida Pender was there - Squizzy Taylor's girlfriend. Mickey introduced me to her. I think their association would have gone right back to the days before I was in the dancing game. I don't know if Squizzy Taylor ever married her or what, but it was the first time ever that Mickey forgot what he was doing on the floor. She was a very charming person to speak to. Had a beautiful voice. Funny how different things strike you. I could have just closed my eyes and listened to her talk. Like honey. Just melted in your ears.

We put this show on at Festival Hall. Mickey put it on. We got a couple from Japan, a couple from London, somebody from Europe. We wanted to try and get it recognized as a world event. For some reason or other the major dancing bodies just wouldn't be in it. You'd think all you'd need would be a couple from each country, then we'd have an Australian Title that was recognised world-wide. I think what could have ruined it was that other people started having Australian Titles in Sydney or Brisbane - all over the place. When you get more than one, it's no longer an Australian Title. So, through being a bit greedy, they ruined it.

In 1937 Mickey told me that he'd be going to London and he thought he'd better check with me as to my position because he'd have to take a partner with him. I had a discussion with my husband and he wasn't over impressed because he'd split up with his partner Ruby. So we came to the conclusion it would be better for me to step down and for Mickey to find someone else.

There was a young lass I knew by the name of Dorothy St. John who was a very good ballet dancer. I knew she was unattached because she danced ballet - no partner. So I mentioned her to Mick and he said, 'Send her in and I'll have a run through with her.' He was quite happy with her ability, taught her and took her to London with him.

We put a show on to help him with expenses and fares. It was a big night and everyone turned up. We gave him the proceeds. When he was going I got big hearted and said, 'I'll give you all my press cuttings and things to take with you.' That's why there's little to show of my time as Mickey's partner.

Those days you went by ship - no flying. The cricket team was on board so, to pass the time away going across, he used to teach the cricketers how to dance. He did very well in London. They gave him so many write-ups. They thought he was absolutely marvellous. In Melbourne, of course, he was known as number one and I was very lucky to have had that opportunity to learn from him.

I'd had three chances to go overseas and I'd knocked 'em all back. So I thought, I'm never going. And I didn't.

Chapter Five: One Nite Stand

I had been very lucky to dance with Mickey Powell. I went straight from the beginning to the top. Short cut. He wasn't worried about whether I could dance or not. As long as I could keep time. As long as he had a partner that suited him. His routines were nothing to do with ballroom at all. That's why I liked it - it was different. Instead of letting all I'd learned go to waste, I suggested to my husband maybe we could put some exhibition into the ballroom. My husband had a very natural style for ballroom. All you had to choose from in those days was the Quickstep, Slow Foxtrot, Tango and Waltz. Bill did a beautiful Waltz. He had a very rhythmical body. He kind of weaved into each movement so that's why, later on, I thought we won't give the Waltz away. We'll just put some of the exhibition in with it. People loved that type of thing.

So, having practised for some time in the lounge room of our house, we thought we were ready to try it. First time we ever put it on the floor, I think, was either at the Casino or the Ziegfeld. Bill had a very open personality and he was extremely popular. People loved watching him Waltz. So we used to do the Waltz - sixteen bars - then we'd leave each other, come back together and he'd pick me up and spin. Then when I came down we'd continue on with the Waltz and do the same maybe twice. Always finished up with something spectacular. The audience understood the waltzing part of it and to see a bit of flair in the middle of it really got 'em in. No one had, to my knowledge, ever done it before. Not with ballroom. Not here or England. We more or less started off a new trend.

After we'd danced it a few times and it proved to be so popular, we got quite a few breaks from round about. The chappy who had the Locarno Ballroom, Arthur Hearndon, gave us two nights a week to teach there. Tuesdays and Thursdays I think. We used to run the dancing class but most learners don't like doing too much....

We became resident dancers. We were very fortunate. We took over all the jobs Mickey had before he went overseas. For two nights we'd do the Casino in Brunswick, two nights we'd do the Ziegfeld Palais at Glenferrie. We also did the Trocadero Palais in the city, the Orama Ballroom in Footscray, the Palais de Danse in St. Kilda and the Caulfield Town Hall. Palm Grove came later. It wasn't so popular. We also got on at the Heidelberg Town Hall. Allen Burnell opened that up as an experiment. Big success. At the Melbourne Town Hall we'd either put on our own show once every few months or we might go and dance there for somebody else. To be a resident dancer you had to hang onto your job because they were hard times - plenty of people after it. Pretty much the depression times then. It was a good living but that's why I never had any children. Never had enough time to spare.

Most places used to have championships that would wind up at the end of the year. Then they decided, instead of competitions every week, they'd have resident dancers who'd put the floor show on. It was a change over from competitions to entertainment. We were lucky enough to be in on the ground floor. They still had championships at the end of the year but they didn't drag them out so much.

The only things I hated doing were the 'Spreading Chestnut Tree' and the 'Lambeth Walk'. When they first hit, we had to do them to show the public. I never felt so silly in all my life doing that 'Spreading Chestnut Tree'. That was only a small period of time though. Just a matter of showing people and once they'd looked at it, that was enough.

From there we had a very successful time and I was joined then by a chap called James Cane. He was the professional champion and very good. The three of us - between us - we did very well. We were a good combination. We were a team for eight years. We did everything together. Worked in the same places. Went to the same places... I danced with both partners, sometimes trio, sometimes individually.

Bill Glennon and I dancing the Jitterbug at our first exhibition in Melbourne.　　1937

Jim Cane.

39

The Palais de Danse was the place. That's where the championships were held every year. The man who managed it, Mr. Kerwin, was a real business man. He never mixed with the dancers. He didn't know them. He was just an out and out businessman. They had the biggest bands and they used to put the shows on and supply all the trophies. He had a good business head.

We pretty much had control of Melbourne and we also did performances in country centres. There was a place at Geelong - we'd take a bus load there and we'd have the band from the Casino. The man in Geelong who employed us was Laurie Slack. He owned a big picture theatre there. They'd have the pictures going on while the dance was in progress. You could please yourself whether you wanted to dance or watch the picture. We went to other country towns a couple of times but not very often. Another man we worked for was a very go ahead person named Cyril Bright and he owned a jeweller's shop. He had the Brunswick Town Hall and the Ziegfeld. He was tied up in the money of these different places.

A tailor by the name of Lever in Melbourne offered to make our clothes for publicity. He made me a white suit and he made my husband a suit and in return we had to tell everybody where we'd had them made. From there on, every show I went to, my clothes were always provided. In Sydney I got most of 'em from America. Up here in Brisbane - Solomon Lou.

When I was about fifteen my father bought me an autograph book. One of the little rhymes went - 'I'm just a blue eyed blonde that happens to be fond of...' and it was signed Tommy Davidson. Tommy had a big band - fifteen piece. I never dreamed at the time I would get to know him personally. After all those years, he did a special recording of 'Dark Eyes' for me in five different tempos.

Nine thirty or ten would be floor show time and before we went on, we had a theme song, 'Dancing in the Dark'. When it got a bit out of date Artie Shaw, the band leader, did 'One Nite Stand' for us. That would have been about 1941. It was a good name so we used it for our floor shows. Didn't have the same meaning as it does now!

The first couple we taught the same type of work to were people called Jack and Joyce Bosley. They were excellent. They went to London and did the stuff we had pioneered. Over there it was a sensation to see someone doing a beautiful Waltz and the next minute, up in the air and spinning. They had lots of publicity. I'd have to say Australian dancers led the field in that type of work. It had never been seen in Europe then. Now it's taken for granted.

Chapter Six: The Samba and the Rumba

Young Apollo was the chappy who used to pull buses up Bourke Street with his teeth. He was an Adagio dancer - balancing girls as he walked around, then dropping and catching them again. It's more refined than Apache. I met him through a young lass I worked with and, while he never came into the ballrooms, I thought this work has to have some good in it. So I had him come down to teach and I started to pick up some handy hints. He taught the three of us how to hold. He was very helpful - especially with the Bolero. The Bolero is more sexy than straight out Apache or Adagio.

You know how they spin holding one leg and one arm? Well, he'd teach you the knack of letting go. Bill could let me go and I could keep spinning on the floor. He also taught me how to make myself lighter. I was an asthma sufferer and my breathing was pretty bad. This improved it. When you're about to go into a lift, you take a deep breath beforehand. Soon as they put their arm on you and throw your body upside down, you twist yourself on the way and take that big breath. Then they can get you round the back of their neck. You hold your breath till you've finished the spin - sixteen bars of it - then as they throw you out of it, you're still light as a feather. Your legs are tight together and your arms are tight together and there's no weight for the partner. When you hit the floor you just let it go. You're right. You're fully stretched. All that Latin American stuff was just coming out. The Tango was back - it had been around since before the war and it had gone through phases of popularity. The Rumba - which is probably of African origin - had that Spanish influence too and when it came out in the movies I'd learn it and we'd put it in the shows. I loved Latin American. Every time a movie was released with it, I'd make sure I saw it.

Then there was the Samba which was new. It really only caught on in London after the Second World War but I got it from the movies and I had this bright idea. I thought, why not make the Samba and Rumba all part of ballroom?

The Victorian Society of Dancing was run by a woman called Dorothy Gladstone. I don't know if she was ever a dancer herself but I suppose you'd think of her as on a level with Jennie Brenan. She was at the top of the business. She was President of the Victorian Society of Dancing. Everything to do with ballroom had to go through them. When I suggested the Rumba could be a part of ballroom, she didn't want any part of it unless it was done through her members. Because I'd never done any exams or competitions she didn't want to see it. However Arthur Hearndon was a member so I approached him and said, 'If I teach you the Rumba movements, would you help me present it to the Society?' He agreed. He was a very nice man. The next time there was a convention, he and I went on the floor. We danced the Rumba - the old square Rumba - to let them have a look and see what they thought of it. They were quite impressed. They thought it was most.... different. But they were still very small minded about it. They were most reluctant to put it into the competitions. Later on, as it started to catch on, we changed it to an offbeat Rumba which was much more interesting.

Then all the variations came into it and it was accepted everywhere - in every state. But they were very hesitant at first to include it professionally. Thanks to Arthur Hearndon, at least I got it out there on the floor for the Society to look at.

Without him I could never have got it off the ground. The only other thing to hit at that stage was Jive, but the Americans brought that out.

Jim Cane and myself (amateur) at the 1937 Ballroom Championship in Melbourne.

Jim and I posing for a studio shot. 1937

1937

We kept working the Melbourne circuit and putting on shows for quite a few years and we were teaching pretty well full time. Sometimes we'd put a couple of teams together and challenge Sydney to a competition. There was a man up there called Jack Musgrove who'd do all the arrangements in Sydney and we put on some very successful shows. I was to meet him again some years later when I went there to live. The team thing got everyone in. Great publicity. It was good to work in another city too. It got us known just that bit better.

At the Palais Royale in the Melbourne Exhibition Buildings there was a dance run by the Dennis Brothers. Down one side of the dance floor there was, like, a little studio where, after you'd paid your admission, you could come over to where we were teaching and learn for nothing. When you were good enough you were allowed to go out on the main floor. That was a strategy to get people to come whether they could dance or not. We'd be teaching up till about ten o'clock. It was there that a chap called Alf Davies came looking for a new partner. Alf had been taught by a man called Charlie Ring who was a ballroom stylist. Beautiful dancer and very good looking. He always wore white tails. I used to teach him the Rumbas and Sambas and he'd go over to England and get lessons in ballroom in exchange for teaching them the Latin American stuff. Charlie had given Alf all the polish and poise for ballroom.

This young girl was amongst the beginners at the Palais Royale - a pretty red head. Her name was Julie Reaby. I introduced them and Alf danced with her out in the main ballroom and he finished up marrying her. They were number one dancers. They were the first Australians ever to win a world title. They won it two years in a row so they must've been good. When he and Julie came back to Australia, they got in touch with me and said, 'You've done so much for us, Jean, that if there's anywhere you want us to dance, we'll do it.' I think I put 'em on at Festival Hall or somewhere and I lined up all the teachers to have lessons from them. It was nice that they hadn't forgotten me.

I met Alf in Sydney some years later walking through Coles or one of those places. He had a job on the newspapers. Alf and Julie Davies had gone on to judge at all the major championships and gave exhibitions and lectures. They remained one of the longest reigning champion dance couples in Australia.

Another thing that happened when I was teaching - Bill and I were giving lessons over at the Casino. There was this chap from Queensland named Tommy Omhdal and his partner who were both professionals. We were giving them some routines to take back. My husband was walking around showing how easy it was to keep your partner up in the air. Because our heights weren't very much different it was easy for him. Plus he'd done a lot of wrestling so he was very strong. But poor young Tommy was tall and his girl was tall and thin but, well, he'd paid for the lesson so we had to keep at it till he got the knack.

Bill had me up there showing how simple it was but he got carried away and forgot and just let go! I landed straight on my head! I was a bit fuzzy for a while. It was a long way down. I've had some funny things happen to my head. No wonder it comes up in a lump!

There was a funny experience happened over at the Casino too. Cyril Bright - who I've already mentioned - had that and the Brunswick Town Hall next door. The Town Hall was for old time 50:50 stuff and the Casino was all modern. We used to work at the Casino then rush in next door, put the floor show on then go back. This night I was dancing with my husband and Jim Cane. We were doing the Bolero for the Town Hall floor show and I used to wear this open, frilly dress with a halter top that just tied at the back of the neck.

When Jim took me up in the air and I was sliding down the front of him, the back of the halter neck got caught in his vest. As I got to the ground and spun away, it just undid the back. So the result was I had nothing on in the front! You couldn't wear a bra doing that kind of work. I thought - what am I going to do? I was spinning away - not a stitch on top! I heard the band falter a bit. They got a shock! It's a big hall, that

Town Hall. A lot of people. So I picked up the skirt and pulled it up in the air and kept spinning. Spun myself off. Out to the exit. The two partners were standing there like two stunned goats. They didn't know what had happened. But the audience loved it! They were up on the balconies cheering.

The manager berated me. He said, 'Next time you do a show like that, you do it in the Casino. The modern place. Never mind here in the old time....!'

A bloke called George Osborne booked us to dance in Albury. His family had been pioneers of Albury and he owned half the town. He engaged us for a one night show. Well we got off the train and we were given the star treatment. They'd converted a skating rink into a ballroom. It was Albury's premier ballroom.

The show went over really well and when we spoke to George later, he said there was this bloke called Pivot Smith. He was a big jeweller. He was interested in engaging us for a few months. Albury needed somebody like us, he reckoned, or they'd get left behind. They offered us a wage for the floor shows and gave us the use of the ballroom for teaching. Plus they'd throw in our accommodation. So we agreed. We had plenty of pupils too. They'd come in for miles.

The Osbornes were a big family and they were spread all over town. In all the best places too. I got to know a girl called Wilga Osborne who, strangely enough, came to marry my father later on. There were also the maiden aunts - two old ladies who owned a house near the railway station. I remember going there once and there was a tabby cat under the stairs. I sat down to pick it up and I was just stroking it when one of the aunts came out and saw me. Apparently it was a wild cat no one could get near. They were all amazed. But see, I'd grown up with animals. I was used to them.

After we finished at Albury we decided to go and stay with my mother for a while up in Sydney. Before we left, Pivot Smith, George's partner, took us to his jeweller's shop and he said, 'Jean - pick anything from the window. It's yours.' Well, there were watches and diamonds - and he had said anything. I picked out this red medallion - just a little thing. I think he was a bit surprised that my choice was so modest. He'd been so good to us.... He said, 'Are you sure?' Anyhow, he went inside and came back with it in a velvet box.

We took the train to Sydney to stay with my mother at the Cross. Didn't do any dancing up there. We were just helping out. My mother was living in a guest house and the woman who owned it was from New Zealand. When she got to meet us she got enthused about changing the place into a coffee shop or a dancing studio. She finished up asking all the guests to move out. My husband and I set the place up as a coffee shop and we worked there for a while just having a night time show.

My mother at this stage had a business there in Kings Cross. It was a mixed business behind the Mayfair Hotel. There was a Chinese cafe, then there was a lane, then there was the Mayfair. Mum had her business right on that corner. Kings Cross was exciting back then - not like it is now.

Mum used to give everything to everyone for nothing! People were ticking up left, right and centre! She was a real softie - that's where I get it from. After she'd had the shop a few years, her husband finally said, 'I think you'd better give this business away. All you're doing is keeping all the no-hopers around the place!'

There was a girl who also came from Melbourne staying at the guest house where we'd moved to. She was Chinese. Judy Wong He. She had this little niece with her - real cute. One day we went to the beach at Bondi. I used to go there all the time when I was in Sydney. I couldn't swim. I only went out as far as my neck. I just used to sunbake near the water. We'd been there a while and I was taking this little Chinese girl for a walk up the beach. We were only up to our ankles. Then I heard someone talking about a big wave so we went further up the beach to try and see it. You could sure see it alright. It was huge. All the boys went off on their boards to catch it. It was so high you could see it from way out.

When it came in, it hit the edge and dug out a hole about six feet, dragged everything out with it and drowned all the people that couldn't swim. There were casualties laying all along Bondi Beach. As the life savers were bringing them in, they were just sort of placed along so the boys could go out again for more. And this life saver - he got sucked under himself.

I always thought to myself, thank goodness I had that little Chinese girl with me 'cause if I hadn't, I'd have been in the water where those people were. Must have been a tidal wave or something. First one I've ever seen. I thought I must mention that because people would have forgotten.

We weren't over-enthused about running this coffee shop for too long. Then the woman who owned it started getting my husband to do all the odd jobs - as well as us running it. When she wanted him to wash down the front stairs every morning, he jacked up. We talked about it, he and I, and we decided to go back to Melbourne. I think the place later became the Pink Pussycat.

Things in Melbourne were pretty bad - wasn't a lot of money about. But we got all our jobs back quick enough and did a lot of teaching. One couple I taught to dance was Italian. Their name was Mamanna. The old chappy couldn't speak a word of English but the mother could and they owned the baby shop, the tobacconist's, the hairdressing salon - all the shops from Bridge Road in Richmond - from the corner down. The Town Hall and the Richmond Baths were directly opposite. They had a lovely home in Burnley in the main street there and it had its own ballroom.

The daughters all ran the shops and one of 'em, Sadie and her husband Stan Dixon, wanted to dance. Now he was a short, fat little chap and she's a dumpy, dark little girl. Not exactly what you'd expect for dancing. Anyhow I felt sorry for them because everyone used to have a bit of a laugh at their expense. I'm a bit of a softie. I thought, here they are trying as hard as they can and people are laughing at them. So I gave her a bit of ballet. I thought well, this might get some of the fat off her - you know. She was very determined. They practised and practised and they both trimmed down. I put 'em on at the Melbourne Town Hall for a show. Nobody could believe it! The determination had taken over and they were good at what they did. And when they went on the floor this night, the people who knew them got the shock of their lives! They did such a wonderful job they staggered everyone.

The mother never forgot the fact that I'd helped 'em do that. When I had trouble with my second husband - the one that died - they repaid me by letting me go and stay at one of their places there in Bridge Road. I used to go down to their house every weekend. It was very nice. They never forgot.

NEXT FRI. NIGHT
MELB. TOWN HALL
One Night Stand
By JEAN MONTEZ
featuring
GRAND FINALS
DANCING
CHAMPIONSHIP
MODERN AND OLD TIME
Plus Challenge N.S.W. v. Victoria
for Latin American Rhythm.
RHUMBA, SAMBA, TANGO.
Floor Shows by Australia's Leading
Professional Ballroom and Fancy
Exhibition Dancers.
Brilliant Music by Melb.'s Ace
Sweet Swing, Dixieland and Rebob
Band. Radio Vocalists and Stage
Stars.
Compere: Bon Gibbins.
Mod. and O.T. Non-Stop Dancing
8 till 12.
TICKETS 3/6, AT GLEN'S
Hear Billie Hyde on Drums and
the Splinter Reeve Splinettes, with
the Famous Bachelor Boys Rhythm
Kings.

46

Sydney   1937

47

SATURDAY, 17th FEB., 1951
at SILK'S Ballroom
BON & NOEL GIBBINS'
PRESENTS A BIRTHDAY TRIBUTE TO
JEANNE MONTEZ
AUSTRALIA'S LOVELIEST DANCER & BRILLIANT ARRANGER

who has partnered Australian leading Professional Dancers including the following—
MICKEY POWELL, JIM CANE, BILL GLENNON, MICK DAVIS, HUMPHREY DUKE, SYD CAVE, BILL FREEMAN, JACK AYRES, ARTHUR HEARNDON, CHAS. FROULOP.

and has arranged Professional Exhibition Routines, for many champions including—
MICK DAVIS — SHIRLEY REID
FRANK SOUTH—MURIEL WATTS
(Both couples at present overseas)
also for—
ALF DAVIES — JULIE REABY
FRANK KAYE — BERYL HANSON
DENNIS BRAMHALL—ANNE SULLIVAN
CHAS. FROULOP — IVY PATON
CHAS. FOLEY — SHIRLEY ROBERTS
SEL HANCHETTE — SHIRLEY BONE

ARE YOU A GOOD DANCER?

ASK YOURSELF THESE QUESTIONS

A. Do your partners look pleased and happy when you dance with them?

B. Do you see a look of disinterest appear on their faces after you have travelled a few steps across the floor?

A. Do you glide over the floor effortlessly and in time to the music?

B. Do you find it hard to move freely and easily?

A. Do your partners say to you, "I enjoyed that dance immensely," and ask you for another?

B. Do they escort you off the floor and not ask you to partner them again?

A. Are you surrounded by partners all anxious to have the next dance with you?

B. Do you decorate the wall and sit out most of the night watching other people enjoy themselves?

A. Do you feel confident and at ease when you step on the floor with your partner?

B. Do you feel nervous and shy, knowing full well the dance is going to be an effort?

A. Do you enjoy success with the opposite sex and see others looking at you enviously?

B. Do you feel neglected and lonely at a dance, wishing you were being paid more attention by good partners?

What is your rating? If you have a majority "A" you are a good dancer. If it is "B" our advice to you is don't wait another minute, slip in and have a lesson and see how easy it is to learn. Your dividends in increased confidence will be enormous.

HOW MANY LESSONS WILL IT TAKE ME?

This question is asked time and time again—do you know that the average beginner knows enough to go on the floor after the first three or four lessons? You can potter around for years trying to pick it up, when for the sake of having half a dozen lessons you learn right from the start. For the few shillings you spend on learning to dance you will gain something that will give endless pleasure and happiness.

THE ONE SECRET OF BALLROOM DANCING POISE

This can be taught in one lesson. It is simply the carriage of the body, and once this is acquired, dancing becomes effortless and a pleasure. This balance and control of the body is taught to mannequins and film stars, and learning this through dancing is the short cut to achieving those admiring glances.

Show at Leggett's – Bon Gibbins and myself making the presentations.

Chapter Seven: The War Effort

War broke out. Everyone's life changed. To travel anywhere at night was difficult. Everything was blacked out. Car lights, trams, all the railway stations - everything was dark. We were managing the Heidelberg Town Hall for Allen Burnell who made a lot of money out of war machinery. He went on to open a place in the city called the Dug Out. It was near the corner of Collins and Swanston Streets. You know the shops on the corner of Collins and Swanston? You know the arcade there? Downstairs was a coffee shop. If you went through that arcade it would take you round the back way into Little Bourke. Renee Rose or something was there and you'd go down the stairs and the Dug Out was below. It was for any of the boys on leave. It was all put on free for them. Paid us less than five pounds a show but that wasn't bad money in those days. I had a day job somewhere as well so I made a good living really.

A lot of people who danced weren't drinkers but they'd get together with the musicians and have music sessions. They loved it. At one stage Ackland Street, St Kilda used to be all coffee shops - all the way down. Only an odd tobacconist or something here and there. The musicians would all gather there at the end of their shows. We used to go down and we'd travel all the way from say, Heidelberg or somewhere, just to listen to the musicians.

In Glenferrie, across the road from the Ziegfeld, there was another skating rink and when I was younger I went skating there with my father. See, skating rinks were perfect to convert to ballrooms for obvious reasons. They changed this one to Silk's Ballroom and that was run by Bon Gibbins, the man who started Moomba, the annual Melbourne festival. It has art exhibitions and entertainment and the huge float parade where they close off all the city streets.

One night a week we taught dancing at the Eureka Youth Club - behind all the big factories around Collingwood and Carlton. It was held at the Tattersall's Club. The kids only had to pay two shillings a week to become members. That two shillings entitled them every night of the week, if they wanted, to learn to speak correctly or to dance. We used to teach dancing on Thursday and on Tuesday there would be speech training and they had some man who'd been in the Spanish Civil War who used to lecture about what happened over in Spain. Very interesting. It took off at a great pace and the kids were coming in from everywhere. Then all the communist stuff started to creep into it. Anything to do with communism everyone was down on. That ended up finishing it.

There were a lot of ads about for people to help with the war effort. I thought, I should be doing something too. One of the girls I was teaching at the Eureka Club said 'I'll get you a job to help the war effort. I'm out at the munitions factory.' That sounded alright to me. So she gave me the particulars and I fronted out there.

When I got there they took me out to this little hut. Only two people to each hut. Reason being, if it blew up only two would get killed! We used to put this dynamite through a - like a sausage machine and I used to turn the handle. As it dropped out, it dropped through a little hole in the bottom and these little trolley trucks would come around to pick 'em up. The end of the fortnight when I went to get my pay, the payslip had so much for working and under that it had 'danger money'. Next time I saw my father I said, 'What's 'danger money' for?'

My father and I were very close and when he looked at the payslip he said, 'Oh Jean, I wouldn't stay there if I were you! If you want to help with the war effort you'd be better off to go to Victoria Barracks doing shorthand-typing.' My father was a great pusher - don't wait for jobs to come. Go after them.

So I went to Victoria Barracks and saw the woman in charge and what do you know - they were short of typists. I got straight on. I think I only lasted three weeks at the munitions factory. Of course, if I'd only used my head, we were putting shows on everywhere for the services - the Airforce, the Dug Out and a hospital for the Yanks down at Frankston. I was already working for the war effort.

There was one Airforce show on at the Princess Theatre where we were doing a Latin American routine - a Rumba. Throughout the routine - every sixteen bars - we'd throw a lift in. It was pretty exacting work because you had to come out right on the beat. We got through the routine and the last lift was up and around the neck. As my partner threw out his arms like a cartwheel, I heard something split. You could actually hear it - the taffeta. Fsssst! I thought now, what can it be? I only had this open, frilly dress on and a little pair of briefs. There wasn't much of 'em. It could only be one thing. All of a sudden I felt something flapping around my legs and I thought, my God! It's my knickers!

When I went into the lift, I was supposed to have my legs in a certain position for the balance. Well I couldn't. I had to keep 'em together! If I'd had 'em up - I don't know if you could see anything or not, but anyway my partner, poor devil, he got me up there alright but when he found I was in a different position, he wondered what was wrong. I had my right leg kind of curled around my left. I had to keep 'em together like that. We kept dancing though and when we got off he said, 'What in hell happened back there?'

I said, 'I just split my pants!'

A big night I remember - we went down to do Palm Grove where Bobby Gibson was playing. This particular night after we'd finished our floor show, one of the American lads in the audience - they called out that he was the Harvest Moon Ball champion in America. He and his sister had just won the title. He jived and they were urging him to come onto the floor. They asked me if I would dance with him. So naturally I had to say yes. Bobby played this real jivey music and the American was spectacular. He was a trained ballet dancer. He could do anything. I didn't have to do much - just keep in time. He did the lot. I had seen Jive before. See, the music to me.... music's always been movement and it was very easy. It was just an even beat and you could fill in and do what you wanted to. What he did was almost solo. He'd grab me by the waist or by the hand - swing me out and swing me back in. Then off he'd go again. It brought the house down because one of their own lads had been given a chance.

I think that same night we had Artie Shaw down there. He was playing his clarinet with Bobby Gibson. They got up and played together. It was quite a big night. From there on we decided to include Jive in our own shows at the Melbourne Town Hall and the people liked it. I just made up all the lifts and throws - as long as it came out on time. My husband was a real versatile dancer. He only had to be shown a couple of times and because he was also an amateur wrestler, he had broad shoulders. It was just no trouble for him - he was very strong.

Dad was often at the shows too. He loved the music. The only time he ever danced with me was one night at the Heidelberg Town Hall. I was there with Bill. We put the floor show on and after it was finished I went up to the microphone - you know how impulsive I am - and I pointed him out. My father was sitting up in one of the little boxes upstairs and I called attention to him. I knew he'd love it and I said that was my father and I'd like him to come down because I wanted to do the old time Waltz with him. He came down the stairs with his chest out. He looked as much like a dancer as all get out but they played the Waltz and we went around the floor once. Everybody clapped and he thought that was wonderful.

We still took teams to Sydney during the war and we'd go by ship. The ships would have to go way out because of the mines and nearly everyone got sick except me. However, dancing took a bit of a lull around then and that's when I switched round to doing the show at the State Theatre. I was in my twenties then and full of confidence. I was ready to try anything.

Airforce show at the Princess Theatre.

★ BILLY GLENNON and GEORGE McWHINNEY
PRESENT
SIXTH ANNUAL

ONE NITE STAND

AUSTRALIA'S MOST FAMOUS DANCE SHOW

MELBOURNE TOWN HALL
WEDNESDAY NITE ----- 27th NOVEMBER

JEAN MONTEZ DAVIS
From Trocadero, Sydney

We proudly present our NEW SHOW

SWING AND DANCE BAND
FESTIVAL
10 - BANDS - 10

NON-STOP DANCING ------- 7.30 to 12 p.m.

Tickets now at Allan's.   ADMISSION -- 3/11 (incl. Tax)

1946

Chapter Eight: *Star Spangled Freedom*

They were good days but they weren't easy. You had to hang on to what you had. The three of us - Jim Cane, Bill and I - we'd worked together for so long, I was getting a little bit.... not fed up, but the life was becoming tedious. I didn't want anything more to do with ballroom dancing. I'd never felt at home with it. Just dancing backwards - that's all the girl is doing. How can you express yourself following the male lead and dancing backwards? I suppose I'm a nut but that's how I felt. So I thought to myself, I'll turn to face the front. I'm not going to be dancing backwards all the time! So I didn't.

There was an ad in the paper for someone to do a dance solo for the show 'Star Spangled Rhythm'. They wanted a band, a singer and a dancer. It was a show and a movie put together for the American Marines and visiting soldiers and it was going to open at the State Theatre.

The movie 'Star Spangled Rhythm' was made in 1943 and it featured all the top stars from America. There was Vera Zorina who did 'That Old Black Magic'. Betty Hutton was in it. Eddie Bracken, Bing Crosby, Preston Sturgess.... The Americans used to be standing in the passageways to see it. They brought Daniel Maas out from America as the conductor so there'd be no jealousy among our own musicians. Smart move.

My lucky break was auditioning and getting the part for the solo dance routines and that made me independent of having partners. I still did a bit of the exhibition work but not a lot. Things fell my way. I was very lucky. I'd had enough of ballroom. All the bickering and.... See, I can't stand people fighting over things. The jealousy that goes on.... So the three months that I worked there, I sort of moved away from my two partners and friends of years and got into a different way of life - you know? I didn't have to dance with anyone any more. I could do what I liked - which to me was marvellous.

The band was all local musicians. I think even Horrie Dargy might have been one - I'm not sure. They all finished up top of the ladder in their work but they were just kicking off then. They had this tenor who was a well-known singer about town. He sang a Spanish number from one of the balconies and when the music came on for my cue I had to go on and dance. I had three different numbers and three changes. Because the dressing rooms were such a long way down, I used to just slip a dress off at the side of the curtains. No one there but the old bloke who pulled 'em backwards and forwards. I didn't have any worries.

My routines had nothing to do with the movie. I did whatever Daniel Maas selected. Can't remember the other numbers - only the first one because this tenor used to stand on a balcony to sing it. As he was up there singing, the conductor was down in the pit with the band and I'd come in from the side of the curtains with the old castanets. When I look back, I was game 'cause I didn't know a thing about dancing solo. I'd always loved the Spanish music though and it all came pretty easy. See, ballroom dancing to me - even though it's graceful and nice - I don't feel as if you're giving.... what's inside. With this I never did the same thing twice. I just used to make it up as I went along. The music was no trouble. I knew it so well. I enjoyed the freedom very much.

It was a terrific movie. I could never understand why it didn't make a comeback. As its name suggests - it was full of stars. The last couple of weeks there were a lot of Marines stationed down at Frankston. Ones that all got killed on.... where was it? Guam? Somewhere they were all wiped out. They used to practise down at Frankston and on the last couple of weeks the show sold out completely. The boys were standing in the aisles all the way up to come and see this movie.

THAT OLD BLACK MAGIC

Words by JOHNNY MERCER
Music by HAROLD ARLEN

Paramount's STAR SPANGLED RHYTHM

MUSICAL SCORE

'THAT OLD BLACK MAGIC'
'SHARP AS A TACK'
'A SWEATER A SARONG AND
A PEEK-A-BOO BANG'
'I'M DOING IT FOR DEFENSE'
'ON THE SWING SHIFT'
'OLD GLORY' · 'HIT THE
ROAD TO DREAMLAND'

FAMOUS MUSIC CORP., • 1619 BROADWAY, New York City, N. Y.

Circa 1944

I was living in Batman Avenue, South Yarra when all this happened. We had a flat just over the bridge and the Riverside Hotel was on the other side. There was nothing else there, just a track for the horses. The Tan Track. You'd walk out of our flat, cross the road and the track started. Then there was the bridge that took you over to Punt Road. Batman Avenue was a real deserted place. The trams went past and there was a bus that would take you over the bridge. That's where that radio announcer Eric Welsh drove his car straight off the bridge into the Yarra and drowned.

Because it was so deserted over in that section I was frightened to travel. That American soldier - Leonski - used to pop up everywhere when you least expected it. He murdered one girl over near the zoo and one in Russell Street.... I wasn't even game to go home on the little bus. So I decided that I would move into the city to Collins Street and I found a place there where you could just have a room for the night if you wanted. I'd only have to walk up a little way, cross the road and I was at the State.

I left the flat and everything in it. It was full of antiques. I had a bit of a thing on them at that stage. I bought a lot because antique shops were opening up everywhere. When we sold the place, the man who bought it did so on the condition I left everything there, as it was.

That was more or less the beginning of my break up in the marriage. The fact that I got the job by myself at the State and I never used to go home.... I'd stay in the city because of the closeness. Those three months of separation....how can I put it? When you're with somebody day and night all the time, then all of a sudden you have a separation, you think clearly. I'd never thought about myself. I'd always been trying to please other people.

Bill and I got divorced and for the first time in my life I felt free. I was very happy. I had reporters from People Magazine and the newspapers coming for the story. I just said, 'No - no comment about anything.' We were still the best of friends as far as I was concerned.

Unfortunately I don't have any photos of my wedding and not many of the dancing. I left 'em all with my mother-in-law. I didn't like to take 'em from her. I felt mean - you know. Everything I had to do with that marriage, I left in her hands.

Chapter Nine: *The Tivoli*

The Tivoli would have been just after 'Star Spangled Rhythm'. A couple of people I boarded with in Collins Street - Lennie McDermott and Rene Nicholson - we decided we'd try The Tivoli. Rene was dancing with Gerry Hales. She was a very attractive young girl. She'd won the South Street Ballarat competitions and she was looking for something new. Lennie was a singer from Western Australia and had won the Sun Aria and a few other things.

We went up and did an audition and Rene went in as a showgirl. Naturally, I said I'd be dancing. They had ballets and that sort of thing so I did what I'd just done at the State. What they went in for those days - the more clothes you had off the better. But the old devil who was running it - Parnell - didn't tell me what I had to do until it was time for rehearsals.

When I was going to school, I knew these two sisters - Myra and Yvonne Slater. We more or less grew up together from the age of about seven or eight. Yvonne married Athol Smith, the photographer. He was German. When Parnell sent me round there to get some publicity photos, I was very happy that my own girlfriend was there to do all the draping with the clothes and everything. Knowing her all those years I immediately felt at ease. Didn't worry me. That's where that photo with the lace came about. I've never had any qualms about nudity of any sort 'cause at the State Theatre I used to have to change on stage. So Yvonne put the lace across and they took some photos and then she said, 'This one I want you to hold it out the back like that.' Meant I had nothing on in front. She could tell I wasn't too keen about it. She said, 'You don't have to worry because everything we take you'll see first.'

When the session was over and done with, I made some appointments to have dancing photos taken at a later date with my partners. After a couple of days the first proofs were ready and I had to go back and see them. But they weren't proofs. They were the finished products. They were photos about four feet high! There was one with the lace in front of me and one with the lace behind me and I said, 'Well I'm not too keen about that one.'

'Don't worry about it,' they said. 'Whatever you say can be used, we'll use.'

In the meantime we'd had the dancing photos taken. Athol Smith was a very clever man with his photography. He made those ones up life size. They were huge. If we had a show on we'd put one at the door as you walked in. It was almost as big as me standing there. But needless to say, the one Parnell picked was the one without any clothes on. Then I found out that the scene he wanted me to do was not dancing at all. He wanted me behind two curtains holding the reins of a great big dog. With all sorts of nothing on! A silhouette. I immediately told my father because, those days, if you broke a contract they could take you to court.

When I explained it all to him, Dad got his back up. He said, 'I'll deal with this. Don't you worry about it.' He got in touch with Parnell and said, 'You're not to use my daughter's photos. She doesn't want that. She was engaged as a dancer, nothing else. You're not to display her pictures.'

In the meantime I got in touch with Yvonne and told her what had happened and said, 'Whatever you do, don't supply him with anything.'

It all must have fizzled out because I never heard any more about it. Because I was engaged as an act, I had a good out. So that was my big brush with The Tivoli. I never worked there. You had to be very firm with men like that. Both Lennie and Rene went ahead with it and had no trouble at all but it was a different position for me. Not like these days of course. I could probably sue him for breaking the contract!

The photo with the lace.   1943

LENNIE McDERMOTT

EXT FRIDAY NIGHT — MELBOURNE TOWN HALL

THE GRAND FINAL OF

MODERN and OLD TIME CHAMPIONSHIPS

Don't miss this huge Dancing Extravaganza. "Jeanne Montez" Presents

ONE NITE STAND

TO SUPPORT MARGE JONES, MISS AUSTRALIA QUEST ENTRANT.

SPECIAL FEATURES: CHALLENGE MATCH BETWEEN N.S.W. AND VIC. FOR LATIN AMERICAN RHYTHM DANCING—SAMBA, RUMBA AND TANGO.

A HUGE FLOOR SHOW FEATURING MICK DAVIS, MILLIE MEAKIN, SHIRLEY REID, BERT WATSON, VERA CLARKE, CHARLES FOLEY, SHIRLEY ROBERTS, DENNIS BRAMHALL, ANNE SULLIVAN, SEL HANSETTE AND SHIRLEY BONE.

BRILLIANT MUSIC BY MELBOURNE'S ACE BANDS

THE BACHELOR BOYS' BAND, THE SPLINTER REEVE'S SPLINTETTES AND IVAN LOEL'S SWEET SWING. WITH BON GIBBINS AS COMPERE.

AND LEADING RADIO VOCALISTS AND STAGE PERSONALITIES AND BILLIE HYDE ON DRUMS

YES ! IT'S A GOOD NIGHT YOU MUST NOT MISS—FRIDAY NEXT, NOV. 18.

DANCING AND VARIETY FROM 8 TILL 12. THE 1949 SHOW OF SHOWS.

TICKETS 3/6, OBTAINABLE FROM GLEN'S. 800 BALCONY SEATS FOR NON-DANCERS. This Space Donated by SILK'S BALLROOM, Glenferrie, the Home of Dancers. FRIDAY and SATURDAY NIGHTS, Melbourne's Super Shows. Danceland's Very Best Rendezvous.

Chapter Ten: *Jeanne Delysia Montez in Sydney*

Around the end of 1944 when 'Star Spangled Rhythm' had finished the three months in Melbourne, the show went to Sydney. Melbourne and Sydney were great rivals so I suppose that's why they didn't transfer the musicians. Just the show. I was left hanging in limbo until they made up their minds whether I should be engaged to do it up there. I wanted to get away from Melbourne for a while after my marriage break up and the trouble at The Tivoli so I thought I'd go to Sydney regardless of the show. At least, with the show up there, I wasn't going with no hope of a job. There was a good chance I was going up to something.

Before I left Melbourne I changed my name. I thought I'll start in Sydney under a different name altogether. I won't know anybody and it'll be great. I'd just hope for the best. Well, I did that. I've still got all the papers - the legal change of name. I had always worked under the name Davis, then I changed it to Jeanne Delysia Montez. Delysia Montez was, I think, the name of the Lady In Waiting who married my great grandfather, the butler Davis.

When I got to Sydney.... everything had seemed so great, you know.... till I arrived. Then I thought to myself, what have I done? I'm alone in another state. I don't know anybody and I'm sitting in the hotel room feeling very dejected. All my friends were missing. I didn't think I was so smart by then.

On the second or third day I was walking along Kings Cross - the main street there - and I saw two of my friends from Melbourne. I was never so pleased to see them in all my life! They said, 'We're going to the Trocadero tonight. There's a big ball on. Come with us.' I thought how nice it would be just to be with somebody I knew. The three days prior I'd more or less just sat in my hotel room or walked up and down the street. Knew nobody. Not a soul. I had been to Sydney before but only on visits with my mother or my husband, taking a team up or something. But I didn't know people.

However I took the opportunity of going with them and when I went that night to the ball at The Trocadero, the manager there, Mr. Jack Musgrove, recognised me and came up and said, 'Oh how nice to see you!' I thought well, that's good. Somebody remembers me! He knew me from when I'd taken a team of dancers up by ship and challenged any four from New South Wales at The Trocadero, see. That's how I'd got to know him. He'd put the show on and paid all the expenses. He said, 'What are you doing up here?'

I said, 'I'm living in Sydney now.'

He said, 'Would you be interested in a job?'

I said, 'Nothing I'd like better. What would I have to do?'

He said, 'You brought those people up - put that show on. You've had plenty of experience. You could come in as our public relations or entertainment manager. Over the past years we've had nothing but Americans in here. Everything we used to have is gone. What I want you to do is reintroduce balls, championships and floor shows. I'll give you a retainer and whatever you can get over and above our normal take of a Wednesday and Saturday night, we'll go half each.'

I said, 'That sounds alright to me.' So that's how I started putting on shows. I'd go to all the talent quests that were around and about Sydney and if I saw anyone who I thought had a bit of potential, I'd give 'em a build up and put 'em on. I had them coming up from Melbourne too which was very handy. I had a lot of contacts there.

DEED POLL DECLARING CHANGE OF NAME.

KNOW ALL MEN by these presents that I the undersigned JEANNE DELYSIA MONTEZ of 96 Collins Street Melbourne Actress now or lately called JEAN MARY GLENNON DO HEREBY on behalf of myself and my heirs and issue lawfully begotten ABSOLUTELY RENOUNCE AND ABANDON the use of my said name of MARY JEAN GLENNON and in lieu thereof assume and adopt the name of JEANNE DELYSIA MONTEZ and for the purpose of evidencing such change of name I HEREBY DECLARE that I shall at all times hereafter in all records, deed, documents and other writings and in all actions, suits and proceedings as well as in all dealings, transactions, matters and things whatsoever and upon all occasions use and subscribe the said name of JEANNE DELYSIA MONTEZ in lieu as my name in lieu of the said name of JEAN MARY GLENNON so abandoned as aforesaid.

AND I THEREFORE HEREBY EXPRESSLY AUTHORISE AND REQUIRE all persons whomsoever at all times to designate, describe and address me and my heirs and issue by such adopted name of JEANNE DELYSIA MONTEZ only.

IN WITNESS whereof I have hereunto subscribed my adopted name of Jeanne Delysia Montez this *ninth* day of *February* One thousand nine hundred and forty-four.

SIGNED SEALED AND DELIVERED by the abovenamed JEANNE DELYSIA MONTEZ in the presence of

Jeanne Delysia Montez

B. Sher
Solicitor

65

The Trocadero Palais

Balls, Club Parties, etc.
specially catered for

●

MELBOURNE'S PREMIERE DANCING RENDEZVOUS

JUST OVER PRINCES BRIDGE

SOUTH MELBOURNE. S.C.4

30th August 1946

Miss Jeanne Montez,
Trocadero,
SYDNEY.

Dear Jeanne,

Many thanks for your ring re the "Summer Championship". Mick Powell gave me all details on his return, and we will be pleased to co-operate with you and send our couple to Sydney.

Would you let me know as soon as possible the approximate date of the final, so that I can arrange the heats accordingly.

Mick tells me that you and your partner anticipate coming to Melbourne in the near future, and I would be glad to arrange an exhibition if you will let me know when.

Of course if this "Summer Championship" becomes an Annual affair, we would naturally expect the final of next year in Melbourne.

Kind regards,

Yours truly,

A. Sullivan

Samba – Women's Weekly
featured a double page
showing all the movements.
Demonstrated in Sydney,
Brisbane and Melbourne.

With Jim Cane.

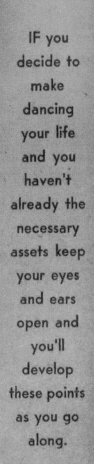

IF you decide to make dancing your life and you haven't already the necessary assets keep your eyes and ears open and you'll develop these points as you go along.

Here is the story of an Australian girl who has really made the grade — Jeanne Montez, of Sydney's Trocadero.

From an article in 'Bachelor Girl' magazine – with Jim Cane.   1947

METRO-GOLDWYN-MAYER
PTY. LIMITED

G.P.O. BOX 2576E
CABLES AND TELEGRAMS
"METROFILMS," SYDNEY
CODES
BENTLEY'S AND CINEMA
TELEPHONES
M 4291 (4 LINES)

HEAD OFFICE
20-28 CHALMERS STREET, SYDNEY, N.S.W.

June 23rd, 1947.

Dear Miss Montez,

I have pleasure in extending an invitation to you to be
personally present at a special preview screening of the
new Technicolor romance, "FIESTA", which will take place
on Tuesday, July 1st, at our theatrette, 20 Chalmers
Street at 2-30 p.m. sharp.

"FIESTA" stars Esther Williams and introduces MGM's new
artist, Ricardo Montalban, who has been hailed as a new
screen sensation. The cast also includes Akim Tamiroff,
John Carroll and Cyd Charisse.

I feel that you will be particularly interested in a dance
which is performed in this film by Ricardo Montalban and
Cyd Charisse, which has great possibilities for adaptation
in the ballroom. If, after seeing the film, you are also
of this opinion, we would like particularly to tie-up with
you in introducing the new "Fiesta" dance to the Australian
public.

In view of the limited seating capacity in our theatrette
I regret that this invitation must be strictly limited to
one person from your organization.

On receipt of this invitation would you be so good as to
'phone Miss Brady at M4291 and advise if you find it convenient
to attend.

We are,

Yours faithfully,
METRO-GOLDWYN-MAYER PTY. LIMITED.

H. A. Carleton.
Director of Advg. & Publicity.

HC:MB

70

Mum had been living in Bellvue Hill at that time and I lived just down from the Cross - Rosalind Gardens. It was no time before I was established at The Trocadero and Mum decided she and her partner had had it so she came to me. We lived at Kings Cross for a while, then we went to Rose Bay and then we got onto this big house opposite the convent in Vaucluse. We had to sign up and pay up front for so many months because the owners were going away. They were very fussy as to who got their house. It was a lovely place - beautifully furnished. The furniture was all kind of gold edged. And beautiful balconies. My mother was fond of nice things and she wanted it. I thought well, alright, we'll have it. It meant that I had to travel by bus every day from Vaucluse to The Trocadero and be home at night because neither of us could drive. In many ways, the fact that I did so well working all kinds of messy hours, was because Mum was with me. Sometimes she'd come to The Troc but if she didn't want to, when I'd get home she'd have my dinner ready for me and she made sure I always got a good eight hours sleep.

All the people who came up from interstate, we'd put up at the house without having to pay expensive hotels. We kept the costs down. My mother was a great help. I probably couldn't have done it without her. I got to the stage where if anyone asked me out, they'd say - you can bring your mother with you. We used to go up to Sammy Lee's place on a Sunday night to play poker. She used to love that. She was the sort of person who could fit in anywhere. Everyone loved her and she could make herself at home. She enjoyed every minute of it.

Mum and Bill had separated. Someone must've been hard to get on with. He was a brainy, easy going sort of bloke but Mum just didn't want him. She was a very definite woman. Under no circumstances would she have him back. Even years later, here in Brisbane, he came to the house and he begged her to go back with him. No. No way. Very definite woman. Stayed with me right to the end.

At that stage Rumbas and Sambas were becoming really popular. Latin American dancing started off overseas then we started doing it here. It had taken a bit of a lull so I revived it.   I liked the Spanish music. I did a little bit of Flamenco dancing too. Never learned it but I could do it. I just learned it from watching. The music seemed to be there, inside.... you know? That might have been passed down from the Montez family. God knows where! I can't account for it in any other way. I didn't do any of the heel stuff because to do that you have to be stationary. When I was dancing I couldn't be stationary. I had to move because when I had ballets and things behind me, to stay on one spot would be boring.

I mostly got the routines through seeing the movies. The music appealed to me, Rumba... Samba... La Fiesta - that's the Mexican Hat Dance. All the stuff that Cyd Charisse and Ricardo Montalban did. I loved that music and because I did, I naturally used to go and watch the shows. La Fiesta took me to Melbourne, Sydney and Brisbane. I got all the stuff by memorizing it from the movies. In the end the people from the theatres must have told each other because they used to get in touch with me and say, 'There's going to be a dance routine in this next movie. Do you want to come and see it?' So I'd go along and they'd run that section through for me and then I'd put it in the show. When the theatre put the movie on, we already had it publicized for them.

There was a big Gene Tierney movie we publicized once and Cinesound filmed us doing it. They sent over the outfit she wore in the movie 'Leave Her to Heaven' and I had to model it. They mentioned the name of the movie and said it would be released soon and I just walked out in her clothes. At one stage they were going to give me the outfit but that went by the board.

I was a dedicated worker and Jack Musgrove never once queried anything. If I came up with an idea I wanted to put on he'd say, 'Well you know the rules, Jeanne. I don't mind putting out the money but you've gotta get the results.' He was marvellous. I don't think we had one flop. It was no time before I had all the balls back on in the place again. I had the championships running and he even let me employ eight girls.

Then I got the idea of putting into the show all the Rumbas and Sambas that I'd tried to get going down in Melbourne. Jack Musgrove was one hundred percent behind it. He thought it was great. So he let me put on all these people and I had four professional couples - one from each state. I tried to spread it round amongst the states. While I had the couples in the corners all dressed alike, doing the ballroom version of Rumbas and Sambas, I had the girls in the middle doing the real Sambas. Whatever I'd seen on the movies. Then all I did - the last chorus - I'd toddle down the stairs, get in the middle of 'em all, do a few spins.... it was all over. Lovely! I didn't have to do anything! Sydney was the place where I first felt recognised for what I could do.

So after all those years from when I tried to get the Victorian Society of Dancing to look at the Latin American stuff, it finally became popular. I knew it would. Oh, they decided, finally, it wasn't so bad after all. Then it was accepted everywhere - even the off-beat Rumba and all the variations. Went into the championships and everything! But they were very, very hesitant at the beginning. We ended up sending over to London all the Latin American and exhibition dancing routines that they could have got themselves from America. I suppose you might say, as far as ballroom went, Australia led the field in that type of work.

RITZ
Ballroom
TO-NIGHT

PRESENTING

MONTEZ &
FREEMAN

Direct from Sydney Trocadero
in Latest Latin-American craze,

SAMBA

72

Cinesound at the Trocadero, Sydney, filming the Stand-In Club presentations to publicise the Gene Tierney movie 'Leave Her To Heaven'.   1945

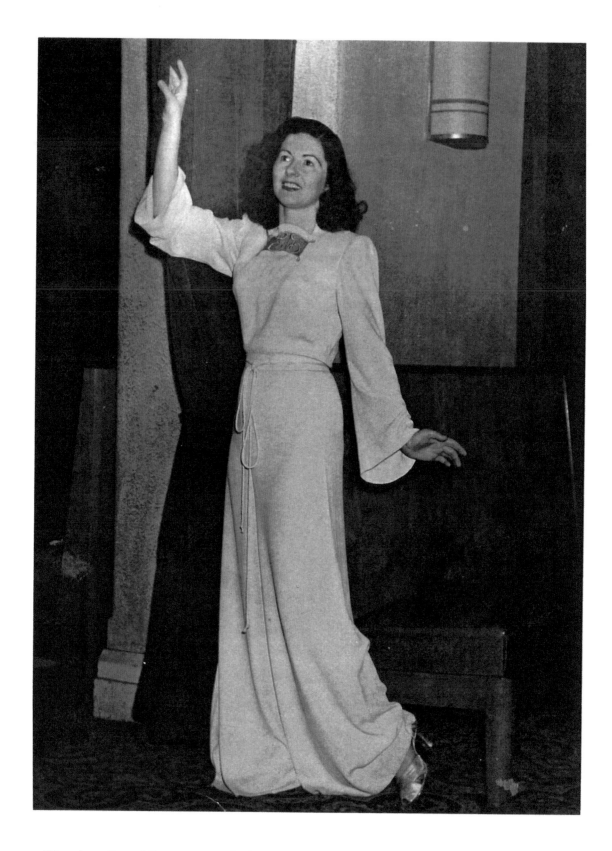

Wearing Gene Tierney's outfit from her movie 'Leave Her To Heaven'.   1945

"SERVICE ABOVE SELF"

ROTARY CLUB OF SYDNEY

TELEPHONE B 5934 • PRUDENTIAL BUILDING, 39-49 MARTIN PLACE, SYDNEY, AUSTRALIA • BOX 2532, G.P.O., SYDNEY

6th September, 1948.

Miss Montez,
The Trocadero,
George Street,
SYDNEY.

Dear Miss Montez:

Although both Mrs. Rigby and myself expressed our
thanks and gratitude to you for the care and interest
you took in training the Debs. who were presented
to Sir Leslie and Lady Morshead at our Rotary Ball
on 3rd September, I felt that I should write and tell
you that in the opinion of all those present the
dignified and confident bearing of all the young Ladies who .
were presented, was solely due to your inspiration and
training. It was our pleasure that you and Mr. Robinson
were able to be our guests for the evening.

If you will send a note of your professional charges I
will have it attended to at once.

Yours sincerely,

A. Les. Rigby,
PRESIDENT.

75

TELEPHONE: BW 6934

MACQUARIE STREET, SYDNEY, N.S.W.

Sydney Hospital Ball

Under the distinguished patronage of
HIS EXCELLENCY THE GOVERNOR and MRS. NORTHCOTT

President:

    Mrs. J. K. Schartl,
      "Green-lees," Gordon.
      JX 1225.

Vice-Presidents:

    Mrs. K. Cudmore.
    Mrs. Hamilton Kirkland.
    Lady Paul.

Honorary Secretary:

    Mrs. S. S. Blake,
      Birtley Towers,
      Elizabeth Bay.
      FA 3608.

Honorary Treasurer:

    Mrs. R. Bull,
      33 Wolseley Road,
      Point Piper.
      FM 4369.

Miss Montez,
C/- Trocadero,
George Street,
SYDNEY.

Dear Miss Montez,

        On behalf of the Sydney Hospital Ball Committee I have very much pleasure in thanking you for training the debutantes and also for arranging for the floor show.

        We have had many comments as to the success of the ball and feel that it was largely due to the excellent training of the debutantes and for the floor show which was a pleasant surprise to many at the Ball.

        Again thanking you and with best wishes.

        Yours sincerely,

Muriel Blake

      HONORARY SECRETARY.

FOX SOCIAL CLUB

43-51 Brisbane Street, Sydney
———N.S.W.———

•

Telephone: M 6621

4th
Nov.,
1947.

Dear Miss Montez:

I hope you will forgive the delay in thanking
you for your courtesy and co-operation in
providing your Ballet for our Function.
You will no doubt be interested to learn that
it was a huge success and the proceeds will
considerably swell our FOOD FOR BRITAIN funds.
Your floor show was voted one of the highlights
of the evening.

     With sincere thanks,

               Yours truly,

               Marjorie Sparrow.
               ORGANISER.

WILL PERFORM "SAMBA" HERE

The Samba, the new dance Princess Elizabeth requested in a London nightclub, will be demonstrated in Brisbane dance halls this week by Sydney professional dancers, Miss Jeanne Montez, and Mr. Billy Freeman.

The Samba is claimed to be something entirely different from any other dance, and is done to a fast jungle tempo. It is based on the Mexican hat dance, in which the dancers swirled wildly round a hat on the ground. The couple nearest the hat at the end of the dance were betrothed.

Music for the Samba is fascinating and catchy. Nearest approach to the new dance is the rhumba square. The Samba craze is sweeping England, and is fast supplanting the rhumba for popularity in the United States.

Miss Montez, whose blue-black hair and magnolia complexion show her French-Spanish origin, wears a midriff frock of red green, blue and lemon, with a slit skirt, for her demonstration of the Samba.

WILL DANCE SAMBA IN SHOW WEEK

Miss Jeanne Montez and Mr Billy Freeman are arriving in Brisbane this afternoon by Skymaster from Sydney. They will demonstrate the Samba, one of the latest dances of Latin-American origin.

The samba. which is having a great vogue in London, is a successor to the tango, rhumba and conga.

Miss Montez and her partner will be seen in leading ballrooms during Show week.

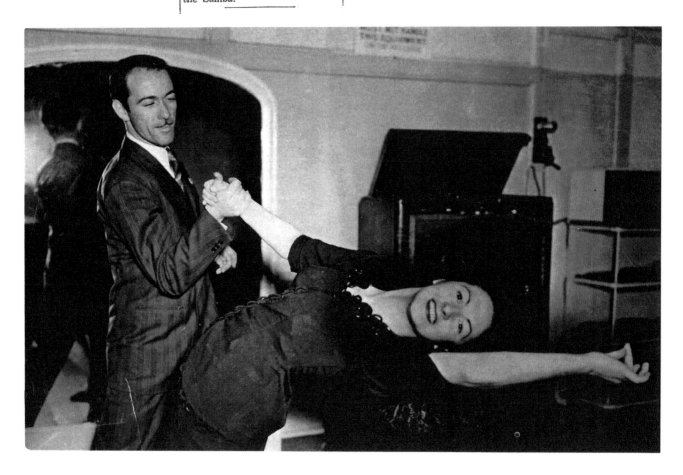

Bill Freeman and I.   1946

Chapter Eleven: *Miss Australia*

Through the day I often went down to Bondi. That was my relaxation. I'd just lie on the beach and sunbake. This particular day it was pretty windy. There weren't many people there. I had a towel over my face and I was laying face down. My shoulders were covered but I forgot my legs. I went sound asleep and when I woke up, my legs were burnt pretty badly. I went home and changed then went to work. In the morning when I got up, I'd had my legs bent in bed and I couldn't straighten them. Mum took me to St Vincent's Hospital in a taxi and they bandaged me right down to my ankles. I wore bandages for about two weeks. Couldn't dance or anything. I still get pain there.

Except for that silly mistake, I loved Bondi. I'd just lie on the beach or on the rocks where the shark net was. There were sheds there where you could change but they've all gone now. There used to be two old chaps there who belonged to the Surf Club - they were brothers. Their name was Saunders and one of 'em, Charlie, used to massage the life savers. I got to know them because I had permission to put on shows at the Bondi Surf Club. Charity shows. It was a big place. You'd walk up the stairs of the Surf Club and at either side was a ballroom. You weren't allowed to charge for a Sunday show but as the people came in they'd put a donation in a box. It covered itself well and truly then you'd give the rest to a charity. No one got paid. They all did it just 'cause they wanted to.

I danced all over the place in Sydney. The Wentworth Hotel, Marrickville Town Hall, Surreyville, the Rooseveldt, Grace Brothers. There was a beautiful ballroom at Grace Brothers. We put on shows there. There was some connection between The Troc, the Rooseveldt and Hoyts Theatres. The directors from the three companies would have meetings at The Trocadero. Made it easier for me to put shows on all around Sydney. I was permanently employed at The Trocadero of course and Jack Musgrove did everything in his power for me. Let me have a private flat behind the bandstand where I had my own shower and a sofa to rest on. I had all my clothes there too. Jack never once put a hand out of place. Never entered my head either. The only time he ever showed any indication of interest was once when I went up to Brisbane to dance. He said to me, 'Jeanne, if you go away I've got a feeling you'll never come back.' And he had that real sad look on his face. That was the only time he ever showed any sort of feeling.

I said, 'Of course I will.'

He said, 'Who are you going with?'

I said, 'This time I think I'll take Bill Freeman.' See, I could just pick any partner. Lucky, wasn't I? I'd had enough of being with just one. It didn't work out with me. I had four professionals there and I could just pick any one. I felt at home with them. We all rehearsed together and thought along the same lines. I've been lucky all my life like that. I've worked in Melbourne, Sydney and Brisbane with lots of men and I've never once had any problems. Some used to be a bit keen but never once did they make any approach.

The man who booked us up in Brisbane was a chappy called Tibby Challenger who was the best known name in Queensland when it came to dancing. He ran and owned the Ritz Ballroom in the Valley and every dancer who kicked off from Brisbane, he pretty well started. He and his wife Aidy. He brought myself and Bill Freeman up from Sydney to do a show at the Brisbane Town Hall for the Duke and Duchess of somewhere or other. I don't know if you'd call it a command performance. They just brought us up because they wanted something different. Then a few months later, Tibby came down to Sydney with his wife and daughter. The daughter was going to America to marry some navy chap. They stayed in Sydney a couple of days and I put them up at my place. Tibby and I became very good friends

Away from the ballrooms though, I sometimes got more attention than I wanted. One of my days off

I took the bus to the beach and I got off to walk down towards the main road when these two young lads walked up and asked me where this particular street was. While I was telling the one on the right hand side that I wasn't sure, the one on the left grabbed my arm and stuck it right up my back. Stood right next to me and said, 'Where're you going from here?'

I said, 'I'm going to visit my girlfriend.'

He said, 'Well you know what we want.'

I lied when I said, 'She's home on her own.... Come on, we'll all go together.' I knew her husband would be there that day because he was a shift worker. He was a big bloke too and I was thinking fast. I couldn't think of anything else to do.

The bloke on the right looked a nicer type. He was all for it. But the other one wasn't so sure. So we walked down a couple of streets and as we walked through the front gate of my girlfriend's house, she had already seen me coming. How lucky that I knew someone in Bondi. Whether she gathered something was wrong, I don't know, but before I even knocked on the door she opened it and there was her husband standing behind her. Those two blokes just went for their lives! The very next day in the papers there was an article about a woman home alone with her little kiddie who opened the door to two young chaps and they pushed their way in. They gave her a bad time. I wouldn't be a bit surprised if it was the same pair.

I had a ball in Sydney. I used to go to all the local talent quests in my spare time. I was always on the lookout for talent. There was a chap at Surreyville who wanted me to give a friend of his a chance. You know that young lad, Doug Parkinson? I put him on at The Troc for a couple of nights. He was only a boy but he was quite good. I think he ended up resident singer over at Surreyville.

Knew a lot of people in the business too. People like Toni Lamond, Elaine McKenna.... We were all from the same period. We never got together as friends because dancers were a race of their own. The only time I'd ever strike them was if they were on at the same place to do a number. There was nothing close but I knew 'em all by name.

At The Trocadero I met people like Ozzie Pitworth the golfer, Edwin Duff who was a singer, the guitarist from Django Reinhart's band, the Ozzie Nelson band, Sid Factor - Max's brother, Vivien Leigh, Veronica Lake, Bob Hope, Frank Sinatra....

I had dinner with Sid Factor one night. We went on to a nightclub and the hat check girl there was a friend of mine. I was feeling a bit strange and she looked at me and said, 'You don't look well. What's wrong?'

I said, 'Well I was having a drink with Sid and I went to the ladies. When I came back and finished my drink I started to feel a bit strange.'

She said, 'You're not going out anywhere! You're going upstairs to rest!' I was lucky she was there to help me. Never went out with him again.

I had these Stand-In Clubs going very successfully at The Troc at this time. The idea for them just popped into my head. I thought, instead of pushing dancing down everyone's throat.... it was too commonplace. Everyone was dancing. So we started having competitions for movie star look-alikes. You've got so many chances of someone who looks a little bit like somebody else. Even old Edwin Duff. He looked like Danny Kaye - same face and everything. It was a huge success and some of 'em - you could hardly tell the difference between the stand in and the movie star. I was supposed to look like Margaret Lockwood and I even got an offer to go to America to be her real stand-in. See, I was also tied up with Hoyts and the Union Theatres.

Bill Freeman and self. Bill held the NSW Championship for many years.

Presenting . . .

JEANNE MONTEZ

Syncopation's Representative For "Miss Australia" Contest

Top Left:

Miss Jeanne Montez, Syncopation's Candidate, with Syncopation's Editor, Jim Hanley, and Committee Secretary, Jim Cane.

A well-known ballroom personality, Jeanne Montez has organized ballets and floor shows for many night spots, and is currently engaged at the Sydney Trocadero.

Miss Montez and her committee will be organizing, in future, shows and musical presentations, to raise funds for Miss Australia. Further particulars will be announced in future editions.

Printed by Cunpress Printing Ltd., 168 Castlereagh St., Sydney for Syncopation Publishing Coy., 231 Kent St., Sydney.

Miss Australia Quest – Committee, sponsor Jim Hanley (Syncopation Magazine)
and myself.   1947

**THE
AUSTRALIAN SINATRA
ASSOCIATION**

In support of Syncopation Musical and
Dance Magazine's Candidate in Miss
Australia Quest.
in aid of Kindergarten Union & Legacy

JEANNE MONTEZ
PRESENTS ITS FIRST BIRTHDAY

SINATRA CONVENTION DANCE
TROCADERO, MONDAY, JUNE 23

and Featuring

★ **REX WILLIAMS**
**AUSTRALIA'S OWN
FRANKIE SINATRA**
No Autographs, by request, thank you.

★ **MONTEZ BALLET**
REVEL IN THE BEAUTY OF THE
AUGMENTED BALLET IN SOUTH SEA
MAGIC.
Sorry we haven't a Stage Door.

★ **MIRIAM WHEELER**
TEEN AGE WONDER CONCERT
PIANIST
Hear Chopin's Glorious Polyanaise as it
should be played.

★**JIMMY PARKINSON**
THE TROCADERO'S OWN SWOONER
CROONER.
Jimmy has a special line-up, bow tie
and all.

★ SINATRA JITTERBUG CONTEST
SASHES SPECIALLY DONATED BY FRANKIE SINATRA SENT DIRECTLY FROM HOLLY-
WOOD. SEE AUSTRALIA'S CRAZIEST JITTERBUGS DRESSED IN SLOPPY-JOES, PEG-
GED PANTS, AND WHAT HAVE YOU FIGHT IT OUT IN ONE GLORIOUS COLOR
FUL BATTLE OF DANCING.

At this first birthday convention dance of the Australian Sinatra Associa-
tion will appear representatives from each state and all country officials.
Other Fan Clubs supporting Convention: Alan Ladd Club, Ron Randell Club,
British Film Fan Club. All celebrities will be interviewed by a leading
Sydney Radio Station in the foyer for an Australian wide hook-up.

**MUSIC BY FRANKIE COUGHLAN IN SINATRA MANNER
ADMISSION 3/-**
DON'T MISS THIS FAST MOVING SHOW WORTHY OF HOLLYWOOD
ITSELF!

One day Jack Musgrove said, 'Now, Jeanne, why don't you go in for the Miss Australia?'

I said, 'Well I can't. I'm a Mrs.'

He said, 'You don't have to go through with it but you're raising all that charity money at Bondi and you're a publicity girl. We'll get someone to sponsor you and the publicity won't do you any harm.'

I said, 'I'll think about it.' I wasn't really fussed. I've never liked having my photo taken. It's funny isn't it? It's been a thing with me all my life.

Then I started to think, I suppose I could just for the publicity. Suddenly the chappy from Syncopation Magazine, Jim Hanley, said, 'If Jeanne's going to be in the Miss Australia, I'll sponsor her.' He came up with the bright idea of Sinatra. At this particular stage Sinatra was the number one bloke. Anyone in the news like he was back then had lots of supporters. Even though he wasn't a popular bloke, he still had a good voice and personality. Jim said he would write to Sinatra's agents to get them interested and the way we got around it was we started forming Sinatra clubs right around Australia. They were like fan clubs - same as the Stand-In Club, see. It was a way of entertaining the young kids because there was nothing much offering. Those days people did try to entertain young kids. The Sinatra Clubs started off as little groups that used to meet at different places and listen to Sinatra's music. People flocked to them. When the agent in America realized how much we were doing for their publicity, they became very interested. See, Sinatra was coming out. Then each member of the Sinatra club decided they would nominate me for Miss Australia on his behalf and the agent got behind it. That's how it all happened.

We also did a tour of the major country towns between Melbourne and Sydney with a seventeen piece teenage band for the Miss Australia Quest. We called the shows One Nite Stand and we travelled by train - parlour car. It finished with a big show in Sydney at The Troc where there was a Sinatra challenge to any vocalist who reckoned they could sing like him. It was all to raise funds for Miss Australia.

I met a lot of people in the time I was at The Troc. Horrie Dargy was one. He was a nice chap. He married one of the girls from The Tivoli. He had a very good band that he took to entertain the troops during the war. When he came back he couldn't get a job anywhere. I'm a real softie. I used to think, what a talented man and he can't get a go here in Australia. He could play the mouth organ like you wouldn't believe. So I said to him, 'I can't give you a permanent job but I can feature you for one night at The Trocadero with the revolving bandstand.'

So when Frank Coughlin's band went round we just went straight on with Horrie. One band would stop and the other would start. Jack Musgrove said, 'What's this going to cost us?'

I said, 'Don't worry. This man's just been entertaining the troops overseas and he's trying to get a start here again. At least we're helping him try to get back into showbiz.' I didn't follow what Horrie did after that but he must have done alright. A nice chap. One of the very few genuine ones you meet.

Then there was Dianna Hartt. She used to do a bit of modelling for me when I had the shows. I'd get these nice looking girls to walk down the stairs while the other girls were dancing. They didn't have to do anything – just look good. She was also a showgirl at the Sydney Tivoli. One night while all the girls were changing out the back of The Tivoli, one of the heaters went over and the place caught fire. Most of 'em got out except poor Dianna. She copped the lot. She ended up with these frightful burns all over her body. What we did, we had parties to raise money for her to go over to London for skin grafts and that sort of thing. Her mother had a nice home in Rose Bay and we'd have the parties in her gardens. I'd let all the girls at The Trocadero know and they'd all turn up in support. She finally went and had a lot done but she was never quite the same.

That's how things were in Sydney. Did lots of shows. I even had a woman there to keep an eye on the girls so the mothers would know there was no hanky-panky and everything was right. They were funny those girls. I'd give a routine to one of them then I'd have to make sure the next one had something different. I used to make them pick their own tunes and whatever tune they picked, I'd work on. So at least they had the pleasure of saying, 'I've chosen that myself.' I remember one couple chose 'Flower Drum Song'. That wasn't easy to work with!

I managed the entertainment at the Sydney Trocadero from 1944 until I got married again in 1948. It gave me a good name in the dancing and show business industry.

RITZ
Ballroom
Presents
Jeanne MONTEZ
AND
Billy FREEMAN
Direct from Sydney Trocadero.
in the long-awaited
much-debated
SAMBA

Jeanne Montez

PRESENTS THE MOST AMAZING SHOW OF THE YEAR

ONE NITE STAND

TROCADERO, Wednesday July 9

★ **INTERSTATE BALLROOM PERSONALITY CONTEST**

In this contest you will enjoy the sparkling beauty of Australia's loveliest girls. See the N.S.W. final and on the same night, the final of the interstate contest. Last year's competition was won by the beautiful Victorian, Alison Logan. Who will win it this year? The 25 N.S.W. finalists will be judged by Diana Hartt, Maurice Le Froy, and Richard Warburton, Editor of "Batchelor Girl" Magazine.

IF YOU ADMIRE AUSTRALIAN BEAUTY, DON'T MISS THIS SENSATIONAL CONTEST

★ **ONE NITE STAND**

Ballroom Contests. Amateur and Novice Sections. See Sydney's most graceful couples in this brilliant event.
JUDGE: BILLY GLENNON

★ **MONTEZ BALLET**

A farewell ballet specially arranged by Jeanne Montez for Diana
Don't say we didn't warn you, it's
DARING! BEAUTIFUL! CAPTIVATING!

★ **JITTERBUG CONTEST**

No One Nite Stand would be complete without a Jitterbug Competition. They're crazy, but it's fun!

ENTERTAINERS' FAREWELL TO AUSTRALIA'S
BRAVEST GIRL

Diana Hartt

The entertainment world of Sydney will give a dazzling farewell to Australia's bravest and most popular girl, prior to her departure to U.S.A. via Paris, London and New York, then on to Hollywood. Come and meet the celebrities of the theatrical and artistic community of Sydney at this colourful farewell. Guests invited:

Chips Rafferty, Roy Rene (Mo), Hal Lashwood, Dick Bentley, Al Thomas, Dawn Anderson, Joy Brewer, Pam Hookam, Ruby Lacy, Bill McColl, Don Baker, Kay Pearce, Tivoli Ballet, Lloyd Barrell, Muriel and Paul Nicholls, David Brockhoff, Jack Burgess, Bob Pollard.

---

2 BANDS:- FRANK COUGHLAN'S BAND,

Admission 3/- Including Tax   RALPH MALLEN'S GUEST BAND

YOUTH Campaign

Conducted by

FEDERATION OF NEW SOUTH WALES POLICE-CITIZENS BOYS' CLUBS

AND

THE ANTI-TUBERCULOSIS ASSOCIATION OF N.S.W.

Address all Communications to:

ANTI-T.B. ASSOCIATION OF N.S.W.
Youth Campaign Committee
33 MACQUARIE PLACE, SYDNEY

Phone BW 4040

29th October 1946

HELP TO SAVE OUR YOUTH FROM T.B.

CONFIDENCE BUILDS MEN

X-RAY CLINIC SERVICE

Miss Jeanne Montez,
c/o Trocadero,
503 George St.,
SYDNEY.

Dear Miss Montez,

I have been given the pleasure of conveying to you the thanks of Miss Diana Hartt's Committee for the very knid co-operation and help you have so willingly given to functions in aid of the Youth Campaign.

The spontaneous and generous help of kind and charitable minded people like yourself has done so much to make the Youth Campaign such an outstanding success, and, knowing the worthy objects of the Campaign, I am sure this will give you a warm glow of satisfaction.

Yours sincerely,

E.H.Williams,
Anti-T.B. Assn. Youth Campaign Committee.

AUSTRALIAN BROADCASTING COMMISSION

264 PITT STREET

SYDNEY

G.P.O. BOX 487, SYDNEY

NCE ....

1st July, , 1948.

Miss Jean Montez,
C/- The Trocadero,
George Street,
SYDNEY.

Dear Madam,

We believe you will be interested in the feature
"The Teen-Agers" which will be heard on the Interstate
programme at 9.15p.m. on Thursday, 15th July, 1948.

Mr. Colin Simpson, the writer of this feature has asked
us to let you know the time of the programme. We hope
that you will be able to listen and that you will enjoy
the broadcast.

Yours faithfully,
AUSTRALIAN BROADCASTING COMMISSION

J.C.R. PROUD
Acting Director of Features.

1947

TROCADERO

— Presents —

Nite in Hollywood

See Australia's Stand-ins for the stars
in association with

Frank Coughlan's Swing Carnival of Music

WEDNESDAY, 28th JULY

SPECIAL BAND PRESENTATIONS

Frank Coughlin (Australia's most outstanding band leader will surprise you with his versatility by playing for you the favourite numbers of your most popular American band leaders.

GLEN MILLER'S

American Patrol

STAN KENTON'S

Back to Sorrento
Intermission Riff

TOMMY DORSEY'S

Sentimental over You
We'll Git It

BUNNY BERRIGAN'S

Can't Get Started

LOUIS ARMSTRONG'S

Pennies from Heaven
Saints Go Marching

WOODY HERMAN'S

Woodchoppers Ball
Golden Wedding

Also a host of other numbers that will bring back memories to you from "Broadway Melody," 1928 to "Road to Rio," 1948.

SHOW GIRLS !   FLOOR SHOWS !   SHOW GIRLS !

HARLEM JITTERBUGS

The real low down on

Harlem Boogie and Blues

SPECIAL ADDED ATTRACTION—
**Grand Final Novice Championship
Popular Vote Section
Winner to be
Challenged by Champions
GORDON ROGER, BERYL NORMAN**

Also the following Artists will astound you with impersonations of the following Hollywood stars.

BING CROSBY	AL JOLSON	HEDY LAMARR
FRANK SINATRA	CARMEN MIRANDA	DOROTHY LAMOUR
KATHRYN GRAYSON	PAULETTE GODDARD	AVA GARDNER

Posing for Pix Magazine   1948

Chapter Twelve: Musicians' Club

Kings Cross was a bright spot during the war years. Everyone would get together and enjoy themselves. You'd see them at the California and those places. On the other side of town near the fire station there was this downstairs place where the gays went. In those days they had to be careful where they met because the intolerance was even worse then. There was a chap from New Zealand who was the first one to put an act together. I was fascinated when I first saw him. He must have appeared at The Troc before I ever worked there - that's how far back it was. I can remember looking at him and thinking, fancy him being gay. I couldn't work it out. See, I'd never known anyone gay before I went to the Cross. Years later I got to know many of them personally and, after I'd finished with the dancing, I gave all my costumes to Les Girls.

My mother went away on a holiday to Melbourne for three weeks and while she was away I met this man called Alva Robinson. He was tied up with the American small ships. He was an Australian but he got a job on the ships as a refrigeration mechanic. He had a nice personality and was very good looking. Very well known around The Cross. People liked him. His brother was one of the head blokes on the Sydney newspapers.

Alva was very charming. Couldn't do enough for me. He got so much respect from the people at The Cross that I just accepted it. He knew everyone there in the early days. We used to go to coffee shops and places like that. I only knew him three weeks and I married him. I thought why not? See, I'd never had a home life of any sort and I must be a very easy person to convince. I don't like hurting anyone's feelings. Find it hard to say no. Jack Musgrove gave me the wedding and I was married at The Trocadero. Seven tiered wedding cake. Everyone there got a piece. We had all the stand-ins as bridesmaids and groomsmen. It was called "the wedding of the year". Made all the papers and magazines. It was a big do. The year was 1948.

They started putting different things on at The Troc then. When rock and roll was starting to become popular in the fifties I used to teach some of the bands routines - you know how they do while they're playing? But it was never like it used to be.

I kept teaching and did a bit of modelling. Pix magazine paid me for a job - an article about photography. The heading on it was 'PIX Cameraman Makes An Old Master'. One of their blokes - a chap called Ivan Ive - worked out this technique that gave his pictures the patina of the old masters. He used a stippled screen that he borrowed from a newspaper block-maker and photographed it. Then he took a picture of me dressed in Renaissance style and printed the two negatives together. He didn't use any special lighting or anything but the effect softened the image and made the finished product look like an old painting.

They were interesting jobs but I wanted to get back to producing shows.

The Musicians' Club was there in Pitt Street. Horrace Lindrum had a billiard room underneath. I saw the chap who was in charge of the club and asked him if he'd mind if I put a late show on. I wanted to get into something that would keep an interest. I wanted to make it for the show business people, starting at eleven and going through to three or four in the morning. The chap said that was fine so we opened it. Alva had all the connections.

It was a well-known spot. We served coffee and that sort of thing and when the Sydney musicians knocked off work wherever they were playing, they'd all come up. It was a real session from then on 'til the early hours of the morning. They were able to have drinks because out the back we had these huge fridges and all the musicians would have their names on their drinks. So we weren't selling it. We had this little peep hole like you'd see in the movies and we'd look to make sure they were members. If you weren't a member, you couldn't come in. I had rather attractive young girls waiting tables and it was a great get-together for musicians.

I got the idea from the coffee shops in St Kilda, but there, there were so many of them that the musos would spread out. In the Musicians' Club they were all there together. They were fighting each other to play. Used to cost me nothing. We had some good sessions up there. We used to get home about five in the morning. Eyes'd be dropping out. But still it was good.

What finished up happening was, we used to take all the musicians up to Cliffy Evans' Dancing Studio in Pitt Street and they'd rehearse and copy the American bands down to a tee. Stan Kenton had one of the largest bands ever put together in America. They'd listen to his records and copy them. Couldn't tell one from the other. Then on a Sunday at the Bondi Surf Club they'd all come and play. Amazing talent. Talent was just everywhere but they never got a chance. Unless it was imported it was no good. So we had the Sunday dancing at the Surf Club with this terrific band. Everyone loved it. They used to come up, drop their donation in, go inside and enjoy the music. Just come as you are - beach wear. Casual. Sunday afternoons...

My husband Alva was very good at cooking. When he was a refrigeration mechanic on the ships he learned how to do it. While he wasn't doing mechanical work he was helping the chef. Funny how things happen, isn't it? Everything just fell into place. He was such a likeable person - you couldn't help but like him. I never had any idea that he would be involved in drugs 'cause I never drank or anything.

During the war while he was on the ships, they were taken POW and tied up off India for quite a few months. They weren't allowed ashore or near any women. All they could do was stay on board. They couldn't go anywhere. He used to have all these papers and he'd say to me, 'Never let these papers out of your sight.' That didn't mean a thing to me. I probably would have received a big payout from America - the navy - when he died.

He started to hallucinate and whatever was going through his mind he thought was actually happening. He'd hop out of bed and throw his arms around, fighting people. He was a real case. If he was taking drugs then, I never knew, but I gathered, being at the Cross.... I never look for anything wrong with anyone. Never even thought about it. Never entered my mind. He'd pour a glass of wine and just drink it like a glass of water. Just couldn't stop him from drinking. When he'd go to sleep of a night time, he'd wake up and he wouldn't be with you. He'd be back in the war or wherever. He was a little violent sometimes so I used to have to lock the door. I'd get home of a night and he'd just be sleeping on the bed and if I didn't feed him - hand feed him - he wouldn't eat anything. I tried to handle it by myself without worrying anyone else.

JEANNE MONTEZ, Hostess Australia's Loveliest Ballroom, Trocadero

presents

One Nite Stand

Jeanne introduced the One Nite Stand to Sydney for the first time in 1946. Since then it has become to be regarded as the most important dance function of the year. She has been responsible for the introduction of many new ideas into the N.S.W. dance programmes, most noticeable of them being the South American dance sensation, "Samba." She is undoubtedly Australia's most versatile dancer, having partnered such champion dancers as Billy Glennon, Jim Cane, Micky Powell, Syd. Cane. Bill Freeman and Jack Ayres.

96

The Musicians' Club was still quite successful. Until one night - the big fridges at the back where we kept all the name-tagged drinks, one of 'em defrosted and all the water went through the floor and down onto Horace Lindrum's billiard tables. That caused a stir! He came up and said that there was water all over his tables and it was all from our place! I forget the chap who managed the Musicians' Club at the time but he had to take the full brunt of it all. Because he was responsible. So that sort of finished the late night shows.

Alva and I decided to go to Melbourne. Get away from The Cross for a while. We'd been married for nearly four years and I was confronted with something I'd never been up against in my life before. Couldn't understand it because he was such a perfect gentleman. He tried to adjust his life but he just got worse. It was taking me down too so I went to see this doctor friend of mine. He was a Collins Street specialist who used to work at The Herald years before. I sort of grew up with him. We were friends. I introduced him to Alva without saying he was a doctor then I went to him myself a couple of times because I wasn't well.

He said, 'Jeanne, you're in a bad way. You're on the verge of a nervous breakdown. You've got to do something about it.' So I thought about divorce. And you wouldn't believe it but I was staying at a hotel in Melbourne and I ran into that clairvoyant woman again. I'd left Alva in the November but this woman told me, don't sue for divorce. Just wait a while. She was right.

The last twelve months of my marriage were very hectic. I couldn't do anything with him. He'd had it. He went downhill so fast and he died of a heart attack in January 1952. He was only thirty-two. Very young. Everything he'd given me I returned to his family. Those papers, a locket that belonged to his mother. I gave it all back to them. Then I decided I'd give dancing away completely. I'd had enough. I took a job relieving back at The Herald. That's where I met old Harry Hopman. I started having blackouts then too. The worry could have kicked it off. But I wouldn't know for sure.

Chapter Thirteen: Cloudland

The Mamannas came to my rescue. I'd known 'em for years by then and they were very good friends. One of the daughter's husbands was running a hotel and he said, 'Jeanne, if you want to have a job and be away from dancing, I'll get you a job in a hotel.' I thought that'd be great 'cause no one would ever expect to see me in a hotel. So he put me into a hotel right up the top end of Spencer Street Station. He managed one in Swanston Street but he also had control of the Spencer Street one. He said, 'We don't have to be in a rush or anything. Just take your time and you'll pick up the serving.' I was quite happy 'cause it was only a little pub and I settled down and started to get over my problems.

Only twice in my life I've cried. Once when my old cat was put to sleep and the other was when my Grandmother Marnie died - and when I say cried, I really let out the lot. It wasn't 'til much later but it was all churned up and it was just waterworks everywhere. I was doing a show at Silks Ballroom and I didn't even realise that she was sick. I hadn't seen her for a few weeks but I got this feeling I should go and see her. And I thought, what on earth out of the blue made me do that? It was about eleven-thirty when I got a taxi from Glenferrie and went over to her house at Malvern. When I arrived it was after twelve. My uncle lived there with her too. I said, 'I don't know what made me come but I just wanted to see my grandmother.'

'Well,' he said, 'I think you're just about in time because she's very low.' He was a funny bloke. Wouldn't you think he'd have let us know? I walked in and she was lying on the bed in a coma. I just picked up her hand and held it and that night she died. I was just so pleased that I was in Melbourne at the time it happened. A few days passed and she was being buried. We went to the funeral at the church. The whole family turned up. All my cousins who I hadn't seen in years were there. I was there with my father. Then in front of all my relations, I just up and.... an absolute river of tears. For me it was so out of character. I'm not usually the type. But she was a lovely person and she and I were very close.

Wasn't until a month or so after she died I was showering and I went out to dry myself. I looked in the mirror and thought, that mark on my leg has gone. The potato. I double checked and I got another mirror looking for it this way and that. It had been there all my life then suddenly there was no sign of it. It was so strange that after my Grandmother Marnie had died, it had gone.

Life went on though. I was working in the pub, keeping my head down, so to speak, then one day this bloke walked in and said, 'Jeanne Montez!' I thought - oh no! Somebody knows me! His name was Tom Connelly and he was working for the Melbourne Metropolitan Board of Works. Like the Water Board. He'd been in the navy during the war and he'd seen one of my shows at The Troc. So I gave him a bit more attention than the others 'cause I was trying to keep him quiet. Didn't want him to be telling everybody.

The first time I met him socially was at a party over at South Melbourne given by Judy and Elaine McKenna. He was a very caring person and as I got to know him better he used to come by after work every night to make sure I was alright. He lived way over at Brunswick - a long way. I was a bit run down at the time and he used to come over to look after me - cook meals, do the right thing. He turned out to be a very, very down to earth, lovely person. He was an only child too and he had quite a history. He was also a football umpire at the big AFL games. I married him that same year and we were married for twenty-eight years. His thing was hotels. He loved hotels. So naturally I went into them with him. I helped him as much as I could.

Tom Connelly

SURRYVILLES
Biggest Event!
4 Big Shows in One

NEXT TUESDAY, 25th JUNE

Sensational Dance Demonstrations

★

JIM CANE -
LAUREL WILSON
PRESENT
SLOW FOX TROT

•

ST·AN WRIGHT -
LORNA EVANS
PRESENT
THE TANGO

★

Jim Cane & Jeanne Montez

★

BILL FREEMAN -
JEAN ERICKSON
PRESENT
THE WALTZ

•

JACK AYRES -
JEANNE MONTEZ ·
PRESENT
THE RUMBA

★

These Eight Dancing Stars are all members of
JEANNE MONTEZ SCHOOL OF DANCING
Private Tuition : 11 a.m. - 7.30 p.m. Daily.
TROCADERO BALLROOMS, GEORGE STREET, SYDNEY. 'Phone: MA 6431

APPLE PIE EATING CONTEST	★	B—— DRINKING CONTEST
IT'S A CREAM	Plus . . .	IT'S A SCREAM
SKIPPING STAKES	NOVELTIES THRILLS	GIRLS' SCOOTER RACE
WE HOP YOU LIKE IT	PARTY DANCES	Introducing MISS BERNBOROUGH

. NO POPULAR DANCE AT TROCADERO ON TUESDAY, 25th JUNE.
P.S.—IT'S "MOVIE BALL" NIGHT.

We were married on September 12, 1952 and Tom really looked after me. Only for the Mamannas and Tom, goodness knows where I'd have been. The only thing he wanted in return was to dance. Tom had never danced as a professional but it was his one ambition. I thought to myself, gee this is going to be hard because, whilst he had a good appearance and a good personality, he just didn't.... His dancing was OK. No worries about that. But it just wasn't there, you know? You can tell. However, I thought if that's what he wants to do, the least I can do is dance with him. So I lined up a show and rehearsed him but when they wrote it up in the paper.... there was a singer around called Dennis O'Conner. They put the wrong name in. They had my name and Dennis O'Conner doing the floor show. Tom was most disappointed. So I had to make good and do another show. You wouldn't believe it but I teed up a job in the Melbourne Botanical Gardens kiosk where I'd sang once when I was a kid.

Tom was a good average dancer but he was particularly good on The Charleston. So I decided to teach him a Charleston routine. There's not too much finesse in that and he thought it was great. He had a very nice, easy smile. Always had a happy smile. When the band went into the intro, we both came out - one from either side - doing The Charleston. The people were all enjoying it and they were clapping in time like they do.

Next minute, I heard a real roar go up. We'd split and gone in different directions and when I looked back, he'd fallen over and was sitting on the floor on his bum and they all thought it was part of the act! They didn't know that he'd fallen over! When I turned around and saw him, all I could do was laugh. He looked so funny. With that, the band joined in. They were still playing. People were killin' 'emselves! I thought to myself, well now I'm in trouble. I'm going to have to make the rest of this a joke, otherwise it's going to spoil it. I can't be serious now! So I Charlestoned over and put a couple of funny movements in of my own and helped him up. When I helped him, I pretended I tripped. Got myself up again. Then we did another sixteen bars of the routine till he knew where he was up to and we carried on. Then I tapped him on the shoulder, gave him a little bit of a push and Charlestoned off. He followed me. Didn't have a clue what he was doing, just copied me. He wasn't embarrassed. He didn't care. He just kept going! Didn't have much choice, did he?

We hadn't even done the chorus when it happened and I was thankful it was a short routine. I'd have been substituting stuff for too long. It's not easy to be funny for a couple of choruses of music if you haven't worked it out beforehand. But when the audience started to laugh I couldn't stop laughing either. Always got to be one time! That was the beginning and end of Tom's dancing career. That brought us up to Brisbane in '52. So I'm in another state again with another name, starting from scratch.

We were very fortunate when we first came up here. All the hotels were booked completely because it was Exhibition time and we had nowhere to stay. I picked up a paper from the Gold Coast and we just chose this name at random and rang the man and said, 'We're strangers in town. We need some temporary accommodation.' He said that yes, he had some.

We said, 'We don't know how to find your place or anything.... '

He met us at the Southport Station, drove us down to his flats and he became a very good friend. His name was Skennar. When we went to Brisbane to live, he had a house at Coorparoo that he let us have. So everything fell into place. And our next door neighbour was Kevin Allen. When he and his wife had their first child, they wanted us to be godparents. That's how that relationship started. I've known Kevin and his wife nearly as long as I've known my husband. We lived there for quite a while 'til we built our own place.

The first person I looked up in Brisbane was Tibby Challenger. He was, as I told you, the number one man in Queensland. If it hadn't been for his foresight.... He just had that bit of drive that was needed. I believe that years ago on the south side there used to be a Trocadero. I don't know where but that was where he used to dance. Then when he left over there, he bought The Ritz Ballroom. He started training couples himself then he let it out to Sandy Robertson. Jack Busteed used to be there. Norm and Nancy Berg, Dick and Nola Orchard.... Tibby Challenger did a lot for dancing in Queensland. Always doing things for other people.

When I went to see him, he suggested I talk to the people who ran Cloudland - I think it was Mrs. Winters and Mrs. Roach. Two sisters. He came with me to see them and they gave me the job on the same terms as I'd had at The Trocadero. So I began teaching exhibition routines to the Brisbane professionals and putting on shows at Cloudland. I was there for quite a few years - until about '65 or so. I did the same thing as I'd done in Sydney. I'd see a movie, train the couples and put them on the shows. I was on a percentage but I was a bit of a softie. Half the time I'd give the money back or take all the professional couples down to Sydney or Melbourne and pay their way. It was an interesting life and pleasant but of course eventually I went into the hotels with my husband.

In 1952, after we'd moved up from Melbourne, I went to work as a shorthand typist at the Amalgamated Engineering Union. They had a big dispute while I was there. Biggest one they'd ever had. Lasted three months. O'Malley was the railway chief. Healey was the fire chief. The man I worked for was Merril. They used to all get together and have a few beers in the hotel opposite The Ritz Ballroom. They'd go there to discuss business. Everything was done nicely.

I hadn't been too well when we moved but soon after I got this job I began to feel very tired all the time. I was really pushing myself so I went to a doctor by the name of Burke-Gaffney in Coorparoo. I was still getting blackouts and he couldn't work it out. I'd pass out, come to an hour or so later and I wouldn't know I'd done it. He sent me for some blood tests and they found that all the red cells were being eaten up by the white ones. Leukaemia. They were quite worried because there was nothing in those days for a cure. Vitamin B12 had just been discovered in Germany but Health and Home Affairs hadn't tried it on anybody. My doctor asked me if I'd be willing to be a guinea pig. I agreed so they used to give me these injections in the arms. They were great, long needles and once I got home afterwards, I'd take a hot bath to try to stop the pain. I gave up work for about twelve months so I could rest and they must have done the trick 'cause I'm still here. Funny though, when I had the stroke, the pain was in my arm right where they used to stick those big needles.

Coming up to 1956, both Mickey Powell and myself tried to get ballroom dancing into The Olympics. We both tried very hard - even went to the trouble of arranging a show down in Melbourne to coincide with The Games. We got a lot of publicity about it but, no, they didn't want it.

The show was at Leggett's Ballroom. I think it has burned down since. The couples were all billeted in guest houses down the line a bit. Frankston way. I tell you who arranged it all for me. Bon Gibbins - the man who started Moomba. He got all the accommodation and of course, he was running the show. Some of the couples I trained for that show went on to bigger things. John Blake and Laurel Wilson were two of 'em and they went to Europe and won the exhibition championship. When they came back, if I had championships up here at Cloudland, I'd bring 'em in as judges. I'd make sure I brought judges from Melbourne and Sydney so that there was no favouritism or anything. It sort of worked out pretty well. Kept me in touch with all the states.

There was another big show we did in Melbourne. I'm pretty sure it was at Festival Hall. I took professionals and amateurs down from Brisbane to compete. It was a big championship. Jack Busteed was with us as a judge. We had a woman chaperone.... About thirty or forty people.

We had to get a charter plane from ANA or TAA - one of the big ones. A Viscount I think. Special pilot to take it - bush pilot. Trip down was great and on the way back, we dropped one couple off in Sydney. They were competing in the championships there too. Then we came on home. As we approached Brisbane, the pilot received word not to land in Brisbane but to take the passengers off at Coolangatta. So they told us over the intercom - please put our seat belts on. There was a huge cyclone in Brisbane. We'd be landing at Coolangatta and there'd be transport to take us to Brisbane.

Exhibition routine to 'Peter Gunn'. L-R: Dick and Nola Orchard, Bill and Fay Johnstone, Barry and Mirth Quinn, Kevin and Betty Beunion.

Me dancing solo.

OLYMPIC DANCING CHAMPIONSHIPS

QUEENSLAND STATE TITLES

ARRANGED BY JEANNE CONNELLY
On behalf of the Management of Cloudland

Cloudland Ballroom

FRIDAY, OCTOBER 19th, 1956

To select a team to represent Queensland in the Olympic Dancing Championships (Regd.) to be held in Melbourne during the Olympic Games.

PROFESSIONAL BALLROOM CHAMPIONSHIP

(Slow, Waltz, Tango, Quickstep)

The greatest of all championships ever to be staged in Queensland. You will see the cream of our Professional Dancers competing for the honour of representing Queensland in Melbourne for the Olympics.

PROFESSIONAL EXHIBITION TEAM

Two Queensland Exhibition Dancers will be selected to challenge other States in Victoria. The two couples selected will be part of the Queensland team to Visit Melbourne during Olympic Championships.

AMATEUR BALLROOM OLYMPIC CHAMPIONSHIP

(State Title)

This contest is open to all Amateur Dancers in Queensland. Dances to be Slow, Waltz, Tango, Quickstep.

(Trophies presented by Sandgate Australian Rules Club).

AMATEUR OLD-TIME OLYMPIC CHAMPIONSHIP

(State Title)

Invitation to all Old-time couples to compete for the above title. Dances to be Swing Waltz and Danube Schottische.

(Trophies presented by D. Robinson, Jeweller, 186 Edward St., City).

QUEENSLAND'S OLYMPIC JIVE CHAMPIONSHIP

Open to all-comers. Slow and Fast Jive Routine. See our greatest exponents of Jive in this thrilling contest.

Who will be the champions ???

Jeanne Connelly, James Cane

COUNTRY TEAMS MATCH

All country centres are eligible to enter one or two teams into this unique contest. Watch our Country Champions battle for the Olympic honours.

Who will be Queensland's "Miss T.V."?

This contest will be held in conjunction with 4BH Broadcasting Station and all contestants will be personally interviewed by popular Studio Manager, Mr. ALLEN BRANDT. You will actually see the girls as they would appear on Television. (Trophy by E. H. Burton, Rex Arcade, Valley).

105

John Blake and Laurel Wilson.

Everyone put their seat belts on and relaxed. My husband and I had two seats right opposite the doorway, facing all the other passengers. We could see everyone's face. The weather was fine. Couldn't see any trouble but the pilot must have got another call. Don't land in Coolangatta. Come on straight to Brisbane. So he told us to keep our belts on till he got under way again, turned out over the Gold Coast and across it and, as he did that, we must have hit the eye of the cyclone out at sea.

The plane gave a couple of bumps then dropped like a lift. We went straight to the bottom. You could feel the plane.... how can I explain? It was just like somebody gripping it. We all had our seat belts on luckily - except for the hostess. She'd just come out with some refreshments and she went straight to the top of the ceiling. She was hanging from the top of the plane by her head! Next thing I saw, out of the pockets of the kids in front of me there were combs and pens and everything - rising out of their pockets and floating around the cabin! It was like seeing a movie - you don't believe it. You could see their faces. They were grasping the seats. Some were screaming, some were sick.

My husband grabbed the hostess's legs to help her. The bobby clips holding her little cap were coming away. Sliding upwards out of her hair. It all happened quickly but it didn't seem so at the time. They did say later that only for the fact we had a bush pilot who was used to all conditions, we probably would never have made it. He came out underneath the cyclone while the waves were splashing over the nose! That's how low we were!

There was another plane in the area too. Brisbane was worried that we might have collided in those conditions but we finally arrived up there safely. Everybody was half dazed and there were doctors and ambulances standing by at the airport. There was a mad rush to get off. One girl - Joyce Tuesley.... she would have only been eighteen or nineteen....her arm was seized up from gripping. Jack Busteed dropped to his knees, kissed the ground and said, 'Never again!'

How that pilot did it I'll never know. Everyone was congratulating him. Without his ability we would never have made it. He saved all our lives.

Looking back, I led a bit of an exciting life, I suppose. Both before and after the plane incident, I did a lot of travelling. I'd go up to Maryborough and Bundaberg to examine the kiddies for ballroom dancing and new vogue. Sometimes I'd be working until two in the morning because so many kids were interested. They'd come in from the farms. We'd present 'em all with a trophy to say that they'd passed. Bronze medals.... silver.... gold. It was a bit of an incentive for them. I used to go up with Col Ogilvie. He's still running it. At Nambour I'd call on Kevin Stoddard. Then, to give all the country teachers a bit of a go, I'd put championships on at Cloudland. That brought the country people and the city people together. Mostly I travelled by plane - up until that bad trip. Only once I went up by car with Nola Orchard. There were so many kiddies going through, I had to have someone to help me out. I took Jack Busteed as well.

After that horrible plane trip, I only did one flying trip on my own. I was feeling a bit off with the thought of flying, but the man I sat next to was a preacher or something from London. I think his name was Badderly. They made a big fuss of him when he arrived in Australia. I had the seat next to him and he was a very pleasant person to talk to. Very English. He must have had the right connections because we arrived safely that time!

Doing an Astaire – Rogers routine (Swing Trot) from the movie 'Barkleys of Broadway'
with Mick Davis.   1949

Chapter Fourteen: Hotels and Siamese Cats

Alady who had a business a few doors up from where we lived said she was going on a cruise. I was sitting there with my mother and Tom and she said, 'Jeanne, why don't you come with me?' Mum and Tom piped up and said, 'Yes, why don't you, Jeanne?' So I said OK. They all got the shock of their lives because they didn't think I would. I went away in January and I think I got back in May. It was a pure bluff job. I did enjoy it too. I went to Singapore, Manilla, Hong Kong, Japan, Bali and Keela. I didn't dance. I slept just about all the time. I was really crook. It was the greatest tonic I think I ever had. I was away from everything.

My husband Tom was dead keen to get into hotels. His real ambition was to own one and he'd had a passion about it all his life. Never worked in one before but he got a position at the Embassy Hotel up here in Brisbane. He got an interview with Laurie Quinn who owned quite a few pubs around and when Tom went to see him, Quinn said, 'Yes, I'll give you the job but your wife has to be here with you.' Tom explained that I was running Cloudland and had nothing to do with hotels. Quinn said, 'Well this job calls for marriage. You've got to be here on the job together.'

When Tom told me, he looked so disappointed 'cause he wasn't going to get it. I thought, well he's put up with a lot with the dancing so I'll do the right thing and I'll go with him. I went down to see this Laurie Quinn and told him I wouldn't go in the kitchen because I didn't know the first thing about it. But I didn't mind doing the reception. He said, 'That'll do me. So long as you're on the premises.' He was a funny bloke.

I didn't give notice at Cloudland. I just said I wouldn't be able to devote as much time. I took the hotel job very much against my will. Tom would do the bars and I'd do the reception and of a night we'd both do the meals. This Quinn, he wouldn't let us live there. He used to keep people down a bit. We'd have to go across the road to The Exchange where we had a suite. Now the man who managed The Exchange, Laurie Coleman, he lived there too but he only had a room. It annoyed him too. When his father sold his business up in Mackay, they decided they'd buy a hotel of their own and the first thing he did was offer Tom a job. In the meantime, we'd taken a job at The Redland Bay Hotel and we worked there for a bit while the Colemans found a pub they could buy. When they finally did, the job offer was still on so I said to Tom, 'It's up to you - do you want to go down and work with Laurie Coleman or do you want to stay here?'

He said, 'We'll give it a try.'

So we left Redland Bay and went straight down to Coleman's. Tom had the pleasure of running the business and it suited him down to the ground. He was good at it. We all got along famously. The family was all musical. Loved music. Laurie loved the fact that I was tied up with Cloudland. We used to put a floor show on Friday and Saturday nights and he lived all the week for that.

It was The Manly Hotel. Quite a magnificent place. Beautiful dining room. Right on the water. Someone had been way ahead of their time when they built it. There weren't too many tourists then. They'd built suites that never even got used. Tom and I got it going and Coleman wouldn't let a night go by unless I sang the blues. He loved that sort of music. He used to sing himself. So did his sister and his father. One of the other kids played the organ. They'd all get up when the floor shows were running. They weren't really brilliant but they were good enough to entertain. They didn't give a damn how many people were in the audience. They just did it 'cause they loved it so much.

We had a lot of artists on those shows. Don Burrows, George Lawrence, Peter Allen.... he and his brother came and they were both very young. We got such a good reputation as a hotel - not for people staying there because it was too dear - but for the shows.

Then in 1965 the job in New Zealand came up. Tom got an interview with this Mr. Reddiford. He was the man sent here from New Zealand to interview people from every state. I think he was English. Mr. Milner was the man in charge of it all and there was also a man called Barney Ballin. He came into the picture because he was tied up with all the soft drink factories over there. In the South Island you had the Milners and the Ballins who controlled everything.... motels.... hotels....factories.... They were on the same boards as each other, you know?

I didn't want to go to New Zealand - partly 'cause I'd have to fly. Finally I thought well, I've never seen New Zealand. I'll go to the interview and see what happens. I went in and there were all these directors sitting around.... Ballin, Lorimer, Reddiford.... They said, 'And what do you know about hotels, Mrs. Connelly?'

I was being very smart because I didn't want the job and I said, 'Nothing.'

They said, 'What about running of food and kitchen?'

'Wouldn't have a clue.' My husband looked daggers! I said, 'I can't cook. Never been able to.'

They said, 'Well what do you do?'

I said, 'I'm a professional dancer.' I thought, that'll fix 'em! They'll think I'd be hopeless around the place.

I nearly died when they pulled us back in and said, 'That's *exactly* what we're after. We want to start entertainment over there.' I thought, oh no! Put my foot right in it!

The United Services Hotel was the number one place in New Zealand. We got the job and tidied up our affairs here. Rented our house that we'd built at Ekabin. I had two Chinchilla cats there I had to find homes for. They wouldn't let cats into New Zealand. You could bring 'em out but you couldn't take 'em in. I gave these two beautiful cats to a lady who lived alone and she loved them. The bloke that took over Cloudland went into bands. He asked me to stay and teach the bands the movements - like, choreograph their music. He kicked off a lot of performers. Bands were just forming and getting their recording done. Normie Rowe had only been there a short time. The Bluejays and a few others - they were recording when I left. I first met Norm in the office at Cloudland. I hadn't heard him sing. He was sitting at a desk and playing around with a typewriter. It wasn't until years after I realised it was the same chap. Very pleasant to talk to. Only a kid then.

We went over to New Zealand in December 1965, just before Christmas because we were there for Christmas Day. We came back then to get everything together to move permanently and we were only there a month when decimal currency came in.

At first Mum didn't want to come but I was only over there for about two weeks and she changed her mind. She was a very capable person. Never drank but she smoked. I could go anywhere and leave her on her own and she knew everyone within half an hour. She just had the way about her. Funny - I had plenty of guidance from my father in the first half of my life then I had my mother in the second.

We worked in New Zealand for two years. It was a pretty upmarket hotel. There were eighty-seven on the staff there and I'd say a lot of 'em were gay. There was a special chef for everything. One used to bake cakes, another did salads and nothing else. Then another bloke'd do all the roasts and one would look after the silver tray service. There was one man in charge of the lot but each had his own section. Big business. They were all good workers.

The same group of people who owned the United Services owned other hotels over there, but ours was number one. We used to get a lot of guests from London and America. Old Prince Charles had stayed there once. They kept his special suite and it was never used by anyone else again - even though he didn't come back. Everything was very la-de-dah.

At first the staff were a bit hard to get to know. Took me a while. I suppose they felt, when the opportunity came up for a manager, why not get someone of their own? Why go to Australia? We had to sort of fight against that for a while but after about three or four months I got to know them all pretty well. They were a good bunch of people.

The Queen was scheduled to stay with us at one stage. It was all arranged and we'd done all the preparations. As the Queen and Duke were coming through in the car from The Britannia, some little kid fired a gun right across where the cars were. It was quite innocent really. They got to the hotel and the old chap from the church opposite was there to greet them. He's all done up in purple velvet pants - real Pommie type stuff. She came in and everybody had to curtsy but she only stayed a short while and went back to the ship. She was going to stay for a few days at least then she was going further up north but the kid with the gun finished that. And they'd spent millions on security guards. She wouldn't take any chances though.

We had a young girl - Margaret. Big girl. Part Maori. A real hard toiler. She could carry three or four plates on one hand. Really good at her work. She'd looked after the Queen on a previous visit and evidently the Queen was so pleased with her work she gave her a special medallion. She was very proud of it. We brought her back to Australia with us in the end.

We had a local clientele too. They'd come in after work for a beer and they'd arrive on the machines they used on their farms. No putting on side there! Drive up to the door and in you'd go. We opened up this Under Twenty-One Club and because they all joined it we got a big following. We had a big door that used to keep the sound in so they could rage on and have loud music. Because of that we used to get invited to a lot of parties. We didn't often go but when we did.... you'd walk through the door - girls to the right, boys to the left.... Boys all got a bottle of beer straight in their hand. No glasses or anything. Rough and ready but this was how they did things. Same as their bulk beer. Came in tankers.... like oil tankers. They'd just plug the line into the pub and let it run through like petrol! Terrible! Beer used to come out black. How they drank it I'll never know.

Friday night was all businessmen. They were a bit - gay. They'd come and have dinner.... drinks, champagne, the works.... with their boyfriends. Tables were all taken by couples. They never brought their wives or families because that was their night. Just the way things were. Three of the boys who were working for me over there joined up with Les Girls. They are talented people and they'd always do you a good turn. Nothing's a trouble. As far as work was concerned, you couldn't fault 'em. Most reliable.

One night I was going to see that show 'Hello Dolly'. It was a big night with the cast and invited guests arriving at the theatre - that type of thing. They all asked, 'Mrs. Connelly, when you get dressed, can we have a look at you?' I had some beautiful clothes then that had been made for me when I danced. I wore this royal blue sequined dress - just plain, split up the side. I thought, I'd better do the right thing so I went down to the kitchen through the back way so the boys could have a look.

The naughty boys, they didn't tell me they'd schemed up to have a car with one of them all dressed up to arrive at the theatre. While I was in the kitchen, they organised it all so I wasn't involved. The people at the theatre thought it was the 'Hello Dolly' cast. These blokes stole the thunder because they arrived first, and when the real cast came it was a bit jaded because they'd put everything into the hoax arrival. They were full of tricks like that.

New Zealand was where I got my favourite cat. Tai Che. The vet had imported a Siamese cat and the story went that the King and Queen of Thailand gave one of their pedigree cats to the British Royal Family. My cat, I think, was his great, great, grandson. It's all there on his papers. The woman who bred the kittens was swamped with orders. Everyone in Christchurch wanted a kitten. I got one of 'em but the only reason I was allowed to have it was on the condition that the vet neutered him so I couldn't breed. Looking after his own interests, I guess, but that was OK. I ended up bringing that cat back to Australia with me.

People at the hotel in New Zealand were marvellous. They wanted to send us overseas for three months staying in America and London but Tom wouldn't be in that. He wanted his own hotel. So we came back to Australia and we decided, before we settled down, we'd go on a cruise. Tom's mother said she'd come too. Everything was booked and we were ready to go then she suddenly said if we cancelled the cruise, she'd sell her house and that would give us enough money to buy a hotel. Complete waste of time!

She and Tom bought the Mayfair Hotel at Warwick and she came with us to run it but they just didn't hit it off. They never had. They were too alike. I wouldn't have any part of it. I said, 'If you're going to run a hotel, I'll work for you. You can just pay me a wage. I'm not going to be involved in the financial part of it.'

My mother was with me at this stage and he had his mother so, to take it all round, it wasn't a hundred percent huge success. You could imagine! Finally I went back down to the Gold Coast and Mum came with me. Within about six weeks my husband was there too - so here we go again!

Sookie.

Chapter Fifteen: *The Gold Coast*

I stayed on the Gold Coast for quite a few years and I was teaching. I opened a studio down there. This time jazz ballet was becoming very popular so I taught that. The chappy who used to run the dancing there - Harry Brooks - I taught him. He was quite a good dancer and I just gave him exhibition routines and stuff like that. That sort of thing appealed. Ballroom was very nice but you see one, you've seen the lot. The couples used to like doing exhibition just for a change.

The Gold Coast to me was only a place you'd go to relax but this time I stayed quite a while. I put on a few shows. I used to do Kirra Lifesavers. Did one at The Chevron - I think it was. It was a championship and I was asked to judge it and help with the arrangements. So I got in touch with Bruce Small and asked him would he mind coming down to do the presentations. He brought that bike rider with him - Oppy. They were old friends. The both of 'em ended up on stage all night presenting trophies. Bruce Small loved to do anything like that. He was a very helpful person. He'd be in anything for you. He liked his publicity.

I lived one block away from the beach front. Ted Skennar let us have a flat there in Orchid Avenue. I used to see that bloke going up and down the beach spraying people with oil. Bird on his car. Bird on his hat. A real character. The bikini was becoming real popular too. Plenty of business for him.

My friend Val Daley, she did very well with bikinis. Jo Stafford actually brought them out and Val started making them too. Her factory was right alongside the RSL Club and she got these bikinis out and they went like hot cakes. Put them through all her shops. She had quite a few through Brisbane. Did very well. Her sister was the one who owned Baxter's Restaurant.

Years before in Melbourne I used to teach this bloke dancing. His family had stalls at the Vic. Markets. They were in seafood. He had a brother called Jack. I don't want you to use his real name so I'll just call him Jack. He fell off a truck when he was a kid and they put a tin plate in his head. I didn't know him. I only heard about it from his brother. So this young chap walked up to me on the Gold Coast and said, 'Jeanne.' I thought: who in the name of all fortune's this? He said, 'Don't you remember me? I'm Jack. You used to teach my brother.'

I said, 'Oh, of course I do.' Well from there on I was his long-lost friend. He asked me to come around to his flat because he wanted me to meet somebody. Wanted me to manage him 'cause he knew that I'd been in that type of business. So I went to his flat and he introduced me to the bloke. It was Ricky May! But I couldn't really help him - not that he needed much help. He had a beautiful voice. A person with a voice like that - they couldn't help but be successful, with or without a manager!

There were all these people at the flat playing cards and Jack took me inside where he had this beautiful stereo. God knows where he'd got it! He said, 'I want you to have this for the studio.'

I said, 'Oh no - I couldn't do that. You keep it.'

'No,' he said, 'I want you to have it.'

I thought, oh well - best not to make a big fuss. There were a lot of people there whom I didn't know. I didn't want to get him into trouble. So I just kept quiet and hoped he'd forget about it.

Then he went on to tell me how he'd been sent back to Australia from London because he was in the Biggs train robbery and he got caught. He spent quite some time in jail over there but I'd defy anyone not to like him. He just had that way. Even all the blokes and the wardens in the prison liked him. He said, 'We're having a big party. You've got to promise you'll be there. I've got a lot of friends coming and I want you to meet them.'

I wasn't too keen on going to any party but I'd promised so we went. We didn't intend to stay long.

He held it at a big hotel restaurant right opposite my new studio. A tall building. I'd better not tell you the name of that either because of what happened! We went up there and he introduced us to a number of guests. They were amiable people and we were soon made to feel at home. Jack had a little lady friend up from Brisbane and he was the perfect host. The champagne was flowing and the food was all beautifully prepared.

Every time we went to go home though, he'd say, 'No - don't go yet. Stay.' So we were there among the last. Everyone's ordering up anything they wanted. When it was time to leave, we got in the lift and he said, 'I'll come down with you.' And he said to the chap who was bringing the drinks, 'I'll be back in a few minutes. I'll see you when I come back. I want you to bring something up to the room.'

When we got down to the ground floor, he walked out with us. He never went back! Next time I met him, which was about two weeks later, he told me what he'd done was, he'd booked in as a Doctor Somebody from South Australia - 'cause he *had* come from South Australia. They thought he was an important man and when he ordered all this, it was just put on his bill. So the hotel paid for the lot! I knew he was a villain! Cool for those days!

I had another interesting experience with that man I told you about before, Charlie Ring whom I'd known for years. He was the one I told you always danced in white tails. He was a beautiful dancer. We were supposed to be doing this overseas tour. Charlie Ring was first to go, then when he came back we were going to take his place. Well he went and when he got to Singapore he got himself into all sorts of trouble with someone's harem. He was charming - a good looking bloke who'd get away with murder with the women. When he got involved with this harem, they were going to shoot him so he came back to the Gold Coast and that was the finish of the tour.

Then he got in trouble on the coast. He was at dinner one night and in those days you didn't get a table to yourself. They had long tables where you sat with groups of people you often didn't know. He'd brought this young girl up from Sydney for a holiday and it turned out her boyfriend was a Sydney gangster. A bloke at the table was one of his thugs and when Charlie went to the toilet this bloke followed him out and bashed him. Hit him with the toilet seat. When he was taken to hospital he must have given our name as the only people he knew in Queensland. The detectives came to our place and said, 'You know a chap called Charlie Ring?'

I said, 'Yes I do.'

They said, 'Well he's up in Intensive Care. We'd like you to come up.'

God, what a mess he was. Really chopped up. His face was cut to pieces. When he got out of hospital he went downhill a bit so I gave him a few jobs judging at Cloudland to get him back on track. Course, now all his ego had gone because he was so badly scarred. He got well enough up here then he decided to go back to Sydney to make a new start, but in a few months he died. They buried him in his white tails - the way he wanted to go.

We lived alternately on the Gold Coast and in Melbourne for a long time. We'd be up here for say, three months then we'd get a bit fed up and we'd go back to Melbourne. Then back up here. Travelled by car. Tom's mother lived in Melbourne and finally we went down there and stayed between about 1970 and '77. I was working in a hotel - the Railway Hotel in Prahran. Tom went to work for UBD. He'd had hotels. Tom was an Aussie Rules football umpire and for a while there I was giving the footballers lessons. The papers beat it up as ballet lessons but of course it was really for technique in getting off the ground to mark the ball. I taught them how to jump higher and use their feet better.

Christine Jorgensen

Dad died in 1977 when I was sixty. Only been to a doctor once in his life. He had a heart attack. We came back up here again after that and we lived in Brisbane. We worked down on the Gold Coast at weekends for a bloke called Claude Carnell. Funny that I knew men with similar names. There was Carnell, Parnell and Burnell. Claude Carnell had the Playroom. Claude put on people like Johnny Farnham and Johnny O'Keefe too in the old days.

I helped Claude with the shows and Tom kept an eye on trouble. That's where I met Christine Jorgensen. It was a very interesting case at the time. Probably not now. But Christine was the first to ever have a successful sex change operation. It had never been attempted before. He was in the Marine Corps. American. There were big stories about it everywhere. After he'd had the operation he went to live in Switzerland with his aunt, then came out into the entertainment business and made a fortune travelling all over the world.

One of the best acts I've ever seen. Good singer, lovely to look at - but he was a fair dinkum change. He had to have this special curtain so he could step behind it and he was so slim that he could have three dresses on and, as he'd close the curtains, he'd just unzip one and come out wearing something different. It was a good act. People were flocking from the south to come up and see it. He was a very clever performer. Really polished. They'd never seen anything like it before. At that stage gays were just coming out into the open - as entertainers. It was all hush-hush before.

Edwin Duff was another talented bloke I knew too. When I was at The Trocadero in Sydney, I used to get him up for the shows and put him up at my place. He'd come out in the morning with his hair in rollers. He used to be in the Stand-In Club. Looked just like Danny Kaye. I met him down the coast years later. I was with Tom and my mother and we walked into the RSL at Surfers. This bloke came up and he had a big medallion hanging down the front of him. What was it he called me....? 'Mamma Montez!' I thought, who's this? It was Edwin.

I did a bit of singing at the RSL at Surfers. Even at the hotels where I worked in Melbourne I used to sing. Johnny Bruce - I sang with his band sometimes. He made a few records. People liked it because my deep voice was a novelty. I sang a lot of blues and numbers like 'Barefoot Days' and 'Sunny Side of the Street'. I still only had a repertoire of about six numbers! It was either take those or none! It was always just a fill-in sort of thing. The voice I had - you either liked it or you didn't.

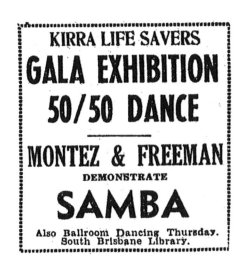

118

Chapter Sixteen: A Stroke of Bad Luck

The stroke was caused through stress. But originally I went through a storm gutter on the corner of Adelaide and Kent Streets. I was crossing the road and, as I put my foot forward, a kid coming down on a motorbike never stopped and I stepped back. As I stepped back with my right foot, it went straight through the drain. Of course my toe was pointed! Straight down - and I had the veins sticking out, up in the air. I went to the chemist across the road and he sent me to a doctor.

The storm water drain was dirty. Hadn't been cleaned in years. The grate was all raggedy. I probably could have sued the City Council but the man I was working for at the time I think worked for the Council as a solicitor. He said there was no good suing them. They had no money. I think it was a square off. The day after it happened the Council put in a new grate. I finished up with thrombosis there and that thrombosis - the clot - they said one day could travel. So when I had the stroke, it could have taken all those years to have got to my head. We'll never know.

There were other things that could have caused the stroke. As I told you, I got dropped on my head when I was dancing and when I was a kid, I was hit by a swing. I had those blackouts too - but they never came up with any explanation for them.

I'd been to visit some friends at Stone's Corner the day before and the next morning I had to go to town. While I was getting ready, I felt a bit off. I couldn't pinpoint anything but I could feel a real dragging at the side of my mouth and around my arm, right where they used to give me those vitamin B12 injections when I had leukaemia. It was like a big steel band there - someone twisting. I thought I was having a heart attack. The pain in my arm was really bad and I was always given to understand that if you get a pain round there it's usually a heart attack. So I was just taking it very quietly. Just lying on the bed. Not moving.

I laid down there for a while then the lady next door came in and I made her a cup of coffee. We sat down and talked and she told me she thought I was having a stroke. I didn't really know what a stroke was but it didn't feel too bad. I didn't feel nauseous or anything. Just pain. From the mouth there, it was pulling right down to where you see the tendons going up in my arm. You know, my father always taught me that nothing hurt. You'd always get better. So I laid down again and it took from about ten-thirty in the morning till five in the afternoon for it to actually happen.

At about five Tom came home from work. He always came in the front so when the doorbell went I hopped out of bed to open it. In the meantime I'd had the stroke. The old cat's with me and I sat up to get out of bed. As I stood up, the right leg worked but the minute the left one touched the ground it was gone and I went straight back and hit my head.

When my husband heard the flop, he ran round the back 'cause the back door was always open. He got panicky and said, 'You'd better go straight to hospital!' No, I didn't want to go to hospital and he knew better than to argue with me if I'd made up my mind.   I said, 'I'll go tomorrow.' So I took a sleeping pill and got back to bed. The old cat didn't leave my side. He sat next to me on the bed and turned his face away so he didn't breathe on me. I'd trained him to do that. He wouldn't leave that bed. He just stayed there. I lay there all night, massive stroke, bleeding.... I slept through it!

Next day I went to hospital. The ambulance came to carry me out. I was like a ton of lead! They took me into emergency on this trolley. Oh they didn't wheel it slow. They ran! I heard 'em say, 'There's a woman here - she's had a massive stroke and she's *still alive*!' I thought, that sounds cheerful! Never had any feelings of panic - only pain. After they'd taken the scan they said where I'd hit my head had moved the clot and started the bleeding at the back. Probably saved my life. One of the nerves it must have hit was my sight. Instead of having to wear bifocals, I don't have to use glasses if I don't want to now. That's about the only thing it improved!

They transferred me from the main hospital over to the special section and there I stayed for five months. They couldn't understand how I'd slept through the whole night. I saw the scans they'd taken and even three months later you could still see the bleeding down the back of my head. Inside.

I was there from January until about Mother's Day - May. About March they let me go home for weekends. Course, you can just imagine me in hospital. Not allowed to do anything. Trying to pass the time away. There were fifty women in the section I was in and I could converse with three! It drove me mad. At meal times they'd deliver all the food in containers and there was a great, long table where all the women would eat. I couldn't eat with the others. Some of them would be sitting there sound asleep. Some would stick their hands in their food to eat.... I used to eat on my own. I got on the right side of the sister because I'm a real fad on food - as you can well imagine. I ate salad the whole time I was there. The sister would wheel me out onto a kind of little balcony out near the kiosk. It was much better.

All you'd do all day is have breakfast then sit and wait until your name went up on a board. Then you'd go into the gym for half an hour with the physiotherapist. There were fifty women to get through. After your thirty minutes' therapy, you'd go back and you'd sit and wait for your meal at night. Then you'd wait for the night to pass by. There was a TV there if you wanted it. I never read or anything. I nearly went round the bend trying to get out. You just sit - all day, all night long.

I was lucky because Tom would come down every day. He was a very, very good person. He didn't just come down to say hello to me but he'd go to all the other ladies as well. He just had that way about him. They all looked forward to him coming - even the ones who didn't understand. That's why it was so sad when he finally arranged to give up his job so I could be home and he'd be with me. That's the only reason they finally let me out. To think that stupid accident had to happen and he was gone before his birthday.

Tom was completely lost 'cause we'd worked together for so long. Twenty-eight years we'd been together. He was working at the RSL at Moorooka but he couldn't put his mind to his work because he was at the hospital every day. So I said, 'Look, give it away. Just stay home. By the time you look after the cat and you come down looking after me, that's enough.' So he did that. Then, after a few months they decided they'd let me go home first of all on weekends.

It was a great relief to get home - even for a few days at a time. We had a fairly large house and it was all glass. Big eighteen by eighteen foot patio glassed in - at the back and even the next room. It was a real airy place. You could look out across to the TV stations, it was so high. And the old cat used to follow me wherever I went. I'd sleep out the back sometimes. I'm a fresh air person. I like all the windows open. The cat would be there with me. When I went for that trip a few years before, my mother looked after him. He absolutely wrecked our lounge suite. She said, 'I gotta tell you - I couldn't stop him.' Must be their way of showing that they miss you. He never left my side the whole time. No matter where I was, he was there too.

They decided they'd let me go home permanently under Tom's care. I was home on the Friday.... Saturday.... Sunday Tom had some people up for Mother's Day. Older people. I think he cooked them a turkey or something. He was good at that. These people had a couple of little dogs. When we were saying goodbye to them, one of the little dogs ran away with its lead trailing. Tom put his foot out to stop it running onto the busy road and as he did, he slipped and fell against the kerb. He cut his head. Then the following Tuesday he was driving me down for physio and he hit the car into the gutter. We got down to the hospital and while I was waiting my turn I said, 'Tom, you don't look too good. While I'm waiting here, why don't you go to casualty and just get it checked out?' Next thing I know they're wheeling him upstairs. You wouldn't believe it but he'd had a stroke too. It had travelled right down his back. He could move his hands but he had it down the back of his neck. Now, I don't know if it was the dog or the accident. So easy for it to happen.

That meant that Tom would be in hospital for a few weeks at least. The doctors said to me, 'We'd better take you back too.'

I said, 'No way in the world. Now I'm out I'm not going back.' So I stayed home with my old cat. He knew I wasn't well. Like I said, the house was all glass, high on a hill and on the corner of the street. It had openings everywhere. Sookie would go around to every window and every door to check - just like a watchman. Then he'd come back into the bedroom and hop up on the bed. I never went to bed until about one in the morning - same as I do now. I'd be up half the night. If anyone came near that place, the cat would know. He was wonderful company. I doubt I'd have made it through without him, just sort of having him around, actually guarding the place.

I used to get a taxi to the hospital 'cause I couldn't walk. I'd go every day. I'd only been ten days out of hospital myself - in Tom's care. He was conscious for just ten minutes. He was in a coma. He'd been laying there for almost a week when I saw the blood coming on his lips. I went out and got the male nurse and said, 'I've been wiping my husband's lips and there's bleeding.... '

He got the doctor down straight away and oh.... big panic! Things wheeling everywhere! They sent me home and the next morning I got there early 'cause I was worried. When I went in here's this great big bottle and tubes coming out of him with all the blood. It had gone into his lungs. That's what killed him. They told me when the car hit the kerb that day, he'd gone forward and bitten his tongue. Course, being in pubs for so long, they put it down that he had sclerosis. But he died of biting his tongue and he bled to death. See, here's the death certificate - Thomas Richard Connelly died at age fifty-three on May 22, 1980.... About two days before his birthday.

The doctors were a bit worried about me. I had no telephone or anything. They wanted me to go back. I said, 'I'm not changing. I want to stay home.' After being five months in hospital – as if I didn't know what to do by then....! There was a lady came to clean the house and a sister would come twice a week. See, I was still pretty sick and I couldn't use my arm. I'd sit and watch TV and have towels full of ice on my leg. My left hand was badly twisted and I iced it so much that, when it was frozen, I'd pull it round. But I'd be lucky to get it back much at all. The old cat used to sit with me all the time. I often think to myself, if I hadn't had him it could've been a different story. He wasn't a young cat - he was thirteen. When he died, I had him buried in the back yard. So there I was, alone again.

Chapter Seventeen: Kilkivan

Like I told you, back in 1952, Kevin and Sis Allen lived next door to us at Coorparoo. We were Godparents to their children. When we moved away, we hardly ever kept in touch unless we were passing through the same state. Now it could have been just coincidence but - and I remember the date - on the 4th of July, 1979 Sis Allen died. She'd had a heart attack. I was down at Baxter's Seafood Restaurant that particular night. Just before midnight I had one of my blackouts. They stuck me in an ambulance and took me off to hospital. When I came to and Tom came in to get me, I was alright again. It seemed funny that I'd blacked out the exact same night as Sis died but, like I said, probably a coincidence.

Later - after Tom had died and I was living at home alone, I was awoken by one of these horrible feelings I used to get. They were horrible feelings. You feel like - all around you there's electricity. A tingling. It's a sensation. In those days I used to get to the stage where I thought, I won't open my eyes. But there's no good fighting against it. I opened my eyes and there was a woman standing in the doorway. When I looked close I saw she was a tall lady - not small by any means - standing in the doorway, just smiling at me. I could see every detail about her. Because she was a biggish woman, she sort of filled the room. It was only a small room. She was wearing a kind of brown dress and it had a bow on one side. It was Sis Allen.

I was so taken back, the next day I thought I had to tell somebody. You know how you feel? I thought the only one to tell was the daughter. The closest one to her. I told her that I'd just had a vision of her mother and I could describe in detail what she was wearing. She naturally got in touch with her father and he phoned me. He said, 'I'm coming up your way. I'm going through to Emerald to dig sapphires. I'll drop in and see you.'

So Kevin called in and we were discussing it. He said, 'You're not going to believe this but I've got a photo at home of Sis and she's wearing exactly what you've described. She made the dress just before she died to wear to a wedding.' I finally saw that photo and it was exactly what I saw. It makes you wonder 'cause there was no way in the world I could have known those things. It is a bit unreal.

Kevin came to see me a few times after that and he got the garden going for me to grow a few vegetables. I said, 'Don't plant anything there. That's Sookie's spot.'

'Oh,' he said, 'He'd be way under by now.' He put a heap of vegetables in but not one grew in that place. Nothing. He used to say, 'There's a bit of a witch around here somewhere!'

We finally decided to buy a Toyota bus - mobile home - and travel around Australia. I tried not to let the problems from the stroke get in my way. I married him in 1981 in Mudgee, NSW. Then the rest you know. We ended up buying a block of land here in Kilkivan in James Street behind the Museum. When we sold it, we bought the house here in Harding Street. Look, here's a photo of Kev when he was taken in as a J.P. He was a J.P. - yeah. Fancy me keeping all these photos for you....!

Author's Note.

I met Jeanne in 1996 when I was entertaining at the Kilkivan Bowls Club, across the creek from her house. As she began to tell her extraordinary story, an odd set of coincidences in our lives became apparent. That we had both been in the entertainment industry was the catalyst for our friendship; the following additional parallels in our lives were a surprise to us:

Jeanne grew up in Auburn/Kew Victoria, the same area as my mother did. (Ch. 1)

Marnie isn't a common name but her grandmother and I both adopted it. (Ch. 1)

Jeanne and I started performing at three. (Ch. 1)

At around eight I, like Jeanne, took piano lessons but was discouraged by the teacher because of memorising, not reading, the music. (Ch.1)

At ten years of age, we both entered a highland dancing competition. (She won; I came third - I'm not a dancer, I'm a musician!) (Ch. 1)

At about sixteen I also secured a job at the Herald Office in Melbourne through my father, who already worked there. I worked in the pictorial library. (Ch. 3)

While employed by the Herald I, like Jeanne, had my first big break into showbiz. (Ch. 3)

Sydney was where I also gained most recognition. I even worked some of the same places as Jeanne. (Ch. 10,)

I once had a very vague association with Squizzy Taylor through the family of one of his close acquaintances. (Ch.4)

When I was first married, I was living in Mudgee, NSW. (Ch. 17)

Flying from Sydney to the Gold Coast in a chartered plane for an engagement, I too had a close scrape with heaven.... (Ch. 13)

Like Jeanne, I have been a wanderer, only occasionally returning to Melbourne. As she did before me, I worked for extended periods in Sydney, the Gold Coast and Brisbane. Fate eventually brought me to Kilkivan to live – just as it had Jeanne. Kilkivan, for both of us, simply seemed the right place to stop.

It was as though I had followed her on a parallel journey through life - thirty years later.

On March 10th, 1997, two weeks after I had recorded the last tape of her life story, Jeanne Delysia Montez passed away. She had defied the disabilities from the stroke so bravely and for so long, but the Queensland summer had not been kind to her. I guess she just grew weary of the fight. She died in the Gympie Hospital with her cousin and next door neighbour John Stapleton beside her. The service two days later in St. Kevin's Catholic Church in Kilkivan was a peaceful time attended by her local friends, but her ashes did not remain here. However, for me St. Kevin's is her final resting place.

Jeanne's gift of the colourful, lively Latin American routines to modern Ballroom dancing is now taken for granted. Her relentless energy to have them included into the championship categories has, to date, gone unwritten, yet Jeanne and her countless, talented colleagues were the force behind the changes. They redefined the Ballroom genre from the precise and graceful movements of the courtier to the rich, athletic excitement of modern Dance Sport. Every competitor in the modern art of Ballroom Dancing owes some of these unrestricted routines to Jeanne and her many gifted friends.

During her fascinating career, Jeanne lifted many hopeful artists to the heights of success. Because she asked me to write her story, perhaps I will, as a writer, become the last.

Thanks, Jeanne.

INDEX TO NAMES

Printed in Great Britain
by Amazon

35265658R00069